A
MERCILESS
PLACE

A
MERCILESS
PLACE

The Lost Story of Britain's Convict
Disaster in Africa

EMMA CHRISTOPHER

OXFORD
UNIVERSITY PRESS

OXFORD

UNIVERSITY PRESS

Oxford University Press, Inc., publishes works that further
Oxford University's objective of excellence
in research, scholarship, and education.

Oxford   New York

Auckland   Cape Town   Dar es Salaam   Hong Kong   Karachi
Kuala Lumpur   Madrid   Melbourne   Mexico City   Nairobi
New Delhi   Shanghai   Taipei   Toronto

With offices in

Argentina   Austria   Brazil   Chile   Czech Republic   France   Greece
Guatemala   Hungary   Italy   Japan   Poland   Portugal   Singapore
South Korea   Switzerland   Thailand   Turkey   Ukraine   Vietnam

Copyright © 2010 by Emma Christopher

First published in Australia in 2010 by Allen & Unwin

First published in the United Kingdom in 2011 by Oxford University Press

www.oup.com

Oxford is a registered trademark of Oxford University Press

Library of Congress Cataloging-in-Publication Data
Christopher, Emma, 1971–
A merciless place / Emma Christopher.
p.   cm.
"First published in Australia in 2010 by Allen & Unwin" — T.p. verso.
Includes bibliographical references and index.
ISBN 978–0–19–969593–5 (hardcover : alk. paper)
1. Penal transportation—Great Britain—History—18th century.
2. Penal transportation—Great Britain—History—19th century.
3. United States—History—Revolution, 1775–1783—Influence.
4. Prisoners—Great Britain—History—18th century.
5. Prisoners—Great Britain—History—19th century.
6. Convict ships—Great Britain—History—18th century.
7. Convict ships—Great Britain—History—19th century.
8. Penal colonies—History—18th century.
8. Penal colonies—History—19th century.   I. Title.
HV8949C47 2011
365'.34—dc22   2010049032

1 3 5 7 9 10 8 6 4 2

Printed in Great Britain on acid-free paper
by Clays Ltd, St Ives plc

CONTENTS

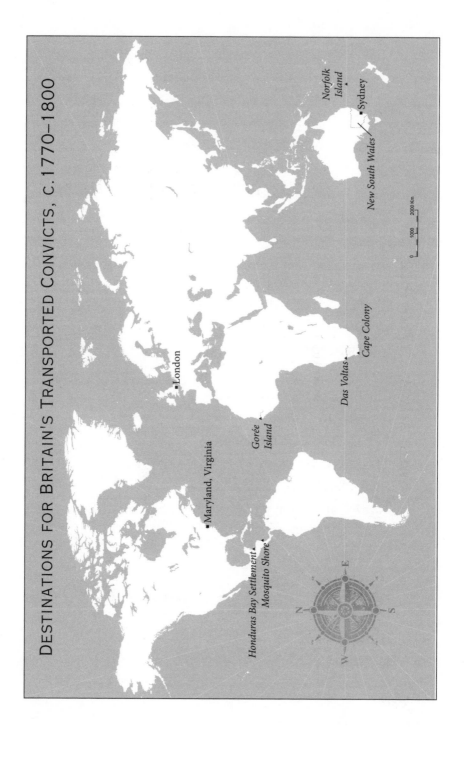

DESTINATIONS FOR BRITAIN'S TRANSPORTED CONVICTS, C. 1770–1800

London

Maryland, Virginia

Honduras Bay Settlement
Mosquito Shore

Gorée Island

Das Voltas

Cape Colony

Norfolk Island

Sydney

New South Wales

0   1000   2000 Km

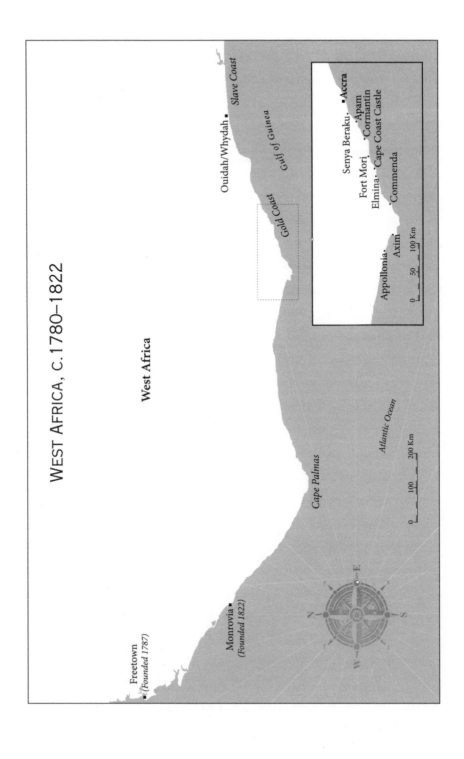

WEST AFRICA, C. 1780–1822

West Africa

Freetown
(Founded 1787)

Monrovia
(Founded 1822)

Cape Palmas

Atlantic Ocean

Gold Coast

Gulf of Guinea

Slave Coast

Ouidah/Whydah

Senya Beraku
Apam
Cormantin
Fort Mori
Elmina
Cape Coast Castle
Commenda
Accra

Appollonia
Axim

0   50   100 Km

0   100   200 Km

INTRODUCTION

Gorée Island, West Africa, November 1781

Trying to regain their land legs, Thomas Maple and his brother Joseph shuffled unsteadily off HMS *Mackerel* and into the blinding sun. They were a long way from London and the house they had burgled in Swinton Street near Bagnigge Wells, where Nell Gwynne had once entertained King Charles II. Beside them was another convicted housebreaker, Job Massey, a widower who had been unable to explain away some ribbons in his possession. John Plunkett, a sailor who had been caught stealing some gilt-framed mirrors, was less disoriented but awkwardly trying to hide a stigma. Beneath the cuffs of his shabby uniform he curled his fingers over his thumb to hide the fact that he had the letter 'T' for thief branded into the soft flesh of his hand.

Alongside the Maple brothers, Massey and Plunkett were some youths growing up in the criminal system. With the uncertainty of the long-since orphaned, Thomas Field claimed in court to be 'about seventeen' but his age was noted as sixteen when he boarded the hulks to begin his original sentence of hard labour on the River Thames. A clerk had guessed that John James Smith was only fourteen when he had joined the ship.

William Cheatham was said to be 'a boy' when he was convicted of shoplifting at London's Old Bailey, along with his Fagin-style boss. His criminal overlord, Patrick Madan, had already become known as 'the famous Madan' and should have been standing alongside Cheatham on the parade ground at Gorée. The fact that he was not was a saga in itself, another escape which added to Madan's legend.

At the head of these criminals, teaching them to drill no less, was William Murray Mackenzie (alias Jefferson, Williamson, Taylor, Ward, Brett and a multitude of other assumed names), a man whose infamy rivalled Madan's. His appointment as drill sergeant of these indentured convict soldiers meant that the ranks were a crooks' hierarchy with teaspoon thieves, pickpockets and a host of petty chancers guarded by a man whose criminal career had begun with stealing a footman's coat while the servant's master was enjoying the services of a brothel, and had progressed to relieving the capital's jewellers of diamonds, emeralds and large sums of money. In fact William Murray Mackenzie had avoided a one-way trip to the gallows, it was whispered, only because he was the black sheep of one of Britain's most influential families.

To observers that warm November day, the new arrivals were a very sorry sight. Most were stunted from having grown up malnourished, their faces were pockmarked from disease, and having shared out the uniforms of the few well-dressed men among them, all were poorly clothed. Rather than marching proudly with heads held high, as they had been ordered to do, they stumbled tentatively off the ship. Hidden beneath their trousers, telltale scars revealed why they were so unsteady: the abrasions of iron fetters were still clear around their ankles. For some of them it was the first time in years they had been released from their metal cuffs.

Gorée was a short stop on the way to their real destination, the slave-trading forts of the Gold Coast on the southern shores of the bulge of

INTRODUCTION

West Africa, where the cold waters of the Atlantic give way to the sultry Gulf of Guinea. Gorée was little more than a way station, but as it was the first time they had set foot in Africa and experienced life at a slave-trading post, it seemed to be a window to the future. We can picture them still: frightened boys and men far away from everything they had ever known. Beyond the uniforms worn by the garrison, there must have been little which seemed familiar at Gorée.

Most had led parochial lives until this point, their experiences closely circumscribed by poverty. Some had been born in rural squalor and had gone to the city in search of work, but even there they had joined the urban-born in venturing only from dosshouse to pub, chophouse to market. Life rarely encompassed more than rambling the streets in search of employment, warmth and food, and if these failed to materialise then any opportunity to stave off starvation for the time being would do. Being caught shoplifting or hooking a purse from a pocket was not so much a matter of shame as sheer bad luck. Only the rather better-to-do could afford the luxury of seeing morality in the ownership of a handkerchief or teaspoon.

As bad luck went, though, this was well beyond the usual run of things. Bad luck was being tied to the pillory while others threw mouldy fruit or eggs. Bad luck was the painful laceration of flesh as the rhythmic beating and retreating of a whip marked out the required atonement for the committed crime. Rotten luck had previously involved seven or fourteen years, or even a life sentence, banished to the American colonies, a punishment recently replaced by hard labour on the River Thames. The worst luck involved standing in front of a braying crowd with eyes covered, waiting to feel the hempen halter tighten as the world dropped away. But even the most terrible luck of all had never before led to Africa.

3

Standing at the head of the convict troops were two men who were equally disenchanted at finding themselves in West Africa. When Captain Kenneth Mackenzie and Captain George Katenkamp had addressed letters to King George III each patriotically offering to raise an independent company, this was not at all what they had intended. Implicit in their offer was that they and their new company would go to America, where the war to suppress the rebellious colonies was going unaccountably badly. Reading between the lines of those letters it is still possible to see the dreams the offers encompassed: of being a saviour in their country's hour of need, of playing the hero when all around were failing and, not least, receiving the substantial prize money the government would pay for successful campaigns. There was scant hope of any of those being achieved in Africa. It was a terrible comedown. Looking at the two poorly maintained forts and the House of Slaves, never mind their ragamuffin, rowdy convict troops, it was evident that they had been sent on an inglorious mission.

Kenneth Mackenzie's feelings about the assignment were made clear in a letter he wrote to the War Office from aboard the *Mackerel* only a week before setting sail. It was an eleventh-hour plea to the government to change its mind. Regretting the expedition he had been earmarked for, he gently sought to protest his destination, intimating forlorn hopes of going to the frontlines in America or even of rejoining his old regiment in India. His reasons were articulated frankly. 'Africa does not promise so many dimonds [sic] as Asia,' he wrote. It did not do, of course, to question the War Office and he was careful to beg 'Pardon … for letting a Syllable escape from my lips or pen, that has the least appearance of reluctance to the service I am going on'. His unwillingness to go to Africa was obvious.[1]

The man who met the two captains as they strode ashore understood their frustration all too well. Commandant Joseph Wall, governor of Gorée Island, was equally disenchanted with his lot. The position of ruler at Gorée was what an eighteenth-century gentleman called a 'choke-pear': a role so unwanted and difficult it could cause a man to stifle and choke. Wall himself had ended up there thanks to a penchant for debauchery and dissipation which had driven him to debt. By his own admission he had spent his adult life 'a zealous votary to Hymen, Venus and the fickle Goddess; in a word, fortune-hunting, intrigue and the gaming-tables'. He too wished for the possible glories of America.[2]

As it turned out, Wall, Mackenzie and Katenkamp were too late to join the fray in America anyway. While the convict-soldiers were at Gorée, unthinkable news reached London. As they had been sailing to Africa, General Cornwallis had surrendered to George Washington at Yorktown. Prime Minister Lord North took the news 'as he would a ball in his breast'; pacing wildly around the room he declared repeatedly, 'Oh God! It is all over!' The King apparently took the news with more fortitude but the monarchy would be rocked by the crisis all the same. In the coming months the King would go so far as to draft a letter of abdication.

Aside from the general hand-wringing and malaise this would bring in Britain, it also meant that the inauspicious arrival of this motley band of convict-soldiers in Africa would mark the start of one of the British Empire's most bizarre enterprises. With the American War of Independence all but lost and hope of restarting the transportation of convicts to the Americas dwindling fast, Britain had begun sneakily banishing its criminals to West Africa. Now the disastrous news meant this continent would become the potential new home for many more unwanted felons.

The problem, as they would soon discover, was that the only real employment for the newly arrived malefactors, and for all those who followed them to Africa, would be acting as guards at the castles where distraught captives awaited sale to a passing slave ship. The government could scarcely have found a place where criminals could cause more chaos if they had deliberately sought one out. It was, to say the least, an extremely unwise idea.

The components of the disaster, though, would outrank all that even the most cynical of prophesiers could have imagined in November 1781. Before the scheme was abandoned, it would have run the gamut of piracy, treachery, mutiny, starvation, poisonings, allegations of white women forced to prostitute themselves to African men, and several cases of murder. And some of the worst offences were not committed by the convicts. For Kenneth Mackenzie, George Katenkamp and Joseph Wall, whatever disasters they feared that November day, they surely did not conceive the awful truth of their destinies. One of them would be dead within weeks. The other two would become a pair of the most reviled men in Britain, found guilty of crimes many times worse than those of the highwaymen, forgers, petty thieves and pickpockets they had under their command.

As it all fell apart, the British government decided, rather belatedly, that from then on their banished criminals should go to the farthest reaches of the globe, as far as possible from anywhere they could cause chaos and disrupt trade. So the events set in motion by a few hungry criminals' boots scuffing Gorée Island's hard dirt would end on the shores of New South Wales in the continent the world now knows as Australia. This story has been strangely ignored by history, but is no less epic for that.

Let us go on a brief tour of 1781. We will meet three 'tribes' on our tour: Londoners, especially the working-class men and women who lived in the city; the Fante, who lived on West Africa's Gold Coast and had long been

Britain's ally; and the Eora people of what would soon become known as Sydney Harbour.[3]

At the centre of the world known to the convicts was the great city of London, the hub of the British Empire. Then the largest city in Western Europe with a population approaching one million, it was home to vast extremes of prosperity and poverty. Since being rebuilt after the great fire, London had enjoyed a period of rapid growth and the wealthy lived in enormous luxury. Twenty years earlier, a year after ascending to the throne, George III had spent £6898 5s 4d on a dinner for the Lord Mayor of London, a sum which was well in excess of a lifetime's earnings for most of the city's inhabitants. The wealthy decorated their houses with gold leaf and marble finished off with unique objets d'art, and when their contemporaries gathered in these great mansions for balls, the women wore jewels worth fortunes around their necks, wrists and fingers and in their hair. Getting a headache from the weight of your diamonds was an occupational hazard. But only around two or three per cent of the population lived in such style.[4]

Below them, another twenty per cent or so of the population formed the 'middling sort'. They could enjoy the circulating libraries which had just come into fashion, the newly popular activity of strolling around the city's parks and gardens, and there were art galleries and concerts. The city's coffee houses, exclusively the preserve of men, were also very fashionable places to eat, drink, read the many newspapers the city produced and, most of all, do business. Boxing, cricket, gambling and cockfights were common leisure pursuits and buying a lottery ticket kept hope alive for those who had not had any luck at the gaming tables. At home their wives supervised the cooking of feasts of mock turtle (calf's head), pheasant, snipe and roast turkey, followed by apple pie and sweetmeats.

The people who concern us most, though, are the other Londoners, the majority of the population who lived at the reverse end of the social scale. More than three out of every four of London's citizens were working people, and of those more than half of the adult male population was unskilled. The average family lived in one single rented room, ate meat scraps and bread tainted with chalk, alum and even ash to make it white, wore clothes that were little more than rags and had lost the majority of their children in infanthood. Being jailed for debt was commonplace, charity was scarce and the dreaded workhouse was the only real alternative to starvation for many.

Some of the poorest boroughs were those around the docks, to the east of the old walled city. Limehouse, Whitechapel, Wapping and Stepney were where the working poor lived and laboured in dye, manure, glue, paraffin, lampblack, match and bone-meal factories. These were the districts where seamen rented shared bed space when they came ashore and spent their earnings in the many pubs and brothels. They were utterly wretched certainly but, a century before Jack the Ripper roamed the streets, not the most awful places in London. That vile 'honour' went to St Giles in the Fields, where people lived in perhaps the worst conditions of any in London's thousand-year history. The area now roughly confined within Charing Cross Road, New Oxford Street and Shaftesbury Avenue, St Giles was where William Hogarth set his painting *Gin Lane* showing 'the emaciated young man, the drunken woman with syphilitic sores, the suicide, the hasty burials *in situ*, the child about to fall to its death'.[5] The people lived in dank basements and garrets, several families to a room during the daytime and as many as could be crowded in at night. The even worse off just paid to sleep with complete strangers of either sex crammed into the filthy beds of a boarding house. Alcohol and sex were the currencies of the street; consumptive coughing, haggling and fighting the soundtrack to the sordidness.

It was not just the dilapidated buildings, stinking basements and fetid alleyways which kept honest householders and merchants from the neighbourhood. The poverty was so extreme, hope the long-dead casualty of gnawing hunger, that its dispossessed residents had created a world turned upside down. Renowned as a sinkhole of criminality, crooks and conmen ruled the area, protected by those who glorified lawbreakers as working-class heroes. Cocking a snook at the superciliousness of the affluent, they made a virtue of the cunning and conniving their everyday survival necessitated.

In this kind of neighbourhood it was easy to see why Josiah Tucker wrote that London was 'no better than a wen' while, more famously, to William Cobbett the city was 'the infernal wen'. It was, in fact, a strangely fitting dig in another way too. Wens—a wart, sebaceous cyst, tumour or goitre—were thought to be cured by the touch of a person just as they passed from life to death. So hangings were the perfect opportunity for the sufferer to find their cure. The afflicted waited in the crowd ready to rush up at the appropriate moment, women even baring their breasts if that was where the protuberance was. Similarly, the city's lawful citizens hoped that a regular purging at the gallows would rid them of their unwanted elements.[6]

Unfortunately for the honest, the crime rate was just about to soar at the end of the American War. It was the same throughout the eighteenth century; crime rates dipped for the duration of the recurrent wars as young men, the most common perpetrators, were away. Conversely, peace brought with it both a real and a perceived rise in crime. As the current war came to a close, King George lamented 'the number of idle persons that this peace will occasion'.[7]

9

His Majesty's fears soon came to pass. Violent crime in particular rose to unprecedented levels by the mid-1780s and became a major concern. Newspapers began to report numerous stories of gangs of men, thought to be discharged soldiers or sailors, who were running amok. Some believed that the demobilised men were simply too lazy to return to their homes and instead hung around thieving whatever they could lay their hands on. *The Times* bemoaned the large number of soldiers and sailors 'who went abroad to fight for their country, come home to starve or be hanged'. The Old Bailey's dock saw a succession of soldiers and sailors in the 1780s.[8]

There was some sympathy for former soldiers fallen on hard times, but often not a great deal. The general perception among the upper and middle echelons of society was that crime was caused by laziness, sloth and general abandonment. Low wages, unemployment and need were not considered to be motivating factors. Rather, men and women too lazy or corrupt to find a legitimate way to get subsistence for themselves and their families simply turned to crime instead. In fact, it was believed that crime was a class problem, with an entire criminal class terrorising their more virtuous compatriots. Jonas Hanway, philanthropist, founder of the Marine Society and early advocate of the umbrella, published a pamphlet in 1772 which professed to explain the 'dissoluteness which reigns among the lower Classes of People'.[9]

In truth, though, when food prices rose and times were hard, prosecutions for theft increased noticeably. This was especially true in the years around 1783, when a period of rising food prices coincided with the demobilisation of around 130,000 men from the army and navy. At that time, around twenty per cent of the British population 'was destitute' and unable to buy enough bread to feed their family even if they had no other expenses whatsoever. In this situation, alongside the organised mobs and professional criminals who still went about their scams and evil doings, crimes which smacked of desperation greatly increased. Women stole more often. Both men and women stole foodstuffs and other goods of minor value in crimes which were plainly neither organised nor well thought out. The number of people accused of petty crime who had previously borne a good character rose dramatically.[10]

A few of those who paraded through the Old Bailey's dock were of African origin. A relatively small number of black people had lived in Britain for decades, a community recently boosted by the outbreak of the American War. In fact their ranks would soon be greatly increased by Royal Navy ships bringing back those who had fought on the British side and now found themselves homeless, a group which included many men of African origin. Black sailors would have been a familiar enough sight to the people of London even before the war, as too were black prostitutes, seen as having niche appeal to customers. The capital even boasted an all-black brothel. Black beggars, entertainers, street-sweepers and hustlers were all part of the large crowd of men and women who eked out an existence from these occupations.[11]

More common still were black servants, quintessential symbol of a white nobleman's wealth and rank. At a time when newspapers advertised 'Turkish Wash' to make ladies paler and therefore more attractive, a pageboy's value increased according to the darkness of his complexion. He was a pet whose tasks included holding the good lady's smelling salts and decorative fan, combing her lapdog's fur and carrying the train of her dress if it was in danger of dragging in the dirt. Georgiana, Duchess of Devonshire, who delighted in all manner of new trends from hot-air ballooning to ostrich-feather headdresses three feet high to political campaigns—the first time a lady had seen fit to spend time on the hustings and considered a shocking deviance by many observers—had a black pageboy. Older black servants were fashionable too. It was said that one lady's 'black running footman is one of the finest figures ever seen, of an African complexion' and (despite the qualification) 'when in his tinsel apparel, is full as striking an object, as Sir Watkin Lewis in his aldermanic robes'. William Hogarth famously depicted black servants of all kinds in his paintings.[12]

But familiar as people of African origin were to working-class Londoners, unknown Africans, the inhabitants of the continent itself, were mysterious at best, a terrifying menace at worst. As the convict-soldiers stood on the parade ground at Gorée, the world was still six years away from the day when 'twelve determined men' would sit in a small printer's shop in London and mark a new beginning in the crusade against the slave trade. It would become a campaign which attracted a quite remarkable following: refined society ladies refusing sugar in their tea and mass meetings of ordinary people whipped into a frenzy of indignation against this moral outrage. But in 1781, the very idea that an African in chains was 'a man and a brother', as the popular publicity image of the abolitionists would soon beseech the British public, was all but inconceivable. Really only the Quakers had already taken a stand against slavery and the slave trade and anybody espousing such beliefs was generally regarded as a crackpot.[13]

Africa was a place which most Englishmen of the era held in terror. Large swathes of the interior of the continent were still unfamiliar and though they were no longer filled on maps by imaginary ogres, unicorns and strange man-beasts, the idea of Africa as wildly mysterious still pervaded opinion. The notion that Africans practised cannibalism was slow to fade, repeatedly bolstered as it was by many a slave trader's assertion that he was in fact a humanitarian saving his tragic cargo from certain demise.[14] Even if not eaten, the idea that a pale-faced visitor might be dedicated to one of the continent's bloodthirsty gods as a ritual sacrifice was ever present.

For most Britons, especially perhaps the uneducated ranks of indigent poor from which most of the convict-soldiers were drawn, the people who lived in Africa remained naked idolaters, so libidinous they might procreate with a monkey just before killing a man to dedicate him to a deity.[15]

Such prejudices were fed by opportunists who provided exotica for British people to gawp at. Sometimes, after being shown in London, they toured the country. An 'Æthopian Savage' had even been taken to Exeter, George Katenkamp's home town, where he had been displayed in the local pub. The price to see this 'satyr' was one shilling for gentlemen, less for servants. Given that 'this animal sits in a chair, with a club in his hand' it was most likely a chimpanzee, but even animals like bears had been shaved, dressed and displayed to the gullible British public as African men.[16]

Actual people of African origin were put on public display too. These were, after all, the years between the arrival in London of Omai from Huahine, a 'noble savage' introduced to the King and Queen and celebrated in London society, and the far less noble sideshow displaying Sara Baartman. Known as the 'Hottentot Venus', she was shown around Britain and France, scantily clad, so that visitors could gaze in astonishment at her large buttocks. Before her there was Mrs Amelia Lewsam, 'the greatest Phænomenon ever known', a woman of African origin evidently suffering from albinism. Having originally been offered for sale as a child of about five, she was still being presented in the 1780s as a marvel with 'all the features of an Æthiopian, with a flaxen woolly Head, a Skin and Complexion fair as the Alabaster'. She was often displayed at Bartholomew Fair, the yearly grand August event at which at least one of the convicts arriving in Africa had been a visitor. Benjamin Value had admired Amelia and the other 'freaks' on display, the acrobats, jugglers, wrestlers and wild animals and had then pocketed some lace, ribbon and thread from one of the stalls. It was a theft which eventually led him to Gorée.[17]

For all that was unknown about Africa, there was one thing eighteenth-century Europeans knew about it only too well: the place was deadly. One group of British men who travelled regularly to Africa, or at least its coast, were sailors engaged in the slave trade. They took back to their homes tales of mystifying fevers which came and went so that no man could say whether he was cured or about to die; diseases so merciless half the crew of a ship could be stitched into their hammocks and thrown overboard within the space of a few days; stomach complaints that made the sufferer shit white, green, orange and all the colours of the rainbow; parasites that could swim around the blood and then deform part of the body as they emerged; and the omnipresent risk that a man would suddenly and irrevocably lose his eyesight for no discernible reason. All those who hung around the docks of the East End looking for the chance of a quick penny knew only too well the seaman's ditty:

> Beware, beware
> The Bight of Benin
> For one that comes out
> There's forty went in.

In actual fact, though, the African people the convicts would most come into contact with were the Fante, who had been well known to the British (and vice versa) for decades by this time. As far back as the fifteenth century Europeans had visited Fanteland and by the 1780s, 'generations of literate Africans had learned to hold their own in the white man's world'.[18]

The slave trade and the presence of Europeans had profoundly affected Fante society by the 1780s. They had long established themselves as middlemen between the Europeans at the coast and the interior of Africa where few of the visitors ventured. It was an approach which had made them both powerful and relatively wealthy, and had kept more of their own people out of the oppressive holds of slave ships than might otherwise have been the case. At the beginning of the eighteenth century Willem Bosman had written that their territory was only a narrow strip of coastline nine or ten miles in length eastwards from Fort Mori, but by the end of that century they held control of all the land along the Gold Coast from close to Elmina to near Senya Beraku. Their territorial gains had in no small part been won with guns they had received in exchange for slaves traded to other African traders and Europeans.

Their lives had been significantly changed by their military superiority. The Fante men and women the convicts met with were living in a society utterly different from that their parents and grandparents had known. Education had promoted the idea of individuality and seniority based on achievement and success rather than lineage, profoundly altering the way things had always been. The wealth created by trading with Europeans had also greatly changed the power structure of their society. The growing group of mixed-race people—half Fante, half European—embodied the meeting of the two cultures. Margaret Priestley, in her study of Irishman Richard Brew's life and descendants, concluded that the Fante 'showed no small capacity for the assimilation of alien cultural traits, and indeed alien blood'.[19]

For all that, there were many aspects of Fante culture which the convicts would have thought, at best, very odd if they had become aware of them. It was not so much that, along with their sometime enemy the Asante, they were Akan people who believed that the Fante people all shared a common origin. Nor necessarily would the fact that the Fante were a matrilineal society have seemed very strange, as they had enough patrilineal traits to have confused far more educated observers than British criminals. But belief in a supreme being who stopped interacting with earthlings after an old lady pounding *fufu* struck him with her pestle might have seemed outlandish to say the least (never mind that the Europeans' own supreme being had a son, born to a virgin, who could walk on water). More strange still to the British visitors would have been the many lesser gods, local deities, ocean and river spirits and the act of throwing drink onto the ground as a libation to their ancestors.[20]

Yet however peculiar the Fante seemed to the convicts—and it is hard to imagine how alien the dirty, pallid, half-starved convicts were to the Fante— they were nowhere near as unfamiliar as the third 'tribe' of our tour—the Eora. Living on the banks of what we now know as Sydney Harbour, the Eora, fittingly enough for a people pretty much left alone by the rest of the world for forty thousand years, took their name simply from the word for people: *Ee*, 'yes', and *Ora*, 'here' or 'this place'. The adult members of the tribe would have remembered the strange day years earlier when some floating islands of people, huge white wings flapping above them, had passed mysteriously by the harbour. Others had heard rumours of this weird event from their kinfolk along the seashore, some of whom had even met the spectral visitors. They could not know that soon, as a result of the events told in this book, the Bérewalgal or 'people from the clouds' would reappear, this time to stay. To the Eora, it would mark the end of time.[21]

Mori, Ghana, August 2006

Only a few miles away from Cape Coast Castle but several worlds adrift, the locals were unprepared for visitors. There had been some negotiation to move boxes of tomatoes and bananas so that I could get the car through, but eventually I was defeated by the narrowness of the gap between ramshackle homes, and still there was no sight of what I'd come to find. Jumping down from my air-conditioned world into their dusty all-too-real one, I was surrounded by the inquisitive smiling faces of the women, half-dressed children and a few self-important men. They laughed.

I explained that I was looking for Fort Mori. For a second, the puzzlement on their faces made me wonder if I was in the wrong place or pronouncing it imperfectly, but then I realised that their bewilderment concerned why I would want to do such an outlandish thing, not where it might be.

A short walk around a steep corner led to the ruins of the fort. All that is left of it are two walls, precariously balanced close to the edge of a sheer cliff above a dazzling sea. They tower jarringly above the crude single-storey African dwellings, symbolising the now-crumbled power Europeans once had on this coast and the devastation they left in their wake.

While most of the other old slave-trading forts of the coast have been beautifully restored, monuments to the terrible suffering that occurred here and the modern-day tourists' wish for a place of memorial to visit, Mori lies forgotten. At Cape Coast, just down the road, a full-scale tourist industry is in place, with parking bays for coaches and swarms of youths for whom the visitors are the main chance to earn some cash. As many of those who arrive are the descendants of the victims who were once shackled in the castle's dungeons, loaded onto ships and taken across to the Americas for sale, there is of course something ironic in all this. The descendants of the sold have returned with more money in their pockets than the descendants of the sellers can ever hope for.

Mori is untouched by this world. There are no guides, no hawkers, no other tourists, no scam artists and certainly no Smithsonian-funded exhibits. I'm left alone to wander through the rubble, take some photographs, and wonder how the remaining parts correspond with pictures I've seen and descriptions I've read. I look for any signs of where the slave dungeon might have been, but it's too derelict to make it out with any degree of certainty. I ask the locals but am answered only with shrugs.

Laughing, always laughing, the women take my hands to help me climb back down over the uneven ruins. 'You've come from far!' they cry, and I don't tell them exactly how right they are. Presumably they think I've come from Britain or maybe the USA, but the reality is I've come all the way from Australia (a journey made via London), where I had first gone to trace this story and then found myself staying. And I'm looking for the ghosts of convicts, not slaves.

I've been on this coast several times before while studying the slave trade, so in another way my journey back here has been a long one. While living in North America and writing about the slave trade I became interested in the links between the transatlantic slave trade and the transportation of British convicts. Ships, captains, merchants, even victims were what I initially had in mind. Donald Trail, for example, the slave trader turned convict transporter whose ship had the worst death rate of all the vessels which took convicts to Australia and who subsequently stood trial for their murder. Or the black slaves who somehow escaped their bondage, got to Britain, committed crimes in a desperate effort to survive, and ended up being sent to Sydney for their crimes.[22]

Right away, though, I discovered that convicts had been dispatched to West Africa, to the slave forts of the region, after the American colonies had been lost and before 'Botany Bay' had been decided upon as the site for a penal settlement. I was intrigued. But I found that almost nothing had been written about them. The fact that there were convicts sent to Africa is quite well known to historians of early Australia but normally dealt with in a sentence or two. Who the convicts were and what happened to them has been seen as untraceable, lost.[23]

However, I knew where to go looking for these lost men and women. Any historian of the slave trade who has studied the copious letterbooks, ledgers and accounts of the Royal African Company and its successors would know where to begin. Often little more than their names was obvious at first, inscribed in the documents from the forts to which they had been banished. But with their names I knew that it would be possible to trace them back to England, to their appearance in the dock, usually for the most paltry of offences. I wanted to try to understand the lives of these men and women whose destiny had intersected with a bizarre period of British history. Too late for America, too soon for Australia, they had been sent out to live and die at the pivots of the transatlantic slave trade.

So this time I'd come back to Africa not to study the manifestly evil—how man could have inflicted on man the iniquities of the slave trade—but to gaze in wonder at the oddness of times past and the old British world's multiple, complex ways of holding people captive. Being in the places they once stood, it seems amazing, even now when it is only an eight-hour flight from London, that people were banished here for their crimes. Standing in the sentry boxes and walking around the ramparts of the renovated forts like Dixcove and Apam, it is no more comprehensible than it doubtless was to those who had to endure it.

Mori was the place I most wanted to visit because it was Captain Kenneth Mackenzie's headquarters back then and was somewhere I'd never been before; scarcely heard of, indeed, before I began researching this book. Among these ruins are the bones of many British convicts who lived and died here. The 'slave dungeon' I searched for once held not just human African merchandise but also the most abject of white men.

Much more than anything, though, being in West Africa brings to the fore the very morality of writing this book. Is it simply wrong to write a book about those who walked the walls dressed in redcoats when those who suffered so very much more can have no such history written to reveal their names and their individual stories? I am only too aware that the tragic victims who passed through the various castles' dungeons are almost totally silent in this book. It is as the record implies: to the castle guards they were scarcely more than merchandise which had to be carefully watched. I wish that they could tell their story too, of how the men in this book were their captors and oppressors. I wish it were so.

Amid the twelve million or so Africans who left from these forts, never again to see their homeland or to taste any degree of freedom, seen as scarcely human by their captors, the sufferings of a few hundred British convicts seems so inconsequential, so trifling. But it is still an important story to tell and the ripples this African experiment set in motion sealed the fate of the Eora people too. I can only hope it does all three tribes justice.

Chapter One

BOUND FOR AMERICA

In the 1770s the Strand was a place where all London's ranks rubbed shoulders. A gentleman might stroll with a lady on his arm and admire the wares in the street's stores but then find himself ambushed by a cutpurse or a 'bung nipper', waylaid by a wan cockle seller or accosted by a tuppenny prostitute. Behind the respectable facade of the window displays and carriages on the main thoroughfare were dark alleyways and courtyards where semi-feral pigs, poultry and destitute souls huddled together for warmth. The smell of animal manure, unwashed bodies, human excrement, wet straw and rotting food scraps often spread to the street along with the thick, choking smoke from coal fires. The well-to-do lady might feel the need to carry a pomander to counteract the stench.

In the late afternoon of 14 July 1773, as jeweller George Farquharson was beginning to put away his more valuable wares and thinking about closing up for the evening, a well-dressed customer entered his Strand premises. The man had some paste costume earrings he claimed to want to exchange, but after casting a discerning eye over the jewels on offer nothing the shopkeeper showed him took his fancy. He took a liking though to a mahogany case filled with green-handled cutlery and asked for it to be delivered to 16 Mead's Court the following day. Farquharson was only too pleased to oblige.

Later that evening Farquharson noticed that some silver and diamond earrings were missing, and over five shillings from his till. Of course he suspected some ne'er-do-well sly scoundrel from the streets rather than his gentleman customer. Shopkeepers and other honest citizens of the era considered the poor to be wholly responsible for the crime wave they were enduring. Gentlemen and their ladies were generally thought to be beyond reproach. The closest thing London had to a chief of police, Sir John Fielding—who carried out his role despite being totally blind—provided a colourful example of contemporary opinion. He described the underprivileged class as a 'black fountain' from which robbers, cutpurses and all manner of other dishonest villains gushed forth.[1]

The following day, however, when Farquharson ventured along Piccadilly and up Old Bond Street to Mead's Court to deliver the silverware, he found that there was no number 16. The penny dropped.[2] Even so, William Murray was away and clear, and that was by far the most important part of succeeding at eighteenth-century theft, a century before the distinctiveness of fingerprints was discovered. He had gone straight to a pawnbroker in Princes Street off Drury Lane and pawned the earrings, getting in return a locket he had hocked some days before and six guineas. Again his clothing had made his case. 'He was dressed very genteelly,' the pawnbroker recalled. 'I had not the least suspicion of their being stole.'

Murray next paid a call on goldsmith Constantine Tealings who kept a shop in Duke's Court off St Martin's Lane. There his modus operandi was similar and again he was successful, getting away with silver buckles and some earrings. Two days later he was at the shop of Jenkin Jones. He stayed around three quarters of an hour playing the gentleman accustomed to having tradesmen at his beck and call. His sense of entitlement well honed, he sent Jones and his employees running hither and thither with earrings, necklaces, shoe buckles and all manner of things he pretended an interest in. 'Being a man of a genteel appearance I had no suspicion of him,' Jones admitted ruefully. After he had gone Jones noticed that an elaborate diamond and emerald set buckle worth £9 was missing.

Three weeks later Murray was spotted by an acquaintance of Farquharson's and arrested. Though positively identified by Farquharson, at first Murray fervently denied the claims, professing high dudgeon that such an insult be laid at his door. But after a grim night in the watch-house he began to waver. He admitted that 'he was in unhappy circumstances' and had stolen the earrings but offered to go and get them back from the pawnshop if the jeweller dropped the charges. Farquharson refused.[3]

Hauled back into Newgate jail, 'London's notorious prison republic', Murray knew the ropes only too well. His list of crimes and arrests was already lengthy, starting with the time he and his partner in crime Richard Johnson had stolen the livery coat of Robert Edwards, Sir Francis Knowles's footman, while Sir Francis was patronising a bagnio in Soho Square. Then they had been lucky and had walked away with only sore heads and some bombastic swaggering to show for their night behind bars.[4] Twice he had been held in Newgate on charges of housebreaking but both times had got off scot-free when the case came to trial. On one he had been acquitted because a cry of 'fire' had alarmed the neighbourhood just as he was breaking in through the shutters of a house. He had hardly managed to stop himself smirking when the judge at his trial ruled that as he had not stolen anything this did not constitute an offence. Admittedly the other case had proved stickier as he had been caught in the act. Nevertheless, some carefully chosen words and promises had persuaded victim Simon

Abrahams not to testify in court. Rumours of bribery would dog Murray for years to come.[5]

He had also been in Newgate earlier that year when, for once, things had not gone in his favour. He had been accused of having stolen three pairs of white silk stockings from Thomas Tolley, whose shop was also in the Strand. Stockings were part of every gentleman's dress in an age when breeches were cut to just below the knee to reveal a nicely shaped calf, which along with manly comportment and favourable prospects was thought to be irresistible to the ladies of the age. On that occasion, Tolley had caught him with the stockings in his top hat before he left the shop, meaning that his guilt was all but incontrovertible.

In court Tolley had proved a resolute opponent. Murray, like all accused, was hearing his accuser's claims for the first time, and though he was far more educated, eloquent and guileful than the vast majority of terrified illiterates who paraded ceaselessly through the courts, appallingly ill-prepared and powerless to defend themselves, for once he could not talk his way out of trouble. Worse still, Judge George Perrot had slipped a black cap on his head as he pronounced Murray guilty. All prisoners knew what the black cap meant. The sentence was death.

It was hardly a surprise in one sense as death was by far the most prevalent punishment on the statute books. It was the penalty for so many crimes it was said that no-one even knew the exact number. They included stealing hedges, fruit from trees and timber; damaging orchards; taking fish from ponds; being in the company of gypsies for a month or more; having your face blackened in disguise; damaging Westminster Bridge; pilfering from a naval dockyard and even cutting down a small tree. For children aged seven to fourteen years, 'strong evidence of malice' was enough, officially at least, to send them to the gallows. Approximately 225 crimes carried the harshest punishment by the late eighteenth century.[6]

But the theft of goods worth less than forty shillings was not punishable by death, and the three pairs of silk stockings Murray had stolen from Tolley were valued at thirty shillings. Nonetheless, Murray had three months in Newgate's condemned cells to mull over the injustice of his sentence, growing fearful that his time was near. In the end events had gone in his favour. Judge Perrot (whose main claim to fame had been opening the prosecution against the insane and drunken Lord Ferrers, who would be hanged for murdering his steward, thereby giving him the dubious distinction of being the last lord of the realm hanged as a common criminal) eventually relented and recommended him to the King's mercy. On 16 April Murray had walked out of Newgate with a free pardon.

Now, less than four months later, he was back there again, back among the crowded mass of reprobates awaiting trial and the lice, rats, fleas and diseases that followed them everywhere. Again he worked potential rationales through his mind, by day confident that he could outwit his accusers; he had more chance of being found innocent this time, having been arrested weeks after the crimes. In the long reaches of the night, though, cacophonous howling all around, he must surely have wondered if a crossroads had been reached.

After a two-month wait, he was back at the bar of the Old Bailey, where the light deliberately reflected onto his face so that those watching could try to ascertain more clearly his guilt or innocence. The first signs were good, as Constantine Tealings was not there, perhaps alarmed by the fees prosecutors had to pay—subpoenas, recognisances, the indictment, the officer who swore the witnesses in court, the doorkeeper of the court, and the crier and the bailiff could add up to as much as £3. Cases regularly collapsed when the prosecutor failed to appear. Perhaps a visit by Murray's numerous shady acquaintances had persuaded him to stay away.

The other two jewellers were there, however. George Farquharson was the first to state his case, which Murray tried to undermine by suggesting it was all a most unfortunate case of mistaken identity. But Farquharson stood his ground, insisting that he was certain that the man in the dock was the guilty party. William Murray, Farquharson told the courtroom, had been wearing a sky blue 'showy' embroidered waistcoat at the time he had robbed him of the earrings and money. It was all over quickly. Justice was notoriously perfunctory in the eighteenth century. The judge slipped on the ominous black cap and declared that Murray should pay for the larceny with his life.

Despite that ruling, there was more to endure. Jenkin Jones had to have his day in court. He related the circumstances of his case against Murray, also declaring himself certain of the accused man's identity. He, though, was prepared to cut his losses, agreeing that the thief should escape the death penalty if he undertook to return the stolen item. Once again found guilty, for this crime Murray was given a sentence of seven years' transportation beyond the seas. It was rather hypothetical given the earlier ruling. Even the most vengeful of governments could not transport a man who had already been hanged.[7]

So Murray was returned to the condemned cells. This time he had to wait three long months in the squalid conditions, his life hanging in the balance once more. No longer a promising case for reform or a first offender, and with stolen goods far and away in excess of forty shillings, he knew he was unlikely to survive.

Murray had a couple of things in his favour, however. Since his earliest arrests he had been playing a name game with authorities, giving a variety of names and aliases whenever he was apprehended. So far, his name had been recorded at his various Old Bailey trials as, in the order of his various offences, William Mackensie, William Murray, Kenerth M'Kenzie, and now

William Williamson alias M'Kenzie. Eighteenth-century spelling mangled people's names often enough, but this was clearly something else. Murray (as I have chosen to call him to differentiate him from the man who would one day be his captain) claimed a proliferation of names as his own. As the years went by they would become more fanciful and most probably did not have any meaning, but these early names were all rough versions of the truth.

The Murrays and the Mackenzies were both powerful Scottish clans who had scores of kinship ties. The Murrays, who date their history to a Flemish settler in the twelfth century, had scattered lands throughout Scotland. William had been the forename of many of the prominent members of the clan. The name Kenneth Mackenzie was also significant. Aside from the man who would one day be the captain of his army company—and if he could have foreseen that turn of events, how he might have enjoyed the stunning irony—Kenneth Mackenzie was the clan name of the Earl of Seaforth and the current incumbent, the sixth earl, had that very name. A line of peers stretching back to Coinneach MacCoinneach (Kenneth son of Kenneth) in the fourteenth century, their name had been corrupted to the more anglicised Kenneth Mackenzie.

Who was the man behind all these names? It was a question which would cause considerable confusion. His identity and criminal record often obscured by all these aliases, who exactly he was would trouble the lawmakers for years and become a subject of speculation in London's many broadsheets.

Murray was also lucky with the timing of his capital sentence. Soon, Britain would start hanging a far larger number of the great unwashed. By 1785 there were twice as many hangings in Middlesex as there had been in 1780. London saw a huge fourfold increase in the same years. By 1784 it was remarked that so many men were awaiting execution that if all their sentences were carried out England would become known as 'the Bloody Country'. The years from 1780 to 1788 have been called 'an orgy of public slaughter'.[8]

In the meantime capital sentences were often reprieved. Women could 'plead their belly', as pregnancy provided at least a temporary respite from being hanged. The benefit of clergy was also still used, though for fewer and fewer offences; by it, felons secured respites for being able to mutter Psalm 51, known as the 'neck verse': 'Have mercy upon me, O God … Blot out my transgressions. Wash me thoroughly from mine iniquity, and cleanse me from my sin.'

More often still, capital sentences remained a way for the monarch to hold the ultimate power over life and death. With a flick of the pen and regal benevolence, he and his ministers could save a condemned man or woman, or could summarily command that they should meet their fate. The grand godly presence could play with his condemned subjects as pieces on a chess board, moving them around as he saw fit. Regularly, far more often than granting free pardons like Murray's previous reprieve, he decreed that they would be saved from death if they went to his American dominions. Small wonder that Americans were known as a 'scape Gallows race'.[9]

On the final day of November 1773, William Murray learned that his neck would again be saved. The price would be leaving Britain for fourteen years, banished to the American colonies.[10]

The following month, Murray shuffled out of his cell and into Newgate's 'press yard' where the blacksmith positioned a chisel over the rivet securing his manacles and struck it with a hammer. For the first time in months he could move his legs freely. But there was a heavy price to pay for this liberation, as instead a halter was fixed around his neck. It was part of a chain of iron collars which attached him to other departing convicts:

three men who had conspired together to take a ewe, another who had pocketed some almonds, and a man who had stolen six dried herrings while he was drunk. There was even in the chain the clichéd small boy who had picked one single handkerchief from the pocket of a gentleman in Fleet Street.[11]

They set out at dawn, but already the route down to the ship was lined with friends, family, partners in crime, neighbours and a host of other gawkers who turned out for the spectacle. Like hangings, this passed for entertainment in the raw days of the 1770s. Watching the banished shamble past on their last walk through the capital's grimy, polluted streets was not quite as electrifying as an execution, for there was no cataclysmic climax as the grand themes of life and death were played out before the crowd, yet the same element of Londoners turned out to watch this diversion, to make jokes and to amuse themselves with the creativity of the colourful invective they yelled at the chained men. The people in the coffle were ready with droll rejoinders and shouted back with their own ribald humour. It was gallows humour without the gallows. If any in the coffle managed to show their fine criminal skills by purloining a hat or wig from an onlooker who got too close, the crowd erupted in laughter.[12]

The walk from Newgate to Blackfriars' Bridge passed the Old Bailey where they had been judged and learned their fates and then went close by the Fleet jail, sarcastically known as Bartholomew Fair, where debtors whiled away their days. Then the coffle shuffled past St Bride's church, few pausing to look up at its towering spire (the original inspiration for layered wedding cakes) where Samuel Pepys had been baptised and Benjamin Franklin had advised on suitable lightning rods the previous decade. Heading towards the river they passed Bridewell, on the site of St Bride's Well, a place so infamous its name had become a generic appellation for all prisons. Then, by the elegant arches of Blackfriars' Bridge, they were loaded onto lighters which would take them to the ship.

At the end of the journey the *Justitia* waited for William Murray and the rest of the chain gang. Two hundred and sixty tons, the old wooden vessel was making its ninth consecutive trip to Virginia with expelled prisoners. Captain Finlay Gray was at the helm.

The *Justitia* was owned by Mr Duncan Campbell, Esquire of Black-heath, London. A former ship's captain who had once sailed aboard HMS *Dove* and the slaver *Methuen*, he had retired from the sea and become a wealthy merchant and man of some standing in the community. In 1758 he had gone into business with John Stewart, who held the monopoly on shipping the capital's convicts away to the American dominions, a trade they combined with bringing back tobacco in the empty ships. It was a lucrative business. Not only was a sum paid by the government for every convict transported, the felons sold in the colonies for between £8 and £20 each. On average, Stewart and Campbell had shipped away 473 banished men, women and children each year and since 1772, when John Stewart died, the business had been Campbell's alone. He was also one of London's top ten tobacco importers.[13]

Aside from being the man behind convict transportation, Campbell was part of the West India lobby, the group of men who campaigned in London for the interests in the slave islands of the Caribbean. His plantation in Jamaica, Saltspring, had come to him not by hard work and investment but by marriage. In his youth he had made a judicious match with Rebecca, the daughter of a planter, and upon her father's death he had inherited the plantation and all its accoutrements: machinery, tools, the grand plantation house and animals as well as the men, women and children he owned as slaves. Campbell's correspondence veered between the trials and profits of slaves and the trials and profits of shipping convicts.

Murray and the other Newgate passengers waited aboard ship, conscious only of their own unfolding tragedies. Slowly the ship became more crowded as convicts from other jails arrived in dribs and drabs. Eventually they numbered 170. They celebrated Christmas of 1773 anchored close to shore and saw in the New Year of 1774, the last most of them would ever spend in their homeland. In January, with a creak of timber and a hauling of ropes they set sail, leaving England behind them.

Long before the era of global communication, being banished abroad was a type of death. Those who were literate could and did write letters back home, but for most their children would be orphaned just as surely as if they were being nailed into a wooden box and lowered into the ground. Transportation of a spouse was usually considered to be a de facto divorce as the chances of ever seeing the other person again were slim. Quite often transported felons were leaving their families to a life of penury or the workhouse; their going meant that their children would have to survive as best they could alone on the streets without income or protector. Even for those without families, in a time when neighbourliness and community were of great importance and individuality was far less prized, to be forcibly removed from family and friends was a wrenching loss of personal identity. This was just as the British government wished it to be. Many transportees—like Murray, reprieved from death—were nevertheless dead to England and those who remained behind.[14]

Almost 50,000 men, women, boys and girls had been shipped to America as convicts in chains by the time Murray made his journey into exile. They were not the worst of offenders. Britain's murderers had gone to the gallows to feel the weight of the rope noose around their necks and then had their bodies anatomised, an additional punishment for those who had killed: to leave them mutilated as they faced their maker. Women found guilty of forging coins had been burned at the stake. Plenty of petty thieves had also swung from the gibbet beside highwayman and murderer as justice in eighteenth-century England could prove a capricious beast. In many ways, those who went to the Americas were the lucky ones.

Still, there had been many utterly pitiful people with tragic stories among the America-bound convicts. The stereotype of beggars being transported for pocketing a handful of food was not entirely wrong. In 1746 Francis Otter, whom the court acknowledged to be 'a poor creature', had been sentenced to transportation for fourteen years for stealing a single loaf of bread. Similarly, Jophoenix Smith, a resident of St Giles in the Fields, had gone to Maryland for stealing some bacon. Numerous young children were also among those shipped away. In 1719 John Easton, 'a small boy', had been cast for transportation for stealing three iron bars; the ship's records reveal that he was 'sold to Richard Snowdon' for his crime. Elizabeth 'Little Bess' Armstrong, only nine or ten years old, had travelled to Virginia for stealing two spoons. Others were not villains at all. Irishmen who resisted English rule, supporters of Monmouth's Rebellion, wandering vagrants, Scottish Covenanters and children of the 'swarming multitudes' had all gone en masse.[15]

What few in Britain realised as Murray and his shipmates set sail aboard the *Justitia* was that after all the decades of shipping away thieves, pickpockets, shoplifters, prisoners of war, conmen and wandering tramps, the days of convict transportation to the Americas were numbered. Murray would be one of the last to suffer this particular form of punishment for in the American colonies the drums of war had begun to beat.

In December 1773, while Murray had been waiting aboard the ship which would transport him away from England any day and Rebecca Campbell's family grieved her loss, a group of fifty or so Bostonians wearing headdresses and face paints in a caricature of Mohawks descended on the docks at Griffin's Wharf. Climbing aboard the *Dartmouth, Eleanor* and *Beaver*, they tipped their cargoes overboard. Within the space of a few hours, £10,000 of East India Company tea was emptied into the water in protest at Britain's taxation policies. The Boston Tea Party, as it would afterwards be known, was a major stepping stone on the path to revolution.

As well as taxes and representation, transportation of convicts from Britain was one of the main sources of the colonists' grievances against King and country in the tumultuous days of 1774. Murray and his shipmates were not just entering a political minefield, they and their ilk were a significant part of the problem. The tensions had been building for some time. In 1757 politician and lawyer William Smith had written of imported convicts as 'a herd of the flagitious Banditti'.[16] Two years later Benjamin Franklin contacted the *London Chronicle* complaining that transportation was 'an insult and contempt, the cruellest perhaps that ever one people offered another'. He famously suggested that rattlesnakes could be sent back to Britain as a fair exchange for the 'Human Serpents'.[17] A decade later a writer in Maryland using the name Philanthropos again used the media to rail against convict importation. British and Irish felons were 'vermin forced on us', he complained, and he questioned whether the colonists should go on letting England 'disgorge the foulest pollutants from her jails upon us'.[18]

It was all a far cry from the earliest days of transportation, when many of the American colonies had petitioned eagerly for convict servants. Virginia had first received a shipment of felons in 1618, seven years after Governor Thomas Dale had originally requested them. In 1640, Thomas Verney of Barbados asked his father in England to arrange for the transportation of one hundred prisoners from Bridewell jail so that he could use them as labourers on his plantation. In the 1680s, planter Christopher Jeaffreson even left his home on St Kitts and travelled to

London to personally arrange a shipment of felons to be transported for sale back on the island. Jamaican and Antiguan planters similarly requested and received shipments of convicts, and even tiny Nevis received over a hundred convicts in 1722. On the mainland, South Carolina, Pennsylvania and Maryland as well as Virginia received felon workers. The colonies desperately needed the additional manpower.[19]

As the islands' staple crops had grown more profitable, though, they had switched increasingly to slave labour. Sugar proved hugely lucrative as most of Europe developed a sweet tooth and by the 1680s planters in colonies like Barbados and Jamaica were among the wealthiest men in the world. Rich as Croesus, they could have any labourers they wished for, and they chose African slaves. Though they were more expensive than white servants, the advantage was that their terms of servitude never expired, going on ad infinitum, a yoke to be endured by their children, grandchildren and every other generation of their descendants. Thoroughly disposable and with fewer legal rights than their convict counterparts, they were planters' drudges of choice. The days when white servants could be bought, sold, gambled away, willed or mortgaged by their masters were over.[20]

On the mainland too African slaves increasingly became the mainstay of the labour force. South Carolina had a black population majority by the first decades of the eighteenth century. There was no longer any need for white troublemakers and as early as 1712 South Carolinians passed a law fining any ship's captain who imported convicts.[21]

Only the Chesapeake colonies of Virginia and Maryland, where the staple crops were less profitable and grown in smaller-scale operations, accepted convicts for most of the eighteenth century. Two-thirds of all the convicts banished to the Americas went to these two colonies alone. But in this region too, especially after Bacon's Rebellion, increasing numbers of African slaves were imported: for every ten new workers standing on the auction block, six were African slaves and the other four were British servants. The small Rappahannock region, for which Murray was destined, had imported 10,000 African slaves in the first half of the eighteenth century.[22]

Though Virginia and Maryland still accepted shipments of convicts at the time Murray sailed, trouble was most definitely brewing there too. For decades it had been thought that imported British convicts were responsible for almost all the crime committed in the two colonies. In the 1720s, Hugh Jones wrote in *The Present State of Virginia* that imported convicts were 'the poorest, idlest and worst of mankind, the refuse of Great Britain and Ireland, and the outcast of people'. 'The abundance of them,' he wrote, 'do great mischiefs, commit robbery and murder and spoil servants, that were before very good.'[23]

There were also suggestions that transported convicts were causing slave labourers to be unruly. In 1751 the *Virginia Gazette* published a letter claiming that 'most well deserve Hanging at home' and that in the colonies they 'corrupted and spoilt … other servants and Negroes'.[24]

The media meanwhile speculated that they brought with them 'gaol-fever' (typhus). In 1767, there had been discussion in the *Maryland Gazette* about the rights and wrongs of convict versus slave labour, with the spectre being raised of convicts arriving laden with infectious diseases which then spread to the American settlers and their valuable African slaves. Three years later Landon Carter, one of the region's foremost planters, wrote that so great was the fear that arriving convicts had spread 'Jail disorder' that 'every death that has happened in the neighbourhood has been imputed to that cause'.[25]

Cramped below decks, nauseous for the first few weeks from the endless rocking of the ship, unaccustomed to the nasty salted food and rank water, Murray's oceanic voyage can hardly have been a happy time.

Some captains used whips and thumbscrews on rebellious prisoners, and long days at sea were thought so traumatic they could cause a man to lose his mind, suffering hallucinations which would make him jump overboard thinking himself on luxuriant grassy fields. The women convicts were said to 'do no work except whoring wantonly in every corner of the ship'. On Murray's voyage, twenty-five-year-old Lydia Heathcote certainly seems to have impressed one of the seamen with her 'fair complexion', as he later helped her and some of her friends escape.[26]

On 3 March the ship sailed through the heads into Chesapeake Bay, all aboard comforted by the sight of land and calmer waters. Passing the entrances of the James and York rivers, the old *Justitia* finally turned into the Rappahannock.[27] When allowed on deck the convicts could see in the distance the grounds of Mount Airy, the Palladian-style villa built for planter John Tayloe, and the extremely grand Sabine Hall, owned by Landon Carter.

Thirty miles upstream they finally reached their destination. Leedstown was a thriving colonial port on a site which had once been the village home of King Passassack of the Rappahannock people. Northern Neck, as the area was called after its geography, was the home of George and Martha Washington, who occasionally travelled over from Mount Vernon to dine in Leedstown, and fourteen-year-old James Monroe, who would grow up to be the new nation's fifth president. It was also home to many imported convicts. Fifty years earlier Governor Gooch had said that the people of Northern Neck were 'of a more turbulent and unruly disposition than anywhere else' because of the number of transported convicts who had settled there. Nonetheless it was thoroughly respectable by the 1770s, with inns, stores carrying a variety of European and West Indian imports, eating places and a huddle of houses.[28]

Murray and other prisoners were to be sold by Thomas Hodge, Duncan Campbell's factor in Virginia who imported hundreds of convict servants in the last years before the American Revolution. Eager to make a profit, Hodge arranged a public notice advertising the sale of 'upwards of 150 healthy servants—men, women and boys'. In Purdie and Dixon's *Virginia Gazette* this announcement ran alongside a plea for the capture of a runaway slave named Matt, who walked badly having lost some toes to frostbite, and the return of a lost 'red and white no horned' Guernsey bull. On the same day, the *Justitia*'s human wares shared space in the rival Rind's *Gazette* with an appeal for the return of a 'half Indian fellow' named Jack Brown, who had run from his owner, the sale of 1700 acres of land in Orange County, and notice that a 'small negro boy' had been found in a wagonload of wheat. The paper appealed for his owner to claim him.[29]

Thomas Hodge proved himself to be an adept salesman, talking up the value of his merchandise. Most saw banished convict servants as dishonest undesirables, undernourished, ill-educated and untrustworthy. Hodge saw only opportunity and potential profit. Among the new arrivals on the *Justitia*, Hodge claimed, were many skilled craftsmen and women. They included 'smiths, cabinet makers and carpenters, joiners, shoemakers, tailors, bricklayers, peruke makers and hairdressers, bakers, weavers, schoolmasters, mantua makers and seamstresses, a printer, a copperplate printer, a gardener and surveyor, a dyer and a tanner'. The ship was represented as a veritable floating artisanate, with farmers and country labourers making up the remainder of the cargo. A ship full of petty thieves had been transformed somewhere in the middle of the Atlantic Ocean into a company of respectable workers.[30]

Hodge was prepared to extend credit to prospective purchasers wishing to buy this human merchandise, just as many slave merchants did. Many of his customers were probably grateful for the service as male convicts sold on average for £12.[31] Although the value of the pound sterling was around twenty per cent less in Virginia than in the mother country, this equated to two years' wages for a housemaid in London, or one year's pay for a low-quality coachman. To most ordinary folk it represented a large sum of money.[32]

Come 16 March the scene was set. Bidders stood around and took their pick of men like Samuel Beal, 'an incorrigible rogue' who had deserted his family, Patrick Dunn and Timothy Bray, who had stolen a hay bale, or William Agar, who had been caught wearing a stolen shirt. Planter and merchant Thomas Montgomery, who also oversaw slaves, decided upon the Allen brothers, George and John, both likely looking lads in their mid-twenties. Others were sold over the border into Maryland.[33]

For Murray and his shipmates, their sale on the banks of the Rappahannock was the moment of realisation of what they would truly suffer for their crimes. Even for those who had been destitute in Britain, accustomed to overcrowded jails and then herded aboard ship, this was considered to be a whole new level of humiliation. How could that furtive act of slipping a hand into a gentleman's pocket to fish out a handkerchief, or climbing in through that tempting open window to take goods which, when pawned, would stop your children going to bed hungry yet again, how could they be reconciled with this? But the might of the British government had decreed it be so.

The horror of the experience has been described by others who had gone to the auction block. William Green wrote of his sale after being banished to Maryland for seven years: 'we were all put on shore in couples, chained together and drove in lots like oxen or sheep'. Prospective purchasers viewed them 'as the dealers in horses do those animals in this country, by looking at teeth, viewing our limbs, to see if they are sound and fit for labour'.[34] James Revel, sentenced to transportation at Surrey in the early 1770s, wrote similarly of his experiences after arrival in Maryland:

Some viewed our Limbs, turning us round
Examining, like horses, if we were sound.

Revel, like other indentured servants before him, also compared the convicts' lot with that of African slaves. He warned his countrymen to avoid crime, otherwise they would, like him, be 'Sold for a Slave because you proved a Thief'.[35] Henry Woodford, transported for stealing four brass candlesticks, had protested that he and his shipmates aboard the *Susannah and Sarah* were 'sold for Slaves', which he considered to be 'worse than Death'.[36] William Murray left no account of how he felt as he stood on the auction block, but accustomed to diamonds and the finest white silk stockings, we can only assume he must have been utterly mortified.

As William Murray walked away from the *Justitia* he steps fleetingly into the shadows beyond where historical records can trace him. It could be that he found a way to escape the auction block that was far more legal than that taken by Lydia Heathcote and her fellow runaways. The truth was that the rigidities of the British class system had not entirely been left behind as the old country slipped over the horizon: there was still some leeway for a man who had once had silk stockings and a top hat to his name, even if he was now a banished felon.

Two decades before Murray's banishment a man named John Poulter had written about his criminal activities, including a section regaling the reader with advice about 'the way that convicts return from transportation'. He suggested that the best method was to bribe the captain of the ship going over, allowing the prisoner to be recorded as a free servant. In that way, they would then be at liberty. In fact, the *Justitia*'s owner and contractor, Duncan Campbell, claimed that it was legitimate to let felons buy off their servitude, as 'their punishment was only banishment'. In many ways he was correct, as Britain's laws made no clear case as to whether transportation was merely exile or included some element of hard labour.[37]

The £12 or so needed to secure any such arrangement was a considerable sum, well beyond the means of the majority of Murray's shipmates. But for Murray himself, £12 would have been equivalent to about two debauched nights out in London if he factored in 'supper, a bath, and a fashionable courtesan'.[38] It was far less than the proceedings from a single successful jewel heist. Just like the time when the judge had declared him innocent after a fire had prevented him from breaking into a house (an event which must have seemed so long ago), perhaps Murray could not help but be rather amused at the arbitrariness of the seemingly august British legal system. Money, the handmaiden of class and status, could apparently make any number of indiscretions vanish to dust.[39]

Equally, though, as Murray seems to have let money slip through his fingers like water, it is quite possible that he had no choice but to endure being sold for his labour as a common criminal. Given what came later, it is tempting to envisage William Murray toiling as a convict servant in Virginia, where white labourers often worked alongside black slaves.

Most of those who arrived on the *Justitia* went to work in the tobacco industry which employed black and white workers. Tobacco was everywhere in the Chesapeake. The region was overwhelmingly rural and tobacco plantations were relatively large, as one field labourer could work around fifty acres. Planted in late December or early January, transported from the seedling beds to the main fields throughout April and maybe into May and June when the leaves were about the size of a dollar, pruned and weeded for several months, harvested in September, even then the process was far from complete. After that the leaves were hung in barns to cure then were 'stripped', 'stemmed' and 'prized' until they formed a solid mass. Around March or April, the time Murray arrived aboard the *Justitia*, the finished product was finally ready for shipping away to market. Another year's crop was by then, of course, already in the ground.[40]

Virginian society held tobacco dear to its heart. It was what the grand estates at Mount Airy and Sabine Hall, seen from the *Justitia*'s deck, had been built upon. In the 1770s tobacco accounted for over three-quarters of the colony's exports; in England there was a huge market for the addictive crop. More than this, tobacco cultivation was a way of life in Northern Neck; it defined the seasons, social life, a man's status and even his sense of self.[41]

Although the majority of the heavy field work was done by African-American slaves—George Washington, for example, owned 227 men, women and children—convict servants were also still in demand. Many planters employed both servants and slaves in the process of tobacco cultivation. Convicts in fact regularly compared their situation to slavery. James Revel claimed, 'we and the Negroes both alike did fare', stating that he had been forced to work 'among the Negroes ... at the Hoe'. Elizabeth Sprigs wrote home to her father from Maryland in the 1750s that she had been 'tied up and whipp'd', was nearly naked and was 'slaving during Masters pleasure'.[42] There were plenty of accounts of convict servants wearing iron collars, iron fetters and even 'horse locks and chains'.[43]

In reality, by the later eighteenth century such comparisons were but a linguistic device to emphasise their sufferings. The difference between selling a person's labour power and his bodily being may have seemed only a legal nicety to some, but to those who stood on the auction block it was the difference between sovereignty and chattelism, freedom for your children or an inherited lifetime of bondage, a future with some hope or a continuous, ruinous battle against despair.

The word 'slavery' was fast becoming what it still remains today: a trope for all manner of suffering and even mania (fashion slave, slave to love) as well as a system of bonded labour. This is why American republicans, some of them slave-owning planters, used the term 'slavery' to complain of their subservience to the British crown. George Washington, for example, unabashed slave master, wrote that the British government was 'endeavouring by every piece of Art and despotism to fix the Shackles of Slavery upon us'.[44]

William Murray, then, was certainly no chattel slave while he was in Virginia. But he was in close contact with people who were. Over forty per cent of America's people of African origin lived in Virginia at the time of the Revolution and Murray would have been able to see these black bondsmen and women from sun-up to sundown engaged in backbreaking labour on the land.

Although it is hard to imagine Murray working as a common labourer—educated and astute, he probably found his way to a better position quickly even if this was his lot—he could well have worked closely with slaves. We can imagine him perhaps as an overseer, ordering slaves around as they went about their daily tasks, all the while ingratiating himself with his owner by offering to help with the bookwork and by charming his master's wife. He could even have formed bonds with slaves as George Newton, one of his shipmates aboard the *Justitia*, seems to have done. Newton would soon flee his owner along with two slaves named George and Tim.

Or perhaps the darker-skinned men and women dressed in uniformly dour clothing made of cheap, no-nonsense fabric were a curiosity to Murray and he could scarcely envisage that within a few years he would be living in their ancestral homeland. In fact for a man with such pretensions to gentility, they were probably one of many things about the colony which seemed dreadfully outré. A Londoner with a taste for the finer things in life and accustomed to living in Europe's biggest city—the heart of the British

Empire no less—he in all probability turned up his nose at the post-in-the-ground homes with their clapboard exteriors and dirt floors, these strange chattel labourers, the maize they ate and a whole host of other colonial oddities. Though many white Americans followed the English fashions in clothes, furniture and decoration as best they could, even the people themselves might have seemed strange to Murray, being around three and a half inches taller than their English counterparts. Murray was not a small man, but accustomed to living among the British urban poor who were shorter even than their rural compatriots, he could well have thought himself in a land of giants.[45]

Murray had a stroke of good fortune, for the timing of his period of transportation to Virginia was fortuitous. In some ways he had been sold into a hornet's nest of resentment against the country he had left. Leedstown, where he first disembarked from the *Justitia* and set foot in the American colonies, had been the site of the first resolutions to defy England over the Stamp Act a whole eight years earlier. Virginia was the colony with the least divisions over the question of independence and the fewest people who allied themselves with King George, though Leedstown later became an infamous 'sink' of Toryism. Whichever side a person was on, though, whatever his political persuasion, it was clear by the summer of 1775 that there were problems ahead. By then the colony was hurting from the British blockade of ports; the acute lack of salt, used in food preservation and cattle feed, was proving an especial problem.[46]

Soon people started to leave. By June of 1774, George Washington's friend and neighbour George William Fairfax had sold all his 'mostly new, and very elegant' worldly goods, let out his mansion house and retreated to England. Then things escalated as the Quartering Act was passed, requiring colonial residents to let British soldiers into their homes. In response, the First Continental Congress was held at the beginning of September to coordinate a response to that and other of the 'Intolerable Acts'. The situation was fraught, as those loyal to the King were bathed in tar and then rolled in feathers to mark their lack of patriotism. Murray was definitely astute enough to see where things were heading. As an educated and wily man, he could hardly have failed to be aware of the many announcements in the newspapers that men were leaving for England, fearful of their prospects if they stayed behind.

On into the next year the tensions heightened. In March 1775 Patrick Henry stood on the steps of St John's Church in Richmond, Virginia and uttered the immortal words: 'I know not what course others may take; but as for me, give me liberty or give me death.' By June the governor, Lord Dunmore, left Williamsburg and took refuge aboard HMS *Fowey*. In November he would issue his famous declaration that all slaves and indentured servants in the region would be freed if they sided with the British. African-Americans began flocking to the British despite dire warnings of their fate if caught.

In this climate of chaos and insecurity, it was easier for Murray to sneak away than it otherwise would have been. Certainly no runaway advertisement appeared in the local media for him as it did for many convict deserters. And there were many reasons for him to head north to the much bigger cities of Philadelphia, New York or Boston, where there were far fewer men who knew him to be an imported convict supposedly serving a fourteen-year sentence. In the anonymity of the crowded urban centres there were also far more opportunities for him to return to his existence of trickery, scams and stings. A man who had lived the majority of his life in London would have felt more at home there than in Virginia's rural backwaters.

If Murray headed north from Virginia, attracted by the greater prospects in New York or Philadelphia, he would have found rising disquiet among the populations there too. Philadelphia, the largest city in the colonies with around 42,000 people, was home to meetings of the Continental Congresses and so played host to George Washington, Samuel Adams and Patrick Henry among others. The citizens of New York, closer to the centre of the conflict in Massachusetts, looked on as fighting broke out in Lexington and Concord at the start of 1775. By May it was said that 'there never was a more total revolution at any place than at New York'.[47]

All over the colonies many of those loyal to the king made the painful decision to leave for England. By the middle of 1775 in Boston a number of loyalists were embarked on a ship bound for London. By July, the *Polly* and the *Mary* arrived in Britain with some of New York's fleeing supporters of the King. All believed it would be a short-term retreat, a fleeting place of refuge until the King's forces had subdued the rebels.[48] But what for them was a temporary withdrawal to safety was a sliver of a chance to Murray. He boarded one of the ships of returning loyalists, assumed an identity as one of their number, and made the reverse crossing of the Atlantic Ocean. He had been away only eighteen months.

Chapter Two

MR JEFFERSON AND PATRICK MADAN

Among the highways and byways of filth, grime and deprivation which London had in abundance, numerous pickpockets, shoplifters, burglars and a host of other illicit chancers were incessantly huddled in rotten dens pledging oaths to form gangs. Alliances were generally fleeting, but in a world in which a lifetime might last until the next quarter sessions, solemn promises to stick together and, if caught, to 'die mute' were weighty rites. They were to some extent the pivot around which all-important seedy social networks—very young boys eager to move up the ranks, favoured molls, trusty publicans and their network of fences—revolved. Or at least they were until nightfall, for who knew what new circumstances dawn might bring?

In this underworld, an Irishman named Patrick Madan rapidly became a well-known figure in the early 1770s. He had been set on a law-abiding path by his father, an honourable man who had ensured that he could read and write and placed him as an apprentice with a bricklayer and builder in London. But by the age of thirteen or fourteen he had parlayed those skills into the 'sport' of 'flying blue pigeons', as stealing slate from roofs was known. Unable to get work as a builder because of his very dubious honesty and his involvement in the Spitalfields weavers' riot, he joined with a notorious gang of outlaws. When he was caught picking pockets he was sent away to sea by his uncle, the navy being a familiar reform school of the era for errant sons and nephews. He sailed to both Jamaica and Greenland.

His period at sea definitely did not reform him. Returned to London, he became a skilled and fearless thief, the bane of the night watch and constables. He also became a gang leader, standing at the head of his own faithful band of brigands, for thanks to his strength, daring and charisma 'a number of thieves of lesser consequence gladly hastened to his standard'. All had 'arrived at the summit of sin'. He also took up with 'the daughter of a noted bawd, to whose artifice he became a wretched dupe'.

One of his favourite scams was rather similar to Murray's. Affecting the dress of a country squire with a 'silver capped whip' he would take one of his much younger conspirators into a shop on the pretence of having brought his son to town to shop for a gift for him. Numerous items would then be surreptitiously slipped beneath the clothes of both man and boy.

His exploits became so notorious that he was believed to have been involved in a startling number of crimes. Among his unsubstantiated exploits was housebreaking in Hackney at the tender age of fifteen, a capital burglary in which he and two accomplices stole £700 worth of banknotes, and highway robberies using a pistol and threatening language. Rumour even spread that he was the fifth missing man of a gang of Irishmen who had murdered a watchman on Westminster Bridge on Christmas Day 1769. It is very unlikely that he participated in this crime—or, perhaps, some of the others—but as his fame spread he was believed to be guilty of almost anything. His charisma and reputation was a double-edged sword. At one point he was apparently cast for transportation to suffer fourteen years in the colonies like Murray, but was reprieved before he was sent away. He then turned his attentions to receiving stolen property and became celebrated among thieves for always treating fairly those who came to him with stolen items. His house was also a favourite thieves' haunt because it had a double-door 'privy conveyance' in the back yard which allowed people to slip away undetected if the police should appear.

After all these escapades, both real and alleged, he was finally put into a very awkward situation by a crime of which he was reputed to be innocent. On 9 April 1774, on a proverbial dark and stormy night, members of his gang were out and predictably up to no good. Near the Shepherd and Shepherdess pub on City Road in Islington, William Beckenham and John Dobbs were held up by two footpads armed with a pistol and a cutlass. After stealing some money from Dobbs and then sending him on his way, they turned their attention to the trembling Beckenham. One man put the barrel of the gun in Beckenham's mouth as if to blow off his head and then, holding him prisoner for ten minutes, stripped him of his watch, around forty shillings, his coat and waistcoat.

Five weeks later Patrick Madan and a man named Michael Brannen were arrested for the crime. When Brannen was spotted by a constable who knew his pockmarked face all too well, he was still armed with the gang's horde of weapons. Desperately flinging the guns into a ditch he fled on foot, but was soon caught and the pistols retrieved as evidence. Worse still, when the watch arrived to arrest Patrick Madan, he got out of bed and put on the coat which had been stolen from William Beckenham.

For the law, Madan's arrest was quite a coup, as he and his gang were suspected of numerous offences. When he appeared at the Old Bailey in early July, authorities also laid four other highway robberies at his door, three of them alleged to have all been committed on 8 April.

But these hastily added charges were hopelessly bungled as none of the victims showed up for court. One of the victims later claimed that he had missed the trial through misinformation and not from any 'affection for the prisoners'. William Beckenham was there, though, and presented his evidence well enough to convince the jury. Madan and Brannen were sentenced to hang despite Madan's plea that he had received the stolen coat but had not been one of the armed highwaymen.[1]

Convicted of a more serious crime than petty theft, having used weapons and threats in his offence and with no high social background to count for him, Patrick Madan stood little chance of earning a reprieve. He was warned in court 'to buoy himself no longer up by the prospect of a pardon'. His twin sister, a courtesan to a lord of the realm, petitioned for clemency for him, but in vain. He had only a little over six weeks to wait as his hanging was quickly scheduled for 19 August. The law wanted such a menace dispatched to meet his maker as soon as possible.

When the fateful day came around, Madan was loaded into a cart at Newgate for his final earthly journey to the Triple Tree at Tyburn. Like so much else in English law, it was an occasion replete with tradition. An overseas visitor to the capital, on seeing the procession to a hanging, reported his astonishment at the lack of 'delicacy' shown and recorded that the condemned commonly dressed either 'in mourning or in the dress of a bridegroom'. Usually the damned were allowed a drink at some pubs along the route, the Bowl Inn and the Mason's Arms being favourites, which partly accounted for why the two-mile journey could take up to three hours.

The other hindrance to the carts' progress was the huge crowd, as traditionally hanging days were public holidays. Some of the assembled mob threw dead cats and dogs into the air to mark the occasion. Madan's gang were there bellowing encouragement to their hero, while wags shouted offerings of a 'pint on the way back'—the origin of the expression 'on the wagon'. History does not record whether Madan had already at this stage earned sufficient notoriety to merit the crooks' honour of wearing the white cockade of mockery or to receive a nosegay from one of the hordes of prostitutes standing outside the Church of Holy Sepulchre. There were certainly plenty of them there if he did. The newspapers reported that more than a hundred of the lowest sort of women and a crowd of boy pickpockets attended the hanging, along with Jack Rann, alias Sixteen String Jack, one of the most notorious crooks in the country who would himself suffer at the fatal tree later that year.[2]

Britain's hanged met a ghastly end. There was no careful calculation as to the necessary length of rope for a person of their weight, meaning a protracted and painful suffering was possible as they dangled from the scaffold. The same year as Madan's parade to the gallows, a professor of anatomy wrote that 'the man who is hanged suffers a great deal' as, far from being rendered unconscious by the initial drop, 'for some time after a man is thrown over he is sensible and is conscious that he is *hanging*'. There were even cases of the hanged being resuscitated. Hanged bodies had livid and bloated faces, sometimes with eyes bulging from their sockets and distended tongues. They were uniformly soaked with urine and faeces.[3]

Like the procession from Newgate, these ghoulish displays were public entertainment. Spectacle and melodrama as well as punishment, the moment of death was the apex around which the legal system turned. Huge crowds of 30,000 or so watched executions in London, with people paying to observe from adjacent windows or rooftops or to stand on a cart in a nearby street. Then, with everything in place, those soon to be launched into the next world had a chance to speak their final words from the gallows. Supposed to be an opportunity to ask for forgiveness and repent of sin, for some it was a chance to show their continued defiance. Dying with 'face', or showing the appropriate degree of insouciance, earned the cheers and admiration of the crowd. Long prayers were booed; those like thief Tom Austin who cheekily asked a woman selling curds and whey if he could have some won the crowd's delight.[4] Patrick Madan managed to outdo them all.

With the noose already around his neck and final prayers said, a man named Amos Merritt, a known criminal suspected of a string of offences, stepped forward from the crowd and proclaimed that he, not Madan, was responsible for robbing William Beckenham. The crowd agog, a messenger was hastily sent to the Secretary of State, who immediately sent a respite for Patrick Madan. While Madan's shady associates bellowed their appreciation of this madcap eleventh-hour escape, the rest of the crowd heckled loudly and jeered at being deprived of the fun of a hanging. Nonetheless, as the two other highway men scheduled to be launched into eternity that day felt the noose tighten around their necks, Madan was merely a spectator. Quite what had happened remained a mystery. Many claimed that Amos Merritt, hardly the repentant suddenly feeling the weight of his conscience as another man stood ready to be hanged for his crime, was really one of Madan's own criminal crew who had put his neck on the line for his gang leader. Others maintained that Merritt really was guilty and had been forced by the many underworld characters who admired Madan to come forward to save him.[5]

The saga did not end there. As it turned out Amos Merritt would not be required to make the ultimate sacrifice on this occasion, as when the case was retried at the Old Bailey, Merritt was acquitted. By then it was impossible for any jury to know who to believe. But his days were numbered all the same. Less than five months later he replicated Madan's journey from Newgate to Tyburn for a burglary he had committed a month after his release. Madan was reported to have said a 'solemn farewell' to him in the cart conveying him to Tyburn, which on this occasion had the unusual spectacle of 'two mutes on horseback' riding ahead of it. Meanwhile Patrick Brannen, Madan's alleged accomplice in the Beckenham theft, was offered a respite and, like Murray before him, sailed on the *Justitia*, which was this time bound for Maryland. Patrick Madan returned triumphantly to his gang, now a criminal celebrity.[6]

Pat Madan could hardly afford to be chastened by his brush with death. He knew no other life than that of law-breaking, had no other expertise than as a criminal overlord and had learned nothing from his experiences other than how much he loved playing to the crowd. What was reckless abandon to the middle classes was spirited defiance to the subset of society Madan inhabited, the difference in perspective being also a difference in possibility to do things any other way. He did not manage to stay out of trouble for long.

Caught in the act of trying to mug a lamplighter, he was confined to a watch-house where his ever-loyal gang members made a dreadful mistake. His friends had seen him captured and quickly sallied around the nearby streets recruiting a crew to launch a rescue attempt. As it turned out, his intended victim had declined to press charges, effectively meaning that the crown had no case and he would soon be freed. Unaware of this turn of events, the mob, armed with cutlasses and iron bars, attacked the watch-house where Madan was being held. They damaged the building, stole from the keepers, and bore Madan jubilantly away. One man allegedly lost two fingers in the battle. When the newspapers heard that the same man who had so recently and dramatically escaped the gallows was engaged in yet another affair it became a something of a cause célèbre.

Neither Madan nor his liberators were free for long. Before the end of 1774, Madan and no less than twelve of his partners in crime were imprisoned in Newgate awaiting trial for this escapade. Madan's fate in particular looked grim; when watchmen searched his home, where they had arrested both his common-law wife and one William Thomas, they found keys 'of different sizes', pistols (one of which was loaded), a vice and files used for making duplicate keys, a crowbar and some bricklayer's trowels. Another report said that authorities also found among Madan's belongings a 'pocket book with vellum leaves, containing an account of houses that he intended to be *done over*, viz. a clear-starchers in Fetter-lane; a slop-shop in Wapping; Flexman over the water; Bailey in Islington; Ayliff-street; Five-foot-lane over the water; a shoe-maker's in Tower-hill; a baker in the Minories; a grocer in Whitechapel; a grocer in Virginia-street; No. 42 Watling-street' and so on down to a 'corn-chandler in Crispin-street'.[7]

On Saturday 19 April the thirteen men appeared for trial at Hick's Hall. Authorities were spooked by the menacing-looking mob which waited to watch the proceedings and sent for a party of guards in case an attempt was made to free the prisoners. After hearing the case three men were sentenced to seven-year terms of imprisonment. Nine others, including Madan, received five years each, while the final man was told that he would be imprisoned for three years. It was a punishment almost unheard of in an era when imprisonment for long periods was rarely considered, and the men 'begged hard for transportation' instead. For Patrick Madan his sentence must have particularly riled as he should have walked free from the original mugging. At a separate trial his wife, Elizabeth Castle, fared better, being sentenced to one month at Clerkenwell Bridewell.[8]

As Madan and his allies began their painfully long sentences rotting away in Newgate, another blight on the British law authorities returned to plague them once more. In the middle of 1775, William Murray strode ashore in Britain, illegally returned from banishment in Virginia.

Returning from transportation was one of Britain's many crimes punishable by hanging, but the cocksure Murray felt certain he could cheat the law again.

Between Virginia and London Murray had conceived an astonishingly brazen plan. Despite the precariousness of his position if caught, rather than hiding the fact that he had just returned from the crisis-stricken colonies and attempting to lie low, he used it to his advantage. Having seen and read about the loyalists' problems while in America and having returned to Britain during the flight of some supporters of the King, Murray audaciously claimed that he too was a loyalist. His allegiance to King and country had provoked him to give up his American fortune and return to London, he maintained. His new act was that of dispossessed gentleman martyr.

Murray's ploy was playing on the identity crisis the upheaval and subsequent war precipitated in Britain, for it was unclear to most people whether the rebellious Americans were 'them' or 'us'. Americans were spoken of as 'our Brethren, *Englishmen* as we are, our own Flesh and Blood' and the King's chaplain, Henry Stebbing, stated simply 'they are part of us'. At this early stage there were plenty of people in Britain who had sympathy for the rebellious colonists' complaints and many vehemently resisted a conflict they thought of as a civil war and believed would be ruinous to all involved. Americans were spoken of as kinfolk; it was inconceivable to many British people that they would become a separate entity, much less that the government would engage in a bloody war with its own citizens.

From 1774 onwards American loyalists began arriving in Britain. Seeking sanctuary from the gathering storm clouds and the prospect that their neighbours might get entirely too handy with a barrel of tar and a sack of feathers, they disembarked from their transatlantic voyages hoping to reconcile the two nations they thought of as home. They believed their stay in Britain would be short as the King's troops would quickly defeat the rebels. It was not to be, of course, and many were in severe financial difficulties as hopes for a speedy resolution faded. Searching for work, some found that their colonial talents were unwanted in London and the provinces. In a step they never thought they would have to take, their dignity deeply wounded by the need to resort to such extremities, some of the refugees were forced to beg for government assistance. As the crisis dragged on, fortunes simply vanished.

In this climate of confusion, Londoners were susceptible to believing fake claims that a man might have given up his land, business and possessions in the colonies and returned 'home'. Numerous people had sympathy for such a plight. Murray was also helped by the fact that only ten Virginian families had arrived in Britain by 1775, meaning he was less likely to be identified as a fraud than somebody arriving from, say, Massachusetts. Boston and the surrounding region had seen far more of its citizens resettle in London during the first years of the conflict.[9]

To assist in his subterfuge he adopted a new alias. Murray now became William Jefferson. What bare-faced cheek led him to assume the surname of Thomas Jefferson, one of the foremost critics of the British government—who a year later, at the age of thirty-three, would draft America's Declaration of Independence—while acting the role of returned loyalist can only be imagined. With his eye for exploiting any available opportunity, he had likely been using this name since his time in Virginia, where it certainly would have had plenty of cachet by 1775. Returning home, he saw the continued benefits of being a Jefferson rather than a Murray or a Mackenzie or any of his other names. It added to the authenticity of his pose as an American and it separated him from his earlier life of crime. More to the point, using the name of somebody who was an even greater thorn in the side of crown and country than a scoundrel like himself was an ingenious prank. His criminal comrades surely enjoyed the joke.[10]

As returned loyalist William Jefferson, martyr to his devotion to King George and the good people of Britain, Murray lived a life of luxury, gaiety and dissipation. He employed servants and self-importantly drove around town in a vis-à-vis, a type of two-person carriage where, as the name suggests, the occupants faced each other. So successful was his act, so convincing his air of respectability, that he began to socialise with London's moneyed and powerful. Apart from being tremendous fun for Murray, it was also a very shrewd ploy. A gentleman driving grandly around town in a carriage was the last person one would suspect of being a returned convict transportee.

Unsurprisingly, he did not acquire all the fancy trappings of his new life legally. He saw no point in suddenly adopting such a conservative habit as paying for merchandise and services. Rumours circulated that he ordered many items from craftsmen and shopkeepers and then disappeared, gaining credit through his apparent social status but then reneging on the debt. He augmented this with a bit of outright shoplifting, reluctant to waste his old skills when something took his eye.

He thoroughly enjoyed the flamboyant life the metropolis provided, now with the added frisson of knowing that he was mocking the law with every raised glass or placed bet. He returned to visiting prostitutes, something he had shown a penchant for in earlier years, choosing those who were a cut above the street girls who called out to prospective clients from the city's alleyways. In the 1770s, 'sporting' men could purchase *Harris's List of Covent Garden Ladies* or *Man of Pleasure's Kalendar* or *The Man of Fashion's Companion*, publications which allowed the discerning man to choose a woman he desired before calling at her premises. Lacking even a smattering of their Victorian successors' prudery, women of the era thought nothing of advertising their bodies as having 'two beds of down for Cupid to sport on' or a 'coral lipped mouth of love'. A Miss Wilmot even advertised that she had pleasured King George's brother and that any other man might share the royal experience for a guinea if he could overlook the fact that she had syphilis. Perhaps rather mercifully, we are not privy to Murray's partialities and peccadilloes.[11]

Murray's luxurious life now included operas, theatres and concerts as well as Soho's brothels. Theatre-going was a common activity in the eighteenth century, and one which often required far more from the audience than simply to sit, watch and clap politely at the end. Contemporary audiences were rather more rowdy than that. In 1762, the Prince of Brunswick had written that while attending a show at Covent Garden 'the eagerness of a titled and fashionable mob was such that the male part fought their way with drawn swords'. Meanwhile, 'the females fainted, and lost shoes, caps and ruffles'. Even King George noted one occasion when there was such a great throng in a Drury Lane theatre that 'many people were almost suffocated' and he seemed quite surprised to find out that there were no deaths. More to Murray's liking would have been the observation that in the mêlée many people managed to get in without paying.[12]

Murray also patronised Oxford Road's Pantheon. Since opening a few years earlier, the Pantheon had quickly become an extremely fashionable venue for London's upper classes, and was estimated to have taken over £3000 in entrance fees in its first year alone. A 'Palace of Pleasure', it was 'an extravagant hybrid of Roman and Byzantine architectural styles' which attracted peers, government ministers and wealthy merchants as well as the attendant courtesans or 'demi-reps', 'jew brokers' and 'lottery insurers'. The building consisted of fourteen ornate rooms and a centrepiece modelled on the dome of the mosque of Santa Sophia in Constantinople.

Edward Gibbon would say that 'in point of ennui and magnificence [it was] the wonder of the XVIII century and the British Empire'. The masked balls were events which attracted huge crowds as those attending arrived in opulent carriages, wearing immensely ornate costumes and swathed in jewels, while the lower classes stood agog at these displays of unimaginable wealth, a few doubtless hoping to pick a pocket or two.[13]

As usual, Murray had an altogether grander plan to profit from one of these events than a stealthy handkerchief lifted from a wealthy reveller's pocket. Paradoxically, it would prove his downfall. Having demonstrated his aptitude for life's larger masquerades, his rollicking months living the high life would be ended by his conduct at a masked ball.

On the day of a Pantheon masquerade in February 1776, jeweller George Ragsdale was in his shop in Bond Street which ran off Oxford Road through fashionable Mayfair. The customer who arrived to borrow jewels for the ball was 'dressed very genteel, with a sword', Ragsdale would later say, explaining why he had happily gone along with the man's request. Murray, using the name Jefferson, chose a diamond pin and asked for it to be delivered to a lady at nearby 16 Hanover Square. Half an hour later, the jeweller was told by an acquaintance that the houses in Hanover Square were not numbered, and shortly after that his daughter Harriet noticed that a diamond ring worth £7 7s was missing from their display. By then Murray, still dressed in formal attire and bearing a sword, had pawned the ring for £5 5s.[14]

Back at the Old Bailey once more, Murray's tale was that he had received the ring from a Captain Mansell of the 15th Regiment who, as desperately bad luck would have it, was out of the country and so could not testify to this. Another witness to this fact was, according to the accused, suffering from the ravages of smallpox and so was also unable to attend court. A woman named Martha Lee, without whom he had claimed he could not possibly receive a fair trial, was not in court either. Needless to say, this explanation was no more believed than his previous protestations from the courtroom's bar, and once more he was condemned to death. For the third time the shadow of the noose hung over Murray's head.

This time he was held in Newgate until September of that year where, although condemned men like Murray were held in separate cells, he would surely have got to know Patrick Madan and his gang. Prisons in the 1770s, Newgate especially, were not the closed, tightly guarded affairs common in the present day. Rather they were a great conglomeration of all that was sordid and base crammed into one dingy space. Not all living within were even prisoners. Countless people might be crowded into these spaces. Prisoners' poverty-stricken families, plus dogs, pigs, poultry and other animals were tenants. Rats were everywhere.

Great hordes of visitors also filed through the cells. Prostitutes sold their wares in the overcrowded wards to anyone who had the money to pay. A host of other petty hawkers and pedlars passed through hoping to secure some trade. On top of these were the visitors who, having paid the jail keeper for the privilege, were free to parade through to experience this most base and abandoned of scenes as entertainment. Convicts themselves also had to pay for any number of services: 10s to enter the jail upon arrest, 18s 10d to leave if acquitted or released, and 2s 6d for the use of a bed rather than the usual damp straw. When Murray had left in the coffle bound for the *Justitia* and Virginia, he had been made to pay 14s 10s for that luxury. Criminals regularly had to go back to their life of crime to pay the jail fees, or else they would just swap the felons' side of the premises for the debtors' side.[15]

Nobody even pretended that a thieves' marketplace did not prevail. The prison reformer John Howard wrote of English prisons as places where 'sloth, profanness [sic] and debauchery' reigned. The economy of Newgate ran on bribes and backhanders, the object to win over enemies and to buy large quantities of alcohol to make the days pass more quickly and to numb the acute discomfort. Many managed to keep their former 'businesses' running while they were in jail. Jenny Diver, a notorious pickpocket who was particularly skilful with a false set of arms, managed to acquire so many stolen goods while in Newgate that she had amassed 'nearly sufficient to load a wagon' by the time she was transported to Virginia in 1738. That two leading criminals such as Murray and Madan never crossed paths in Newgate seems very unlikely.[16]

By this time, conditions in Newgate were worse than ever as the outbreak of the American Revolution caused a level of overcrowding far more serious than before. Although Britain would make some attempts to reinitiate the practice of shipping convicts to America at a later date, the last transport from London before the revolution had sailed in October of 1775. It was the faithful old *Justitia*, now under the captaincy of John Kidd. After the *Jenney* sailed from Newcastle with its cargo of felons, this lack of an outlet for convicted criminals caused an acute crisis in Britain's jails. It was the end of an era. When the American colonists declared independence in July 1776 Murray and Madan were both incarcerated.

Yet again Murray's miraculous good fortune continued. While in jail he used some of his time to write a petition appealing for clemency, which must have impressed. Still known by the name of William Jefferson and so distanced from his earlier crimes, Lord Weymouth wrote to the Recorder of London on 11 September 1776 asking if Murray was a fit object of the king's mercy. If he knew any of the details of the affair, Weymouth might have had some sympathy, having been an inveterate gambler in his youth and the talk of the court for his dissipated lifestyle and accrued debts. Only a judicious marriage and noble connections had ensured his respectability, though even as Secretary of State he retained a reputation for gambling, drunkenness and a rakish lifestyle.[17]

By this time Murray had somehow acquired an incredible number of respites and acquittals, and although his timing was fortuitous with the war causing more administrative chaos than usual, he clearly had an extremely powerful redeemer working somewhere behind the scenes. Certainly the Earl of Seaforth, Kenneth Mackenzie, whose family Murray claimed to be part of, could have exerted influence, but there remain other possibilities. Another name which he often used, and which in fact he had used back in 1771 and 1772 when his life of crime was just beginning, was the name we know him by: William Murray.

William Murray was also the name of the Earl of Mansfield, a judge (presiding over the landmark case which set slave James Somerset free) and politician who, like the Seaforth family, was from the Scottish highlands. Throughout the period of Murray's criminal career, Mansfield was Lord Chief Justice to the King's Bench. He was definitely powerful enough to have helped Murray. It could even have been the case that he had not knowingly helped the felon, but that Mansfield's subordinates knew of his relationship to the criminal William Murray and so tactfully recommended respites to avoid offending their boss. Mansfield had numerous siblings who lived in London and Murray could well have been related to one of them. Mansfield was known for his indulgence to his family, unconventionally having his illegitimate mixed-race niece Dido Elizabeth Belle live with him at Kenwood House.[18]

Another possibility was John Murray, Lord Dunmore. Governor of Virginia at the outbreak of the American Revolutionary War, Dunmore was a Scot like Murray and perhaps some family connection through marriage linked the two men in some way, making one feel compelled to defend the renegade other. We can only speculate. Certainly the patronage of either of these men would account for the unprecedented, not to say extremely unorthodox, number of respites Murray was given.

At the time, though, the media speculated that it was a Lord of the Treasury who was Murray's benefactor. In 1776 the five lords were Lord George Onslow, Francis Ingram-Seymour-Conway (who was known as Viscount Beauchamp), Charles Townshend Baron Bayning, Charles Wolfran Cornwall and First Lord of the Treasury, Lord Fredrick North. North was, of course, also serving Prime Minister from 1770–82. Cornwall went on to be Speaker of the House, whereupon he became notorious for hording porter under his chair and taking a swig when the debates became boring, as they all too often did. Quite which of these august gentlemen was thought to be helping Murray the newspapers of the time were, unfortunately, too polite to say.[19]

Whoever his patron was, another respite was agreed upon, and two days later Secretary of State Lord Weymouth wrote out a formal list of men reprieved from their sentences of death. The name William Jefferson was the ninth of eighteen who would escape a date with the hangman.

Chapter Three

LONDON IN FLAMES

Murray's latest respite was no generous amnesty. He and the other reprieved men had been chosen to endure a new method of punishment, a stop-gap arrangement hastily put in place when it became clear that the American conflict was not going to be quickly resolved. With the jails more overcrowded than ever and fears that criminals were running unchecked through the streets, it was decreed that old, unseaworthy dismasted ships would be anchored on the Thames to house prisoners. To the horror of some—the *London Magazine* wrote that it was very foolish to 'preserve the breed' in Britain—the bill had been given the royal assent in May 1776.[1]

This was not the only innovative feature of the plan. Those incarcerated on the hulks would perform 'hard labour' for the duration of their sentence. So Murray's respite told of the work he would have to do to save his neck. He was destined to perform 'hard Labour for the Term of Three Years in raising Sand, Soil and Gravel from, and clearing the River Thames and other services for the benefit of the Navigation of the Said River'.[2]

Duncan Campbell, the man who had previously held the monopoly on shipping convicts from London to America, was the first contractor, which was fortuitous for him in several ways. 'A very considerable part of [his] Fortune' being in the Americas, he needed another source of income quickly and a place to hold the convicts he could not now ship away. The first hulk was the *Justitia*, and on 11 November 1776 Murray was delivered aboard.[3]

Duncan Campbell tried, in his rhetoric at least, to do his best for the convicts. But his efforts were in vain. Conditions on the hulks soon became nightmarish. Bobbing along at the sides of the river, then the centre of London life and bustling with traffic, their doleful inhabitants a daily sight dragging their manacles along as they performed gruelling tasks, the hulks became the epitome of extreme suffering and the lack of restraint shown by the government. To the poor who lived and laboured all along the Thames they represented yet another sign that those in power would break them at all costs, no matter how small their offence.

The hulks became known sarcastically as 'Campbell's Academy' precisely because there was so little chance of the men held there being reformed. Working ten-hour days in the summer, sloshing around in the cold water, permanently wet for seven hours each day in the winter, they were fed inadequately and were housed below decks where they could not stand upright. A man who was on the hulks the decade after Murray said that the work was so heavy it was 'fit for a horse to do' and that it had rendered him 'entirely a cripple'.[4] It was hardly the way to persuade a man of the benefits of honest labour. The men on the hulks were said to be depressed and despondent beyond anything found in conventional jails, an amazing claim given conditions at Newgate and many of the provincial prisons.

Typhus was a constant threat; the continual dysentery epidemic spoke of extremely poor sanitation and substandard drinking water; all those aboard were infested with lice and lived among rats, and half were also suffering from the ravages of venereal disease. This was no inconsiderable problem: syphilis, in its advanced stages, causes the rotting away of bones, cartilage and internal organs. Victims become cadaverous, hardly able to stand let alone perform hard labour. It also triggers blindness and madness, and while the hulks were intended for desperate criminals, in truth some of those housed there were paralysed, blind or insane. The sick convicts slept on the floor of the forecastle with only a few planks separating them from the healthy.

One in three of the convicts on the hulks died. They were buried in the yielding but unconsecrated ground along the Thames's banks by the Royal Arsenal, nameless and discarded in death as they had been in life. At first, those who died were buried with a modicum of decorum, but eventually there were so many dead that bodies were just cast into a common grave.

By 1777, a number of other men who would one day in the not-too-distant future be destined to stand to attention in the army's ranks, Murray watching over them on Africa's inhospitable shores, were also toiling on the hulks. Eventually at least forty-six, or almost a quarter, of the men who would be banished to Africa with the companies of George Katenkamp and Kenneth Mackenzie would serve time on the hulks. Most, though, were still enjoying their freedom in 1777, only a small number already breaking their backs on the Thames along with the man who would one day be their sergeant.

Many of those who would later go to Africa were among the most arrant recidivists, not quite worthy of a trip to the gallows but repeat offenders, the unreformed and unrepentant. Thomas Phillips and William Davis were both highway robbers, the former only seventeen years old, the latter starting an agonising ten-year sentence on the hulks in 1777. John Kittenridge, who had been sentenced to hang for housebreaking but was reprieved to do hard labour, was a notorious criminal, known to the good citizens of Chelmsford, Essex by the pseudonym Flashey Dick. Others, though, were far less deserving of this terrible fate, and their eventual journey to Africa was more a matter of random chance and timing than of justice served. Robert Jeffreys, who would one day be a drummer to the army companies, had bungled a mugging and got away with nothing, and only a few years earlier would have gone to Virginia where he would at least have had a fighting chance of a new life. Similarly, it is hard to imagine what fourteen-year-old John James Smith, sentenced at Hick's Hall, had done to deserve such a fate as banishment to West Africa. In 1777, they could not imagine that future however, and longed merely to escape the unspeakable hulks.[5]

Once more it was Murray—not poor waifs and strays like Smith—who was fortunate. Not only did he manage to survive in the extraordinarily hard conditions—beneath the previously dandified exterior was clearly an ox-like constitution—he served only part of his sentence. After a year of the three he was supposed to spend on the hulks, they were so overcrowded that authorities feared a rebellion. Desperate to offload some of his charges, Duncan Campbell recommended that some be pardoned. George Barrington, the celebrated gentleman-thief was among that number. So too was the ever-plausible, wily Murray.[6]

It was not long before he returned to jail. The following month he was again imprisoned in Newgate for housebreaking, with the grim reaper again clawing at his cell door as the total value of his alleged loot was reckoned at well above forty shillings. He had just missed some excitement at the jail as Patrick Madan and his gang, by then imprisoned for three years, had tried to launch a mass breakout the previous month by demolishing part of the building. Around ten o'clock one evening they suddenly began pelting the turnkey with 'pieces of brick, iron, wood' and stones as they tried to knock a hole into the wall of the prison. A female prisoner, Miss West, shouted encouragement: 'Go it, lads, go it, dash away, don't spare them! Liberty! Liberty! Liberty!'[7]

Akerman, the jail keeper, aided by some nearby butchers from Fleet market, rushed into the cell to subdue the rioters, apparently going straight for the chief agitator, Patrick Madan. During the scuffle Akerman's pistol discharged and some said that Madan was shot in the forehead. Other reports said that one of the butchers nearly beheaded Madan with his cleaver. Either way, as if to prove that the desperado was really a coward, the media reported that the infamous Madan fell backwards upon being injured, calling out, '*by Jasus I am dead*'. Their ringleader seriously wounded, the rebels were quickly subdued.[8]

Madan and his accomplice Joseph Hawes, known to all as Joe the Baker, were moved to New Prison after the riot while Newgate was refortified. But most of his co-conspirators were still in Newgate regaling newcomers with tales of their leader's derring-do when Murray arrived back the following month. He was there until January 1778, when he was freed after his alleged victim failed to testify against him.[9]

Murray only stayed beyond the grasp of the law for a month before he was arrested at the Genoa Arms in Covent Garden under a general warrant to search the pub, known to be the hideout of robbers, highwaymen and their fences. He was said to be one of the 'gentry' of criminals held in the raid and his long list of death sentences, pardons and escapes was noted. This time there was no crime he could be held for, but he and the others held in the raid were 'humanely expostulated' by Sir John Fielding to leave their lives of crime and enlist into either the army or merchant marine. Needless to say, the media reported that 'the proposals were rejected with that Spirit of Impudence and Insult which are the sure Prognostications of the abandoned'.[10]

This time Murray was free for several months until Thomas Colcomb, who owned a tambour shop in Cecil Court off St Martin's Lane, caught him purloining one of his finely embroidered waistcoats. But once more, Murray somehow found the means to escape before the matter could even come to trial.[11] Then, within weeks, he was charged with fraudulently acquiring 'an elegant sword' from a cutler named Daltry. By now, with the war causing a backlog of cases, he would fester in Newgate for three and a half months before the case came to trial. There he was reacquainted not only with Madan's gang, who were still enjoying His Majesty's hospitality, but also some new faces who would have the misfortune to share his peculiar fate. William Holloway, a soldier who was said to have led many a young man into a life of crime, arrived just before Murray, charged with highway robbery. Wright Stagg, an eighteen-year-old who was in jail for at least the fourth time in his young life, had spent some time there before, like Holloway, being transferred to the hulks to perform hard labour. When Murray was once more acquitted, he left the others to their fates.[12]

Murray and his feats had not gone unnoticed and by this point he had gained a reputation for daring among the population at large. In early 1779 the *Morning Chronicle* wrote about him as 'the genteel swindler', continuing in a rather tongue-in-cheek vein, 'of whom we have so often made honourable mention'. On another occasion the same newspaper had noted that 'he is a very *genteel* young fellow, and has kept the *genteelest* company *at the hazard table*'. It seems that the media hardly knew whether to condemn or fawn, at one time writing of him as 'a genius'. They held George Barrington, 'the Prince of Pickpockets' and Murray's former shipmate on the hulks, in the same unfathomable regard.[13]

By this time the charges against William Murray were legion. A grocer in Oxford Street told how he had been extended credit on five pounds of tea because he had said that he was an associate of Squire Adams wanting the tea for Mrs Adams. William Gray, a silversmith in Bond Street, claimed to have been tricked into delivering some silver buckles to Murray's lodgings believing that the 'gentleman' would pay later for the items. A breeches maker named Guyon swore that 'Captain Murray' had procured some doe-skin leather breeches with silver buckles, credit being extended as the customer claimed to be recommended by the Honourable Mr Neville. Murray also had yet another alias, having gained a watch from William Edgar in Fleet Street using the name Captain Ward. On that occasion he had ordered a special watch be made by the watchmaker and had then asked to borrow another watch until his own was completed. Needless to say Edgar never heard from him again until he saw him in the Public Office at Bow Street where the charges were heard.[14]

None of these aggrieved parties could get the charges against him to stick, but Murray was soon back before the courts, charged along with an associate of his named Patrick Doyle with stealing a horse. For what would turn out to be the last time, Murray had tried his ruse of being a gentleman of standing in order to hide his thieving. While Doyle played his groom, Murray acted out the role of a well-to-do city gentleman wanting some new horses for his phaeton. Asking to try out a horse, he simply rode off on it. By this time Murray was so infamous that when the horse dealer enquired locally who might have done such a thing he was told that the accused doubtless had his horse. The horse was found with its ears docked at Plaistow Marsh, an area then outside metropolitan London where cattle were fattened for market. Arrested and held at a watch-house on Wych Street, which ran between St Clements, the Strand and Drury Lane, Murray again tried to bribe his way out of trouble. This time he failed.

Defence lawyers were coming into fashion at the time but Murray did not hire one, seemingly having boundless confidence in his own oratorical skills. He was taking a significant risk, as horse theft was considered to be an extremely serious crime in the eighteenth century, one which repeatedly saw culprits go to the gallows. His story this time was that he had gained the horse dealer's permission to take the horse and, far from having maimed and then sold it, he had merely used it as collateral to borrow £17 in order to bail Doyle out of a 'spunging house' (a temporary debtors' prison). What he made no attempt to explain is quite why the dealer would have agreed to any such arrangement. Doyle said nothing in his defence. It was pointless anyway; once more the judge slipped on the black cap, and both men were sentenced to death.[15]

Murray was immediately returned to the dock where he was tried for another jewel theft. It closely resembled his usual modus operandi, but this time his act of respectable gentleman had met an unexpected hitch. Leaving the shop with a diamond stud concealed in his clothes, he had been stopped at the doorway by a beggar woman. Propriety demanded that he give her a coin. Used to living by her wits, she immediately recognised a fellow mischief maker and alerted the jeweller. It was only his 'appearance of a gentleman' that made the jeweller hesitate to have him arrested immediately. It was an error of judgement, for it allowed Murray to be acquitted of the offence. Murray's victory was hollow though: a man can only be hanged once.[16]

Murray and Doyle were both removed to the condemned cells in Newgate. These cells were said to be so austere—nine feet by six feet, with four-inch-thick doors and studded walls—that they had caused horror and tears even among felons who had 'affected an air of boldness at their trials'.[17] Murray was of course familiar with these cells already. By the middle of 1779 he had spent in total around sixteen months in Newgate, in addition to the nine months he had laboured on the hulks. It must have taken a considerable toll on his physical and mental strength, surrounded as he was by sickness, wailing, continual taunts from his fellow inmates and the threat of the noose forever hanging ominously just above his head. Yet this was nothing in comparison to the five-year sentence of incarceration Patrick Madan was enduring, a very unusual punishment when Britain rarely imprisoned malefactors for long stretches. Little wonder that desperation had led him to try to escape in 1777, despite the unlikelihood of success.

Pat Madan recognised all the characteristics of the world of Newgate and was adept at negotiating its pitfalls. The back-biting, clannishness and petty rivalries were reminiscent of the world Madan had inhabited since he was barely a teenager. But unsurprisingly he loathed its strictures and longed to be at liberty, free to return to the dark alleyways where he was a hero rather than to remain stooped by the confines of the law. In May 1780, he was exultant that his sentence was almost at an end. But the law had another trick to play on Pat Madan. The very last day before his release from jail he was suddenly charged with another offence. It was claimed that he had committed a robbery while at New Prison in Clerkenwell, where he had been held temporarily. A man claimed to have visited the jail with two women, whereupon he got very drunk and was robbed of two and a half guineas. In truth this allegation was a fairly blatant ruse by authorities to keep Madan jailed, especially as the victim had been too drunk to know what really happened. Madan was really just the 'likeliest person' to have robbed him; in other words, the most notorious. He was acquitted.[18]

Having dodged this last-minute obstacle, on 11 May 1780 Patrick Madan was finally released from jail. Rather ironically, after all that time he missed the biggest and most infamous day in Newgate's history by less than a month. For Murray, Patrick Doyle and the others still inside, the chance of liberty arrived from a totally unexpected quarter.

In June 1780, apparently angry about the increased tolerance of Roman Catholicism in Britain, the poor of London revolted. Called 'the most serious municipal insurrection of the eighteenth century' and 'a calamity, which, in the history of London, ranks with the great plague and the great fire', the riots lasted from 4–9 June 1780 and caused the deaths of between 400 and 500 people. At any time the riots would have been shattering, but coming at a moment when the war in America was dragging painfully onwards and any idea of British military pre-eminence had been quashed, they shook the establishment to its foundations. First their colonial children had rebelled, now the poor had taken to the streets right under their noses. London's aldermen hardly knew what catastrophe would befall them next.

The rioters were ostensibly allied behind the renowned eccentric Lord George Gordon, who had raised a cry of 'No Popery!' in response to a relaxing of laws against Catholicism. The third son of the Duke of Gordon, Lord George may have been nobility but he was also an iconoclast. Two years earlier, in his maiden speech in the House of Commons, he had rounded on the Prime Minister, exhorting him not only to end the war in America but rather ill-advisedly calling the British soldiers engaged in the conflict 'butchers'. Less restrained still on the matter of religion, one of his parliamentary colleagues thought simply that he had 'a twist in his head' when it came to his loathing of Catholicism, a 'whirligig which ran away with him if anything relative to religion was mentioned'.[19]

But Gordon's lack of political savoir faire did not matter at all, to those who took to the streets. Though the riots began with a gathering of 60,000 men to take one of Gordon's petitions to parliament, they soon unleashed an outpouring of pent-up grievances about much wider issues. As protest turned to rebellion, the insurgents attacked symbols that had little to do with religion, but a great deal to do with the disgruntlement of London's lower classes towards those by whom they felt oppressed.

Naturally, the upper classes believed the riots were just an excuse for the poor to go on the rampage, looting as they went. A contemporary cartoon of a rioter was accompanied by the lines, 'Religion he cries, in hopes to deceive, while his practice is only to burn and to thieve.'[20] Perhaps they were not far wrong. The poor of London had decades of repressed anger at their more wealthy compatriots to expel and their sense of injustice ran very deep. And of course in the bedlam there was plenty of opportunity for the criminal elements, those living in St Giles's hovels for example, to break from the humdrum penury of their lives and enjoy some counterculture revelry. An informer told the government that the rioters included '200 house breakers with tools' and '550 pick-pockets'. No doubt Pat Madan was running amok among them; certainly the establishment thought so and dragged him in for questioning.

Given Newgate's notorious reputation for misery, suffering and pandemonium, it is unsurprising that the jail became a primary scene of the mob's displeasure. On 6 June the rioters went to the jail where they were met by the keeper, Richard Akerman, of whom they demanded the release of their associates imprisoned for the previous day's violence. A black man named John Glover was said to have shouted, 'Damn you, open the Gate or we will burn you down and have everybody,' and to have poked the barrel of his gun through the gate. At first Akerman refused, but then asked the government what he should do. By that time the mob had lost patience and set fire to his house, burning it to the ground. When a hundred policemen arrived to help they were surrounded by the braying mob carrying pickaxes, bludgeons and sledgehammers.

Determined to release the prisoners, and their demands for the keys being rebuffed, the mob set fire to the prison gate. Slowly, like a bleeding wound, Newgate spilled out its constricted guts. One writer described it as an erupting 'volcanoe'. Scottish lawyer and writer James Boswell, who witnessed the events, wrote of 'a miserable crew of felons in irons' being liberated 'amid flames and firebrands'. 'The captives marched out with all the honours of war,' wrote the poet George Crabbe, 'accompanied by a musical band of rattling fetters.' Out strode Mary Adey, sentenced to death for the murder of a constable trying to pressgang her husband. Margaret Cunningham, 'a misfortunate girl of the town' who was paid a counterfeit shilling for her services and was charged when she tried to spend it, also took flight. With them was Lucy Johnson, alias Black Lucy, a black woman imprisoned for the theft of some money. In all, over 117 felons fled from captivity. Among that number was William Murray and his accomplice Patrick Doyle.[21]

The destruction was so intense that the following day 'the fire [was] yet glowing' at the jail. By then, the mob had turned its attention to the Old Bailey, where around a hundred men plundered that building too. The mob carried away furniture from the courtroom and burned it on bonfires hastily constructed in the street.[22] Many other buildings were also destroyed during the riot, including a house beside a 'Romish Chapel'. A man named Theophilus Brown was said to have been part of the mob which attacked this building, wearing a blue cockade and shouting, 'Damn his Eyes there should be no popery.'[23] Eventually the destruction spread to countless private dwellings, Catholic schools, churches, clubs, the King's Bench prison, New Gaol, Marshalsea debtors' jail and the toll booths of Blackfriars Bridge. The mob even made an assault on the Bank of England. For several days London was in chaos, the wealthy citizens cowering behind locked doors. The spectre of revolution flared brightly but, ultimately, for only a brief moment. In the end it did not prove to be a predecessor to Paris, as the city returned to order.

Like the riot itself, Murray's freedom was short-lived; he was well known by now and was soon recaptured. Nine days later he was reported to be detained in New Prison at Clerkenwell, wanted for 'escaping from and out of his Majesty's jail of Newgate' as well as his original horse theft. His accomplice Patrick Doyle was still at large, but the rebel John Glover and his fellow black Londoner Lucy Johnson were both recaptured and held at Poultry Compter.[24] The jails in London and its surrounds were soon at breaking point as an additional 160 or so men and women were brought in, charged with being among the lawless mob. Rushed quickly through the courts, the accused rioters knew within days what their sentence would be.

Benjamin Bowsey and John Glover, noted as 'a blackmoor' and 'a copper coloured person' respectively in court, were both found guilty at the end of June and sentenced to hang for their part in the destruction of Newgate and keeper Akerman's house. Theophilus Brown was also sentenced to death for his part in attacking Mary Crook's house, which stood beside a Catholic church. Seventeen-year-old apprentice shoe-maker John Morris and his older half-brother Enoch Fleming were in Newgate too, awaiting a journey to Tyburn for being among the mob which had attacked the house of Ferdinand Schomberg in Hanover Square. Even London's hangman, Edward Dennis—more commonly known as Jack Ketch after the *Punch and Judy* character—was sentenced to death for his part in the riots. Dennis was soon freed, his skills needed to execute his former fellow rebels who now languished on death row.[25]

Such a mass bloodletting as would involve hanging all the condemned was not something for which Londoners ultimately had an appetite however. Edmund Burke wrote that if all the guilty were hanged the public would become 'overloaded and fatigued with a long series of executions, or with such a carnage at once'. To hang them all would resemble 'a massacre [rather] than a sober execution of the laws', he cautioned. Clemency was adopted, although twenty-four were still executed, meeting their deaths around London rather than at Tyburn so as to create a city-wide spectacle of terror. Enoch Fleming was one of those who went to the gallows, swinging from the crossbar on 1 August at the end of Woodstock Street near Oxford Road, leaving his wife and four young children alone in the world. But his half-brother John Morris escaped the hangman, as did Bowsey and Glover. Along with Theophilus Brown they waited in jail to see what penalty the government would impose on them.[26]

Murray was similarly still in Newgate, wondering if this time, finally, he would swing by the neck for his crimes. By the end of the year he was again joined by Pat Madan, who was charged with two new offences. The first, giving a glimmer of a suggestion that the two men had indeed got to know each other in jail and traded tips, was almost an exact replica of Murray's stocking theft from Thomas Tolley, although executed with less élan. On this account Madan was acquitted because one of the witnesses was judged to be too young to understand the oath. On the second count, however, he was not so lucky. In another duplication of one of Murray's feats Madan, along with John Bailey and William Cheatham, stood accused of having pinched some knee buckles from an unsuspecting jeweller. All three were sentenced to death, although the two boys, acknowledged to be under Madan's malign influence, were recommended to His Majesty's mercy. One newspaper reported that there was no evidence against Cheatham regardless of the sentence.[27]

Like poor William Cheatham, other first-time offenders arrived in prison at this most unfortunate of moments. Just in time, in other words, to suffer the most extraordinary of penalties. The Maple brothers, Thomas and Joseph, arrived at the end of 1780 charged with stealing loot including household items, clothing and a copy of Alain-René Le Sage's book *The Devil upon Two Sticks*, which had first been published in France in 1707. These novice thieves—if they were guilty at all, for their guilt seemed far from convincingly proved in court—were destined to share the misfortune of such dyed-in-the-wool recidivists as Murray and Madan.[28]

In early April 1781, Murray learned that he had been offered yet another respite from his latest death sentence. The new Secretary of State, Lord Hillsborough—a man Horace Walpole called 'a pompous composition of ignorance and want of judgment'—wrote a list of names of men whose lives would be saved on condition they joined the army. The first name listed was 'Kenneth William Williams McKenzie alias William Murray'. Among those named under him were John Glover, Benjamin Bowsey, the Maple Brothers, William Cheatham and the famous Pat Madan himself.[29]

None could have even begun to anticipate what awaited them. Nothing in their short, squalid lives had prepared them for what was ahead. If they heard of a very strange respite granted at this time, however, it might have become a little clearer what their terrible fate would be. Later that same month the black woman and thief, Lucy Johnson, was offered a respite from her death sentence for theft on the condition that she went to Africa for the term of her natural life. It was unlike any other sentence handed down for some years to come.

Chapter Four

THE 'BEST SACRIFICES FOR DEATH'

Murray and the others did not know it, but they had become part of a plan the British government had been trying to implement for some time. After all their own sleights of hand, sneaking everything from aprons to diamonds up sleeves, into pockets and down breeches, they were now involved in a much greater subterfuge on the part of the government. After many years of trying to cast some of its convicts away to Africa it had finally, amid the chaos of wartime, found a rather underhand way to do so.

In the late 1770s, when the loss of the American colonies caused the British penal system to go into meltdown, William Eden was the man upon whose desk many of the problems landed. It was fitting that he should be an undersecretary in the State Department during this crisis as he had long been a penal reformer. Legally trained, his heart was really in jurisprudence rather than legal practice and he was influenced by the great legal thinkers of the age. His primary mentor was William Blackstone, whose celebrated orations he had once listened to as an undergraduate at Oxford. But he had also closely studied the continental philosophies of Beccaria, Puffendorf and Montesquieu—for which lowly third son of a baronet like Eden could not be influenced by men who rejoiced in the titles Cesare, Marchese di Beccaria-Bonesana; Baron Samuel von Puffendorf; and Charles-Louis de Secondat, Baron de La Brède et de Montesquieu?[1]

Having absorbed such eminent theories, William Eden was ready to take the drastic steps the penal crisis demanded and to reform the ageing system. He had been behind the Hulks Bill which had seen Murray and so many others labouring on the Thames, but this was hardly a permanent solution to the problem. He also supported the Penitentiaries Act, which aimed to introduce long-term imprisonment for felons. This was a remedy favoured by the prison reformer John Howard, who believed 'gentle discipline [to be] commonly more efficacious than severity' and spoke of his aim that punishment would involve 'softening the mind in order to aid its amendment'.[2] Its most forceful supporter was Jeremy Bentham, who believed that sentences should reflect the severity of the crime and be inflicted with scientific detachment. Despite having such distinguished sponsors, imprisonment remained an unpopular solution as it was tainted by the idea that prisons bred crime rather than solving it. A penitentiary planned for London in 1779 was never built.[3]

The commonly held belief in Britain was that exiling felons was the best option for dealing with crime. Circumspectly turning a deaf ear to the rebuke from American colonists that transporting convicts to them had been an insult, Britons decided that transportation itself was not a flawed policy; rather, a new destination was needed. The answer was a whole new colony.

So those in power started flicking through old maps and atlases, then sorting through correspondence from colonial officials, looking for outposts of British power they had forgotten or overlooked. Where could they dispatch those sentenced to transportation? And as they searched, a potential answer was right there under their noses, beside the vellum ledgers and the burgundy leather-bound tomes. There, within their own government department, was a man who had already proposed a solution.

Back in 1771, before William Murray or Patrick Madan had even begun their criminal careers, William Eden had suggested in his book *Principles of Penal Law* that convicts could be used to man forts in Africa.[4] Africa, dreadful, deadly Africa, would become Britain's new hope. The plan, now hastily revisited, seemed all the more feasible because it had a precedent. Convicts had been dispatched to Africa before, and in living memory at that. Then, too, they had been banished to Africa as part of an attempt to find a new America, a colony as valuable as those on the western side of the Atlantic Ocean. Whitehall's mandarins chose to overlook the failures of the original scheme and see it as a hatchling whose day had finally come. Given what had gone before, this was optimism worthy of fools.

After the British had recaptured St Louis, an island off Senegal, from the French in December 1758 during the Seven Years' War, they had attached it politically to James Island, their old outpost in the Gambia River. James Island was in fact only a 360 by 200 foot 'slab of friable rock' with a rundown fort on it, a building so badly defended it had once been captured by the pirate Howell Davis. St Louis did have a settled population of around 2500 living around its ramshackle fort but it too measured only around 0.6 square miles. Yet somehow the two tiny islands expanded in the British mind—a collective mind very adept at grandiose colonisation dreams—to become a dependency 'beginning at the Port of Sallee in South Barbary and extending to Cape Rouge'.[5]

In other words, control of these two small islands entitled them, they felt, to suddenly declare possession of approximately three hundred miles of the African coast. How far inland the colony might go was not clear but we can be sure it would have been found to be copious enough to encompass any newly discovered goldfields. The population they had so carelessly laid claim to was almost totally unknown beyond their worth as slaves and slave suppliers and their devotion to the Muslim faith. The new British overlords christened the new colony Senegambia. It was Britain's first crown colony.

Behind this audacious plan was one of the oldest motivations in the book: greed. In the 1620s an enigmatic 'merchant and travel writer' named Richard Jobson had travelled to the Gambia and published tales of the 'richest Mynes of Gold in the World' which were 'only twenty daies saile of England'. The prospect of these King Solomon-scale riches was deeply imprinted on the British psyche. Cities where all the buildings were coated with gold and where precious metal could be bought from the unwitting natives for a merest trifle such as a 'scarlet cummerbund' were still dreamed of, boosted again in the 1690s by reports from Royal African Company servant Cornelius Hodges. He claimed to have seen goldfields at Nettico, 'ye Best in all these parts', where gold was so readily available that it had first been found there by a woman looking for turnips. The interior of the country also boasted an unknown place called Tarra, which Hodges claimed was 'as bigg as ye Citty of London'.[6]

By the mid-eighteenth century, men such as economist Malachy Postlethwayt were firmly behind Britain's expansionist policies for Africa. Formerly a staunch defender of the transatlantic slave trade and Britain's role within it, in the 1750s and 60s Postlethwayt moved increasingly to advocating the settlement of Africa as a way to expand all trade. He 'considered the West African hinterland a vast, unimproved common', Christopher Brown has commented, whereby 'his plans for commercial agriculture represented a grand scheme of enclosure'. Postlethwayt died the year after the new colony of Senegambia was incorporated, but other men were eager to follow his example and try to secure Africa's promised riches for their own, or at least the nation's, pocket. Many, like the agriculturalist Arthur Young, believed that if the natives of the region could be taught 'European customs and refinements' the resulting demand for British goods could boost manufacturing and exports. Even Adam Smith was interested in the economic possibilities of the region.[7]

The plans for Senegambia were astonishingly ambitious. Government was to proceed 'in the like manner ... as the American Colonies' and ruled under the laws of Old England. His Majesty appointed Charles O'Hara, the illegitimate son of an Irish nobleman (who would later have the rather ignominious claim to fame of being the only man personally captured in battle by both George Washington and Napoleon Bonaparte), as the new colony's first governor. Under him would be a council of nine men who would take the same oaths and abide by the same regulations and orders as councils in the American colonies. A chief justice, justices of the peace and a sheriff would be appointed to rule 'as if in an English county'. It was an extremely bold, not to say imprudent, undertaking.[8]

O'Hara's instructions when he took up his new appointment in 1766 clearly intended him to rule over more than a military outpost. He was commissioned to appoint a schoolteacher and ordered to ensure the rule of law over places where 'any considerable number of Our Subjects' lived. The Church of England was to be established in the area so that the inhabitants would be 'induced to embrace the protestant religion', although freedom of religion was guaranteed. Nor were all the planned European settlers to reside near the two coastal forts. They were apparently destined to dwell several hundred miles up the Senegal River, where O'Hara and the government imagined there to be 'prodigious quantities of Rice, Wax, Cotton, Indigo and Tobacco'.[9]

During the first few weeks of O'Hara's tenure, hopes were high. He penned enthusiastic dispatches back to London reaffirming everything they had hoped for from their new colony. He spoke excitedly of the unknown interior of the country, where he believed the goldmines were the most profitable anywhere in the world, and claimed that he expected that the inhabitants there would provide excellent markets for British goods in return for the precious metal.[10]

It was not to be. The idea that the place might become a colony anything like the American ones was disabused when the area quickly became a graveyard. When Charles O'Hara arrived he had 300 redcoats with him to form a garrison. Within twelve months of stepping ashore, more than 200 of them were dead, having succumbed to Africa's mysterious plagues.[11] Even Britons aboard ship, which was considered to be much healthier (and in fact did have the advantage of more breezes to blow the mosquitoes away) died in droves. A ship with fifty-seven hands stationed at the colony had to have its crew numbers constantly replenished during their two and a half years at the coast. Only two men from the original complement survived to make it back to Britain.[12]

Yet surely it was wanton optimism which had ever created the scheme in the first place, as the death rate of the region had been known long before O'Hara took up his post. Sailors had visited Africa's shores in considerable numbers for centuries before this time, and had long ago christened the west coast the 'white man's grave'. In fact, the detrimental effects of the tropical sun had been part of the European, and especially British, consciousness amid fears about 'the torrid zone' since their first ventures closer to the equator. From Jamaica to India there were concerns that the climate would do everything from drive a man mad to 'dissolve' his blood, while stripping him of all that it meant to be European. The very quintessence of 'whiteness' seemed to be challenged by the extreme climate. Tropical regions were 'synonymous with lethargy, effeminacy and decay'.[13]

What was particularly terrifying was that Europeans appeared to succumb to native diseases far more readily than local inhabitants. Unlike Native Americans and, later, Australian Aboriginals who would be decimated by diseases Europeans brought with them, in Africa it was the invaders who were slaughtered by the microbes. What if British people, or white men as a whole, were simply not suited to living in tropical climates? What if it was simply not what God had intended? With little understanding of acquired immunity and paying scant notice to the destruction the diseases wreaked on local infants and children, they were quick to attribute African adults' resilience to racial factors. It was one of the justifications for African enslavement in the Caribbean.[14]

With such fears for British mortality and ideas of native immunity, the first instructions sent with O'Hara decreed that he might enlist local African men into the ranks he commanded, so long as their number did not exceed one-third of the total. In London, far away from the reality of this decree, it seemed a sensible solution. But on the ground, Charles O'Hara, who as the illegitimate son of a baron was all too aware of how tenaciously rank had to be protected, fervidly resisted. Using locals to do all the labour of a non-military nature such as heaving, lifting and building was one thing, but O'Hara refused to fill the vacancies in the ranks with Africans. Putting black men into the army would, he suggested, wreck 'that subordination to which negroes submit, and which is essentially necessary in Africa'. Africans, he obviously believed, had to be kept subservient in order to maintain European rule in the region.

He was far from being the only white man in West Africa who thought this way. During the ten years of O'Hara's rule at Gorée, around three-quarters of a million Africans were loaded onto European and North American slave ships to be transported across the Atlantic.[15] Although his own commission had specifically ruled that he was not to involve himself in slave trading,

O'Hara sold at least one shipment of slaves to the French when his garrison was in dire need of food and other supplies.[16] He also meddled in intertribal warfare, which massively increased the number of slaves available for purchase. It was a tactic transatlantic slave traders revelled in throughout West Africa, but O'Hara's depredations were so excessive that he became the spectral bogeyman local mothers used to frighten their children.[17]

O'Hara had another reason to resist enlisting black men into the garrison. He wrote home to London expressing his belief that 'white soldiers would consider themselves ill-used if asked to serve with natives'. Obviously in his mind white soldiers, no matter how lowly, would always think themselves to be above Africans and would judge their dignity tainted by working alongside them. O'Hara certainly had reason to believe this, for hostility to the idea of working with black soldiers was pervasive among officers in the British Army.[18]

O'Hara's objections were so forcefully made that the government backed down. They instead turned to convicts to man Senegambia. It was not a new idea. Since at least the time of the War of Spanish Succession the army had been used as a means of sidestepping judicial punishment. The man offered the chance to join up rather than stand in the dock and face the tough justice of the local magistrates was as legendary as the man who got drunk and awoke with a sore head and a red jacket.[19]

There was another brand of criminal in the British Army too, men who had actually been convicted of their crimes and joined the army not to evade punishment, but rather in lieu of their decreed sentence. Some had been condemned to death and then offered a respite on condition that they serve their country. And it was those who had committed the most heinous crimes who were sent to the places with the highest mortality rates. The East Indies took many: service to the East India Company was said to be 'a shelter from Newgate or the gallows'. Others went out to the

West Indies, where local legislatures complained that the soldiers were 'men of so infamous a character'.[20] Convicts went, that is, to the deadliest of places. One historian has written that a respite to serve in the army was actually 'a mere postponement of punishment which often took the form of a painful death'. They were perfect for Africa's dying grounds.[21]

The threat of African army service quickly became notorious. When in the late 1760s some of His Majesty's officers trawled London's prisons hoping to recruit men for the Americas, they saw fit to 'suggest to them that they will otherwise be in danger of going to Mr. O'Hara's Corps in Africa'. The threat of Africa was obviously enough to induce them to 'volunteer' for any other location, despite the fact that death rates in the Caribbean were also monstrously high, and they might be serving alongside black troops there too.[22]

By 1769, when the huge death rate among the troops at Senegambia was all too apparent and felons were avoiding serving there at all costs, more specific respites were issued. His Majesty began directing that 'Convicts should be pardoned upon Condition of serving in Africa'. For these men, there was to be no alternative. The Recorder of London, James Eyre, wrote that it was a way that the miscreants, ne'er-do-wells and scum could be an 'advantage to the Publick'. Dying in the right location was clearly considered to have some value to the country.

It was not difficult to find enough men from the condemned, as times were hard. The end of the Seven Years' War in 1763 had brought the customary economic downturn and soldiers and sailors were suffering. In 1768 there was a sharp increase in the price of wheat, which was calamitous in an era when many working men spent a quarter of their income on bread. In the East End of London, where many of those selected for Senegambia in 1769 lived, there were industrial disputes, and the previous year there had been riots in support of radical politician John

Wilkes with chants of 'Wilkes and Liberty!' On the night two men named Patrick Burne and Samuel Craycraft were arrested 'there were two men singing ballads about Wilkes' in the street.[23] Burne and Craycraft were to be the forerunners of men like William Murray, Patrick Madan and all the others who would have the misfortune to be marked out to go to Africa.

Fittingly enough, Craycraft and Burne's problems had begun in a pub called the Black Boy, one of the disreputable establishments in Wapping near the docks where seamen, prostitutes, swindlers and other lowlifes eked out a sorry existence. The pub was infamous—the manageress kept two husbands and changed her surname according to which man was closest to hand—and Craycraft was an archetypal drunken seaman who had already enjoyed rather too much of the Ship in Distress's hospitality before he got to the Black Boy. There he was seen 'cursing and swearing, in a lewd woman's company' before then threatening to disfigure the face of a prostitute who had cheated him. Burne was only about sixteen years old and had been part of a gang of pickpockets who had stolen from another drunken sailor. Craycraft became involved, not to defend his fellow tar, but trying to thieve from the thieves. They were both informed on by an Irish boy from Waterford, another of the junior pickpockets, who had been living alone in the slums of London since he was nine or ten years old. At the time of the crime the informer was half naked, having pawned his clothes to feed himself, and confessed that he was 'full of vermin'.

There was a Black Boy Alley in London and in the late 1760s three of the denizens of this unprepossessing neighbourhood were John Fennell, Thomas Fowell and Charles Crew. They were all teenagers at the time of their crime, as young as fourteen, and were employed in such hand-to-mouth occupations as 'driving sheep about in Smithfield' and 'carrying milk for his mother'. They had been part of a gang which had knocked down a lame man who walked the streets of the area selling rabbits. The boys allegedly stole his money and two handkerchiefs. At trial they claimed that he had been drunk and 'with the whores for three or four hours' but the judge did not believe them despite having witnesses who said that their alleged victim had lost his money while drunk. All three were sentenced to death. Then, like Craycraft and Burne, they were chosen to be offered respites on condition that they serve the army in Senegambia.[24]

But problems with the scheme were immediately apparent. Of the twenty-four chosen to go to Africa on this occasion, only six passed muster. Most of the rest were either suffering from fevers, chills and pains which indicated typhus, or were under the required height of five foot four. Their plight exposed the horrendous malnourishment suffered by many of the urban poor in the second half of the eighteenth century. Raised from babyhood on bread, with only occasional scraps of meat or eels for protein and a gross insufficiency of fruit and vegetables, many were shorter than both their forebears and their rural counterparts.[25] Fourteen-year-old Charles Crew and his two partners in crime were all rejected as 'undersized'. They must have been inordinately relieved.

Then, foreshadowing the problems which would taint Britain's later convict plans for Africa, came the objections from those with a vested interest. A man named Robert Browne, who worked as agent to O'Hara's garrison and who owned 'large Property on that Settlement and in the trade of that River', heard that nineteen convicts were aboard HMS *Weasel* about to depart for Senegambia. He dashed off a letter to London in protest, complaining that it would insult the volunteer soldiers to do their 'duty with Felons, commanding Street Robbers'. What was more, the regular soldiers would be distracted from their usual duties by the need to prevent the convicts from 'committing the most atrocious Villanies on the defenseless Natives and upon the Property of Merchants'. The 'Nineteen Sturdy Cutthroats' he imagined them to be—in reality they were petty thieves—could easily escape in a slaving vessel, he protested. Even Browne had to concede, though, that felons were the 'Best sacrifices for Death'.[26]

Whether it was Browne's words which made the difference or not, none of the convicts chosen in 1769 and passed as fit ever left for Senegambia. This was all the more extraordinary given that if they agreed to go to Africa their sentences would have been reduced to only five years, significantly less than the fourteen years' servitude they had been sentenced to serve in America. But the plan never got off the ground. Despite the fact that Lord Weymouth had already begun approving respites on condition that convicts would serve in Africa, and despite the enticement of lesser sentences, all six men sailed for the American colonies to serve out their terms.[27] Little wonder that a decade later the government refrained from telling the new Africa-bound convicts their destination until the very last moment.

There were others, however—less fortunate than Craycraft, Burne and the other chosen men of 1769—who did go to Senegambia. In dribs and drabs some convicts found themselves stationed there, wilting under the sun and dying from the diseases. And as rumour of this punishment spread, it became the fate to be avoided at all costs, a posting which was used as a threat to scare the disobedient, recalcitrant or unruly soldier, and the sentence no criminal wanted to serve. At Winchester, one particularly malevolent character, George Collier, was apparently convicted with 'the Prayers of the Country, that [he] may be sent to Col O'Hara's Corps at Senegal, as he had threatened his Prosecutor'.[28]

In 1778 the *Annual Register* announced that 'All Deserters from any of the Military Corps are in future to be sent to the East Indies, or the coast of Africa, for life', adding that the proclamation 'has been read at the head of every Regiment in Great Britain and Ireland by His Majesty's order' in order to instil fear into the men. The East India Company's service was also notoriously deadly, so both this and Africa constituted a grim punishment. Some weeks later the *Annual Register* outdid its earlier story by reporting a sensational instance of the proclamation being put into practice. A cringing deserter had already been taken out on the parade ground, hood covering his face, the gun held to his head for his execution, when at the very last moment his sentence was commuted to spending the rest of his days as a soldier at Senegal.[29] The soldier's reaction was not reported.

Partly because convicts were going there as part of the British military, Senegambia began to be viewed as a solution to the larger convict problem. In the 1770s two different men both put forward serious proposals that the region would be a suitable place to found a convict colony. Mattias McNamara, who succeeded Charles O'Hara as governor of the crown colony, suggested the 'Town of Vintan' [Bintan] two leagues from a creek of the same name. 'I know no place more fitt [sic] for convicts than the River Gambia,' he wrote to Lord Germain, although he did concede that scores would die and only after the first couple of years would survivors 'be Inur'd to the Climate, and be able to cultivate Lands, build Houses for themselves, and have Provisions in plenty'.

More fancifully, he suggested that 'a material attachment' between the convicts 'and the Natives would soon take place' and that the chief of the region would let them build a fortress for their defence in the town. The scheme should be adopted with haste but kept hush-hush McNamara suggested, so that slave traders would not be able to put forward their objections.[30]

Then John Roberts, who went on to serve as Governor of Cape Coast Castle in 1780, also advocated the Gambia River as a good site for a convict colony, possibly the port of Yannimarrow [Nianimaru], which was about 400 miles from the mouth of the river. It was a place where ships could be repaired, he stated, where the land was 'amazingly fertile and plentifull [sic]' and good corn was easily grown. Roberts thought that a colony in that part of Africa would be a 'Beneficial acquisition to Great Britain', particularly as he also thought that the King of Yannimarrow might be induced to sell some of his land that was already under cultivation for a mere 'triffling [sic] consideration'.

Like McNamara's plan, Roberts's scheme did not doubt that plenty of the convicts transported to Africa would die. In fact Roberts had recommended that 'it would not be prudent' to send more than 150 men and 60 women 'for Tryal' in the Gambia area because of the possibility of the death rate being very high. If these pioneers arrived around November or December they would have time to build up some immunity to the fever before the most deadly season, he suggested, and the fever they had in the meantime could be cured by 'a little Bark', that is, cinchona or Jesuit's bark. Nonetheless, 'after the Europeans have had a couple of years Seasoning' they could live there, he surmised. When later convicts were sent out they could then be nursed through their own seasoning period by these first arrivals.[31]

The government considered these plans carefully, calling John Roberts in to discuss the intended settlement in more detail. Before the appointed House of Commons Committee he suggested that the cost of the settlement in its initial year would be £7049 7s 10d, that its second year would cost £2816, and that by the third year it would be self-supporting. Thomas Perkins, who had visited the area of the proposed settlement buying slaves, agreed with Roberts that the settlement might work. Another slave trader, Robert Stubbs, also supported the idea of establishing a convict settlement in the region but thought that Podor was a more suitable place. This was the location of Fort George, a small fortress built by Charles O'Hara on the site of a French trading post about 135 miles east of St Louis (Stubbs erroneously estimated only seventy miles) up the Senegal River on Morfil Island.[32]

Others who testified to the House Committee were far less positive, however. Richard Camplin, Secretary to the Company of Merchants, reported that almost half of the men sent out to West Africa between 1755 and 1776 had died. Then Charles O'Hara was called. While he thought that Podor was one of the healthiest places in Senegambia, which was not saying much, he estimated that perhaps a third of the convict men sent there would soon die. Convict women, he thought, would very rarely be able to survive, a problem which raised the spectre of miscegenation. Worse still, according to O'Hara, the felons would be at risk of attack from the local people. With no apparent irony, Charles O'Hara stated that 'the Moors and Blacks in Africa consider white men as their property'. Although the British government thought that risking convicts' lives in this way, 'in the place of better citizens', was 'undeniably just', it decided against adopting either Roberts' or McNamara's scheme.[33]

All these events concerning Senegambia had clearly inspired William Eden's declaration that Britain's convicts should go to West Africa.[34] The new plan, though, was not to send them to the colony—which was anyway in tatters by the 1770s and then finally killed by the French ransack of Fort James and recapture of Gorée in 1779—but rather that they should go to Britain's forts on the Gold Coast, much further around the coastline from Senegambia where the Atlantic Ocean became the Gulf of Guinea. The plan was bold but had some sense to it: like the outposts at Senegambia, the forts struggled with recruitment issues and a crushingly high death rate. Black soldiers survived longer, but the same concern with maintaining white superiority existed in the minds of those who ruled the forts just as they had in the troubled consciousness of Charles O'Hara. In many ways convicts were perfect for this deadly, desperately nasty role.

Except that there had always been one huge stumbling block to this plan. While Senegambia was a British crown colony, a playground for

King and country to do with as they wished, the Gold Coast forts were not formally owned by the nation. The British government officially had no say whatsoever in who was employed at the forts and could not foist its unwanted jailbirds on them however much they cajoled.

There was some paradox in this, as the forts were quintessentially British in the sense that their raison d'être was to promote British trade and interests in the region while hindering those of other European powers. Nonetheless, the government had no direct say in their management. The Portuguese had vested their African holdings in the Iberian crown but like the Dutch, Danes and French, the British had originally formed a joint stock company to manage their forts. In 1660 the Company of Royal Adventurers Trading to Africa was incorporated in London, quickly to be superseded by the Royal African Company. This company then managed the forts for eighty years until its final demise in 1752, at which time the forts passed into the hands of a newly created company called the Company of Merchants Trading to Africa. As their name suggested, the dominant idea at this time was that the rights of individual merchants must prevail rather than any monopoly being allowed to form. A group of British merchants, based back home in London, Bristol and Liverpool, had no desire to have convicts under their control.

The reason for the Royal African Company, its predecessor and successor, the forts, the colossal investment, and all the subsequent battles between the companies and their European rivals, was the transatlantic slave trade. In total, more than twelve million Africans were shipped across the ocean during the centuries of European (and later American and Brazilian) trading on the coast. It was an enterprise of which history has scarcely seen the like. It is no exaggeration to say that it changed the face of the known world. Those who profited from slave trading and slaves grew wealthy on a scale which could transform nations: in Britain, France, Holland and the US, banks, corporations, companies and revered educational institutions were built or expanded on wealth created from slave trading or slavery. In Britain, slave traders and plantation owners built grand manor houses, stood for parliament and sent their sons to Oxford and Cambridge. The rhetoric is present still: most Britons know that a 'guinea' was a pre-decimal coin and that brown sugar is also called 'demerara' sugar even if they do not recognise that these names come from Africa's tragic wealth and the name of a colony where slaves grew the sweet crop. In Liverpool's heyday, it had a Gorée quay (the accent had been lost in the move northwards) after the African outpost.

The British had actually been latecomers to the gluttony, arriving on the African coast centuries after the Portuguese. The massive Portuguese stronghold at Elmina was 'the earliest European building in the Tropics', built when 'Columbus had not yet sailed across the Atlantic nor Vasco de Gama into the Indian Ocean'. They held it until 1637 when the Dutch, newly dominant on the coast, routed them. The British only came into the picture in 1664, when they managed to take control of a nearby fortress from the Danes with the help of some local Efutu soldiers. It was captured by Captain Robert Holmes, a royalist who had done all the things required of any self-respecting Englishman in Africa: he had voyaged to Guinea to search for that elusive 'mountain of gold', had annexed Gorée, and had generally marauded around capturing the ships of other European nations. By all accounts he rather overstepped the mark, and without any gold to show for his exploits he was confined to the Tower of London on his return. His one time friend Samuel Pepys was unimpressed, calling him 'a rash, proud coxcomb' and a man who 'played the knave'. Then again, Holmes had also rather overstepped the mark there too, trying to seduce Mrs Pepys.[35]

Holmes's contraventions notwithstanding, the English managed to hold onto the new possession and soon renamed it. From the Portuguese name for its setting, it became Cape Coast Castle. As they set about strengthening and refortifying it as their headquarters on the coast, they could hardly foresee that England—or Britain after the union of 1707—would hold the castle until 1957 when the Duchess of Kent, representing Queen Elizabeth II, handed over control of the new nation of Ghana to Kwame Nkrumah. Far more lastingly than at Senegambia, ownership of a castle would become ownership of a vast block of land around it. Cape Coast Castle would remain the headquarters of British rule on the coast for almost 300 years.

The possession of Cape Coast Castle marked a period of British domination both on the African coast and in the slave trade. Eventually it was the headquarters of numerous smaller possessions dotted along the shoreline, everything from looming castles to tiny 'factories' stretching from Apollonia at Beyin in the west to Whydah in the east. While some of these were little more than poorly fortified mud houses, Cape Coast Castle was four storeys high in parts and extremely heavily armed, being home to ninety-six cannon which included some forty-two pounders, among the largest in Africa. Together (and at times stretching up to the Atlantic coast forts at James Island, Gorée, and Bunce Island in the Sierra Leone River), the forts were the spider's web of British slave trading, ensnaring those who fell victim to its cold-blooded moneymaking while providing a safety net for arriving British traders. During the eighteenth century they would oversee the loading of upwards of 300,000 men, women and children onto slave ships to be taken away to be debased, dehumanised and sold as chattel.

The purpose of the forts in the eighteenth century was to provide for all the needs of passing slave ships. At mid-century the dungeon at Cape Coast Castle alone could hold 1500 captive Africans, in utterly miserable and inhumane conditions, ready to be sold to passing ships.

Other amenities the forts provided included the use of small cells in which to detain mutinous sailors, the assistance of company employees to help quell any slave insurrections that happened while still at anchor, and a few glasses of fortified wine for the captain and surgeon of the ship to enjoy at the governor's table.

Around all the forts small African towns grew up to cater to their needs. Africans provided all manner of services, from introducing British tars to such treats as plantains, fresh fish and palm wine, to supplying medical care to the many who were already suffering from dysentery and malaria or whose backs bore the foul, oozing scars of a shipboard flogging. African women, faced with a society changed fundamentally by the arrival of the European traders, became everything from cheap prostitutes to 'coast wives', as few men risked the lives and delicate mental poise of their white spouses by taking them to Africa. Just like port cities the world over, the forts were small outposts of welcome ready to cater to the whims and wishes of passing sailors.[36]

The forts were also microcosm societies. A fanciful report sent to the British government in 1763 described how 'dignified' Cape Coast Castle had extensive gardens and orchards and that its battlements could be very pleasant for an evening promenade. In truth, although the castle's personnel would occasionally eat together in the garden, perhaps accompanied by African drumming, life in the forts was far from a picnic. Loneliness was a fact of life at Cape Coast Castle as well as the smaller forts, and leisure activities were startlingly few. The officers of the castle had access to a range of books in the library and even formed reading groups, but many complained of the lack of 'sport', as shooting in the nearby forests was forbidden. The most common activity was drinking, and as at other far-flung parts of the British Empire, copious amounts of strong alcohol were consumed under the tropical skies. It was thought that West Indian rum, a product made by many of the slaves who had passed through the castle's dungeons, was a prophylactic against yellow fever. On long dark nights it certainly seemed worth a try.

If the officers' lives were bad enough, conditions for the lowly European soldiers in the forts were excruciating. In her classic history of the British in West Africa, Eveline Martin claimed, 'the English soldiers in the Company's employment were probably by far the most miserable and worst treated of all in the forts, not excluding the negro slaves'.[37] Enlisting for five years, they received a £2 bounty and were promised future wages well above those in the British army. This attractive proposition was all a chimera however, and not only because of the huge death toll and the singularly obnoxious nature of the tasks involved. Should the soldiers survive long enough to endure the injustice, they did not actually receive the promised wages in hard currency, just their calculated value in trade goods. If they proved ineffectual traders, bad judges of character or suffered an economic downturn, they could quickly be in debt. With no way to pay off their liabilities other than to keep working, and not allowed to sail for home on a company ship if they owed any money, service in the forts could turn into ceaseless debt bondage.[38]

It was certainly a heavy burden. Like sailors on a ship, slave-fort soldiers were never truly off duty, their whole lives governed by the ringing of a bell. Against the background noise of colossal waves continually breaking against the exterior walls, soldiers had their watches regulated by this ringing, while twice each night it would awaken them to patrol the periphery. Fatigue was relentless. Yet they also had to be constantly on guard against attack, which could come from any side. Most slave castles had cannon facing out to sea to repulse an attack from a European enemy ship as well as smaller weaponry trained inland in case the local Africans decided to assail them.

But the threat came at least as much from within as without. Each of the slave-trading forts of the West African coast had dungeons where they kept their 'goods'. It was peculiar merchandise: it could rise up and kill its sellers. Slave revolts were always feared and the castles remained in a permanent state of anxiety. The frequent call of 'all's well' was meant to quell shattered nerves but all inside feared the sound of a musket shot which warned of danger. While seamen might get liberty ashore, the soldiers of the forts were stuck indefinitely, forever on their guard, jumping to attention to the sound of that ringing bell. It was often a life sentence.[39]

More often still it was a death sentence. Up to seventy-five per cent of Europeans were consigned to the earth within twelve months of stepping ashore. The pale fleshy bodies which arrived straight from colder climes, previously so infrequently exposed to sunlight, provided tasty temptation to the swarms of mosquitoes which plagued the area. The malaria and yellow fever they carried quickly found its way into the bloodstreams of the newly arrived who had no resistance to these alien African ailments. Not knowing that insects carried the diseases, Africa just appeared to be a place of death and dying. Illnesses nobody understood and for which there was no cure struck men down with even greater savagery than the cruel smallpox, typhus, syphilis and fevers which could carry away the previously vital in England. Mortality stared a man in the face as soon as he stepped ashore in West Africa. At times, the men stood over a former colleague's grave every other day. Sometimes at the smaller forts there were not enough healthy men left to dig graves. When a yellow fever epidemic struck the whole place could become a morgue.

As no-one knew conclusively what caused these curious African diseases, a regime of freezing cold baths, wearing thick woollens next to the skin to 'sweat out' toxins, weekly purgatives, and then the intermittent torments of blistering and bleeding was instigated. Windows were kept shut in case it was the air which carried a fatal miasma. Far from curing disease, these measures can only have added to the harm done and the general lassitude caused by the enervating climate and continual fevers.

With lowly jobs in the slave-trading forts being so desperately unpleasant and perilous, they were far from popular. Struggling to enlist enough men to keep pace with the huge mortality rate the Company resorted to coercing men on the streets of Britain's major cities to sign up, following on a path of dubious legality forged by the East India Company. They kept a crimp at Woolwich Arsenal in London to try to waylay any likely looking men heading for the Royal Artillery's grounds and sidetrack them with those elusive better wages.[40] Despite these tactics recruits were forever in too short supply to match the rate of death of those already there. In 1779 the British had only ten white soldiers in total on the coast and they were said to be 'drunken wretches'. Some had to be promoted to sergeant regardless, no matter what their state of inebriation. There seemed to be no choice.[41]

Yet of course there was a choice, and one which the British government was extremely eager for them to adopt. Still, the Company vehemently refused to accept convicts as potential fort soldiers. In fact they had kept up this dogged rebuff to the government's overtures for some years by the 1780s.

When the matter was seriously proposed again, when the American colonies seemed irretrievable and William Murray and Patrick Madan were awaiting transportation, the Company's protests were nothing short of impassioned. Writing in May 1781, Richard Camplin, secretary to the Committee of the Company of Merchants, forcefully stated their opposition, formulating both practical and ideological objections. Believing that a thief would always be a thief, they argued that criminals would pose a considerable security problem for which they would be responsible. The forts, laden with gold dust, ivory, brandy, cloth and, not least, guns and gunpowder, were hardly suitable places for unruly offenders. Rather, the small number of officers who ruled each fort would be unable to maintain order and, far from protecting Britain's valuable resources, the officers themselves would need protecting against 'such Banditti'. There was a more serious implication in all this than loss of goods, no matter how valuable. Tacit was the fear that any weakness among the forts' rulers might induce the imprisoned slaves to revolt. The repercussions of a pickpocket or petty forger's mischief could, in West Africa, go far beyond a few duped citizens as it might at home. It could all result in carnage, as it regularly did on slave ships.[42]

There was more. The Company argued that Africans 'respect[ed] and adore[ed]' the white man. If lowly convicts were sent to the coast, Camplin argued, this veneration and esteem for everybody with light skin would be damaged as Africans would see that not all pale faces were influential, upstanding and worthy. In fact, the reverence—based, they believed, on long centuries of displayed omnipotence—was apparently so fragile that it could quickly turn to dust. In the presence of convicts, previously awed Africans would 'soon learn to dispise [sic] the White Man', Camplin argued.[43] It was an argument characteristic of the delusion of slave traders, but it also reveals the place that racial ideology had begun to play in their increasingly rabid defence of slave trading.

By the time Camplin wrote these words, it was all too late. The government had already outmanoeuvred the Company. They had decided to release convicts into the regular British army to go and fight in West Africa to try to capture some of the forts held by other European nations. The Company of Merchants had, of course, no say over the might of the British Army, neither the campaigns it chose to fight nor the men it allowed to enlist in its ranks. In sending the felons on a mission which would directly benefit the Company if successful, the government effectively outfoxed them, leaving them little room for complaint. The fact that they always seemingly intended to leave the troops in Africa to defend any newly captured possessions was a moot point.

Indeed, by the time Richard Camplin wrote his harangue against convict soldiers, Murray, Madan, the Maple brothers and all the others were already aboard ship awaiting their departure. But if Camplin and the Company of Merchants were unaware how advanced the plans were, those aboard the ships, even the captains of the independent companies they had been drafted into, had themselves only very recently become aware that they were headed for the most deadly of destinations.

Chapter Five

AFRICA

Aboard ship, those destined for Africa were at least as reluctant to go as the Company was to receive them. For William Murray, it was the second time he had been shipped away to a place where he was not wanted. For all of them it seemed a terrible fate, with the awaiting diseases offering a more prolonged and painful death than the long drop at Tyburn, lacking even the sop of bidding adieu to their old gang mates by going to their death with a flourish. In the minds of the men, the horrendous possibilities all churned around as rumour begat rumour, compounded by ignorance about the place for which they were destined. Stories swept the ship of weird and wonderful maladies which would cause untold disfigurements and pain, cannibals, bizarre man-eating animals and the ever-looming threat that they were going to be the servants of Africans.

If the rank and file were not exactly revelling in their fate, neither were the two men placed in charge of them. When Captain Kenneth Mackenzie wrote his letter home to the War Office in the final weeks before they set sail, it revealed much about his outlook, probably more than he intended.

Besides his overtly stated fears that serving in Africa would not bring rewards of either money or prestige, his dogmatic statements about his loyalty to King and country suggest a man trying to convince himself that his choices were the right ones. His claim that his 'good Highland stamina' would prove 'equal to any Climate or Fatigue' smack of a man trying to bolster his flagging spirits and bravery. He finished with a rather pitifully valiant claim, writing of himself in the third person as if to distance himself from the coming terror. 'Mackenzie shall never shirk from any Service or his Duty, but with a Cheerful heart lose the last drop of his blood when the Cause of his Good and Gracious King demands it,' he wrote. He clearly believed that the venture might prove fatal.[1]

For Kenneth Mackenzie, as much as for the men now under his command, it all seemed to have gone so very badly wrong, and yet he was at a loss to know quite how. Only a few years earlier his future had seemed bright and assured. A military man from a very young age, on 19 January 1778 he had proudly joined the Seaforth Highlanders, then being raised by the Earl of Seaforth from among his estates. The clan Mackenzie had been in financial dire straits since at least the time of their support of the Jacobite uprising of 1715, when the current earl had written despondently, 'All my mole hills made mountains.' The family had managed to regain their lands in 1741 but had to pay a crippling fine and was further damaged by the determination of the government in London to destroy the clan system and disarm the highlanders. By the 1780s the current earl saw the best way forward as raising a regiment which would, he hoped, restore honour, economic security and cohesion to his clansmen.[2] Highland regiments were part of a distinguished tradition, and Pitt the Elder had spoken of their bravery, intrepidness and valour. Pitt had suggested that they again be called into the service of the British nation in its hour of need to quell the rebellious Americans.[3]

The new regiment was to comprise 1010 rank and file, twenty drummers and fifes, two pipers and fifty officers and sergeants. Kenneth Mackenzie, the heir to the Redcastle estates and descended from a younger son of the Earl of Seaforth, was among the officers and very proud of his position.

As part of the Seaforth Highlanders, Kenneth Mackenzie marched down to Elgin for inspection. They bristled with pride when Major-General Robert Skene described them as 'stout men, hardy and active' and rejected remarkably few as unfit to serve. From there they marched to Leith where, to their horror, they discovered that they were destined for the East Indies. They had been promised that they would only serve for three years or the duration of the war, and all knew that they had little hope of returning home from the east in that time.

In a precedent to his later predicament, Kenneth Mackenzie, scheduled to go to a different location to the one he had imagined, perhaps felt cheated out of going to the frontlines in America. This time, however, it was the thousand men under him who felt much more strongly about the matter. They protested that they had formed the regiment on the understanding that they were to serve in America, and what was more they were dissatisfied with their pay and treatment. In a show of force, they marched around the streets of Leith, gathered at Holyrood Park and marched up Arthur's Seat, an extinct volcano from which they could see all across Edinburgh. Kenneth Mackenzie, however, stood firm. When some of the mutineers approached him at Canongate jail, where he had command, demanding that their imprisoned comrades be released, it was said that he bared his chest at them, retorting that 'not a single man would be liberated'.

For the government the situation was dire, as they already feared a French invasion in the south and they panicked at the thought that the highlanders might simultaneously spark a mutiny in the north. They could not afford to take any chances as the rebellious Seaforth men were overwhelmingly supported by the people of Leith and Edinburgh, suggesting that any insurgence would spread like wildfire. Things were so serious that Lord Dunmore, then still expecting to return to his post as Governor of Virginia following the supposed British victory, was called upon to intervene. Diplomacy proved ineffectual, though, and in the end the government capitulated and cancelled plans for the Seaforth Highlanders to go to the East Indies. They were dispatched to the Channel Islands where the French were indeed tormenting their old enemy in one of its bleakest moments.[4]

There, on the small dots of land in the English Channel, was Kenneth Mackenzie's finest hour. The French attacked Jersey on 1 May 1779 with nearly 3000 men in five frigates and numerous smaller vessels and tried to land at St Ouen's Bay on the west of the island. Despite having vastly superior numbers, they were repulsed by the dogged resistance of part of the Seaforth Regiment aided by the local militia. Kenneth Mackenzie was singled out for his bravery.[5]

He was an ambitious man, and one who felt keenly the diminishing of his family's status since the English attack on the clan structure. His father's profligacy had ruined the family finances. He himself had done nothing to redress the problem and things became much worse still in September 1780 when he was dragged into court by his wife, Jean Thompson, demanding a divorce. It was a shameful and rare event: the whole of Scotland saw only one or two divorces per year. The charge was that he had 'given himself in adulterous practices fellowship and Correspondence with lewd and wicked women', adultery and desertion being the only grounds for divorce in eighteenth-century Scotland.

Adultery was generally difficult to prove but Jean Thompson had plenty of evidence. She testified that Mackenzie had contracted a venereal disease in the course of his many 'correspondences' with prostitutes and that one of the women had borne him a son. What was more, her legal council had secured a selection of 'girls of pleasure' from 'bawdy houses' around Edinburgh to parade through the court telling of Kenneth's dubious associations and report what he had paid for their services. At a time when it was reasonably commonplace for men to visit brothels—that 'sport' to which Murray, for one, was partial—it was perhaps the child which had particularly offended Jean Thompson Mackenzie, who herself had borne six children in the twelve years she had been married. Or perhaps it was the flagrant manner in which he went about these affairs, for not only had he allegedly visited prostitutes in the small village of Redcastle where the family lived, but he had made no secret—barring once pulling the bedclothes over his head when seen in bed in a brothel—of his nocturnal activities. A certain leniency might have been granted gentlemen in such matters, but they were definitely required to conduct such affairs with discretion and not bring public humiliation on their wives.[6]

Mackenzie, though, felt his own dignity dented by his affairs being discussed in open court. Worse still, the matter not only offended his pride but also hurt his pocket, as Scottish divorces left the guilty party legally 'dead' while awarding the petitioner whatever he or she would have received had their spouse actually deceased. Jean Thompson's share of the rent from his estates was calculated at £100 (approximately £10,000 in today's terms) per annum. He was to pay this every year for the rest of her life, even if she remarried, as she soon did. In addition, Kenneth Mackenzie was still paying for schooling for at least four of his children by Jean—sons Roderick and Hector and daughters Boyd and Hannah—and for that 'natural son' born as the result of one of his indiscretions. On top of that, work needed doing on the Redcastle estate and to the old house itself.[7]

Yet, rather typically of men born to a certain station but whose elders had already spent, gambled away or wrongly invested the better part of their inheritance, he acted as if the money to maintain his standing was still available to him. He was certain that bigger things awaited him than a commendation for bravery as part of another man's company. He made the bold move to break away from the Seaforths and when they sailed for the East Indies—having finally agreed to go—he was not among their number. He had decided to strike out alone and raise his own independent company.

For Kenneth Mackenzie it was an all-or-nothing decision. The costs involved would either destroy his family or he would be victorious in battle and the prize money would restore them to their former position. He approached George Ross, a fellow Scot who had amassed a considerable fortune from being an army agent and who was elected Member of Parliament for Cromarty in 1780. Ross's business, run from his offices in Conduit Street, London, was contracted to twenty-one regiments, and ten years later would have a turnover of more than £1 million per annum, a remarkable figure at that time. Ross was said to be a benevolent and impartial man, but he was also a man whose only son was reputed to have shot himself at his father's grand Cromarty House residence after an argument with Ross about the right way to carve a joint of meat. 'Little men cannot afford to neglect little matters,' George Ross was alleged to have carped at his underachieving son. He was not a man, perhaps, to whom it was wise to be deeply indebted. Regardless, Kenneth Mackenzie borrowed £800 from Ross.[8]

At around the same time another man was also making plans to raise an independent company of foot. Almost as far away as the small British Isles would allow, George Katenkamp was from a privileged merchant family in south-west England, his father a prosperous German merchant who had married an Englishwoman and settled in Exeter. Herman and Ann Katenkamp went on to have at least five children: three daughters—one of whom married the poet Richard Hole—and two sons. George's brother Herman, named for his father, had gone into the family business and five years earlier had petitioned to become the consul at Messina. His approach, backed by thirteen of Exeter's finest, was successful and he went on to be the long-time Consul General of both Two Sicilies (Sicily and Southern Italy) and later Spain. A successful man, after his death in 1807 he was buried in Bath Abbey alongside his wife. He was said, in the kind of hagiography common to grave inscriptions, to be 'warm, sincere, candid and affectionate ... his Mind, strong; clear and comprehensive'.[9]

The Katenkamps were Unitarians, Exeter being a traditional stronghold of nonconformity. George had been educated at Exeter Academy, a religious institution then in its second incarnation under the rule of Samuel Merivale, a Unitarian minister whose son John would later marry George's sister Ann. One of his classmates was Thomas Gwatkin, later Professor at the College of William and Mary in Virginia and minister to Lord and Lady Dunmore. Exeter Academy was in fact one of the major institutions providing ministers to nonconformist pulpits (though some, like Gwatkin, conformed) and it seems that the Katenkamps pondered whether the church was a fitting career for their son. For most younger sons, without the benefit of their father's business which was the preserve of the eldest and heir, the traditional choices were the church, the law or the army. George Katenkamp, spurning his religious education, chose the last of these. On 26 March 1777 he joined the 1st Regiment of Foot.[10]

As the name suggests, the 1st Regiment of Foot was the oldest infantry regiment in the British Army. By Katenkamp's time it had fought with honour in Tangier, Monmonth's Rebellion, the War of Spanish Succession, the War of Austrian Succession and the Battle of Culloden. After that the two battalions of the regiment were separated, the 1st fighting in the Mediterranean and the West Indies and the 2nd engaged in Canada and then Cuba. During Katenkamp's service both battalions—he was in the second—were stationed in Britain on home service. They were part of the force used to quell the Gordon Riots.[11]

In early 1781, dreaming of triumph, riches and the grateful adoration of their countrymen for their derring-do, Kenneth Mackenzie and George Katenkamp went about recruiting for their companies. Mackenzie would be captain of the 101st Independent Company of Foot, Katenkamp of the 102nd. Recruiting the two lieutenants, an ensign, five sergeants, five corporals, two drummers and one hundred privates each company was to consist of—all over five foot four and between the ages of eighteen and forty—was no easy task when the pick of the population had long been sent to the Americas to fight. Yet they had success. Mackenzie certainly had experience of the kind of tactics needed. Earlier he had been called 'the terror of Inverness mothers' and, surprisingly enough, this referred to his enlisting their sons rather than his pursuing their daughters. He was even said to have been cursed by a witch for kidnapping her son for military service.[12]

In February 1781, in the salubrious surroundings of Cannon Coffee House in Cockspur Street, close to Trafalgar Square, where a gentleman might order a meal and rent a room as well as have a drink, George Katenkamp sat and composed a letter to the War Office reporting that his company was ready for inspection. Mackenzie's letter, with much the same news, had been sent off several weeks earlier, although at that time he was still missing a fit man for one of his subaltern positions.[13]

The man Mackenzie wanted for the position was Alexander Fraser, a former marine who was well suited to the ignominy of African service having been dishonourably discharged from his former company. It was an old story: a 'wench' had turned his head and 'diverted him from his duty'. Mackenzie was sympathetic, recalling that he had 'felt a little of the weight of misfortune myself'. (He certainly had, as his former wife Jean could all too ably testify.) There was another aspect to this story, though, another oblique warning to Mackenzie had he been willing or able to listen. Fraser was actually a relative of George Ross, the agent, but Ross, unlike Mackenzie, was loath to overlook his dalliance and had cut him off without the proverbial shilling. To sons and great-nephews alike, Ross could prove an uncompromising foe.[14]

Meanwhile, as Alexander Fraser's fate remained undecided, the rank and file of Mackenzie's company presented themselves for inspection. Colonel Samuel Townsend and surgeon Gloster examined the hundred men at Chatham Barracks, rejecting thirteen who were too young, too old or too short to meet the regulations. One poor fifteen-year-old was sent away for being knock-kneed. Reflecting the desperate times, however, Townsend was prepared to be lenient, allowing sixteen- and seventeen-year-olds among the ranks, plus three men in their late forties. Twenty-eight men who were under the minimum height were also approved, 'several of them being young, well made and likely to grow', Townsend noted hopefully.[15]

A minority of these men were army veterans, with long periods of service already under their belts when they joined Mackenzie for the inspection at Chatham Barracks. Fulfilling the punishments the *Annual Register* had announced three years earlier, two men were from the Savoy deserters' prison. The vast majority, however, eighty-three of the one hundred men, were new recruits or had served the army for under a year. Townsend wrote that even after he had sent the rejected men away, he still considered the centre rank of the company to be 'indifferent' or inferior, substandard. It was a long way from Mackenzie's jubilant days in the 'stout' Seaforth regiment.[16]

After George Katenkamp's men had undergone the same procedure and all those found unfit returned to their homes, the two new captains thought that their ranks were all arranged. They could not have been more wrong. Unfortunately for Mackenzie and Katenkamp, however 'indifferent' their original recruits may have been, things were about to get much worse. Their hard work recruiting was blithely considered to have been for the good of the country as a whole rather than for their companies alone. Any man who looked at all robust and fit for service was removed from Mackenzie and Katenkamp's ranks and deployed to other regiments which were destined for America. For both men, especially Mackenzie with his precarious finances, it was a terrible blow, not least as it identified their companies as being second rate. An appalling realisation dawned on both men that the mission they were earmarked for was going to involve little glamour or status. As a consequence, it was in all likelihood going to entail scant chance of the prize money for which they were both afire.

Protest as they might, it was hopeless. It was a precarious matter to dispute anyway, as neither could afford to show any sign of disloyalty to Britain or be seen to be reluctant to do all they could to further the loyalist cause in America. In the selection of these two men to go to Africa there was already the intimation that they had been chosen because, of those who offered to raise independent companies, they appeared the most suspiciously 'foreign'. Mackenzie, a highland Scot, and Katenkamp, with his exotic surname, could hardly afford to have their loyalty and devotion to King and country brought into question.

So in the months that followed, their companies were decimated by the insatiable demand for men in the frontline of the campaign for Britain to hold onto her American colonies. By the time of the next surviving rollcall for the two companies, less than half of the original men were still with the independent companies.[17]

For Mackenzie and Katenkamp, ignominy was heaped on ignominy. Shortly after the blow which made them realise that they were not destined for America came a second setback: the men enlisted in the place of those removed for American service were the very dregs of society. Kenneth Mackenzie described them as 'convicts both civil and military taken out of the Savoy, Newgate and the Hulks at Woolwich'.[18] Colonel Samuel Townsend, the man who was responsible for this reallocation of troops, defended his actions by saying that Mackenzie and Katenkamp's independent companies were made 'chiefly' of convicts because of the stringencies of the times.[19] At the Savoy military jail they waived the release fee for thirty-three men who had been sentenced to death for deserting their regiments and then reprieved, and sent them off to join Mackenzie and Katenkamp.[20]

Down on the Thames, some of those aboard the hulks were asked if they wished to join the army and so escape endlessly swilling around 'chiefly in the mud & water' performing repetitive heavy dredging. Most agreed. John Keatch, a labourer who had stolen some copper halfpennies from a house in Wooten, Bedfordshire, chose to join the army when asked. So too did Edward Loach, who had claimed debts against a bankrupt man and been sentenced to hard labour for deception. John Plunkett, who had stolen three mirrors and who would be required to commit far worse deeds in Africa, heedlessly chose the army, unaware of what was in store for him.[21]

Keatch, Loach and Plunkett were serving three-year sentences of hard labour on the Thames—a lifetime, to be sure, when the back-breaking labour, intense cold and damp, total lack of privacy and abominable diet could drive a man to insanity—but surely less time than they expected to serve in the armed forces. Patriotic fervour could evidently strike a man aboard the depressing hulks as much as anywhere else, but for most it was Hobson's choice.

Several of those whose names were added to the list were former soldiers, for whom the choice was probably simpler. Despite their crimes and sentences they would return to something like their former lives. Samuel Rudd was a seventeen-year-old drummer in the Coldstream Guards when he was condemned to death for having stolen money from a drunken Frenchman in St James's Park, London. Offered a respite to seven years' hard labour on the Thames he had served more than three years of that sentence but opted to return to the army when the opportunity arose.[22] Twenty-year-old William Holloway had served in the army for three years but was already said to have led many other youths astray when he was sentenced to hang for robbing a man with some other soldiers from his regiment. He too chose returning to the army in preference to remaining on the hulks.[23]

At Newgate and other jails too, when asked, men chose to enlist rather than remain in the squalor. For many of them the death penalty hung over their heads and the army was their chance of a respite. This was the case for Thomas and Joseph Maple, convicted of burglary in January of 1781. Capitally convicted the same day was another housebreaker named Charles Shepherd, and Abraham Dry who had stolen from a woman selling dressmaking items in the streets. Both opted for army service instead of the hangman's noose.[24] William Dobby, who made a similar decision, was only just out of the army anyway. He had been with the 3rd Regiment of Foot Guards, from which a wing had served in many of the crucial battles of the American Revolutionary War. By the time of his former comrades' rout at Yorktown, which effectively ended the war, he would be on his way to Africa.[25]

In February 1781, the last two convicted men who would join the two independent companies stood in the Old Bailey's dock. Ebenezer Harcup and John Lamb were accused of holding up a farmer in his carriage at gunpoint and stealing money and his watch. Lamb alone was found guilty and sentenced to hang but Harcup was found guilty of another mugging at Golders Green in London. He pleaded innocence on the grounds of having been conscripted at the time, claiming he had been aboard ship when the crime was committed. The judge did not believe him and, like Lamb, he was capitally convicted and then offered a respite to join the army. Harcup should have avoided army service as he was missing a thumb, but unfortunately had shown in one of his crimes that he was perfectly able to fire a gun with his other hand. Like the others, once they were marked down to go to Africa they were removed from Newgate to New Prison.[26]

Of all those who went into the army from the jails and hulks in the last months of 1780 and into the start of 1781, only the notorious Patrick Madan ever had the chance to explain why he elected to go. With arresting simplicity, Madan said that he was 'tired of prison' and so chose any route out of the confining walls when asked. More truthfully, he had few options left and had been dicing with death for many years. William Murray, having languished in Newgate for so long and fearful that he had exceeded his legal limit of respites and reprieves, perhaps felt likewise.

Unfortunately for the authorities, neither Murray nor Madan were men to accept any fate without a fight. Jailer Akerman had already found Madan and his associates, including his acolytes Bailey and Cheatham, in the cells of Newgate with their fetters unlocked and a brace of pistols ready to blast their way to freedom. They had planned to make a break for it when they were in the press yard being prepared to leave.[27]

When that failed they hatched a new plan after being moved to the Savoy military prison. There Madan joined together with William Murray and a burglar named Robert Hill. After the final patrol one night, Madan, Murray and Hill along with some others they had inveigled into their scheme tried to knock a hole in the outer wall of the barracks where they were held. By 2 am they had made a sizeable hole but it was not yet big enough for any of the men to crawl through. Only as day was breaking was it large enough.

Desperate now, with undue haste, one of their allies climbed through to reclaim his freedom. But it transpired that the guards had known what the prisoners were up to all along and had been watching them for their entertainment. When the first man climbed through the wall they shot him dead. Murray, Madan and the others ran to their beds like boarding-school children caught in an illicit feast. Such feigned innocence was pointless of course. The guardsmen smashed into the room and in the ensuing fracas three were killed and another nine wounded. The next day the *Morning Chronicle* reported that 'those notorious villains Madan and [Murray] McKenzie' had been the chief conspirators, and that both men were now 'chained to the floor'. The newspaper expressed gratitude that the event had been discovered before a jailbreak on the scale of the Newgate escape during the Gordon Riots had ensued.[28]

After that the government lost little time in embarking the men aboard the ship which was to carry them away, anxious now to be rid of them before they could cause yet more trouble. On 5 June 1781, they were escorted to the *Mackerel*, which was to take them away from England forever. Kenneth Mackenzie, George Katenkamp, the officers and volunteers had been aboard since the previous month and now watched with a mixture of derision and rising alarm as the most infamous of men shuffled aboard, still wearing the double irons they had been made to endure after their Savoy misadventure.[29]

Murray was listed as number 68 of Kenneth Mackenzie's company, his name also given as Kenneth Mackenzie; it was the name he had used years before when he had slipped three pairs of Thomas Tolley's stockings into his hat. Murray was quick to claim that he was Captain Mackenzie's nephew. Captain Mackenzie almost always vehemently denied any kinship to the younger man, but on one later occasion, when he had plenty of reasons to deny any relationship with his former soldier, he gave a strange reply. Conceding that Murray always claimed to be his nephew, he said: 'I have so many Relations that I do not know; he might possibly be so.' Certainly many of the soldiers in the ranks would always believe that they were uncle and nephew, and their tumultuous relationship would be the axis around which many future events revolved.[30]

Other prisoners also hobbled up the gangplank of the *Mackerel* 'ironed two and two'. 'Irons Chains & other Implements' were ubiquitous on the hulks and in jails such as Newgate, and moving felons in coffles to their transport ships was commonplace so this was unsurprising. Even so, their shackles gave lie to the fiction that they would be indistinguishable from the rest of the soldiers and they always marked them as different, inferior to the men who were now their comrades in arms.[31]

Aside from Newgate-runaway Murray, only two former Gordon Rioters were with the troops as they waited aboard HMS *Mackerel*. Theophilus Brown, convicted for his part in burning down a Catholic church, was there with George Katenkamp's 102nd Independent Company. Also with Katenkamp was teenager John Morris, whose older half-brother Enoch Fleming had hanged in Oxford Road.[32]

Neither Benjamin Bowsey nor John Glover, the two black Gordon Rioters who had been offered respites on condition of their joining the troops destined for Africa, was with the companies however. Glover's sentence was successfully petitioned by his former employer, a lawyer named John Philips, for whom he had been a 'quiet, honest, sober servant' for twelve years. The evidence against him had always been flimsy, with two men claiming that it was a case of mistaken identity. Glover was eventually sentenced to leave the kingdom for three years, and may well have gone to sea.

Benjamin Bowsey also had high-status supporters in his former employer Lord Earlsbury, and Alderman Woolridge, to whom he had written asking for help. But he did not rely on their influence in the end. While under a temporary respite he was transferred to Poultry Compter, from where he escaped wearing a disguise of a 'high toupee' and false ponytail over his own short 'wool'.[33]

Lucy Johnson, the black Newgate escapee whose intended role in Africa was entirely a mystery, was not with the companies either. It seems that the possibility of committing any woman, even a black woman, to do army service in Africa was more than the British government could really countenance when a final decision came to be made and she had been left behind in jail when the male prisoners were boarded on the ships. Perhaps it was Mackenzie and Katenkamp who had objected to taking her aboard, a charge they surely would have perceived as an insult. Sadly for 'Black Lucy' being left behind was hardly a lucky escape. She died in New Prison, probably of typhus, only a few short months after the troops departed for Africa.[34]

Plenty of other ne'er-do-wells had been found to take their places. If Bowsey, Glover and Johnson had seemed, in the decision-makers' minds, to be peculiarly suited to Africa because of their dark skin— and what else are we to read into Lucy Johnson's respite of lifetime banishment to the continent—it appears that others could metaphorically blacken their own complexions through crime. Although some of the criminals had committed very petty crimes and had by a misfortune of timing been drafted into Mackenzie or Katenkamp's companies, the majority were egregious offenders, such as thieves who had stolen the most valuable items or used violence in their crimes. One or two were so notorious as to have criminal pseudonyms, like William Bolton, alias Billy the Flat, whose crimes included picking pockets among crowds watching hangings.

It was only at the eleventh hour that George Katenkamp and Kenneth Mackenzie knew that their destination was the most feared and reviled of places. On 30 May they had received a letter from Lord Germain informing them that they were bound for West Africa to protect the British forts, see if they could capture any of the Dutch ones, and to generally set about 'annoying the enemy'.[35]

Unbeknownst to them at the time, Mackenzie and Katenkamp's fate had been decided at the end of 1780 when Britain had declared war against the Dutch Republic, tired of the Dutch claiming neutrality while assisting Britain's enemies. This onset of hostilities created a new opportunity in the minds of Britain's war planners, accustomed to fighting battles in every arena around the world where their foes had colonies, trade, or merely spheres of influence. The American War had spread to Africa years before and the transatlantic slave trade had been seriously disrupted as ships from Britain, the rebellious American colonies and then France had attacked and captured each other. The Dutch, however, had very attractive possible prizes on the Gold Coast besides shipping, and were already very much weaker than in earlier years. They had tried to rush ships to Africa to defend their twelve isolated forts, but these were taken in the English Channel, leaving their African possessions defenceless.[36] The only problem for London was that their army was already stretched in America and the Caribbean, leaving few soldiers available to attack the Dutch in Africa. The newly raised companies provided an ideal solution while also offering the chance to unload some of the miscreants from the jails.

On 7 June, the *Mackerel* sailed down river to the Nore in the Thames Estuary and by the eighth had joined the other ships with which it was to sail at Deal, Kent. By 12 June they were at Portsmouth. With orders to sail expected any day, the convict-soldiers finally heard what part of the world they were destined for. A man 'convicted of being concerned in the late alarming riots'—almost certainly Murray—then complained that His Majesty's orders were being abused. Technically he might have been right, as his respite and that of several of the others had not stipulated Africa. But of course neither Katenkamp nor Mackenzie could allow this kind of challenge to their authority to go unchecked, and ordered the complainers whipped.[37]

It was not the end of the affair. The angry men declared that 'if the Captain presumed to go with them to Africa, they would scuttle the ship'. Pat Madan, whose respite had specifically condemned him to serve in Africa, was a ringleader once again, along with Murray and burglar Robert Hill. Gathering an angry mob of convict-soldiers around them they desperately tried to smash a hole in the bottom of the ship. As the alarm was raised and the crew hurried to stem the water pouring in, Madan and the others rushed the boats, hoping to get ashore. But order was quickly restored, the incident only going to prove to honest Londoners who read about it in the newspaper what a desperate set of criminals they were.[38]

Murray somehow escaped censure for this act but Madan and Hill were put ashore in jail, deemed too dangerous to be aboard ship. They were put before a court-martial, an affair Hill described as a 'shim sham'. Found guilty they were flogged, receiving upwards of 175 lashes each, then removed to Haslar Hospital to recover. When the *Mackerel* sailed she left the two men behind, but in the months to come the old offender known as 'the famous Madden' would find that his African adventures were not at an end.[39]

After all the excitement of the attempted scuttling, on 21 July the two independent companies finally set sail aboard the *Mackerel* in convoy with HMS *Leander,* the transport *Alligator,* HMS *Ulysses* and HMS *Zephyr.* In charge of the overall naval expedition was Thomas Shirley, a man who had the extraordinarily beneficial career advantage of being brother to Washington Shirley, Vice-Admiral of the Blue. Astonishingly, neither brother had been tainted by their family's notoriety, for their eldest brother had been Laurence Shirley, the fourth Earl Ferrers, who was the last lord hanged as a murderer. Washington, inheriting the title, had even managed to get back the family's forfeited estates. Both brothers' careers had been helped by having commanded ships during the battle of Quiberon Bay during the Seven Years' War, an occasion on which the French Navy had been irreparably damaged. Historians have compared the importance of this battle with that of the Battle of Trafalgar.[40]

Unfortunately for Thomas Shirley, Kenneth Mackenzie, George Katenkamp and all the other men packed to the gunwales on the various ships of the fleet, almost immediately the venture went badly when the wind dropped. Being becalmed was one of the perpetual problems of seafaring in the days of sail, the long days of boredom broken only by the mundane tasks of picking oakum and cleaning. To be becalmed in the English Channel with a cargo of mutinous convicts was bad enough, but to be near to France during wartime was to be a sitting duck.

Then matters took a turn for the worse as it became apparent that the unholy mix of soldiers, sailors and convicts were not the only living things aboard the ship. The fleet's inhabitants began to suffer from sweats and chills, stupor and severe headaches, and welts over the men's bodies. Although typhus could have been carried aboard by anybody, the men from the prisons and hulks were blamed. The volunteers and seamen recoiled ever more from those who had arrived in shackles and chains.

Then came word that the French were nearby and armed. With many of the 200 convict-soldiers affected by typhus and the majority of the seamen also incapacitated by the disease, the ships, saved just in time by prevailing winds, sailed for Cork in Ireland and temporary sanctuary. They escaped the French but could not outrun typhus; 'Twenty or thirty' convict-soldiers died, one of whom was twenty-two-year-old James Gable, who had previously been serving five years' hard labour on the Thames for mugging a lady of four shillings. His respite from the grim reaper had lasted less than three years.[41]

After the deaths at Cork, the small fleet made its way to Madeira, where they again stopped. After some more delays, and taking advantage of the chance to write letters home, they again set sail along the usual slave-ship route down the coast of Morocco and Senegambia. By this time it was clear that the problems of security and control were amplified not by the noted insubordination of the convict troops, but rather by the lack of unity between those placed in authority over them. One of those was Murray, appointed to drill the men aboard ship and try to make them into some kind of functional army unit.

Their arrival at Gorée, off the coast of Senegal, revealed to Kenneth Mackenzie, George Katenkamp and their ragtag band of soldiers the truth of the conditions they would have to face in Africa. It was not only the acute pestilence, although the swellings appearing on every exposed inch of the men's flesh soon testified to those horrors even if they did not recognise their significance. Nor was it just the rivers of sweat dripping down their backs and foreheads as they stood to attention in their grossly impractical woollen uniforms under the vicious sun. Far worse were the stories they heard from the men of the garrison: tales of sickness, scant food and infrequent victualling ships, and the omnipresent spectre of death. The mistreatment was acute, the punishment severe, they reported. It was not idle gossip. One day Commandant Joseph Wall would be a great deal more notorious than any of the criminals who now stood to attention before him on Gorée's parade ground.

The two independent companies were gone before Wall's infamous deed occurred, but they did see at first-hand his method of rule. Hearing that there were divisions between the officers of the companies, he was put in charge of settling the affair. On 7 December he convened a court of inquiry to sort out the matter. The chief offenders were Lieutenant Mawby, from the 101st Company, and Lieutenant Cranstoun of the 102nd. Unable to reach any positive conclusion about the cause of the dispute between Cranstoun and Mawby, and diplomacy not being among his inclinations, Joseph Wall simply told the two men to fight it out between themselves. In the grandest tradition of gentlemanly arguments, the two men dusted off their duelling pistols.

The Honourable George Cranstoun was a man with the kind of scandalous family history which perhaps suited him to taking the law into his own hands. His great-uncle had not only tried to disown his wife by pretending that they had never been legally married, he had then been implicated in a murder case concerning the mistress who had precipitated this act of rejection. When her father had disapproved of her committing bigamy by marrying William Henry Cranstoun, she poisoned her father using tablets allegedly supplied by Cranstoun as a love potion. His involvement in the murder was never proven, however, and the lovelorn woman went to the gallows alone.[42]

On 12 December 1781, the alleged murderer's grand-nephew met with his enemy and their seconds at Gorée. Taking the agreed number of paces apart—ten or twelve was traditional at the time—the two men prepared their weapons. Honour had it that both men point their weapons towards the ground until the last moment, then fire without taking too much time to aim. Mortality rates from duelling had, in fact, dropped significantly for this very reason when pistols replaced swords. In 1790, *The Times* would write that 'according to the system of modern duels, neither party received any injury'. [43]

But George Cranstoun was not a man who had taken to heart the new less-bloodthirsty sentiments in British society, or else he fired a lucky shot. Lieutenant Mawby was mortally wounded and died that evening. Cranstoun was immediately arrested for murder. A court-martial was quickly convened, Wall and Cranstoun were tried for murder. It was a precarious matter as they could scarcely afford to lose Cranstoun as well as Mawby. Predictably, then, he was acquitted and the fleet could finally get on with their regular business. Nevertheless, even with Cranstoun still aboard, they had lost more than a fifth of the rank and file they had sailed with and now one of the thin line of men who stood over them, and they were still a long way from their destination.

Finally, on Christmas Eve 1781, HMS *Ulysses*, *Mackerel* and *Alligator* left Gorée and set off down the African coast, the *Zephyr* being left behind at Gorée for Wall and his garrison's use. [44] The fleet's dwindling ranks were partially bolstered by some soldiers from Gorée 'that Lieut.-Colonel Wall chose to send away'. [45] These were men who belonged to the 75th Regiment—a short-lived regiment that would finally be disbanded in 1783—some of whom were deserters and felons.

It was 8 January 1782 by the time they anchored in the mouth of the River Sierra Leone, in search of potable water and with further problems aboard. [46] Not long after sailing from there, real disaster struck. Captain George Katenkamp, upstanding son of an Exeter merchant and commander of the 102nd Independent Company of Foot, still some years short of this thirtieth birthday, breathed his last. Having survived the fever at Cork and the trials of Gorée, he sickened and died from one of the mysterious maladies which seemed to the men to carry off untold numbers in Africa with little explanation or hope of reprieve. As the small convoy rounded the bulge of West Africa and turned out of the Atlantic Ocean and into the Gulf of Guinea, George Katenkamp's body was sewn into canvas and slipped over the ship's side. The customary hasty prayer service read aboard was hardly the end his family had imagined for their much-loved son upon whose future they had waged so much.

For those aboard ship, too, his death was calamitous. Now they were seriously undergoverned, hardly a promising prospect for two companies of men acknowledged to be, at best, unruly. Lieutenant Cranstoun, surviving dueller and only twenty-one years of age, took command of the 102nd Independent Company.

Worse still, within this misfortune were the seeds of the real problem which was to come. Back in Devon, George Katenkamp's grieving family waited patiently for his belongings to be sent to them. They never received anything. There was no token of their son and brother, much less anything of any value to offset the tremendous financial loss they endured at his passing so soon after raising an independent company. Herman Katenkamp wrote to the Treasury claiming that his brother's belongings had been stolen by Kenneth Mackenzie. It was the first indication that Captain Mackenzie's honesty, the cause of many future problems, was in grave doubt.[47]

Chapter Six

THE BATTLE FOR THE COAST

Tacking around Cape Three Points, all aboard the small convoy hoped that their ill-fated journey would soon give way to more settled times ashore. Occasionally now they passed a flagpole on the land flying a Union Flag, a sure sign that they were among their own, even if dotted among them were the Dutch flags of their enemy. As they passed majestic Elmina, headquarters of Dutch rule and the premier fort of the coast, they realised the magnitude of their mission but encouraged each other with boasts of British military and naval supremacy.

They had grown accustomed to the heat and humidity, but now they were also aware of new sounds and smells, scenery nothing like that with which they were familiar. Many from the independent companies knew only the dense, grey streets of the metropolis, but it was hardly less peculiar to their rural counterparts, who had swapped gently rolling greenery and neatly marked fields for raging surf and sandy beaches with rainforest pressing in just behind. A contemporary wrote that visitors arriving from Europe saw from their ships as they approached 'the snow white sands, the groves of palms, and the golden haze'. The coast, it was said, had 'a Robinson Crusoe sort of charm'.[1]

The landscape was surely beautiful, but there was much about the coast which was far from charming. As the small convoy of ships sailed into Cape Coast's roads on 5 February they found five slave ships bobbing in the tide. This was a much smaller number of vessels than was often found there, but nonetheless the true nastiness of the trade was apparent to the arriving troops. While three of the ships had only just begun their slaving and so were probably reasonably clean and ordered, the *Gascoyne* of Bristol and the *Gregson* of Liverpool were nearly ready to leave. Captains William Chalmers and Thomas Seaman had almost finished negotiating for the purchase of the 590 and 670 Africans respectively who were crammed below decks.[2] Even at this point the stench from such vessels, where the men commonly lay in their own excrement, was infamous. By the time they reached the western side of the Atlantic slave ships were said to reek so badly that passing vessels could smell them before they appeared on the horizon. The men of the arriving independent companies would have seen the paradox of the coast as they pulled alongside the noxious ships: the beauty of the scenery and the ugliness of the trade which prevailed there.

By a strange coincidence, a ship which would become one of the most well known of all in the years to come was bobbing at anchor in Cape Coast's roads. Seven years later the *Brookes* would be drawn by William Elford at the Plymouth branch of the Society for Effecting the Abolition of the Slave Trade. The stylised image of stick figures packed below her decks would set the campaign alight and go on to be one of the most commonly recognised images of the slave trade. In 1782, however, when the convict-soldiers saw it, the *Brookes* was newly built and on her first voyage. Her first captive African slaves, the cargo for which she had been specifically built with air ports to prevent them suffocating, had been loaded only a few weeks before the convoy hove into view.[3]

With no time to lose, the day after their arrival off Cape Coast Castle, Kenneth Mackenzie, George Cranstoun and Thomas Shirley went ashore, leaving Murray drilling the convict-soldiers aboard ship. At Cape Coast going ashore involved an exhilarating but perilous ride from ship to shore, a distance of maybe a mile or two, aboard a small canoe that coasted and dipped over the crashing waves to get the passengers close enough to the beach for them to wade ashore. It was highly skilled work with techniques passed from father to son. An English seaman making the same journey wrote, 'It was very exciting to be perched on a puncheon of rum, or a bale of goods, while twelve naked savages were driving the canoe along like a weaver's shuttle—keeping time with their paddles to a chant struck up by the steersman, in which, at intervals, all hands would join.'[4]

Waiting in the castle for the new arrivals, ready to extend the usual offering of food, drink and the use of the guest accommodation, was Acting Governor Jerome Bernard Weuves. Little is known of Weuves; given his name there is some speculation that he had joined the English from the nearby Dutch forts, but other sources claim that he was Swiss. Richard Miles, the usual governor, had gone home to England to answer charges against him relating to alleged dishonesty in private trading. He had actually been cleared of wrongdoing and reinstated at the end of 1781 but had not yet returned to resume his command, so Weuves was the man in charge when the troops arrived.[5]

Governor Weuves had mixed feelings as he watched the canoes bring Mackenzie, Shirley and Cranstoun ashore. Although he and the rest of the Company of Merchants continued to be extremely hostile to the arriving convicts despite their soldiers' uniforms, they were itching to steal some Dutch trade. The problem for the Company was that the Dutch were much better than the British at keeping their stores filled with the goods which the local African merchants wanted. The 'much superior Influence among the Natives' this created seemed best attacked by driving the Dutch from their forts, as the British were simply unable to supply the types and numbers of goods their competitors made available.[6] It had been a serious problem for decades. Ludewig Ferdinand Rømer, a Dane who was on the coast in the 1740s, noticed that he could spend an entire day at Cape Coast Castle and see no trade, whereas at Elmina there was never half an hour without some business taking place.[7] So while Weuves hated the fact that convicts had been dispatched to the coast, he could not stop himself from hoping that they could secure military victories over the Dutch which would destroy their trading supremacy.

The castle Kenneth Mackenzie found himself in was by far the strongest British fortification on the coast, especially as it had been recently revamped by the Company of Merchants. In the 1750s, Justly Watson had informed Britain that 'a forty gun ship could reduce this castle in a few hours to a heap of rubbish', a report so damning it had led the Company to embark on a serious scheme of refortification. In the years that followed most of the structure had been either repaired or totally remodelled, some older sections helping in the process by falling down before they could be demolished. Despite all the work, castles in West Africa required permanent attention as bits constantly let in water, fell apart or gave way. Keeping them in anything even approaching a sound condition was an interminable task.

Mackenzie's judgemental eye also looked upon 'rotting gun-carriages, which frequently fell to pieces', a courtyard of farm animals awaiting slaughter, and the (to him) strange sight of mulatto men dressed as soldiers. Between them and the haunting absent-presence of the slaves locked below ground in the newly constructed slave dungeon, there could be no mistaking what part of the world he found himself in. On the other hand, there were the accoutrements which Britons everywhere felt the need to have with them, as if to lay claim to the distant land as a small outpost of home. At Cape Coast Castle these included 'fine Spode china and Georgian silverware', wine decanters, paintings (doubtless including ones of the King and Queen), a billiard table, ten volumes of Shakespeare and four volumes of Chesterfield's *Letters to His Son*, which gave 'advice on how to behave with the manners of a gentleman even when you are not'. It was all essential stuff.[8]

The following day, the men got down to the business of plotting their attack. There was some confusion as to what the government actually intended them to do as they had received contradictory instructions. At the end of May, Lord George Germain, Secretary of State for the American colonies, had written to Kenneth Mackenzie instructing him that his main objective was to take Elmina from the Dutch. Five weeks later he had issued similar instructions to Thomas Shirley. But the ships had also carried with them another letter from Germain to Shirley marked 'secret'. In this, Germain instructed that 'Finances will not admit of offensive Measures against the Enemies of Great Britain' and that as they did not have enough men to hold on to all the British forts they should concentrate on retaining Cape Coast Castle, Anomabu and Commenda alone. Germain, a man who had once been 'adjudged to be unfit to serve his Majesty in any military capacity whatever' after he was accused of cowardice at the Battle of Minden, even contemplated that they might lose control of the jewel in their West African crown, Cape Coast Castle.[9]

Around the table at the castle, all the men gathered into the small council of war determined to roundly ignore Germain's secret instructions. To the Company men like Weuves there was too much at stake, not least an opportunity to steal some Dutch trade. Thomas Shirley was a proud

Englishman and determined to do his duty. He would not flagrantly disregard the instructions in the letter but would attack Dutch forts if the opportunity presented itself. And Kenneth Mackenzie was desperate to earn some honour for his disreputable company and urgently in need of some prize money to begin to pay his debts. The letter's contents were quietly forgotten.

Rather than embarking on a low-key defensive mission, the fledgling war council ambitiously conspired to strike first at the heart of Dutch operations on the coast. Elmina, the headquarters of Dutch rule, and the much smaller structure of St Jago, which stood atop a nearby hill, were only a few miles to the west of Cape Coast Castle. Shirley, Mackenzie and the Company's officers unanimously agreed that attacking these two structures was the best course of action.

Elmina was a formidable target, not least as the Portuguese officer who originally chose its location way back in 1482 had deliberately selected the place because it was protected by the raging ocean to the south and had only land access via a narrow peninsula. By the 1780s it was an impressive complex, housing around 200 white people and between 1000 and 1200 company slaves and encompassing accommodation of almost four thousand square metres. The complex even included a yard for raising civet cats 'whose odorous secretions were twice weekly extracted' to make rudimentary perfumes to mask the smell of unwashed bodies. Outside its walls was a town numbering perhaps 15,000 people. Exactly one hundred years before Mackenzie, Cranstoun and Shirley's time on the coast, Jean Barbot had written that Elmina was unsurpassed in both 'beauty and strength', adding that its walls were so strong as to be 'cannon-proof'.[10]

The smaller St Jago was much weaker. It was here that Jerome Bernard Weuves, Thomas Shirley, Kenneth Mackenzie and George Cranstoun decided to attack, the conventions of warfare decreeing that they should try to take control of the hilltop settlement first and then use that as a base to mount their attack on Elmina.

It may have been a standard battle tactic, but the plan was deeply flawed, and based on a misguided premise. Attacking first St Jago and then using that base to attack Elmina was how the Dutch had ousted the Portuguese from the stronghold in 1637. Recognising that St Jago could be used against them in the same way, the Dutch had fortified the hilltop. In the intervening years they had significantly strengthened defences on the hill. A map from 1774 shows St Jago complete with gun towers, drawbridge, ramparts and quarters for a range of officers and an armourer. What had once been a Catholic church dedicated to St Jago was now the Dutch fort Conraadsburg. But with few other alternatives, and swept away by hubris about British military superiority, the schemers incautiously proceeded.[11]

To boost their chances of success, Shirley, Mackenzie and Cranstoun spent the next nine days bolstering their forces. The plan was to sail towards Elmina, and then use canoes to land as many soldiers as possible while the ships' guns provided cover. At least thirty castle slaves boarded HMS *Leander* ready to fight. These were not from among the hundreds crowded into the dungeons of the slave forts awaiting sale to a slave ship, but were owned by the Company of Merchants Trading to Africa; a crucial part of their purpose, to Britain and all the other Europeans on the coast who likewise held their own slaves in their forts, was to reinforce military strength. Aboard the *Leander* they were added to the muster roll, the writer struggling with their Akan names and recording them with titles like Coffee Badow and Quaco Casso, typical English (mis)spellings of local names which represent the day of the week on which a person is born. Kofi is the male name for a Friday birth; Kwakú for Wednesday.[12]

Meanwhile the *Alligator* boarded two other groups of Africans who would assist the British in their battle with the Dutch. Twenty-eight canoemen, some free and others enslaved to the castle, joined the ship, giving names such as Tom, Billy or Quam, or more elaborate titles like Prince Fredrick. Among them was 'Captain Aggrey' the English name for Egyir, the son of Cudjoe Caboceer, who had been one of the most important men at Cape Coast for over forty years until his death in 1776. Egyir was supreme commander of the African forces at Cape Coast and was paid £60 per annum by the British for his services.[13] Fifteen mixed-race castle soldiers also joined the amassing forces, many of whose Anglo-Saxon names betrayed the fact that they were the children of English fathers and African mothers.[14] These mulatto soldiers were an essential part of the defences of the fort, and with some resilience to native diseases, having been born and raised on the coast, they often lived far longer than their colleagues who arrived from colder northern climates as adults.

Finally, some of the seamen from the waiting slave ships joined the expedition. The *Gascoyne* and *Gregson*, which were nearly fully slaved, could little afford to spare many men as the last weeks before sailing were notorious for slave revolts, but the other captains were happy to contribute the services of their men. The *Brookes*, *Molly* and *Nancy*, all Liverpool vessels, had only recently arrived at the coast and had barely begun purchasing their human cargo. The seamen aboard ship had only long tedious months on the coast, ever fearful of the diseases and with their tasks getting riskier and more unpleasant as the number of slaves increased, to look forward to. Little wonder that they joined in the chance for excitement and the possibility of some prize money.[15]

The forces were finally ready to go into combat. When Murray and the others had agreed to join the army rather than endure their sentences this was what they had signed up for, the penalty they had to face.

On 14 February at 9 am the *Alligator*, *Mackerel*, *Ulysses*, *Brookes*, *Molly* and *Nancy* set off. It was only a short distance westwards to Elmina, from where they would launch the attack. Over the weekend of 15–17 February the *Alligator* scouted out a place suitable to land troops close to St Jago–Conraadsburg and then, firing its guns as cover, effected the landing of sixty or seventy men. Testifying to the rough conditions, two drowned in the surf as they attempted to get ashore. Nevertheless this was an insignificant loss by contemporary standards of bloody warfare and Shirley was impressed, writing in his report of the day's events that he should 'bestow the highest encomiums' on Captain Frodsham of the *Alligator* 'for his excellently well conducted disposition in the Landing, which was most effectually executed'.[16]

On the Sunday more men were landed so that now several hundred were ashore. The British soldiers 'Advanced upon a rising ground.' There they were met by the 'Enemy's Blacks', for the Dutch, like the British, used locals in its armed forces. The battle had really begun, and the first day's fighting went well for Mackenzie and his soldiers. The Dutch were forced to retreat with 'a Considerable Loss', which allowed more of the British troops aboard the ships to land.[17]

Captain Shirley had previously agreed with Captain Mackenzie that when the ships were in a position to attack the fort he would fire one of the lower deck's guns and hoist a red flag 'with an intention that [Mackenzie] should at the same time advance with the troops and storm Fort St Jago'. On 20 February Shirley made the prearranged signal and began the attack. The ships' guns pounded St Jago with 'very hot fire', inflicting considerable damage on the Dutch fort. On into the following day they kept up the attack, hoping to weaken the resolve of their enemy by pulverising St Jago's walls. From aboard ship Shirley and his officers saw the men ashore advancing on the fort and 'being warmly engaged' with the African and mulatto soldiers fighting for the Dutch. From the vantage point of the ships, all appeared to be going well for the British.

In actual fact, those ashore were struggling badly, few even able to approach their target. The problem was that when the ships fired at the fort, the Dutch in the main stronghold of Elmina retaliated by firing their cannons not just back at the British ships, but also at the soldiers ashore. Built as a defence against Africans who would attack from overland as well as Europeans who would arrive by sea, Elmina had cannon trained in all directions. The soldiers running erratically up the hill such a short distance away proved an enticing target to their Dutch opponents safe behind Elmina's walls.

There was another problem. The few who did reach St Jago discovered that the ladders they had with them were too short to scale the fort's walls. In the heat of battle carpenters hurriedly tried to lengthen them. Then the Dutch–African attack was strengthened by the arrival of more men eager to defend their town surrounding the fort, which was also under attack from HMS *Leander*. For the independent companies, made up of men with little or no military experience, it was all too much.

At 11 am on the second day Captain Shirley saw the troops 'retreat *very fast*' and then make 'a *precipitate retreat* to the Ground they at first occupied'. He was stunned. In the mêlée the British soldiers left behind their only field piece (a mobile gun) and the ladders they had taken with them. By 24 February the surviving men were being hastily re-embarked on the naval ships, mission unaccomplished.[18]

There were numerous casualties. HMS *Leander* alone lost one sergeant, two corporals and three privates. The *Brookes*'s captain noted in the logbook the loss of sailors Joseph Edwards, Benjamin Roberts and Robert Thirlwind. Many were wounded, including Captain John Fletcher of the marines, who took a cannon shot in his stomach and hand which led to his whole arm being hastily amputated. One report put the number of dead from the two independent companies at sixteen.[19]

Nine privates from the two companies also numbered among the wounded. John Campion and John Lyon, thieves from Derby and East Grinstead respectively, had stood shoulder to shoulder dredging shale on the Thames and had somehow managed to survive the horrendous mortality of the hulks, the prisons and the typhus outbreak on the *Mackerel*. Now the two old friends were both wounded, far from home in hostile Africa.

Murray had survived unscathed but watched as Wright Stagg, whom he had first met at Newgate, suffered terribly from wounds he had received in the battle. The army uniform and the branded 'T' on his thumb showing his incongruous position, Wright Stagg, denizen of London's gangs and barely out of his teens, paid a terrible price for his crimes. Soon his body could tolerate the pain no longer. His name no longer appeared in the records of the independent companies' men.[20]

Horrendously for the independent companies, Lieutenant Cranstoun was also badly wounded. Unlike the convict-soldiers, he was free to return home and went back to England to convalesce. The Honourable George Cranstoun would survive his wounds, return to the army and eventually be killed in Suriname in 1806, but his loss to the independent companies in 1782 further lessened their ever-weakening chain of command.[21] To all intents and purposes, Captain Kenneth Mackenzie was in sole charge of both companies of rebellious, extremely unwilling men.

The problem with Mackenzie's command was only just becoming clear to those men like Thomas Shirley and those of the Company of Merchants, although the men under him had, hardly remarkably, been questioning his rule for months. Thomas Shirley was incensed at Captain

Mackenzie's behaviour during the debacle at St Jago and Elmina. He wrote in hastily conveyed missives to London from the battlefield that Mackenzie's actions during the battle were 'notorious', convinced that Mackenzie had cravenly ordered a retreat while the battle could still have been won. While lavishly praising the skills, bravery and professionalism of his own men and profusely thanking the captains and men of the slave ships who had assisted him, Thomas Shirley damned unequivocally Captain Mackenzie's conduct. He went so far as to tell the officers at Cape Coast Castle that Kenneth Mackenzie was a disgrace to the British military. Shirley made no formal complaint to London, deciding that he would leave it to those who had fought under Mackenzie to issue a more formal protest.[22] Few officers were left to do so even at this early stage, though, and only one man would survive to attest to Mackenzie's alleged pusillanimity and lack of military skill. He was John Montagu Clarke, an ensign who had served under Cranstoun and Katenkamp. He would prove to be one of Captain Kenneth Mackenzie's foremost nemeses.

Great responsibility had fallen on the shoulders of John Montagu Clarke following the deaths of both Captain George Katenkamp and Lieutenant Mawby, two of his three superior officers in the 102nd Company. He was an experienced soldier, having fought for five years in America during the Revolutionary War and seen action in the very bloody though victorious battles of Lexington and Bunker Hill. In fact his original appointment as ensign of the 102nd Company had been, relatively unusually, one of merit rather than a matter of him purchasing his commission. Even so, he had hardly envisaged that he would be in such a position of power as he now found himself.

It would have been prudent for Clarke to quietly accede to the wishes of Captain Mackenzie, a man now seriously aggrieved by events which were spinning out of his control, but Clarke could not stomach kowtowing to a man for whom he had no respect. If Kenneth Mackenzie had simply not been a gentleman or had only shown himself dishonest Clarke might have been able to save himself by making more judicious complaints against his superior officer. But in Clarke's eyes, Mackenzie had let down the good name of the British Army, and that was unforgivable. Mackenzie was not an effective officer, and worse still had shown himself to be lily-livered. According to John Montagu Clarke, the convict-soldiers of the independent companies had fought bravely at St Jago and had acquitted themselves as well as could be expected, which perhaps was not saying much. But Kenneth Mackenzie had gone half a mile behind the lines during the thick of the fighting and had demanded a retreat, so ensuring that they would be defeated. The veteran of gory Bunker Hill had no time whatsoever for cowardice.

Mackenzie's own report of what happened—his defence of his 'notorious' actions—never reached England, if he wrote one at all. In London they gave him the benefit of the doubt about this, assuming that his account had been lost when the *Alligator* was captured by the French on its way back to Britain and all the dispatches it carried were hastily thrown overboard. In its absence they had only Shirley's and Clarke's accounts of the affair. They could not quite credit how things had gone so disastrously wrong.

The two officers were not the only men who vilified Captain Kenneth Mackenzie. There was a popular revolt against him, with the men from the 75th Company who had been picked up at Gorée, plus the naval men on the ships, all vowing that they would never again 'Act under him'.[23] As a consequence, it was not only the wounded who were put ashore at Cape Coast Castle; the entire two independent companies of men were cast adrift from the expedition after this first encounter because of the odium in which their commander was held. They would play no further part in the fight for the Dutch castles, being relegated to playing a supporting role.

This action was clearly in contravention of both sets of Lord Germain's instructions and showed just how serious the schism was between Shirley and Mackenzie. But it was not only John Montagu Clarke, now confined at Cape Coast Castle with Mackenzie and the rest of the independent company men, who was dismayed by this turn of events. Jerome Bernard Weuves and the rest of the African Company men were equally horrified, for their worst fears were coming to pass. The pretence that the convict-soldiers were there specifically to fight for the Dutch forts had been shown to be a sham. They were to be left on the coast to be fort soldiers. It was exactly what the Company of Merchants had campaigned against for years, and Governor Weuves was livid.

He need not have worried about Mackenzie undermining his command at the castle however. Kenneth Mackenzie had little desire to stay there and be watched over by the Company men. When Shirley and the naval ships captured nearby Fort Mori from the Dutch after only a token display of resistance—the governor proclaimed his intention to defend until the last but then realised his untenable position as the British ships moved in—Mackenzie was quick to quash a suggestion from Weuves that the fort should be blown up.[24] He saw it as a suitable alternative base for himself and his men.

Weuves's suggestion showed how far Mori had fallen from its heyday. To the Dutch, it had been of considerable value in their early years on the coast before they had captured Elmina. From it they had inflicted serious damage on Portuguese trade in the region while accruing their own wealth.[25] For some years it had remained one of their foremost sites on the coast with records from 1645 showing that it then housed three junior trading officers, a sergeant, a preacher, a surgeon, a carpenter, a coopersmith, a garrison of twenty-eight soldiers and 156 slaves. The commander of the fort was paid the sizeable sum of sixty florins each month.[26]

At the time that Mackenzie took control of Mori it was in decline and certainly nothing like the castle in size or fortifications. But it still had a drawbridge leading to an archway into the main yard with a 'garrison [courtyard] about, but not quite, a hundred yards square'. From the main courtyard stairs ran up to the battlements from where the soldiers could keep a watch on events.[27] Most important of all, it stood on a narrow promontory high above a couple of small beaches where canoemen plied their trade and fishermen brought in the local catch. Thus it was only vulnerable to attack from a relatively small area of its back wall, which any assailant would have to climb a steep incline to get to. Kenneth Mackenzie was happy enough to take control there.

Captain Kenneth Mackenzie, his remaining officers (including the disaffected John Montagu Clarke), sergeants including the reprobate William Murray, and the tatterdemalion collection of men under them, made the hike of a few miles to Mori. To the watching Africans it can only have been a sight of fascination, derision and some horror, but the men themselves were still hardly less stunned. It seemed simply inconceivable that they were now in Africa to atone for their crimes. Standing on the battlements of Mori, half a world away from everything they knew, the British legal system must have seemed more bizarre, and less just, than ever. Being sent into the army was odd enough but at least part of a long tradition, but sending men to guard a semi-dilapidated castle on a remote cliff face in West Africa, watching slave ships sail by, was truly the most extraordinary punishment.

Ailing from all-pervading fevers which shook a man to his bones, ravenous, dejected and increasingly perplexed by their mercurial captain, the convict-soldiers tried to establish a routine between Fort Mori's wretched walls. Meanwhile, without them, HMS *Leander* and *Alligator* continued to have successes against the Dutch. Whatever glory was for the taking in West Africa, whatever prize money they might lay claim to, Mackenzie and his men were excluded from it, languishing in their fortress-prison.

Only four days after taking Mori, Thomas Shirley and his men demanded the surrender of Cormantin Fort and soon saw the British flag being raised. Again, Mackenzie dispatched men to defend the new possession, allowing the naval ships to depart.

Riding their luck, on 17 March the *Alligator* and *Leander* sailed to Apam Fort where Governor Morgue quickly struck the Dutch flag and raised the Union Jack. This time Mackenzie's men did not get to the newly captured fort in time and a few men from the ships had to be left behind to defend it until they arrived. The vessels next sailed to the British fort at Winneba in search of more drinking water to refill their casks. Once there Shirley saw that the Dutch fort at Senya Beraku was only four miles away, so losing no time the fleet went and demanded the surrender of that structure also. Knowing that they were inadequately manned and armed to defend against such an attack, the Dutch quickly surrendered the fort which was temporarily put in the care of the Governor of Winneba, Charles Graves.[28]

The capture of three forts struck a death blow at Dutch ambitions in Africa but that was hardly apparent at the time. It just seemed like more of the same, Cormantin, originally a small trading post built by a group of English merchants, having already been the cause of long rivalry between the two nations. When it had been captured by the Dutch in 1655 they had renamed it Fort Amsterdam, retaliating for the renaming of a small and not particularly eminent settlement on the other side of the Atlantic Ocean the previous year. New Amsterdam had, of course, become New

York. Now back in British hands and once more known as Cormantin—the name which gave rise to the name Coromantee in the Americas—it was added to Britain's growing network of forts.[29]

Back in England, the unfolding debacle that saw the independent companies no longer being used to fight for the forts was tactfully hinted at in the media. The *Gentleman's Magazine* announced that the forts of Mori, Beraku, Apam and Cormantin were taken solely by Captain Shirley and his men, suggesting to anybody who knew who else should have been involved that things had gone very wrong, without explicitly questioning why the convict-soldiers were missing from the action.[30]

Kenneth Mackenzie's failure to send men to defend the forts even after they had been captured was an additional fiasco. It was not just a matter of the distances involved or the harsh terrain they had to cross to get there; back at Mori the remaining troops were refusing to be split up and Mackenzie was rebuffing demands to order them to go to the outforts. The Company of Merchants' officials were incensed. On 25 March they wrote to Mackenzie to remind him that 'as by Lord George Germain's Instructions, you are directed to distribute your Troops amongst the Company's Garrisons in Africa, in such proportions as the Governor of Cape Coast shall think necessary'.[31] With so many forts now under British control, the men were badly needed to defend the new acquisitions. Mackenzie, however, ignored these instructions. The Company complained that Mackenzie did not 'shew the least attention to the garrisons under his command, having sent only 2 or 3 men to one, 2 or 3 to another, and not a single one to Bercoe [Senya Beraku]'.[32]

In truth, Mackenzie's refusal to separate the troops and send some away was only part of the problem. He was also rapidly losing control over the rebellious men. Jerome Bernard Weuves later related that Mackenzie confessed to him at an early stage that the men of the independent companies were 'a desperate set, and [he] could not command them, nor could he even go amongst them to quell them'. Certainly the chain of command over 200 men, many of whom were hardly tractable, disciplined soldiers, was desperately thin following the deaths of a number of their officers. Even authorities at Cape Coast Castle were incapable of helping. Weuves believed that the troops' refusal to be separated was an act of mutiny and he thought that they should be punished accordingly. He wished to discipline at least the ringleaders, but could not as he had an insufficient garrison to control them, having 'only 24 or 26 effective Men, mostly Mulattoes'.[33]

Mackenzie was indeed failing to control his troops, as by this time men from the independent companies were not just refusing to participate in the British victories. Alarmingly, they were actively fighting for their supposed enemy, the Dutch. From the first, either in protest at their treatment or merely seeking a way to escape their original sentences, Mackenzie's men had been deserting en masse. By the end of March 1782, only a few short weeks after their arrival on the coast, Weuves wrote that twenty-four men who had deserted from the two independent companies had taken part in an assault on one of the British forts. Weuves thought that 'the Dutch place[d] the greatest Confidence in them' and they probably had good reason, given the desperate position the fugitives would be in if they were recaptured.[34]

This situation became increasingly disastrous in April, when the British met their first serious challenge since their defeat at St Jago. The scene of this battle was Accra, where both the Dutch and British held forts close to each other. Here, the Dutch governor boldly declared that he was 'determined to defend what his Masters had committed to his charge with the last drop of his Blood'. He knew that he could rely on the support of the people living around the fort, especially their main African business partner, Chief Otu.[35] As the British fort was close by, this would, like St Jago, be a battle played out on land rather than one merely won by naval forces. Bloodshed was inevitable.

On 1 April the British 'Sallyed out of the[ir] Fort' and attacked the Dutch possession. The enemy was prepared, though, and put up an impressive fight. 'Great Numbers' of 'Dutch Blacks' were reported to have defended their fort against a relentless British attack. The result was a 'great Slaughter'.[36] Despite the carnage, the Dutch were resolute. The next day the fighting continued with no firm outcome. And so it went on. Day after day, the two sides skirmished, attacking and defending, making small inroads but unable to claim victory. For two and half weeks it remained a stalemate.

Then the British managed to persuade some of their African allies from a nearby region to join the fight. It was reported that 'a Black King from Winward & about 100 of His Subjects' reinforced the British line. This was to prove the crucial advantage, but the British still resorted to dirty tactics. On 18 April men again sallied forth from the British fort and set fire to the small African town which surrounded the Dutch fort. British accounts of the battle recounted that 'at Noon the Dutch town was Totally Burnt to the Ground and most of their Blacks drove into their Fort'. The 'obstinate Siege' was over. Yet the Dutch governor and his men remained defiant in defeat. Rather than suffering the humiliation of having to formally surrender the fort and being made prisoners of war, they slipped quietly away that night. They took the keys with them, forcing the British soldiers to scale the walls the next morning to take possession.[37]

British troops would undoubtedly have needed assistance from an African king's soldiers to bolster their attack, but to Shirley and his colleagues it revealed the complete lack of cooperation from the men of the 101st and 102nd Independent Companies of Foot. Far from assisting

Shirley and his men to conquer the Dutch at Accra, the convict-soldiers continued to run amok. The Company of Merchants' worst fears about the whole enterprise were coming to pass.

Chapter Seven

DESERTING TO THE ENEMY

After the siege at Accra, Thomas Shirley and his men were ready to leave the African coast and sail for the West Indies. Shirley was hardly sorry to go, his pride still wounded by their failure to capture the biggest prize of all, Elmina. The Caribbean, embroiled in the dying moments of the American Revolutionary War, offered him hope of redeeming himself.

Kenneth Mackenzie was even more relieved at Shirley's exit, but as the day for his departure approached Mackenzie found that he was not to be free of naval rule. Two days before Shirley and his ships departed, HMS *Argo* arrived on the coast under the command of Captain John Butchart, a veteran of the bloody battle of Grenada three years previously. Also aboard was John Charlton, a midshipman who had been Captain James Cook's servant aboard the *Endeavour.* He was one of the few men in the known world who had seen the place which would one day be the solution to the disaster which Weuves lost no time in describing to Butchart.[1]

John Butchart heard chapter and verse on Kenneth Mackenzie and his band of renegades from Weuves over dinner at the castle. Long before dessert, Captain Butchart was in no doubt as to how the Company of Merchants felt towards the two independent companies of men (or what remained of them) or their contempt for the British government whose total lack of understanding about the realities of West African coastal society had led them to draw up such a preposterous plan as sending its convicts there. By the time the dismayed Thomas Shirley also added his twopenny's worth of claim and blame, John Butchart must have pictured Captain Kenneth Mackenzie as a veritable ogre standing over an uncontrollable rabble of fiends.

There was another man from whom Butchart could learn about the terrible deeds of Kenneth Mackenzie, as Richard Miles, the governor of Cape Coast Castle, had returned from England. It was very much a homecoming for him, as Miles had long ago become more a product of the castle and its idiosyncrasies than his rainy, windswept birthplace. One of the coast's longest survivors, he had lived in Africa for fifteen years before being recalled to England, was the father of at least seven children by African women, and spoke the local Fante language fluently. He would become Mackenzie's chief adversary.[2]

One particular problem, according to Weuves and Miles, was Fort Vredenburg, or Dutch Commenda. Still in Dutch hands, it had escaped capture by Shirley and his men; they had sailed eastwards of Cape Coast, attacking all enemy possessions there, while Vredenburg lay to the west. The issue confronting Miles and his peers was that it was very close to a British fortress, British Commenda—in fact, the two buildings were separated by just a small stream and were well 'within musket-shot' of each other. Weuves and Miles knew that if they did not attack the Dutch, the Dutch would soon attack them. The British fort was in a precarious position anyway, with Governor Thomas Price sick and no officer in charge of the convict-soldiers stationed there.[3]

The previous year HMS *Champion* had attacked the Dutch at Commenda at the request of Jerome Bernard Weuves, but the mission had failed when reinforcements were sent from Elmina. At Cape Coast Castle the Company men worked hard to restore neutrality after this letdown and tried to persuade numerous privateers arriving on the coast not to attack Dutch targets in the hope that trade would not be too adversely affected. It was, of course, rather a hypocritical attempt in light of the fact that they had initiated the original attack, and the Dutch were not fooled. In retaliation they sent out brigades of their African allies to attack the British fort at Sekondi. After capturing that, they moved onto another fort, Dixcove. Commenda remained a sore point for the British.[4]

It had actually been a particular bugbear to the Company of Merchants since the start of Captain Mackenzie's reign on the coast several months before. They complained that as soon as Thomas Shirley and the naval ships sailed away to attack Mori and the other forts Mackenzie had 'turned his attention solely to enriching himself'. A large part of that complaint was due to events at Commenda.[5]

On 3 March, the day after Shirley and his men had captured Fort Mori, a ship named the *Comte de Flandres* sailed into Commenda's roads. Captain Mackenzie was delighted when he heard the news and quickly dashed off a note to Thomas Price, Governor of British Commenda, demanding that the governor board the ship with the detachment of convict-soldiers he had at his fort. That evening Thomas Price went aboard as ordered. Quite oblivious as to what Price and the soldiers intended, its captain, Jean Hageuron, put up no resistance and was utterly taken aback when Price announced that he was seizing the vessel in the name of the British crown. At the time the ship had a cargo which included the remnants of some iron, copper and brandy which had been the original freight, some ivory and gold Hageuron had already purchased, three young male slaves and a single female slave. It was a valuable prize, just what Mackenzie needed to fend off his continued threat of bankruptcy and disgrace.

Delighted that things were looking up, the following day Mackenzie himself went aboard the ship and formally seized it. From his point of view it had come just in time, as his creditors were breathing down his neck. Richard Miles valued the ship and its cargo at £5000, its owners claimed it was worth double that, but either way the share that Mackenzie, as commanding officer, stood to gain was substantial. Under naval regulations a captain received an eighth off the total revenue from the sale of the captured vessel, an amount which would have paid off a large part of his debts even if the ship only sold for the lower sum. His relief was palpable as he imagined what a difference such a prize might make to his family's beleaguered fortunes. He quickly made arrangements for the ship to sail to Mori where he could better hold it as his prize. Then, while sailing the short distance along the coast, he had the fortune to meet with another ship, the *Nossa Senhora de Assuncao*, riding at anchor. He sent men off in canoes to cut the cables on the other ship so that he could plunder them both at Mori. He and his men then helped themselves to all kinds of clothes, books, food, drink and even the ship's charts, despite being warned by trader Pindar Crawford that he was 'acting notoriously wrong'.[6]

Crawford was quite right, as neither ship was an enemy vessel. The *Nossa Senhora de Assuncao*'s home port was Bahia, Brazil. Aboard the *Comte de Flandres*, speaking in a combination of French and English and through a gaggle of men from among the crew and the fort who professed to speak both languages, Captain Jean Hageuron insisted that while he was a Frenchman, his ship was not French. Mackenzie's grasp of geography was obviously lacking; the ship, as its name all too obviously suggested, was registered in Ostend. Flanders, like Portugal and Brazil, was not then at war with Britain, so the ship had been illegally seized. Mackenzie was beside himself when he realised that the potential prize would slip through his fingers due to what he saw as a ridiculous technicality. Hageuron and his crew certainly looked enough like Frenchmen to him.

He raged not just against the loss of his much-needed prize money; he also knew that he was in serious trouble. Taking a neutral vessel as a prize contravened all international maritime law. So Mackenzie shamelessly changed tactic, claiming that far from having stolen the ship illegally, he had in fact commandeered its trading goods to feed his men and defend Fort Commenda, deeds which might loosely be interpreted as legitimate wartime acts. Few were convinced.

As it turned out, Kenneth Mackenzie would not have had a ship to sell for its proceeds even if it had been a French vessel. Realising that he would have to find another way to raise money, the day after the capture Mackenzie ordered around thirty of the convict-soldiers aboard the ship and told them to sail around the coast trading for him. After that he ordered them to sail back to Fort Commenda, to the domain of the more sympathetic Thomas Price (in trouble for his own part in proceedings) and away from the opprobrium of Miles and the climate of censure at Cape Coast Castle. But as he waited for news and Thomas Price looked out from his fort's wall anxious for the ship's arrival, the time it had been expected came and went. More days passed without word. Then more. Eventually it became obvious that something had gone very wrong.

While Captain Jean Hageuron, adamantly believing in the trust-worthiness and loyalty of his crew, clung to the idea that the ship had met with some disaster and been lost at sea, the more cynical Company of Merchants was less sure. With little faith in Mackenzie's men and sceptical as to how dangerous the waters were on the short voyage along the coast, they believed that the convict-soldiers had overcome the Flemish crewmen and become pirates. They were convinced that the men had taken this opportunity to regain their freedom. The Company men's anger grew as they envisaged the convicts raising the black flag with joyous whooping. They conjured up images of the men taking the four slaves aboard as shipmates, as some pirates, quite scandalously in their eyes, had been known to do. They imagined, as tale became myth with each rendering, that they were attacking honest slave ships and pillaging coastal areas, turning Africans everywhere against the 'legitimate' slave traders.

It was all castles in the air, for no word of the ship or those aboard was ever heard. Nobody would ever know what became of the *Comte de Flandres*. Nonetheless, convinced that they and the venerable Company would be paying for this debacle for some time as the pirate gang rampaged around the African coast, the men at the castle blamed Captain Kenneth Mackenzie for the entire fiasco.[7]

However angry they were, it could hardly match Kenneth Mackenzie's own rage over the incident. Even more of his men had escaped his command, and those left represented but a fraction of the independent companies' former strength. All his exertions on behalf of the British monarch (as he unflinchingly claimed) had come to nought and his reputation had taken yet another serious knock. Most terribly of all, his meagre coffers had not been supplemented by a single, rotten penny.

This long discontent surrounding Fort Commenda formed the background to the complaint which Captain Butchart now heard from Governor Miles. Months after the *Comte de Flandres* had sailed and all hope of hearing from it had been given up, the place was still causing the Company grief. The convict-soldiers were now making less dramatic attempts to escape and instead of making off to sea were simply crossing over to the Dutch at Fort Vredenburg just across the river. The Company complained that they were 'far more hurtful to us than the Dutch themselves, as they are far more desperate'. Butchart resolved to capture the Dutch possession.[8]

Among those living at Vredenburg was William Davis, formerly a resident of Croydon, then a market town south of London. His curious journey from Croydon to Commenda had begun five years previously when he had mugged a man named Ralph Knox, making off with £2 7s 6d. Caught and sentenced to hang, he had been reprieved to spend ten years— almost certainly a fatal stretch—doing hard labour on the Thames. He chose the army instead, and was still in his early twenties when he was wounded in the battle over Elmina and St Jago. When he was sent to Commenda to recuperate he saw an opportunity to escape. As soon as he could, he slipped away and presented himself to the Dutch as a new recruit cum asylum seeker. They welcomed him with open arms and added him to their own growing garrison.[9]

Davis was not only loyal to the Dutch out of fear of being recaptured by the British and made to pay for his disloyalty and desertion. Rather, he was taken by the better treatment he received from the Dutch. He even tried to persuade one of his friends who was still with the British to join him. He and Thomas Field, who was only about sixteen years old when he stole a large sum of money in a canvas bag from a grocer he had once worked for, had become firm friends during their years together on the hulks and then aboard the *Mackerel*.[10]

When it became clear that the Dutch and British were about to fight over their possessions at Commenda—a battle which had actually gone on intermittently for a century and had included futile attempts on both sides to extract gold from a nearby hill—Davis, either surprisingly literate or using the fort's clerk, wrote to his friend Field in haste.

Dating his letter only 'saturday, 5 o'clock', Davis told Field that he was writing the letter because of his 'regard' for Field and his life. His advice was to 'confine the Governor and Captain MacKenzie and make here with the rest of your Comrades, and you may depend that you will all be treated like Gentlemen and you will have your share in the Fort'. The British, Davis warned, could not possibly hold out against 'Ten Thousand Blacks ... and Six Mortars from Della Mina [Elmina]'.[11]

But Davis's warning proved unnecessary. An attack by twenty Dutch soldiers accompanied by fifty African soldiers failed when they were beaten off by the British Company slaves and some of the towns-people, the few soldiers there being sick with 'fluxes, fevers and agues'. When the *Argo* arrived the balance of power shifted further, as the poorly defended Fort Vredenburg was inadequately equipped to defend itself against a bombardment from sea. It was barraged by cannon while Lieutenant Cartwright led the foray ashore. The fort was quickly razed to the ground and the British stormed the ruined fortress. This would be said to mark the moment 'the power of the Dutch on the African continent was totally annihilated'.[12]

In the grounds they found twenty dead or dying men. At least one British convict-soldier who had run away to Commenda was among them. When he saw his old comrades approaching he had 'just time to beg his Life', supposing that he would be put to the sword for his treachery. He needn't have bothered; seconds later 'he breath'd his last', succumbing to wounds received in the battle. It could well have been William Davis, but so many British men were fighting for the Dutch by then that the identity of the dying man went unrecorded.[13]

The Company of Merchants was so impressed by the speedy capture of the fort with little loss to the British, and not a little relieved that Vredenburg would no longer cast such a spell over the convict-soldiers, that they wrote to London asking that Cartwright's bravery be commended to the Lords of the Admiralty. Meanwhile, Davis's letter to Field had fallen into Company hands and was also dispatched to London—marked simply: 'from one of the deserters to one of the troops at Commenda'—to demonstrate to the authorities how ominous the situation had become. Both the good news and the bad news sailed home for England together.[14]

Thinking that the danger from Dutch Commenda was passed, the Company ordered twelve more convict-soldiers to march down there from Mori to defend the new acquisition. But no sooner had Governor Miles overruled the convict-soldiers' unwillingness to stand guard than their captain attacked on another flank; Mackenzie retaliated by sending a note to recall them. In fact Miles probably had exceeded his powers, but given Mackenzie's refusal to send his men to the outforts he felt that he had no choice.

The dispute only worsened when the men arrived at Cape Coast Castle. Now judged by Miles to be weak and ill from their exertions under the beating sun, he ruled that they should recuperate there for a few days before going on to Mori. Mackenzie dismissed this and without further word sent to the castle for the men to return to him immediately. Against his wishes Miles dispatched them, but 'they were met on the Way crawling over Rocks by some of the Company's Officers, who declared they were so weak, that the journey was enough to kill every one of them'. The power struggle was endangering the lives of the soldiers.[15]

Regardless of the Company's high hopes, the capture of Fort Vredenburg did not stop the convict-soldiers from running away. By the end of April 1782, the committee at Cape Coast Castle estimated that between forty and fifty soldiers of the independent companies had deserted to the Dutch, more than a quarter of those who had landed in Africa. When the number lost to malaria, yellow fever, battle wounds and aboard the

Comte de Flandres was added, a sorry percentage of the 200 who had set off from England remained. And from all their positions along the coast, and even from right under Mackenzie's nose at Mori, the men continued to desert in hope of finding a better situation for themselves elsewhere. An earlier Governor of Commenda's declaration that 'it is almost impossible to run away on this Coast', uttered while he watched some recaptured soldiers being 'cruelly flogg'd and pickled', was sorely tested.[16]

Of those who had deserted by late April, two of the eighteen men who had fled together during the Accra conflict caused particular controversy. The escape attempt had been impromptu and hastily conceived, a rope tied to a gun providing the means of escape. Feeling so aggrieved at their treatment that they had little left to lose, and no doubt seeking some alcohol and a full stomach, eighteen men went over the wall and took off into the black African night. They stumbled down the steep incline below Fort Mori and headed to where they thought food and safety might lie: with the Dutch at Elmina. In truth there were few options available to them. Their only other choices were going to the African town and trying their luck there, or sleeping rough in the forest until the search for them was called off. Neither was appealing.

The problem was that between Mori and Elmina stood the imposing presence of Cape Coast Castle. All around were locals who supported the British, or at least knew that they would be rewarded for useful information. The runaways tried to slip past the back of Cape Coast township during the night, but castle officials had been alerted by the watchful townspeople. Weuves immediately sent Patrick Lysaght, officer of the castle guards, with a party of soldiers and Company slaves to catch them. Far more used to the terrain, the pursuers quickly caught up with the deserters. But the runaways were not prepared to surrender without a fight, especially as they were already at the banks of the Fetu River, where 'dutch blacks' awaited them on the other side. As their pursuers approached the deserters plunged into the water, desperately wading to freedom. All but two of the convict-soldiers made it across and into the care of the Dutch, although one was badly wounded in the fight and was reported to have probably died from his injuries.[17]

The two men who were caught knew that they would suffer horrendous punishments for their attempted desertion. One was Thomas Rhodes, a thrice-convicted housebreaker from Hertford who was in his mid-twenties. The other unfortunate man was Job Massey, a few years Rhodes's senior and a widower who had been a gentleman's servant and barber in London before being convicted of stealing some cloth, ribbon and lace. Both had been working their way through five-year sentences of dredging shale on the Thames when they had chosen instead to go to Africa.[18]

Dreading their punishment at the hands of Mackenzie, Massey and Rhodes were initially pleased to be returned to Cape Coast Castle rather than Mori, even though they were ordered into the 'slave hole', as Weuves reported to Ensign Hawkshaw—this was surely an informal name for the small above-ground soldiers' prison rather than the dungeon in which the men and women awaiting sale were incarcerated.[19]

Returned to Mori, things got worse. They were whipped and then thrown into that fortress's 'slave hole'. There the two men sweltered in the airless humidity of the dungeon, eaten alive by mosquitoes, desperate for water to drink and dressings for their wounds.

Rather surprisingly, given that a similar punishment had apparently been inflicted at Cape Coast Castle, this imprisoning of convict-soldiers in the 'slave hole' at Mori quickly became the cause of controversy. What exactly the 'slave hole' at Mori was is unclear, but as it was seemingly only able to hold a handful of men at most, it is likely that this too was the fort's soldiers' prison. Most likely used to temporarily hold those who had been insubordinate to their officers, the 'slave hole' was guarded by a sentry and protected by 'iron bars across, as thick as your fingers, on the outside door; there was a great iron bar came across and a padlock'. At other times, though, the punishment was described as time spent 'with the slaves', and if they really were put in with captives awaiting sale, little wonder that it caused outrage.[20]

Mackenzie would later defend putting Rhodes and Massey, and many others of his men, in the slave hole by claiming it was the only place in Fort Mori that could safely serve as a jail, despite its shortcomings.[21] But anywhere called a 'slave hole' would be controversial to Britons in the 1780s, and not only because of its association with the dungeons where slaves were held awaiting sale to a passing ship; 1782 was only twenty-six years after an event which had shocked the British world—an event which, for some reason, among the countless reports of pointless mass losses of life which regularly arrived from around the globe, had stuck in the British psyche.

In 1756, the newly installed Nawab Siraj-al-daulah had marched on the poorly defended Fort William in Calcutta, a British possession. Although all the white families from the town were sheltering in the fort, it was so inadequately manned that those inside were reduced to putting mattresses against the walls in a desperate attempt to repel an attack. Yet they remained optimistic despite being ridiculously outnumbered, believing that no number of the Nawab's men, 'inferior' Indians after all, could possibly defeat good, solid Englishmen. They were quickly disabused of this misconception when the attack began; they managed to hold out for only a few days before being overrun by the Nawab's forces. On the first night after the capture, the invaders locked some British prisoners—the number was traditionally put at 146—into a tiny jail. The next morning only perhaps twenty-three emerged alive, the rest having suffocated, died of thirst or been crushed to death. The horrors of the so-called Black Hole of Calcutta would become legendary.

There was more similarity with Mackenzie's tactics that anyone would admit. The actual 'Black Hole' in Calcutta was in fact the military prison in the fort, a small section of the barracks measuring around fourteen by eighteen feet sectioned off for soldiers to cool their tempers or sleep off hangovers. It was similar, in other words, to the jails at Cape Coast Castle, Fort Mori or any of the other British possessions dotted along the African coast.

The problem was that the Black Hole of Calcutta had been whipped up to the status of national myth, and in the mythmaking the British had seen some justification for the movement to colonise all of India. Less than a year after the Black Hole incident, Robert Clive—known to posterity as Clive of India—was victorious at Plessey and the course of Indian history was changed. By 1782, the idea that the Black Hole incident had been an example of true British grit and determination in the face of Indian barbarity was all too common. How then could it be that a white man wearing the uniform of the noble British Army was to be found locking his own men into a 'slave hole', especially since 'slave' and 'black' were becoming conflated terms?[22]

Despite this punishment or any of the others Mackenzie meted out, he could not stop his men from deserting. The story of Rhodes and Massey was merely an illustration of what was to come. Men went over walls on ladders during the night, jumped off low parapets while on watch, nipped through doors when nobody was looking and went on errands and failed to return. When an opportunity presented itself, few resisted.

With his men deserting in droves, Captain Mackenzie lost all concern for how he might legally, much less humanely, punish them. Volunteer William Varley, who fled in May 1782 and was quickly recaptured by local

Africans, at least had the advantage of being handed over at Cape Coast rather than Mori. Kenneth Mackenzie, of course, demanded his return so that he could punish the deserter as he saw fit. But both Governor Miles and Dr Stuart Beard, the resident physician at the castle, refused, as while Varley was held in the jail there he became desperately ill with malaria. Angry letters passed between the castle and Fort Mori. Beard demanded that Varley be let out of handcuffs and moved 'to a more airy situation' to give him some hope of survival. Miles, meanwhile, refused to order Varley to march to Mori on the grounds that any such journey would kill him. The arguments proved academic. A few weeks later funds were being allotted for the support of Varley's widow.[23]

Strangely enough, one of the few men Captain Mackenzie still had faith in at this point was William Murray. Out of either desperation or a misguided sense of the man's character, Kenneth Mackenzie appointed Murray to be in charge of the small garrison at Fort Cormantin, one of the forts captured by Thomas Shirley. Later, when so many other crimes had occurred, Kenneth Mackenzie claimed that he had sent Murray to Cormantin to banish him from Mori, where he had been causing trouble. Mackenzie declared that Murray was the ringleader in 'most of the Robberies and Riots' among the troops and so he had sent him to Cormantin 'in hopes by separating him from the Gang to be able to keep some order and Discipline'.[24] Yet if that was entirely true, why had he made him the leader of the garrison at Cormantin? It seems more likely that Murray had yet again shown his talent for plausibility, perhaps suggesting that he was just the man his clansman, who he was still claiming was his uncle, needed to lay down the law at Cormantin while keeping a lookout for any goods which could be stolen. It was exactly the kind of offer which would have appealed to 'Uncle' Kenneth.

Just like all the other men who had fallen victim to Murray's silver tongue, Kenneth Mackenzie soon found that he had been deceived. Murray was thrilled to have his own domain, his own petty kingdom in which to run amok. In one way he did just what his commanding officer had asked. He quickly raided Cormantin's stores for anything of value. But he did not turn the loot over to Captain Mackenzie; instead he took it to the local town and bartered all he could for foodstuffs and alcohol. The carousing when he returned was hardly what the British government had intended when it had sent the men to guard the forts. Then again, it had definitely not intended them to be in charge of entire garrisons.

Murray ruled in the style of a pirate captain—or like the criminal gang leaders he had once known so well in Newgate. And fittingly enough, with him at Cormantin was William Cheatham, the young boy who had been the Artful Dodger to Patrick Madan's Fagin. Ruling through a mixture of terror, laxity and utter dissipation and dissolution, Cormantin under Murray was a world of volatile tempers but honour among thieves, of strange codes of practice where acts of disobedience to the British crown and the Company might win the approval of all.

Tales of desertions from Cormantin became legendary, just as they had previously been at Commenda, but there was no local Dutch fort here to entice the disillusioned. More likely, these were not acts of desertion at all, rather a loose system Murray established of allowing soldiers out into the local African town to bargain for food, drink alcohol, and set themselves up with any local women they found willing. It was not his style to keep too close a rein on his men, especially as he himself had no intention of living by those rules. He increasingly spent time in the local town, indulging his own tastes in women, drink and freedom.

One night William Cheatham and four other soldiers decided to flee from Cormantin, breaking locks and doors and destroying gunpowder during their escape.[25] Quickly recaptured, they were returned not to Murray at Cormantin but to their commanding officer at Mori. William Cheatham and his fellow escapees were whipped so harshly for their transgression that Governor Miles thought they could not survive. He later conceded that 'they are such hardened Villains, that in five days they were all well, and would no doubt desert [again], if they were let out of Irons'. But he did not go so far as to approve of Mackenzie's harsh regime.[26]

By this time the Company of Merchants had begun to despair of Mackenzie's severity in dealing with his troops and were writing increasingly strident letters of complaint to authorities in London. Given that they had very little sympathy for a bunch of convicts whom they had never wanted, their criticisms show, at the very least, how strongly they disapproved of Kenneth Mackenzie. The allegations of cruelty were intertwined, moreover, with criticisms of his ineffectual regime. Not only was he trying to rule with an iron rod, his attempts at controlling his men through these methods were proving disastrous.

The Company's men did recognise the untenability of Mackenzie's situation. Richard Miles questioned 'how in the name of God can it be thought the Lives of 8 or 10 Officers are safe among such a Crew of Felons?'[27] By all accounts Mackenzie's job was a very difficult one, a fact that had been acknowledged before he left England and when there had been George Katenkamp and another six or seven officers to share the burden.[28] By this time Mackenzie was practically in sole command of the two independent companies and had promoted some convicts to positions of power. But he was failing utterly to control the troops. The Company of Merchants' assessment of the convict-soldiers was damning. Jerome Bernard Weuves wrote that the soldiers were 'armed Ruffians' who 'put us in fear of our Lives being always ready to fly to their Arms in order to intimidate us'.[29]

Relations between the Company of Merchants and Kenneth Mackenzie were at breaking point. It was partly an issue of who was in charge. Richard Miles complained that 'Captain MacKenzie ... considers himself entirely independent to either me or the Council, he just says, writes, and acts, as he thinks proper'. In fact the exact relationship between the soldiers and the Company, let alone the chain of command, was unclear, as it was in many similar situations around the world. The real problem was that Mackenzie's motives were questionable. Miles thought that 'almost every thing he does, is in the opinion of the Council wrong' and feared that his actions were 'not the most honourable'.[30]

With at least a quarter of his men having deserted to fight for the enemy, thirty or so having disappeared on the *Comte de Flandres* and others dead or dying from diseases to which they had no resistance, Kenneth Mackenzie's rule was rapidly collapsing. Then, to make things even worse, one of the last remaining officers died. Ensign Hawkshaw had been in a position of power since the other deaths and had been acting as virtual commanding officer when Mackenzie was sick. Now he too was gone, and again rumour and gossip surrounded his death, with many of the men believing he had been poisoned.[31]

For Mackenzie and his men it was ruinous. 'I am left entirely destitute of officers,' Mackenzie wrote to Cape Coast Castle. Needless to say, he soon managed to make a terrible situation worse by angering the Company. Rather impertinently he tried to appoint one of the Company's men, Richard Miles's own brother Thomas, in Hawkshaw's place. Of course the Company, themselves short of men, were outraged and Richard quickly recalled his wayward younger brother.[32] In his precarious position—as the sole captain over two companies composed of rogues hardly there of their own free will—Mackenzie badly needed support from the Company of Merchants Trading to Africa to enforce any kind of secure regime; trying to headhunt the governor's own brother was hardly the way to improve relations.

The British were even in danger of losing two of the forts captured by Thomas Shirley and his men such a short time before. At Apam, 'they had seen Blacks scaling the fort's walls … to try and capture the fort and dispossess the whites'. One sergeant there had felt musket shot 'whisk past his ears' as he walked on the ramparts. Senya Beraku, meanwhile, was in danger of being delivered back to the Dutch, 'which the natives can easily do' as it had only one soldier and one company slave to protect it. Things were falling apart.[33]

Chapter Eight

A PLANTATION WITH SLAVES

In June 1782, Governor Richard Miles wrote a damning assessment of the remaining men of the 101st and 102nd Independent Companies of Foot. 'Such wretches as they are my Eyes never beheld,' he wrote in complaint to London, 'miserable and filthy to the last Degree.' His remonstration grew not out of humanitarian concern for them. There was something obvious in his rhetoric, something which closely reflected the apprehension voiced the previous year that dispatching convicts to the West African coast would damage the racial supremacy claimed by Europeans involved in slave trading. The convict-soldiers, claimed Miles, were a 'Disgrace to the very Colour'.[1]

Miles's grievances echoed into the breach which had developed between Britain and her overseas spheres of influence about the nature and importance of racial designations. By the 1780s, the plantation regions of the Americas were developing increasingly inflexible racial arguments to defend slavery, ideas which would not come to prominence in the mother country until some years later. Race was more or less synonymous with skin colour by this time among the plantocracy of Barbados, Jamaica and Britain's other remaining American colonies, whereas in Britain itself the remnants of the perception that race was invested in a person's lineage, religion and civility still lingered.

The exemplary work of arch-racism in this era, Edward Long's three volume *History of Jamaica*, had been published in London in 1774, the year Patrick Madan dramatically escaped execution and Murray was transported to Virginia. Not exactly a man of restraint and moderation, Long's allegations about men and women of African origin were extensive and sweeping. They were, he declared, 'void of genius'; 'have no plan or system of morality among them'; were covered with a 'bestial fleece' instead of hair and possessed of a 'bestial' smell; were also covered all over their bodies with black lice; and were 'naturally thieves and villains'. What was more, they were doomed to this state in perpetuity as Long believed that they had little chance of developing beyond their current state. While the offspring of slave women and white men in the Caribbean were raised to a better condition because of their magnificent European genes, they were, Long stated—and against all the contrary evidence, it must be said—sterile, just like mules. Whites and blacks were separate species and so could not interbreed. Instead, he wrote, orang-utans (he meant chimpanzees) made perfectly suitable husbands for African women.

Such ideas were not yet widely accepted in England and Long certainly did not represent the typical opinion of the era. In fact, it was the lack of loathing for Africans among certain segments of the metropolitan population—he deeply regretted that working-class white women seemed to him excessively attracted to black men—which most alarmed Edward Long. All the same, ideas about racial differences, in which those of African origin (and later Australian Aboriginals) were always seen as the bottom of the pyramid topped by the superlative Anglo-Saxon, were mounting in popularity. Everywhere the categories of 'Christian' and 'African' were being exchanged for the labels 'white' and 'black'. It was no coincidence that the two groups of people were now represented as polar opposites and by terms which in the English language at least also denoted good and evil, pure and sinful. These theories would grow and mutate into the later abominations of head measuring, and from there to segregation, separation and, elsewhere, apartheid.

In the West Africa of the 1780s, among slave traders like Governor Richard Miles, things were subtly different. They had a heavy investment in the kind of beliefs of racial superiority that their customers held, not least (to adapt an old adage) as it is hard to sell people as goods without seeing them as beings lesser than your own sovereign self. Slave traders saw their African victims purely as commodities, as the terminology—'lots' for auction, 'cargoes', 'refuse slave'—implies. It probably also made good business sense to identify with the social mores of their clientele, and a generous dose of a heady superiority complex made the long, frustrating palavers with African merchants of the coast slightly more bearable.

Those very palavers, though, and all the other day-to-day business which went with being an eighteenth-century slave trader in West Africa, meant that there were more nuanced aspects of racial hierarchies which they could not evade. At all times on the African coast the local people were in positions of considerable power and Europeans could only succeed in the trade with their patronage or at least acceptance. European slave traders stationed in West Africa knew only too well that African merchants, kings, chiefs and middlemen were extremely powerful. Of course this did not mean that they regarded the Africans as equals, and certainly they did not speak of them in this way over a glass of port with their fellow Britons around the table at the castle, but it did mean that the notions of racial superiority they were desperate to uphold were even more precarious there than they were elsewhere.

The words of John Roberts, who was Acting Governor of Cape Coast Castle immediately prior to Jerome Bernard Weuves in 1780, are revealing. Roberts wrote that Africans were 'devoid of every principle of honesty, and strangers to the sense of pity, their whole conduct is at once ungovernable and ferocious'. They were cruel, treacherous, knew nothing of the idea of liberty and had no religion, he believed. To be sure, these are the words of a man with deeply held racial views, but unlike Edward Long, to whom Africans were beasts rendered almost helpless by the white man's powers, Roberts considered them far too powerful for his liking. In fact his cry was this: 'the Europeans in this country should be invested with a diffusive, permanent, and formidable power'. This was a man positing his own and his race's superiority, but from a position far weaker than that of plantation proprietor Edward Long.[2]

A former governor of Commenda had made an even stranger statement along the same lines. 'Compassion is an Impulse ill-bestowed on a Savage,' he wrote, 'whose earliest Rudiments, with regard to an *European*—are to look upon him as his Property, to get whatever he can from him *by any Means*—and in all Matters that regard his own Complexion, never to divulge a Truth'. The man had lamented, 'There is no washing them White.'[3]

There was also a corollary to this unavoidable knowledge that African societies had hierarchies roughly corresponding to Britain's potent class system. As Governor Miles and the Company men attempted to wrest power from the African big men, they had a particular fear of exposing Africans to the poor, lowly and destitute of Britain. If this happened, then there was a theoretical danger of two parallel hierarchies or class systems running side by side, black and white. Slave traders, of course, could countenance no such thing, as it would destroy the ideas of essential white supremacy which they entertained. Crucial to their manifesto was the fallacy that Britain, or indeed Europe as a whole, harboured no such contemptible specimens of humanity as the Africans they traded as slaves. Otherwise, how could they justify the fact that Britain's lowliest were not enslaved when Africans were? The convict-soldiers, expelled from Britain for their crimes, provided far too close a comparison.

The convicts were already on the coast, so Miles could only try to make sure that they kept up the masquerade that they were honest soldiers. His horror at the fact that they were 'dirty and miserable' was intrinsically linked to what he regarded as the honour of white men. The least that the soldiers could do was aspire to be materially above black men. And somewhere in the pragmatism of Miles's comments was a deeper angst. Perhaps poor whites could literally become darker through their degradation and, as in this case, through dirt. He intended no irony, despite the fact that eighteenth-century Britons washed rarely, even in the tropics. To him, poor, dishonest, dirty Europeans were fearfully close to blackness.[4]

The situation would have been distinctly less alarming if the man in charge of the dirty convict-soldiers had understood these finer points; if he had agreed with Miles that at least these were objectives to aim for. Kenneth Mackenzie did not. Worse still, he himself was failing to live up to the Company of Merchants' purported high standards set for white men living on the African coast. He had even resorted to writing letters 'frought [sic] with Invectives of the basest nature', complained Miles, doing his best impression of a shocked, chaste maiden who had never heard such terms.[5]

It was not just his ungentlemanly vocabulary which may have made Miles and his peers suspicious of Mackenzie's status. He was, after all, a

Highland Scot. They were thought dubious to Englishman of the age in terms of their religion (heathen or, worse still, Catholic), civility (lack of trousers), language (Gaelic) and their former doubtful loyalty to the British monarch. In 1739, the Society for Propagating Christian Knowledge had published an article in the *Gentleman's Magazine* under the title 'Of Civilising Islanders in Scotland'. Even as late as 1775, Samuel Johnson had set off to tour the Scottish Highlands as an example of a savage, uncivilised society, and found there some people who, he wrote, 'were as black and wild in their appearance as any American savages whatever'. The men Johnson spoke of were McCraes, not Mackenzies, but few outside of the highlands cared about that. Ideas were changing, not least because of the military service of men just like Kenneth Mackenzie, but whether he was a member of the 'superior' white race was still debatable.[6]

Whatever the reason, his actions were more than a little unsavoury in the Company men's eyes, and they could not make him understand the importance of maintaining the distinction between black and white. The problem was partly that Mackenzie was preoccupied exclusively with his need to pay back to George Ross the money he had borrowed to establish his independent company, and making enough money to save his family from financial ruin. Stuck in Africa, this would be no inconsiderable feat.

It was not his avarice in itself which was the issue. The men of the Company were also preoccupied with money making: Miles himself complained that the governorship of the castle was 'a burden which interfered with [his] private trade'.[7] Since his earliest days in Africa 'as a penniless teenager', Miles had begun to establish an expansive private trading network, buying slaves from almost all of the local merchant families at one time or another. When he became governor at Anomabu and then Cape Coast Castle, his trading continued unabated and he regularly exchanged pewter pots, copper rods, kegs of tallow, iron bars, rum, tobacco, guns, gunpowder and a wide selection of textiles—'romauls' and 'chelloes' from India, English chintz, plain cotton, 'palampores', 'pulicats' woollens, silks and even used sheets—for slaves, gold and ivory. It was controversy over this trading which had caused his absence from the castle when Mackenzie and the convict-soldiers had first arrived.[8]

Miles was not alone in his conducting private business from within the castle walls. Most Company servants made money which went into their own pockets rather than entering the Company's ledgers; this was why the African service appealed to middle-class Englishmen despite the death rate. So it was not Mackenzie's desire to undertake some secret fundraising which alone was the problem. The issue was that Kenneth Mackenzie's methods of enriching himself rocked the core beliefs on which the Company of Merchants operated.

Taking control of some land 'to leeward' of Cape Coast Castle, Mackenzie purchased some eighty or ninety African slaves and set them to work clearing the ground ready for planting. Mackenzie's intention was to grow the same cash crops that slaves produced in the West Indies, an idea that many Europeans had entertained over the centuries. If sugar and cotton could be successfully grown in West Africa, instead of transporting captive Africans across the ocean to be sold to plantations where they would grow the crops, things would be simpler and cheaper.

From the start Governor Richard Miles and the other officials at Cape Coast Castle were, hardly surprisingly, against Mackenzie's scheme. Miles warned him that the venture was 'an idle one', particularly as no-one knew when Mackenzie would be recalled to Britain. Miles was obviously still clinging to the hope that Mackenzie and his men would be deployed elsewhere as part of the regular army. He was reluctant to acknowledge that the convict-soldiers had to all intents and purposes been abandoned in Africa.

Miles and the Company's opposition to the plan was more than a matter of Mackenzie's likely term of residence on the coast, though. The establishment of plantations in West Africa had always been controversial in Europe because it struck at the very heart of the plantation system. If cotton, sugar, indigo and other such goods could be produced in Africa, why were millions of Africans being shipped to the Americas to produce these items for the European market?

In fact several members of the Company, including a former governor of Cape Coast Castle, Thomas Melvil, had attempted to produce cotton and indigo in West Africa in the 1750s in order to bolster falling revenues. Their attempts had been summarily crushed by the power of the West Indian lobby. Members of the Company's committee were called to the Board of Trade in London to explain themselves and were told unambiguously that 'the introducing of Culture and Industry amongst the Negroes was contrary to the known establish'd Policy'. If crops were grown in Africa, the Board of Trade's representatives argued, 'there was no saying where it might stop'.[9]

There was also another issue at stake. Although men like Melvil were certainly not anti-slavery and saw African plantations purely in economic terms, the idea of growing staple crops in Africa was tied up with the abolitionist movement. When Bulfinche Lambe, a Royal African Company employee, travelled to London in 1731 with a letter from King Agaja of Dahomey suggesting that plantations should be established in Africa, it was seen as a threat to the transatlantic slave trade. The idea, according to abolitionists who heard about the plan, was that 'the Natives would sell themselves to us, on condition of not being carried off. That we might settle Plantations &c'. To abolitionists then (almost certainly misinterpreting Agaja's real intentions) the idea of plantations in Africa would mean an end to transatlantic slavery.[10]

A PLANTATION WITH SLAVES

By the 1780s, when Mackenzie embarked on his plantation scheme, the production of cash crops within Africa was increasingly seen as a way not only to end the transatlantic trade in slaves but also to assist in the 'civilization' of Africans. Organised cultivation of the land and trade were as important to most Europeans' ideas of civility as belief in the Christian god and small family units. Consequently, the establishment of plantations within Africa not only threatened the slave trade, they were an important part of schemes formulated by liberal Europeans to 'develop' Africans into 'modern' citizens. Perhaps they would even be able to understand the necessity for European goods, as economists like Malachy Postlethwayt had once hoped. Six years after Mackenzie's plantation was developed, Paul Erdman Isert, a Dane, established a plantation named Fredericksnopel not far from Accra as a 'utopia' where the 'demands of humanity and commerce' were 'harmonized'. African plantations consequently raised ideas entirely antithetical to men like Richard Miles, even if Mackenzie's small-scale scheme was never remotely intended as a way to assist those who worked on it.[11]

Besides this, there was something far, far worse about Mackenzie's scheme. What all the men who had these ideas, from King Ajaga to Thomas Melvil to the abolitionists, shared was an unquestioned belief that it was Africans who would work the plantations. The idea of Europeans working the land in West Africa was unimaginable to all. To be sure, European men might own the land if that was possible, and might even direct operations, but they would certainly not be engaged in manual labour. It was unthinkable. Even Philip Beaver, who led a disastrous attempt to colonise Bulama Island near Bissao with British settlers in the early 1790s and who was unequivocally against slavery, did not propose that white men would cultivate the earth in West Africa. In plans for colonising part of the continent in the name of the British monarch, Beaver wrote that his imagined settlement would produce 'cotton, coffee, tobacco and indigo' which would be 'cultivated by free natives'. The settlers for his colony would be white British men, women and children, but they would definitely use Africans for agricultural labour.[12]

Kenneth Mackenzie had gone long past the point in which he cared how his actions would be interpreted. First, he enticed the castle's white head gardener, Daniel Munro, to join him on the plantation working as an overseer. Governor Miles was furious, warning Munro that he was 'throwing up substance for a shadow'. But other castle employees followed, lured by Mackenzie's pie-in-the-sky promises of riches and luxury.

Incensed, Miles wrote to the Company bosses in London, complaining that Mackenzie was poaching valuable employees who would be very hard to replace. Even if they were ever to return to the castle, they would be unfit for future service, Miles declared, as Mackenzie's actions were turning the men crazy. 'These two or three months past by his *plantation* manoeuvres, [he has] set some of your servants mad, who I fear will not recover their Senses till it's too late to repent,' Miles wrote to London.[13]

It could be that Miles was speaking metaphorically of Munro and the others being 'mad' about Mackenzie's scheme, 'crazy' for the story he was spinning of untold riches. Nonetheless, consciously or otherwise, Miles's words also reflected the notion, rapidly gaining currency at the time, that white men and women were simply unsuited to hard labour in tropical environments. This was a very convenient theory, of course, for those with little skin pigmentation, as it deemed people of European origin to be the natural masters in the tropics while Africans were damned to service by their physiology. Against the backdrop of the debates of the slave trade and the settlement of India, Britons came to believe that white men simply lacked immunity to the prevailing diseases of the tropics. In Africa these ideas formed earlier than in most other British locales. In the

1750s Governor Melvil had written that some white bricklayers he had to help at the castle were useless as 'this is not country for Europeans to work in the sun'.[14] God had seemingly ordained that cultivating crops such as sugar and cotton in stifling equatorial temperatures was not appropriate work for white men.

It was not only a man's physical health which was believed to be in danger. Europeans commonly supposed themselves to have far more developed brains than Africans. It was Europeans who had built mansions and castles, written works of literature, composed symphonies, and who just, well, understood the niceties of civilisation. Who could conceive an African Shakespeare or Mozart? Europeans had circumnavigated the globe and even cast their sights far wider afield when the first new planet of modern times, Uranus, was seen in 1781. It seemed irrefutable to them that their brains were more highly developed than those of Africans and other 'native' people and were, accordingly, far more delicately balanced. Temperate airs were the thing, while a scorching sun could literally drive Europeans to develop a kind of psychosis. To Richard Miles, adopting these beliefs ahead of most of his compatriots because of the nature and location of his employment, even being an overseer like Munro could possibly turn a white man quite mad.[15]

There was only one man who seems to have been losing his mind under the African sun, though, and that was Captain Kenneth Mackenzie. Although he had initially purchased Africans as slaves to work on his plantation, when they deserted (another reason West Indian planters gave for removing Africans far from their homeland) he turned to the only source of labour still available to him. To the horror of those observing, he forced his soldiers to engage in the back-breaking work of establishing his plantation. Without a shadow of ethical consideration about the slave trade or the relative development of Africans, Kenneth Mackenzie's act was far more revolutionary than even men like the abolitionists Isert and Beaver would have considered. He put white men to work alongside Africans. Even worse, his men wore the uniform of the honourable British Army, convicts or not. Miles and his fellow Company of Merchants' employees were aghast.

Undertaking the gruelling labour of turning densely forested areas into open savannah, tearing up trees by their roots under the fearsome sun with its immobilising humidity, were many of the remaining men of the 101st and 102nd Independent Companies. William Copeland, who had originally been listed as number 10 of Mackenzie's company and now, after all the deaths and desertions in Africa, promoted to sergeant, spent around six weeks 'clearing the ground & felling the wood on his [Mackenzie's] plantation'.

Job Cooper protested that he did 'no soldier work' in Africa and just worked at agricultural labour on Mackenzie's plantation. William Reeves, who had initially been with Katenkamp, spent his time digging and clearing the ground ready for planting. Reeves said that for six weeks he was forced to 'work upon a plantation belonging to him [Mackenzie] from six in the morning till seven in ev[enin]g'. For a man who was already in his mid-forties, a considerable age for an eighteenth-century soldier, it must have been especially exhausting work.[16]

In part the Company was alarmed at these proceedings because they thought that it would endanger the soldiers' lives. They were already dying at a distressing rate, which mattered not so much in itself other than that they left the forts short of manpower. Just a few months after their arrival in Africa so many were already dead that those who remained could not defend a single fort.[17] Even Mackenzie himself, despite his vaunted robust 'Highland constitution', had been dangerously ill at one time or another. On these grounds alone, making his soldiers work on a plantation would have been unacceptable, even if no other ethical issues had arisen.

Obviously, though, there was more at stake than the practical concern that this labour removed men from their legitimate duties or would leave them vulnerable to disease. If working on plantations was considered inappropriate work for white men, then how much less appropriate was it for them to be working, as William Reeves related, 'along with his [Mackenzie's] Slaves'.[18]

This was the real cause of complaint for Richard Miles and his associates. The Company of Merchants was appalled that white men had, as they saw it, been demeaned in this way. Foremost among the complaints against Kenneth Mackenzie was that the men under his command 'were not treated as Soldiers but employed upon a plantation which he called his own'. They laboured there 'with the common Negroes'.[19] For the Company of Merchants, this represented far too close a relationship between white men and slavery.

The men themselves were not asked about their attitudes towards this work, although the fact that they grumbled about it is significant enough. Certainly implicit in the allegation was that Mackenzie was treating them as slaves, and at a time when bondage was becoming increasingly repugnant to working-class Britons. It was more than forty years since 'Rule Britannia' had been composed with its popular refrain, 'Rule, Britannia! Britannia, rule the waves; Britons never, never, never shall be slaves', but its words remained as popular and germane as ever. Slavery, it was thought, was contrary to the laws of Britain, and not only because of the Somerset Decision of 1772, which was widely believed to have made slavery illegal in Britain (though in actual fact it was more nuanced than that). If Britain's air was so pure that it freed black slaves from the West Indies or Americas upon their arrival—or so it was perceived—then how much more incompatible with natural law was it that a 'True Briton' could be held in bondage?[20]

For the men of the Company of Merchants there was an even bigger threat to their business than the need to uphold their putative racial code, and that was their main objective of assisting British slave traders. If Kenneth Mackenzie did not appreciate the Company's desire to keep the convict-soldiers separate from the condition of slavery, he was even less conscious of the necessity of maintaining good relations with local traders.

The reality of millions of Africans crossing the oceans in ships did not mean that Africans as a whole were defenceless; far from it. What Mackenzie did not realise was that the population living around his fort was not powerless, it was not the same as a defeated civilian population in wartime. African communities on the coast always had a trump card to play: they could cut off trade, which was the Europeans' reason for being there. The native chiefs always maintained enough control of affairs to disrupt trade if they were annoyed by any merchants' actions. They played European groups off against each other, ceased trading if they disliked the terms offered, and resorted to more bloody tactics if those measures failed. The coastal African traders were never cowed victims of the slave trade and nor were they afraid to fight back. Just a few short years after Mackenzie's time on the coast, Africans violently assaulted the British Governor of Tatumquerry Fort when he attempted to levy a fine on them.[21]

Mackenzie had already shown that he was unwilling or unable to see why the local people should be treated with anything other than contempt. He had whipped an African translator who had been sent over from Cape Coast Castle to Mori to help 'without so much as a Line signifying his crime', much to Miles's horror.[22]

Then he refused to meet local Africans who had some unpaid bills to present. In truth they were probably not Mackenzie's debts to pay, and ever conscious of his precarious financial position he ordered his men to send the petitioners away. But Miles and the rest of the Company men knew that their local allies would not stand for being treated so cavalierly. Captain Mackenzie should at least have attempted to make restitution to them from the Company or some other source.

The larger problem behind these small acts was that no European fort on the coast was self-sufficient. Even those stationed at mighty Elmina and Cape Coast Castle had to deal with the surrounding townsfolk, local Africans, for all manner of things, including most of their food. Fort soldiers were customarily paid mostly in goods which they then bartered at local markets for whatever they needed. They were paid, that is, in 'Merchandize calculated for the purchase of provisions in the Country' topped up by some 'Beef, Pork, Bread, Flour etc.' The trading with locals was done under strict cognisance of what punishment would await if they started any sort of trouble while bartering for food or other goods.[23]

The Company had advised the government before the troops had left England that it would be better to pay the convict-soldiers in the same way—in merchandise for bartering—instead of in the regular manner of the British Army. This might have worked if Mackenzie had laid down similar rules for how his men interacted with the local people while conducting their personal trade. But of course he did no such thing, compelling the convict-soldiers to survive as best they could. Small wonder that they resorted to their talents at thievery and plunder, pickpocketing and housebreaking. Mackenzie seemed to think that the surrounding towns were conquered territory, a subjugated people whose homes and possessions could be plundered at will.

This problem was grossly exacerbated by the fact that Mackenzie was not providing his men with the allowance of food to which they were entitled. It was claimed that the convict-soldiers were 'left to themselves undisciplin'd, and unprovided for with any kind of Stores and having neither Pay, nor Bedding, or Cloaths Allow'd them'.[24] The men themselves certainly felt aggrieved at their lack of food. Job Massey and Thomas Rhodes had said that they were starving when asked why they had run away. Later, when a few soldiers were able to testify about Mackenzie's conduct, they all complained that they had been given insufficient food. William Copeland, one of the men who had worked on Mackenzie's plantation, said that the soldiers were 'almost starv'd'.[25] Nor was it only the convict-soldiers who made this allegation. Most of those who observed Mackenzie's rule in action believed that he was withholding a considerable part of his men's food in order to sell it for his own gain. The Company claimed that he only gave out around half of what the soldiers were allotted, selling the rest among the local people and pocketing the proceeds.

Mackenzie had certainly always been very concerned with the food supply. At times the problem took on a farcical tone. On one occasion Captain Mackenzie at Mori wrote to Governor Miles at Cape Coast Castle, 'the cheese produced to me stinks, I say it stinks.' To which Miles replied, 'I scarce ever saw cheese in this country that did not stink.' He did, though, seemingly with his tongue firmly in his cheek, offer to perform a cheese inspection 'as an act of humanity'.[26] This concern seems to have been contrary to Mackenzie's customary lack of interest in his soldiers' welfare—unless, of course, his intention was not for his men to eat the smelly cheese but rather that he would sell it.

With insufficient goods to barter for their food and little or no control over them, the convict-soldiers were daily causing infractions which sorely tested the peace and tranquillity of the coast. The closely supervised, delicate peace the Company tried to uphold was in grave danger of disintegrating in the places where the convict-soldiers were stationed.

Having committed such faux pas, Mackenzie compounded his crimes, in the eyes of the Company's employees anyway, by refusing to listen to their advice on how to resolve the problems. Richard Miles complained that Mackenzie, new to the coast and unfamiliar with its ways, attempted to extricate himself simply by throwing money at those he had offended. Not appreciating the right amount to pay and the technique of bargaining, he refused to follow Miles's advice and paid out far too much as reparation for his mistakes. The account book at this time reveals numerous 'dashes' paid out on account of 'mackenzie's palaver'. Mackenzie did not learn soon enough that local custom, backed up with just the right amount of 'dashes'—that is, gifts, tips or bribes—had to be taken into account.[27]

Thoroughly alarmed, Miles and the men at the castle sent over a representative to see what was going on at Mori. The man they dispatched was Philip Quaque, the castle reverend in charge of the Company men's spiritual welfare and now also given the thankless task of saving the men of the independent companies for the Lord. In some ways he was a good choice and reflected how seriously the Company took the problem Mackenzie had created. Philip Quaque was, after all, a local Fante man and reputedly the son of Birempong Cudjo, once the chief intermediary between the Fante and the Company of Merchants. Perhaps they thought that if anybody could soothe local feelings without the slave trade being too badly disrupted, he could. But Quaque had long since become a man caught between two worlds.

As a child Quaque had been singled out by missionary Thomas Thompson and became one of three boys sent to England to be educated under the auspices of the Society for the Propagation of the Gospel. In

1765, the other two boys long since dead, Quaque was the first African ordained into the Church of England. Then he was appointed as an SPG 'Missionary, School Master and Catechist to the Negroes on the Gold Coast', a position he would hold simultaneously with that of chaplain of Cape Coast Castle. In late 1765, he sailed for his homeland, which he had not seen since he was thirteen years old, taking along his English wife Catherine.

From the start things had been difficult. Catherine died not long after their arrival at Cape Coast and he had little success with either of his assignments. Despite his flock at the castle being British men faced with their own mortality at every turn, they were hardly model Christians. Most lived openly with at least one African woman, drank heavily, refused to attend his prayer meetings and even mocked his attempts to educate their mixed-race children in an English style.

His attempts at converting his native people were even less successful. The SPG complained that he had 'never been able to fulfil the objects of his mission ... [or] even to make a single convert'. This was not so surprising given that, although he was born Fante, his long years in England had distanced him from his native people. He lived in the English style in a fine house with mahogany furniture and a library and even struggled to speak his native tongue. He married two Fante wives in the years after the death of Catherine but nonetheless remained separate from the society he had been born into.

Quaque himself had to trade in order to survive; his SPG salary was rarely paid and his wages from the Company arrived in the form of alcohol, textiles and tobacco. As with most who survived long enough, this trading had provoked considerable animosity with the Company, so he could doubtless sympathise with Mackenzie's motivation if not his methods. He also pitied the soldiers, abandoned sinners though they were, as they were clearly hungry, sick and far from home. A voice of calm and reason, he was able to rein in some of Captain Mackenzie's less wholesome tendencies. The convict-soldiers claimed that while Quaque was at Mori, Mackenzie had treated them well, giving them their proper ration of food and generally toning down the more merciless of his punishments.[28]

Quaque, having invoked all the powers he could think of—the British government, the army, the Company of Merchants and even God himself—left Mori and returned to Cape Coast thinking that his job was done. He was unimpressed by Mackenzie and wrote with disdain about the difficulties he and his men had caused to society and trade on the coast. But he had done his best, more than anybody else was reported to have done with regard to helping the soldiers get their due. It was not enough. As soon as he left Mackenzie again raised the stakes of devastation.

Meanwhile, yet another problem was brewing. At Cormantin, rather unbelievably, William Murray was still in charge of the small garrison. As might be expected, chaos ruled. Often Murray himself deserted, leaving his men to their own devices. The small urban gangs of St Giles in the Fields had been transplanted to the African coast to run amok in a different setting and where the potential to cause pandemonium was at least as great as in London. Murray was still the master criminal, but now he wore a British Army uniform. It would all end badly—though quite how badly was more than even Richard Miles could conceive.

Chapter Nine

A MUTINY AND A MOST PECULIAR MURDER

Strangely enough, when the first real contest to Mackenzie's rule came, it was not from Murray or any of the other convict-soldiers on the coast, but from a man of very different character. John Montagu Clarke, the ensign who had been so disgusted with Kenneth Mackenzie's behaviour during the lost battle for Elmina, led the first serious revolt against their captain.

Clarke had obviously been at odds with Mackenzie since the start of the expedition, but by mid-1782 felt that he could endure matters no longer. He wrote to John Butchart of HMS *Argo* protesting the soldiers' treatment and conditions. When Butchart declined to get involved, the die was cast.

Kenneth Mackenzie's aggressor was every inch the army man. Clarke had even been 'Born in the Army', he declared, his father being Captain John Clarke of the 59th Regiment. As soon as he was old enough Clarke Junior had followed in his father's footsteps and enlisted in the military. As fate had it he joined just in time to fight in the American Revolutionary

War, and as ensign with the 43rd Regiment he saw action in some of the formative battles of the conflict.

Clarke had taken part in the Battle of Lexington, the opening conflict of the war when General Thomas Gage, governor of Massachusetts, had sent his troops to disarm the rebel militia. It was a quick affair, but was nevertheless the 'shot heard around the world' which began the war. Clarke, having marched with Gage's men, could always say that he had been there at the outset.

He had also been present at the notorious Battle of Bunker Hill. Clarke and the other men of the 43rd had been led by Brigadier General Robert Pigot in an attack on the redoubt on Breed's Hill which had been hastily built by the rebels. Their attack had been met with initial quiet, but when they were close enough to see the patriots' 'country hats' the barrage began. The usual respite as gunners reloaded never came as the Americans had given their best shots two guns each along with a man to load them. It was a virtual massacre, saved only because Pigot realised that he could not carry on and ordered the retreat. British bodies lay in piles and the wounded were everywhere. But General William Howe was not cowed and regrouped his men. Once more they attacked and this time, although there were again heavy losses, the redoubt was stormed. Victory was declared by the British, but the cost was enormous. They had lost over 1000 men, close to half of the number they had on the battlefield.

John Montagu Clarke survived the carnage and fought on, but was taken prisoner in 1778 'soon after the takeing [sic] of Rhode Island'. He later complained that he was treated with 'the utmost Barbarity' by 'the rebels'. While incarcerated he used his own money to alleviate not just his own situation but also that of his men, leaving himself in dire financial straits. In November 1780, by then back in England, he appealed to his commander-in-chief for redress, but he knew that there was little chance of being reimbursed for his expenditure. By that point he had received no wages for a year and urgently needed to earn a living. He had no choice but to find a new job which, for a man like John Montagu Clarke, meant another military position. He chose the role of ensign in Katenkamp's 102nd Independent Company. It was a decision he would quickly come to regret.

As Katenkamp died before reaching the Gold Coast and other officers were also killed either during the voyage or in the early fighting against the Dutch, Clarke was second-in-command of both the 101st and 102nd Independent Companies only a short while after arriving in Africa.[1] He had come to loathe Kenneth Mackenzie, his superior officer, and to deeply distrust him. During the first few months they were in Africa he had on several occasions implored Mackenzie to improve his treatment of the troops. He also repeatedly asked the Company of Merchants to intervene on their behalf.

Clarke's dilemma was not just that he was disgusted at the way the soldiers were being governed and the disrepute such mismanagement would bring to his revered British Army. He also feared that, as second-in-command, if he failed to act in the face of the appalling handling of the men and misappropriation of supplies, he too would be guilty.

The military life was all John Montagu Clarke knew and all that he prized, so his next decision can only be seen as a measure of his desperation: he surrendered his commission as ensign. He later explained this act by saying that he resigned 'not from any dislike to his and my country's service, but to return to England and lay Captain Mackenzie's conduct before the War Office, and to save my own life'. Governor Richard Miles, himself no fan of Captain Mackenzie, gave Clarke an apartment at Cape Coast Castle until he could return to England. Miles, however, cautioned Clarke against taking matters into his own hands.

John Montagu Clarke asked several ships' captains for a passage to London to complain about Kenneth Mackenzie and he pleaded with slave-ship masters to take him away, but none of them would accommodate him. Despite his entreaties, neither the captain of the supply ship *Active* nor John Butchart would agree to give him a berth in their vessel. After these refusals Clarke began to think that it was more than just misfortune preventing him from getting a passage. Mackenzie had deliberately thwarted him, he believed, announcing that any captain who took him off the coast would be fined £7000. Desperate, Clarke made a fateful decision. He was no longer prepared to listen to Miles's counsel. Considering the circumstances were so extreme that radical action was needed, he felt 'authorized to resume [his] commission' with the intention of getting Mackenzie sent home to Britain.[2]

First Clarke went to Fort Mori. There he found that yet again Mackenzie had not distributed the goods intended for the convict-soldiers and, with insufficient merchandise to bargain for food, they were 'so much Emaciated that they could not Stir from the Spot on which they Lay'. It was not only food they lacked but also clothing and bedding. Many were lying on the hard floor, Clarke claimed, with only their regimental jacket as a blanket. Only two had a shirt to wear. Whether from these brutal conditions or disease, two men were hardly able to walk. Clarke held Captain Kenneth Mackenzie responsible, declaring that he treated his troops 'more like dogs than men'. Clarke painted a picture of them 'Praying for Death as the only possible means of Escaping their truly inhuman Commanding Officer'.

Clarke again asked the Company of Merchants to intervene to improve the men's conditions but they refused to get involved. So John Montagu Clarke resolved that he would disobey his commanding officer from then on, reasoning that he could not 'on any account take the smallest

Order from a Man who has proved himself a dishonour to His Majesty's Service'.[3]

Clarke asked the convict-soldiers at Mori to go with him to Cape Coast Castle, where Captain Mackenzie had temporarily gone, to confront their commander. He put it to the men that having been 'wronged of our just dues, with regard to Porter, Pease, Butter, Cheese &c' they had no choice but to follow Mackenzie to demand restitution.[4] He dangled the possibility of new shirts and trousers that were rightfully theirs, and raised the prospect that as a result of their action Captain Mackenzie might even be sent back to England on the *Argo* to account for his behaviour.[5] Some of the men were highly dubious about this course of action but others were prepared to go along with Clarke's scheme. Phillip Brookes complained that he had not received 'a Farthing of pay since I left England' and willingly joined in. So did twelve of the other men. Too sick to walk, some had to be 'carried by Blacks to Cannoes' for the journey to Cape Coast Castle.[6]

On 12 May 1782, Clarke and thirteen soldiers from Fort Mori entered Cape Coast Castle and stood boldly 'up on the Parade', brandishing their weapons and demanding that the Company's soldiers lay down their arms. Cries of 'Mutiny!' rang out through the castle, causing utter panic and confusion among a community forever fearful of attack. Richard Miles, lying in his rooms with a terrible fever, dragged himself out of bed to see what the commotion was about. Astonished to see John Montagu Clarke standing there, Miles challenged him as to his intention. Clarke boldly replied that he had come to seize Captain Mackenzie.

Miles told him, of course, that he would do no such thing. But Clarke was in too deep to capitulate. He shouted back that they would have to kill him rather than arrest him. In that case, Miles roared back, he would order the guard to shoot him. Clarke wavered. Then, knowing he was beaten, he tried to hand his sword to Miles in an act of ceremonial surrender. But Miles was much too angry at events to treat Clarke as an honourable soldier. He refused Clarke the honour of accepting the sword, leaving the ensign to lay it on the castle floor. The castle's soldiers then rushed upon the mutineers and secured them in handcuffs and leg irons ready to go into the slave hole.[7]

Two days after this incident, Captain Butchart, whom Clarke had previously petitioned for a passage to London, went ashore to find out what had caused this act of treachery. For Clarke this presented a discomfiting development as the thirteen men who had mutinied with him were now trying desperately to extricate themselves. They testified that they had been unaware that Clarke had resigned his commission and therefore had no authority over them whatsoever. Only one man, forty-two-year-old Phillip Brookes, stood by his earlier complaint against Mackenzie. He repeated his claim that he had not been paid during his time in Africa. He explained what had happened, saying that Clarke had 'pretended to be a great friend to all of us and said, that he was come to see us righted, in consequence of which I told him, that I had not received a Farthing of pay since I left England'.[8] It would not be the last of Brookes's grievances against Captain Mackenzie.

Unlike Brookes, the other twelve of John Montagu Clarke's small band of mutineers quickly denied that they had any criticisms of Mackenzie. Sergeant Francis Thompson said that he had no complaints about Mackenzie's governance. For men who had just launched an armed rebellion against him, these were astonishing declarations. Their attempts to distance themselves from the affair suggest that the soldiers lived in fear of their commander, and given the style of punishment Kenneth Mackenzie favoured this was quite understandable.

One of the men at Mori who had refused to go with Clarke on his mission made the situation worse for the failed mutineer. Robert Andrews admitted to having received a letter from Clarke in which he stated that he had laid out his plan to arrest Mackenzie. Andrews had shown the letter to Philip Quaque, who was then at Fort Mori. Sergeant Andrews claimed that he had then replied to Clarke, saying that he could not think of participating in such an exploit as he had no idea what Mackenzie had done to warrant it.[9] Clarke wrote to Butchart defending himself, repeating that the soldiers had been starved, mistreated and thrown in the slave hole for any offence. He had been 'their only friend and protector', he said, and feared for them now he had to leave.

While awaiting shipment to London, Clarke wrote letters railing against the weak-willed Company servants who had failed to defend him though they too had plenty of grievances against Mackenzie. Jerome Bernard Weuves had apparently agreed with him that Mackenzie was 'a disgrace', while an accountant named Smith had told him that more than a hundred articles of clothing shipped for Katenkamp's men had been hidden 'in the brandy warehouse' despite the men being half-naked. Dr Beard had apparently gone further and said in Clarke's hearing that 'so hardened a villain should be sent off the Coast'. But none now came forward to agree that Clarke's complaints were justified. Even Richard Miles, so long the archenemy of Captain Mackenzie, did nothing to substantiate Clarke's complaints, leading him to suggest that the governor must have been bribed.[10]

In his letters to the officers at Cape Coast Castle, written from the dungeon, Clarke maintained that his actions, however 'extraordinary', were fully in line with the articles of war. To back up his case he mentioned other army officers who had acted similarly. When Major McDonald of the 59th Regiment had defrauded his troops of their pay and victuals, Lieutenant Despard had confined him for his crime, despite being his junior officer. Despard's conduct 'was highly approved of by all of his Superior Officers', Clarke wrote.[11]

Clarke also wrote to Lord Germain the day he was taken aboard HMS *Argo* to be sent home to stand trial for mutiny. He professed that he had only ever wanted redress for the men, and any notion that he had intended to take control of the castle from the Company and Mackenzie was a fabrication intended to get rid of him. His plea was certainly heartfelt. 'My Lord,' he declared, 'I had the Honor of serving His Majesty five years as an officer in America, in the 43rd Regiment, where the most rigid Discipline was observ'd, and the worth of the Soldier known, the reverse that I found in Africa was shocking to Humanity.' He then stated again his unending loyalty to the British Army, writing, 'If I should be so very unfortunate as to be considered as a Mutineer by your Lordship, and the Court that Tries me, I wish for no Lenity, for when I cease to Serve my King, I cease to Live, rather than be dismiss'd His Service I would wish to Die.' It would be for a British judge to decide. John Montagu Clarke went on board the *Argo* as a prisoner on 16 June 1782.[12]

Ironically, by the time of the alleged mutiny, Kenneth Mackenzie was himself as anxious to return to Britain as Clarke was for him to leave West Africa. In May, Philip Quaque had told Miles that Mackenzie was so sick that he was asking to go home so that he might 'die among Christians'. A month later Mackenzie also wrote to Lord Germain, stating that his health was still so bad he did not expect to live long and begging to be allowed to return home.[13] Not receiving an answer, and by then only too aware of the seditious insubordination swelling, not just among the rank and file but even with the remaining officers, Mackenzie decided that he had to leave by any means possible. He decided to abandon his troops and his commission and leave the coast.

He intended, unsurprisingly, to sail away with a fortune. As any serious involvement in the slave trade had become rather difficult since he had offended so many Africans, he turned to the other item for which the coast had long been renowned. It was, of course, what the area had been named for: gold.

To a man in Kenneth Mackenzie's compromised financial state, the lure of the precious metal proved irresistible. All the Africans wearing gold ornaments; the local merchants who wore bags of gold dust attached to their legs; the cupboards full of the stuff held by officers at the castle—this was an era, after all, of tales of gold nuggets so enormous they took four men to lift.[14]

He was hardly alone in his hunger for gold, as many white men on the coast were trading for gold dust which they intended to take home to Europe with them. It was the local equivalent of a superannuation scheme, even if most never lived to return to England and enjoy their old age. Horatio Smith, Governor of Accra, had £450 of gold dust when he died in 1783. Another governor, Thomas Trinder, who had died in 1775, had an estate worth £7261 9s 1d to be left to his relatives in England, as well as copious amounts of additional gold left on the coast. Trinder's will mentioned 'a free woman named Deborah', who got 'all the Gold and Aggerir Beads she has of mine in her possession, excepting a piece of Gold belonging to Biranquoz King of Akim', and his 'slave woman Abinnabat', who was allowed to keep 'whatever gold' of his she had, as well as being given four ounces of gold 'in consideration of her fidelity and constant attendance'. (Pity Trinder's other slave woman, Bumushu, who was left nothing but a lifetime of enslavement to the Company.)[15]

But Kenneth Mackenzie had no intention of dying in Africa before he could enjoy the proceeds he would acquire. Mackenzie's plan was to trade for enough gold to make his fortune and then sail away, leaving the debacle behind him forever.

Predictably, this very quickly went wrong. Gold dealing was a tricky business as, with no easy way to test its purity, many unwitting slave-ship captains found out far too late that their 'gold' was actually brass filings. The exact problem Mackenzie encountered is uncertain, but his lack of diplomacy and constant bellicosity again hampered his dealings. He got into a quarrel with Buchanan, a man he was trading with, and again his high hopes were dashed. Richard Miles dismissed the entire affair as 'foolish'.[16]

Determined now to abandon Africa and what remained of his men, Mackenzie next raided the Company's stores to see what goods he could acquire. They alleged that he stole more than £1200 worth of goods 'in such articles as Slaves are purchased with'. Next he set about trying to ensure that any money owed to him from his local trading was collected, using his familiar pugnacious manner.[17]

Then he asked Captain Noble of the *Brookes* to take him away. Noble had already purchased no less than 666 slaves and, with his hold absolutely bursting with sad humanity, he was ready to weigh anchor. Mackenzie told nobody at Cape Coast of his plans to join the ship, hoping to slip away unnoticed. His plot was only thwarted because Clement Noble refused his request. When the ship sailed for Jamaica, Mackenzie was not aboard.[18]

Having missed this opportunity to escape, Mackenzie's madness seemed only to increase, his actions spiralling ever more out of control. By now relations between Mackenzie and the Company's men were barely civil. They fought over provisions, goods and command, and their flowery eighteenth-century prose descended into barely veiled threats and insults. At one point Mackenzie wrote to Richard Miles, 'His Majesty sent me here I flatter myself thinking me worthy of my charge. If you think yourself entitled to counteract His Majesty's Intentions, I stand by the consequences of your proceedings.'[19]

Mackenzie at this point conceived an idea to launch another attack on the Dutch at Elmina, even announcing to Miles that he was prepared to pay the huge sum of £1000 towards the costs of African help with the expedition. Richard Miles responded saying that this was a very bad idea given that there was hardly a white man well enough to be on guard duty let alone attack the heavily armed fortress. In fact only five days after the suggestion Mackenzie admitted that he had very few troops who were healthy. Mackenzie's claims that he was expecting more men from Britain at any moment were met with disbelief from Miles and his fellow officers of the Company.[20]

In July a new contingent of Mackenzie's men were sent from Cape Coast Castle to Commenda with the dual aim of defending that fort and dividing the troublesome soldiers. Among those dispatched were Job Cooper, who had been working on Mackenzie's plantation, and seventeen-year-old William Mortimer, a volunteer, and one of the 'undersized' men who had been reluctantly approved at Chatham Barracks the previous year.[21]

Three days after their arrival at Commenda a ship with 'imperial colours', the *St Antoine Almas*, sailed into the harbour. A Portuguese ship was no more a legitimate prize than the Ostend vessel he had captured earlier, but characteristically Mackenzie was unconcerned by this. Asking for '12 Volunteers that did not care for their Lives' Mackenzie recruited men to board and seize the ship. Mortimer and Cooper were among those who offered to try to capture the vessel, having been promised they would get £150 each if they were successful.[22]

Tellingly, Mackenzie promised to take only the same share of the profits, if the ship was seized, as the men themselves. While this may seem like a rare moment of fairness, it also suggests that he knew that he was acting more in the manner of pirate than privateer. Dividing the shares equally among all men whatever their rank was standard among pirate companies, but among privateering ships a strict hierarchy existed in the distribution of spoils.[23]

The twelve men boarded the *St Antoine Almas* and, after a skirmish, successfully captured the vessel. It may well have been that the ship's soldiers were simply unprepared for the attack, not expecting to be suddenly and illegally seized by a renegade band of British soldiers. Triumphant in conquest, Mackenzie kept up the pretence that his men would benefit as much as he himself would. Going aboard he told the twelve victorious men, 'My Lads you have made your Fortunes you have 160 L [sic] a piece.' But, predictably, some of the soldiers would later claim that they never saw a penny of their share.[24]

It is clear that by this time Kenneth Mackenzie had given up all thought of acting as a British Army captain was supposed to act. During the seizure of the Portuguese ship he never attempted to justify the deed as he had earlier when he had taken the *Comte de Flandres*, and made no pretence of having mistaken the ship for an enemy vessel. As with the earlier capture, British politicians would spend several years dealing with the diplomatic fallout from this event, but at the time Mackenzie had plainly given no consideration to the future. It was as if, with his health poor and his men mutinying, he had decided to damn the consequences. Perhaps the scorching tropical sun really had affected his senses, as his contemporaries believed it could. Whatever the reason for his behaviour, he was about to commit an act so outrageous as to make his previous illegalities seem positively unremarkable. The catalyst was the man who had always been a problem: Captain Kenneth's putative clansman, William Murray Mackenzie, alias Williams, Williamson, Jefferson, Taylor, Brett and Ward.

Despite first coming to the attention of the officials at Cape Coast

Castle in the most inauspicious of ways—he was allegedly rude to Governor Richard Miles—Murray had always been a favourite of the captain, ever since he had been selected to drill the men aboard ship on the way out to Africa.[25] Far better educated than most of the convict-soldiers, of a different social background and with his own seemingly endless talent for guile, he had been a natural leader. Whether through an attempt to control him by giving him authority or a very serious misjudgement of character, Kenneth Mackenzie had trusted Murray enough to put him in charge of the garrison at Cormantin.

At some point, however, there was a falling-out between the two men. As Kenneth Mackenzie accused William Murray of stealing stores from Cormantin and selling them for his own profit, it could be that his 'nephew' was more like himself than the older man wished. Emulating his tendency to avail himself of government supplies was clearly not what Kenneth Mackenzie wished for in his acolytes.

As was his habit—possibly in search of wine, women and song—Murray deserted from Cormantin. Recaptured, he was returned to Mori, where Kenneth Mackenzie claimed that he suffered no other punishment 'than reducing him from a quartermaster serjeant ... to do duty as a private'.[26] If this was true, then he certainly escaped a good deal more lightly than other men from the independent companies who attempted to flee. It's more likely he received a whipping and perhaps a spell in the slave hole. Certainly Mackenzie sought approval from Miles to appropriate all Murray's possessions as his own, a request which tells us much about both men.[27]

The way Captain Mackenzie told the story, Murray then took advantage of his leniency by entering into a conspiracy with several of the convicts and other soldiers to commit murder as soon as he was returned to Mori. They connived, Kenneth Mackenzie alleged, to kill both himself and a man named Massey. This was not the convict Job Massey, who had previously been locked in the slave hole, but rather 'a young officer of the Marines who had come up there for his health'. The conspiracy was betrayed by Robert Andrews, a former convict who had been promoted to sergeant. Mackenzie feared that poison had been given both to himself and to Massey, and ordered that two of the conspirators be imprisoned in the slave hole. When Murray himself was arrested Mackenzie claimed that the younger man realised that 'all was discovered' and, losing all hope, resolved that he would at least 'sell his Life as dear as possible'.[28]

According to Kenneth Mackenzie's version of events, the conspirators managed to secretly administer poison to both himself and Massey. The toxin, he averred, 'very much disordered their Bowels'. Mackenzie, though, swallowed 'a great quantity of oil which both vomited and purged him', a cure which he claimed saved his life. He tried to persuade Massey to drink the oil too, but by the time he finally agreed to do so 'the poison had been so long in his Body that his stomach would not receive it'. Lieutenant Massey died the following day.[29]

The truth of this is impossible to verify, although the marine Massey did indeed die around this time. Other witnesses also alleged that he had been poisoned, but Governor Lysaght of Commenda Fort, who considered Massey a friend, believed that he had been murdered by Africans in revenge for having whipped a black man at Mori while he had been visiting Kenneth Mackenzie.[30] This was a common accusation, for it was believed throughout this period that Africans had special knowledge of plants that were poisonous and used them on their enemies. It was a rumour that was taken on slave ships across the ocean to the Americas, where it haunted many a planter and his family whose housemaids had ample opportunity to indulge any such skills. Allowing for the lack of understanding about germs and the need for hygiene when preparing food in this era, it could easily be that Mackenzie and Massey were suffering from some unidentified gastrointestinal problem. Given that it had already been alleged that Ensign Hawkshaw had been poisoned and the climate of suspicion that reigned, any stomach complaints could easily have been interpreted as homicide attempts by the suspicious captain.

Whether Murray was actually planning a mutiny of any kind against Captain Mackenzie is hard to untangle from the wealth of hearsay and allegation that swept through the troops. One soldier testified that he had heard nothing about a conspiracy, another that he only heard about the plot after the fact. Thomas Maple, who shared a room at Fort Mori with Murray, claimed that 'sergeant Murray' 'wished many times to desert and go to the mines [Elmina] and wanted me and most of the people to go with him'.

Then an even more dangerous rumour began to circulate. It was said that 'Murry McKenzie [had] form'd a scheme of Cutting Capt McKenzie's throat'.[31] Job Cooper claimed that a couple of days before the murder he had been sick and was lying down, and had heard Murray say to Robert Andrews: 'now is the time, let us do him out and out'. The phrase, explained Cooper, meant that they intended to kill their captain. Another soldier claimed that Murray had frequently threatened 'to destroy' his uncle 'if he could conveniently'.[32]

Whether it was true or not, a man who locked soldiers in the slave dungeon for running away was hardly likely to let such a potentially dangerous man live freely. William Murray was hauled back to Mori and thrown into jail.

Again Murray had one final throw of the dice. He asked permission from Phillip Brookes, the man standing sentry, to go to the gate of the fort to speak to an African who had some brandy to sell. Needless to say it was all a ruse. Mackenzie was irate when he discovered his prisoner had gone and ordered Brookes to receive 1500 lashes for letting him escape. It was a quantity of lashes which could easily prove fatal. Brookes was tied up ready to receive his punishment as 'at seven bells', or 7.30 am, and was flogged remorselessly until, as he remembered, astonishingly still conscious, 'our bell struck one'. If that was not enough, when he was finally cut down, Captain Mackenzie ordered the horrendously wounded man, folds of skin hanging off his bloodied, mangled back, to be thrown in 'with the slaves' in the dungeon.[33]

While Brookes was enduring his punishment, Mackenzie sent the rest of his remaining sorry band of soldiers in search of Murray. They searched markets, houses and known drinking holes for Murray, but he eluded them. As dusk was falling, they returned empty-handed to the fort to once again face their captain's ire.[34]

The next morning Kenneth Mackenzie heard a rumour that the wanted man was hiding out in the area known locally as Black Town. Never one to tread lightly on native affairs, he immediately ordered his men to begin firing the fort's cannons into the town. As they had not the slightest idea what had occasioned this assault, the attack caused 'great consternation and Alarm' among the inhabitants. Panic spread as mothers grabbed their children and tried to flee to safety, unsure of where to find sanctuary as no native building could withstand even an indirect hit.[35]

They soon found out what had prompted the unprovoked aggression. News spread that a soldier named Murray was hiding among them. Captain Mackenzie had his guns pointed at the town and was threatening to raze it if they did not hand over his soldier. The elders of the town went to meet Mackenzie and told him that they would help locate Murray if he stopped firing immediately. Mackenzie agreed to the bargain, stood down his men and waited. It did not take long. On 4 August 1782 Murray was returned to the fort.

When Murray limped back into Fort Mori, the watching soldiers wondered what punishment the irate captain would inflict on the runaway. Murray had survived whippings and the slave hole and had still not modified his behaviour. Captain Mackenzie decided that enough was enough. Without trial, court-martial or any semblance of legal procedure, he unilaterally declared that he was going to put William Murray to death.

Murray hardly knew what to make of it and nor did the other convict-soldiers. Some presumed it was a joke—though Captain Mackenzie was a very unpredictable man, surely he could not just condemn one of his men to death without recourse to judge or jury? Murray had, after all, always been a favourite and was thought to be the captain's own nephew, his flesh and blood. Murray had escaped from capital rulings so many times before and survived so many occasions when those around him had died—in the squalid cells at Newgate, aboard the deadly hulks, from typhus in Ireland and then from malaria and yellow fever in Africa—that he seemed somehow immortal, unstoppable. But none of his other death sentences had been quite like this one.

Not knowing what else to do, Murray prevaricated, attempting to delay proceedings. He demanded to change his clothes, perhaps thinking that he would give his commanding officer time to calm down. He went to his room and retrieved his army jacket, red in the traditional style of the British Army, with the red facing and white buttons which the independent companies wore. Then, steeling himself, he strode back to face whatever was ahead.[36]

Seeing that Captain Mackenzie's fury had not abated, Murray then asked William Copland to petition for half an hour to pray. Whether he was granted this or not is uncertain; the witnesses' recollections differed. Some said that he was denied this dispensation; another remembered that 'a little of the burial service of the dead [was] read to him, and the Lord's prayer'.

At the last moment Captain Mackenzie discovered that they had no hood to put over the condemned man, a nicety he obviously felt bound to conform to despite having ignored so many others, and he went and retrieved his own nightcap from his room for the purpose. Then Murray learned the manner in which he would meet his end. This would be nothing so simple as hanging, nor a pistol shot through the head. Mackenzie had quite a different punishment in mind.

Murray was taken to a cannon by the soldiers holding him and placed in front of it. His legs were tied to the bottom of the cannon's muzzle, his arms tied above.

The man chosen by Mackenzie to fire the gun was John Plunkett, the former seafarer who had been branded for theft before being convicted of the crime which took him to Africa.[37] When he elected to join the army instead of dredging shale on the River Thames, it doubtless never crossed his mind that his military service would involve killing a brother soldier, a senior officer no less, far away from any battlefield. In the event it would seem that the man who had never been convicted of anything more serious than stealing mirrors baulked at the task. He initially refused to kill Murray, but he was left with no choice when his captain put a pistol to his head and threatened to 'blow his brains out' if he disobeyed Mackenzie's order.[38]

If, as is often said, a man's life flashes before his eyes when he knows death is only moments away, what a life Murray had to observe. There was his youth, when he had turned his back on honest family life and stood in the dock for the first time; his transportation to Virginia; his cheeky masquerade as a loyalist named Jefferson; the high life of drinking, gambling and whoring combined with jewel heists and a notoriety that spread all over London town; and lastly the months at Cormantin and those African women he had got to know.[39] Now, with his 'uncle's' nightcap covering his eyes, his red army jacket on, and bound to a cannon, it finally seemed to be over. Murray Mackenzie begged for mercy then, realising that all was lost, said a final goodbye to his comrades.

John Plunkett fired the gun. The ball shot directly through Murray's chest. He was eviscerated; his body parts scattered below the ramparts. Blood spurted onto the fort walls. The force of the blast was so strong that one of the soldiers holding him had the skin ripped off his hand. Many of those watching, exaggerating what they saw, would always say that Murray had been 'fired out of' the cannon.[40]

The sight was so macabre it shocked the white men of the coast, some already hardened almost to numbness by the trade which was carried on all around them. But then the dead man was white like them, and his coat was the red of the honourable British Army. His death in such a gruesome and improper manner confronted their notion that Europeans were less hot-headed than Africans; that they had laws to control their behaviour and did not go in for impetuous human sacrifice.

Some of Murray's fellow soldiers climbed below the fort walls to collect his body for burial. It was not an easy job. One later recounted that Murray 'was tore all to pieces, all but his head, and his shoulders, and legs, and he had his arms on him'. His torso had been ripped apart by the shot. The soldiers saw 'his kidnies, and his liver and lights [lungs], as plain to be seen as ever any thing was in the world', scattered around, and collected them up for a hasty burial.

Explaining his actions to his adversaries at Cape Coast Castle, Kenneth Mackenzie merely wrote, 'I have sent Murray to the other world by means of a nine pounder to answer for his Conduct in this world.'[41]

Chapter Ten

TROUBLE AT GORÉE ISLAND

On the evening of 6 October 1781, while the small flotilla of ships carrying Mackenzie, Katenkamp and their men was making its way to Cape Coast, in North London Thomas Roster was putting some newly woven woollen cloth belonging to his employer onto tenters to stretch. When Roster returned at around eight o'clock the following morning to retrieve the cloth, it was gone. Fearing the wrath of his boss, and learning that two women had been detained by the watch the previous evening, Roster quickly went to see if they had stolen his missing wool. In the watch-house were two pitiable specimens of London's urban poor who had been caught at four o'clock that morning with the cloth, which they at first had tried to claim was 'an old blanket used at the parish chapel'.

A week and a half later the two women stood in the dock at the Old Bailey. Susannah Billings, who had quickly broken down under the watchman's questioning the night they were arrested and had sobbed through her confession, claimed in court that her accomplice, Sarah Jordan, had given her the cloth and asked her to carry it. Billings' employer and her father were there to testify to her previous good character. Sarah Jordan, on the other hand, offered nothing at all in her defence and could provide no character witnesses. The cloth was valued at forty shillings, the exact minimum value of stolen goods that could earn the death penalty, but in this case it was not applied. Instead, upon hearing the word 'guilty' pronounced, Susannah Billings and Sarah Jordan were sentenced to seven years' transportation. But this was no ordinary sentence of transportation, the kind the newly convicted had heard from the dock for decades. For the first time, a judge at the Old Bailey decreed that Billings and Jordan would go to an unspecified part of the coast of Africa for seven years.[1]

This was an astonishing sentence given that their crime had been neither heinous nor violent. Nor was it an uncommon offence or a particularly serious matter involving goods of great value. Susannah Billings had never even been accused of any crimes before let alone convicted of any wrongdoing. A woman named Sarah Jordan had in the preceding years twice been convicted of theft, and if this was the same woman perhaps the reason for the sentence becomes clearer. A woman of this name had been transported to Maryland aboard the *Justitia* in 1772 and was whipped for stealing a watch in 1778. If she was the same woman, now illegally returned (although she did not stand trial for that offence) perhaps this was why the two unfortunate women were selected to go to Africa.[2]

In reality, the sentence was less to do with the women themselves than with the events which were overtaking Britain. On 17 October, when Billings and Jordan stood in the dock and heard their peculiar sentence pronounced, the country was only forty-eight hours away from the calamitous surrender of Cornwallis at Yorktown, the capitulation which to all intents and purposes ended the American war on land. While male criminals could be sent to labour on the hulks or even released into military or naval service, what to do with women like Billings and Jordan was a dilemma. It seemed increasingly unlikely that they would be able to be banished to America.

The next time the Old Bailey handed down the sentence of transportation to Africa, the reasons why the perpetrator was thought suitable for this punishment were blatantly obvious. In December 1781, Patrick Madan once more stood in the dock. Madan produced a declaration in his defence claiming that he had accidentally been left ashore when the fleet carrying Mackenzie, Katenkamp and the rest of the convict-soldiers had sailed from Cork. He had been disembarked from the ship with all the other sick, and orders to sail had apparently arrived so quickly that he had been left behind. Once recovered, he claimed, he had returned to London to see his wife and child. It was a fanciful tale, but the judge on this occasion gave him the benefit of the doubt, telling him that he would be remanded in custody to give him time to prove these claims.[3]

The truth was rather different. Madan and Robert Hill had remained in Haslar Hospital until July of the previous year, when they had been visited by Madan's mother-in-law, the 'old bawd'. She had hidden a second dress under the one she was wearing and, having got the guard wildly drunk, 'she dressed her son in-law in her own habiliments'. Robert Hill, seeing Madan get away, threatened to tell all if she did not help him to make his escape also. She hastily swapped clothing with Hill, so that when the new guard arrived he found only 'the poor wretched hag' dressed in men's clothing where his two prisoners should have been.[4]

Back in London once again, Madan's sister begged him to leave the country to save himself, but his old life of crime dragged him back. With the perfect excuse of going to console her over her mother's arrest for helping him escape, he went to visit his common-law wife. After he had once again clapped eyes on his old paramour he could not bring himself to leave and 'reigned' again over his old territory, the lord of the slums once more, his legendary status greater than ever. He even taunted the police, sending them word that he was armed with a cutlass and pistols and would attack any man who tried to arrest him. Spotting Madan around London's streets became something of a sport: he was in Islington, Poplar and various other spots, an early and smaller scale version of Lord Lucan. It was not until November that he was recaptured near Moorfields when a beefy apprentice barber knocked him down, allowing the watch to secure him.[5]

After his appearance in the dock in December, Madan was returned to jail as per the judge's orders. By this time even the media was speculating as to how and why such a notorious villain was escaping the hangman's noose when far less infamous felons had swung for their sins. But Madan thought only of new ways to escape and, his old charisma not having deserted him, he quickly found a new gang of desperadoes willing to aid and abet him. He now 'cut through a double floor, penetrated a strong roof, and reached the top of the parapet'. He was fired on by a soldier who was standing watch, forcing Madan and his allies back down to their cells.[6]

After this incident he hated all figures of authority even more than he had before. When two soldiers, James Frazier and William Stobbard, arrived in the prison charged with stealing lead from roofs, Madan grabbed Frazier and 'with a great force and Violence threwn [him] into a large tub of filthy Urine' and held his head under for over a minute. Then he beat him. Stobbard suffered the same fate. Madan threatened to treat 'every Soldier in a like manner for preventing them getting out of Gaol'.[7]

By the following April, when he had produced no more evidence that he had not deliberately escaped from Mackenzie and Katenkamp, he was again brought before judge and jury at the Old Bailey. It was left to James Adair, the Recorder of London, to announce that despite his numerous convictions and escape attempts, His Majesty had once more seen fit to spare him from the gallows. He still had one last chance to be useful to society, Adair said, serving as a soldier on the coast of Africa for the rest of his life.

Madan was hardly overjoyed at this latest display of His Majesty's grand mercy. Suspicious that this was a punishment dreamed up by Adair and his cronies, he insolently demanded that the King's letter be read aloud to him. Upon hearing that the King, at this point utterly sane between his bouts of 'madness', had indeed sentenced him to serve in Africa, Madan's usual sangfroid deserted him. He 'peremptorily cast back the proffered pardon on the Court', proclaiming that he had only ever been convicted on circumstantial evidence. Such a rejection of the monarch's benevolence scandalised the court. In that case, he was told, he would go to the gallows a week hence. Hearing that pronouncement, however, 'his obdurate heart failed within him' and he 'bursted into tears; fell down on his knees, asked forgiveness for his rashness, and humbly implored that mercy which he had refused'. After a moment filled with heart-stopping tension he was once again told that he would go to Africa for the rest of his life.[8]

Back in jail his audacity returned and he was heard declaring 'that the ship was not yet built which shall carry him over to Senegal'. His sister exhorted him to bribe the guards with money and alcohol but in vain. In early May his hopes were raised when Captain R—— and some other prisoners managed to remove their irons with a saw which had been smuggled into the jail in a pie. The attempt was foiled, though, and after that every pie was inspected, the jailers taking off the crust to search for contraband among the meat scraps and gravy. On 15 May 1872 things got worse when his 'companion and good friend' Bernard Isaacs, or 'young Isaac the Jew' as Madan knew him, was convicted of theft and sent to the hulks for a two-year stretch. The same day Esther 'Black Moll'

Allingham, a prostitute, was released after being found not guilty of robbing a Frenchman who, she declared, was 'a man neither fit for God nor the devil; he is neither fit for a black woman, nor a white woman'. Patrick Madan thought he knew what black women were fit for, though, and begged his sister to 'prevail on her to attend me to her own country'. Africa was apparently a very hard sentence for Pat Madan, but he thought that a woman freed by the courts, and who was almost certainly West Indian not African, would be only too willing to accompany him there. Moll declined.[9]

After Madan's sentencing, judges seem to have taken the sentence of transportation to Africa into their repertoire of possible punishments. Around the country the new punishment was picked up unevenly. A judge at Warwick sentenced three men to seven years' banishment in Africa at the Lent assizes in 1782; the same sentence was also handed down in Winchester, Stafford and Peterborough at around the same time. At Lincoln, too, judges had apparently been using the sentence of transportation to Africa for some time. By the summer of 1782 men from Bodmin, Cornwall and Dorchester were also sentenced to go to Africa.[10] Meanwhile, other circuit judges continued to send convicts either to America or simply to some undisclosed foreign locality.

The government, desperation growing over the number of malefactors crowded into its jails, pleaded with the Company of Merchants to accept some more convicts. They had been making plans for this eventuality since at least June when Justice Buller mentioned it to Duncan Campbell, the keeper of the hulks. After many protests, the Company agreed to take a small number, though their capitulation in this was grudging at best. On 2 October 1782, Thomas Rutherford, secretary to the Company, wrote to Thomas Townshend (who had not yet taken the title of Lord Sydney) at the Home Office about their concerns. He reported that the

Company had again considered the matter and was still 'of Opinion, that, the Transporting of such people to Africa would be extremely dangerous to the Company's Possessions upon that Coast'. This was not his only concern of course. The old trepidation was reiterated with new words: 'it would render the British Nation odious to the Natives of the Country, and be thereby a Means of greatly injuring the African Trade,' he wrote. Nevertheless, he promised that of course they would do their best to guard the convicts if they had to receive any.[11]

So the government looked for a ship to transport a small number of convicts to West Africa. The answer was obvious. A slave ship could take them. Not only was it the very place for which they were anyway destined, but they were already fitted out and manned heavily to deal with human cargoes. A small problem was that far fewer ships left on slaving voyages in 1782 than usual, put off by the naval conflict still raging in Caribbean waters. There was one ship leaving, though, a small 350-ton vessel which had originally been a prize taken from the French. It was called the *Den Keyser*.[12]

Mason, the merchant funding the venture, agreed that the ship would carry this other batch of unwilling exiles on the first leg of its voyage. He must have calculated that it was easy money, and money which would be paid to him regardless of whether the ship was later captured in the Caribbean by an enemy vessel. It was a type of insurance that he would have some income from the voyage whatever calamity might befall them. Besides, a few ill-fed convicts could fit in with the woollen and cotton cloth, ironmongery, muskets and alcohol taken to barter for their African cargo. Captain James Waddington, a veteran slave trader, thought it a relatively simple matter.

With the Company in Africa in grudging agreement and a ship to take them, judges at the Old Bailey took to sentencing men to transportation with new vigour. In the September sessions four men were sentenced to transportation to Africa, each for a period of seven years. By the next month, Africa was apparently so accepted as a place of banishment that Thomas Nowland, who stood charged with having escaped from Newgate jail before his sentence of transportation to America could be carried out, pleaded, 'I hope you will have mercy on me, and send me to Africa for life.' In fact he received a more lenient ruling, being resentenced to banishment to America, this time for fourteen years. Evidently the government hoped that some new American destination would also be found.[13]

For those sentenced to Africa in September 1782 there was but a short time in which to say their goodbyes and lament their fate as they loaded onto the ship the following month. John Wood, who had been systematically robbing his employer of silver shoe buckles for a decade, was taken from the common side of Newgate to board the ship. Alongside him was William Woodley, a publican who had bought a watch which had just been stolen by a prostitute working in his premises. Elizabeth Barber, the working girl in question, waited in jail to see where the government would send her.[14]

With Woodley and Wood were ten other felons from the common side of the jail. Sarah Jordan and Susannah Billings were there, marching towards the lighters with the men. Also among them was Patrick Madan, making his second intended journey to Africa, and another five men who had been offered respites from their death sentences on condition that they spend the term of their natural lives in Africa. For two of them this should have been a long time, in theory, for John Ruglass and Samuel Woodham were young enough to be called 'boys' at their trial. They, along with Charles Thompson and William Marsh, had been convicted of theft from a seaman, newly arrived home from sixteen years at sea and with pockets full. Ruglass, despite his youth already a criminal who had been whipped for theft the previous month, had drawn a knife on the victim and, the sailor testified, had threatened that 'they would let my puddings out' if he put up any resistance. Now, ambling down to the Thames, where one of their fellow prisoners managed to pick the pocket of a gentleman watching the spectacle, the four allies had become three, as in June William Marsh had died in Newgate, probably of typhus.[15]

Three days later five convicts from the masters' side of Newgate jail had their prison shackles knocked off and were chained together to make the journey down to the Thames to join the ship. Benjamin Harvey, alias Herbert, like Murray some years earlier, had been found guilty of stealing rings from a jeweller's shop. George Adams was one of a gang of 'sharps' who had lured an Italian whose name was rendered in court as Gospee Capello to drink with him and then stolen his purse, hiding with it in the room of a woman known as Yorkshire Poll. With them was a Jewish man named Daniel Mendoza who had been convicted of theft despite testimony that he had been cutting meat in preparation for the Jewish New Year's celebrations at the time of the crime.[16]

The following day the *Morning Chronicle* announced that sixteen convicts from the capital had been sent on board the *Den Keyser* to be transported to Africa.[17] The list of names they gave was wrong in part, though, as they had inexplicably missed out Charles Thompson, and also had included in the list two men who had been returned to jail, considered too sick to sail by the *Den Keyser*'s captain. One of those sent back to Newgate was John Martin, sentenced to transportation for stealing clothes from the Turnbull family. Noted at his trial as 'a negro', he had been sentenced to return to his ancestral homeland.[18]

Also removed from the ship before it sailed was poor, naive Susannah Billings. Always thought to have been more guileless than Sarah Jordan and perhaps under the power of the other woman, she certainly had a good case to argue that her sentence had been unjustifiably harsh. The government obviously agreed and she received a free pardon on 1 November, and was returned to her relieved father. Shocked by the experience, she never again troubled the country's law keepers.[19]

Sarah Jordan would not remain the sole woman aboard the *Den Keyser*. The convicts from outside London who were destined for Africa had been gathered at Wood Street Compter before being embarked on the ship.[20] Among them were John Cockroft and Thomas Greenwood, convicted at York of 'coining' (counterfeiting currency), a crime which still carried the penalty of hanging for men and being burned at the stake for any women so convicted. Butcher William Harry of Kenfig, on the southern coast of Wales not far from Brigend, had been found guilty of plundering the ship *Caterina* of twenty pounds of cotton, brandy and currants when it had run aground in Swansea Bay.[21] With them was a female convict to keep company with Sarah Jordan. Her name was Ann Evans, and she had been convicted of housebreaking in Hertfordshire. Her haul and its value was this:

One cotton cloak	1 shilling
One cotton gown	5 shillings
Four silk handkerchiefs	4 shillings
Two linen aprons	2 shillings
One gold ring	10 shillings
One linen shift	2 shillings
Two pieces of silk ribbon	6 pence

The total fell short of the forty shillings which meant an automatic capital sentence, but nevertheless Ann Evans had been sentenced to hang for her

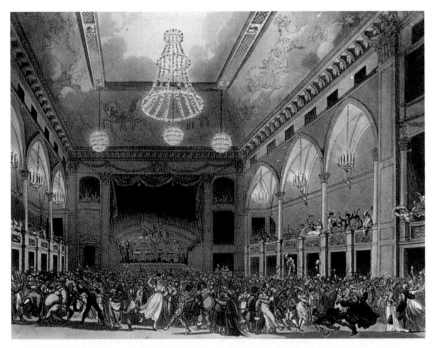

A masquerade at the Pantheon, London, c.1809, aquatint from Rudolph Ackermann's *Microcosm of London* (1808–11), engraved by John Bluck (fl.1791–1831)

The Gordon Riots, 1780 (Mary Evans Picture Library)

'Patrick Madan, Thief', 1782 (British Library)

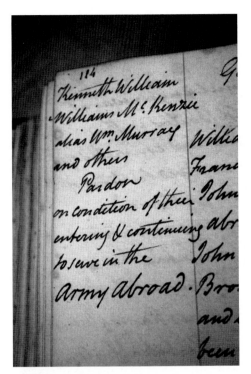

'Kenneth William Williams McKenzie, alias Wm. Murray, Pardon on Condition of entering and continuing to serve the Army Abroad' (National Archives, London)

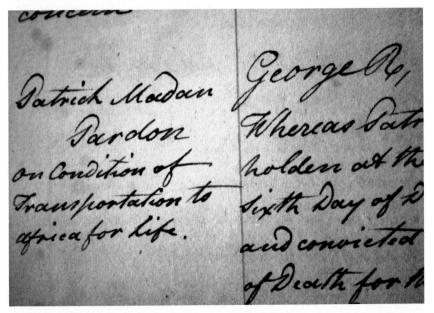

'Patrick Madan, Pardon on Condition of Transportation to Africa for Life' (National Archives, London)

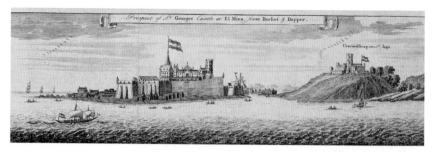

'Prospect of St George's Castle at El Mina [*sic*] from Barbot & Dapper' (University of Virginia Special Collections)

'The Prospect of Fort Nassaw at Mouréé' (National Maritime Museum, London)

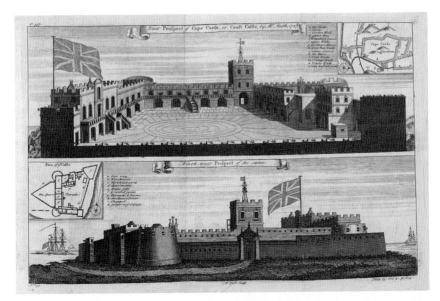

'East Prospect of Cape Corse or Coast Castle' and 'North-West Prospect of the same', by M. Smith, 1782 (University of Virginia Special Collections)

'King Aggri's House at Cape Coast Castle', by Captain W. Allen, 1841 (University of Virginia Special Collections)

Thomas Boulden
Thompson (Mary Evans
Picture Library)

Commodore Edward
Thompson (National
Maritime Museum, London)

'A Fleet of Convicts Under Convoy', 1791 (National Library of Australia)

'A View near Woolwich in Kent, shewing [sic] the employment of Convicts from the Hulks', c. 1790 (National Library of Australia)

'Governor Wall's Ghost', by James Gillray, 1802 (National Portrait Gallery, London)

'Governor Wall contemplating his unhappy Fate, in the condemned Cell', artist unknown, 1802 (National Portrait Gallery, London)

'Four Bucks (Dr Eiston, Hieronymo Stabilini, Francis McNab, Captain McKenzie)', by John Kay, 1786 (National Portrait Gallery, London)

Redcastle, Scotland, home of Captain Kenneth Mackenzie (Emma Christopher)

Fort Cormatin, where William Murray once ruled (Emma Christopher)

All that is left of Fort Mori in the present day (Emma Christopher)

The view from Fort Mori, looking towards the ocean (Emma Christopher)

crime. Later, her respite specified that she was to be transported to Africa for seven years.[22]

The *Den Keyser* was not the first slave ship to transport convicts banished from their homeland, nor would it be the last. Nevertheless, given that slave trading was the real aim of her voyage, the description of how the forty or so convicts were loaded onto the ship is telling. John Townsend, who worked for Akerman the keeper of Newgate, was with the London convicts as they went down to the port to board their vessel. They were taken 'down to the boats chained two and two together' and, once they had been safely delivered, the crew 'ironed them, and put them in the hold'.[23] It was very similar to descriptions of slaves chained 'a right and a left leg, and a right and a left arm' by slave-ship sailors. How John Martin, who had lived most of his life among slaves even if he had always been a freeman, felt about this treatment (though he left the ship soon after) we can only imagine.[24]

After all the convicts, Londoners and non-Londoners alike, had been loaded onto the ship, Captain James Waddington wrote on the register that they were all 'bound for the Coast of Africa'.[25] That lack of a specific destination is interesting, as it implies that neither Waddington nor the government had much idea where exactly they were going. The Company had only agreed to receive thirteen felons at Cape Coast Castle and there were upwards of forty aboard the ship.

Regardless, on 6 November 1782, with all instructions received, the *Den Keyser* set sail. It carried aboard a hastily written note from Thomas Rutherford and a set of instructions from Townshend telling the officers at Cape Coast Castle how to treat the convicts. Townshend's orders should be strictly conformed with, Rutherford cautioned. He would back up these instructions with some of his own, warning them to 'be singularly attentive to prevent as much as possible any Evils that might naturally be expected from such Men'. They were to be kept apart from the regular garrison, he directed, and finished with a reminder that 'necessary Subordination and strict Discipline' were called for.[26]

The *Den Keyser* was no naval ship which could afford to meander to its destination. Mason and Captain Waddington were eager for money and that meant a quick voyage. There would be no hanging about close to England to give Patrick Madan another attempt at scuttling, desertion or any other scheme he could dream up. But rumours spread that he had tried to lead a mutiny just the same. Newspapers reported that he had been strung up from the yardarm of the ship but a letter from Captain Waddington revealed that it was all just idle talk.[27]

So Patrick Madan got his first sight of Africa, the place he had so very narrowly avoided once before, as the ship made its way down the coast of Morocco. Chained below decks, he and the others at least had Bill 'the sailor' Gregory, a convicted highway robber, to ask about the noises and creaking which came from the deck.[28]

Their first stop was at Gorée. Although the colony of Senegambia had long since disintegrated, the garrison re-formed there after the island's recapture in 1779 still had some convicts among its ranks, so it was seen as a potential place to dump more. Joseph Wall claimed that he ruled over 'ranks usually recruited by desperadoes, picked up from convicts from our gaols, or incorrigibles in our military prisons'.

Convicts were seemingly part of Wall's garrison at Gorée from the outset. On his way out to the island in 1780 to assume command, some convicts destined for garrison duty sailed aboard the same ship. Even at this early stage, there was evidence that he would treat convict-soldiers extremely harshly. During the voyage, they were found with their shackles sawn off. Wall fixed on a man named Paterson, formerly a hatter in the Strand, as the most likely candidate to have been able to provide money to buy the saws. Wall ordered him to be hauled up on the yardarm then whipped until his back was raw. Joseph Wall's brother, who was accompanying him out to Gorée, did not have the same disposition as his sibling and, seeing Paterson's injuries, begged Joseph to show him mercy. But his pleas were in vain, and Paterson died from his wounds. Lieutenant Patrick Wall, his mind said to be 'stamped with a melancholy horror' at his brother's actions, was struck down with malaria within days of stepping ashore at Gorée. He 'died expressing horror and execration at the cruelty of his brother' and refused even to set eyes on Joseph.[29]

Although one of his biographers would say that Wall was 'generally beloved by the army' this was hardly the case at Gorée, where Wall was desperately unpopular. His fellow officers grumbled that he was 'of a severe and rather unaccommodating temperament' and ruled with 'rigid tyranny'.[30] He was equally despised by the common men of the garrison who loathed him not just for his despotic rule but also because, it was alleged, he took their pay and gave them goods such as beads and cloth in lieu. Just like Kenneth Mackenzie, he apparently forced his men to sign statements saying that they had received goods that he never gave them. Five of his soldiers even appealed to a passing naval ship for help, stating that, 'Govn Wall will sacrifice us by Inches as he is a Man that will not shew neither Justice nor Mercy to us Miserable Objects.' Before anything could be done to help them, two of them had already been hanged *sans ceremonie*.[31]

If Wall's rule over a garrison which contained former soldiers was already descending into the kind of chaos and brutality which was simultaneously marking Kenneth Mackenzie's rule to the south, the day before Wall's departure from Gorée was when the similarities became too close for comfort. On the morning of 9 July 1782 the garrison at Gorée was told that it was to be paid off as Wall and his paymaster were returning to

England on leave. The problem was that the men were owed some money from before Wall had taken charge and fearing that they would never receive it, they demanded that their commander pay them in full before he left.

Incensed, Wall met the soldiers on the parade ground that evening just before rollcall. Sergeant Benjamin Armstrong was at the front of the crowd and demanded the money owed. Condemning him as a troublemaker who had no right to anything, Joseph Wall ordered him to be tied to a gun carriage and given 800 lashes. As the lashes tore into the skin of Armstrong's back, Wall called out encouragement to the floggers. 'Cut him to the Heart, Cut him to the Liver!' Armstrong pleaded for mercy, but his cries fell on deaf ears.

The following day Corporal Thomas Upton was also sentenced to 800 lashes. He was already a sick man when hoisted onto the gun carriage to receive the flogging and could not survive the whole sentence. The surgeon, who knew Upton 'was not an obnoxious Man', intervened, doubtless saving his life. He was cut down after 'only' 375 strokes of the whip. Then George Patterson, a private in the ranks, was also ordered to endure 800 lashes. He cried out for his brother soldiers to help him, but they were too afraid that they would share his fate if they came to his aid. '[I was] very much terrified at the time never having seen men flogged in that manner before', one would later say.

The reign of terror at Gorée continued. George Robinson, Joseph Shaw, William Evans and Henry Fawcett were all flogged. Joseph Shaw, unaware of his crime, received 275 strokes of the lash. Fawcett, a nineteen-year-old private, claimed that he had only been walking to his post when he had been put in the island's 'black hole' by Wall for some undeclared offence. The following day he was taken out and ordered to strip ready to receive 800 lashes. His crime, Wall then read out, was giving up his bayonet, which he had lost sight of when put in the hole. Only able to stand forty-eight strokes, he collapsed in a dead faint.

Fawcett was taken to the island's small hospital where he regained his strength. The first three men flogged were not so lucky. Upton died on 13 July, Armstrong two days later, and Patterson about the twenty-first of that month. Even 'on the brink of eternity' Armstrong denied that a mutiny had been afoot, insisting that they only wanted the pay they were owed.[32] Robinson, Shaw and Evans, with 'large and deep Ulcers' on their backs, were also thought to have little chance of recovering. Slowly, though, they clawed their way back to life, taking months to pull through.[33]

Like Kenneth Mackenzie, Wall did not go in for standard ways to kill his men. Normally a cat-o'-nine-tails was used for flogging any man condemned to that punishment, but on these occasions the men were lashed with rope about an inch thick. As the surgeon of the garrison described it, it was 'about the thickness of his Finger'. It was more deadly than whip-cord because it bruised rather than cut. Armstrong was 'shitting and pissing blood' by the time he was cut down, 'his back exceedingly bruised and swelled, and as black as a new hat'. John Butler remembered that 'during the flogging of these poor unhappy Men their Flesh was torn off by the Ropes & flew about in large pieces and a great part of it stuck' to his own clothes as he watched on, horrified. 'In all or most of them,' Butler said, 'he could see into the Inside of their Bodies.' One man, knowing that this was all contrary to military practice, took a piece of the rope, soaked in blood, home with him as evidence.[34]

There was something considered worse still in Wall's punishments. Normally the regiment's drummers would have inflicted the flogging, but Wall instead handed the rope to black slaves. Wall, it was said, stood by with his sword, calling them 'Black Buggars' as they did his bidding. When each began to tire they were replaced by another so that the strength of the lashes never diminished. George Robinson remembered later that it was seven or eight 'stout black men' who had flogged him.[35]

It would be the following century before military punishments really became a cause of public outcry, but the soldiers on the parade ground at Gorée that July day in 1782 knew that what they had seen was wrong. No court-martial had been held. Although there was no legal limit on the number of lashes that could be imposed, they had to be given as the result of a court-martial. The soldiers also doubted whether using rope instead of a whip was permissible. What was more, ordering black men to inflict the punishment was against all accepted practice. The system ensured that men were always flogged by their own contemporaries. If, as Charles O'Hara had declared some years earlier, common soldiers would think themselves hard done by if they had to serve alongside African men, how much more did they object to being flogged by them?[36]

These were the events, then, which had taken place in the months prior to the *Den Keyser*'s arrival. Nor were they isolated incidents. Lieutenant Thomas Poplett at the St Louis garrison wrote a list of incidents to illustrate the anarchic state of Gorée: the entire garrison drunk for weeks at a time; prisoners shackled and allowed to starve to death; Joseph Wall had even 'kicked Lieut Fortye of the 75th Regiment' and had 'near Murdered, by Violent blows, Sergeants Smith and Butler'. 'There has been terrible doings,' Poplett related, 'the Inhabitants' Slaves taken by force and sold to a Dane, for spirits to buy all the Men's pay.'[37] On another occasion one soldier claimed that he was whipped purely because Wall had quarrelled with one of his mistresses; another man claimed that Joseph Wall had knocked him down and jumped on his head as a punishment for drunkenness.[38]

Joseph Wall left the island soon after the flogging incidents, leaving the garrison in as much chaos as before. Captain William Lacy succeeded him as governor. Lacy had his wife Harriet with him, so if he too was driven to fury by his African mistresses presumably he kept quieter about it. But in other ways he was as intemperate a man as his predecessor. He had so angered both Kenneth Mackenzie and George Katenkamp when they had called at Gorée on their way to Cape Coast that both men had challenged him to a duel. He had refused. During the events of July, Joseph Wall claimed that Lacy had approved of his actions. Some of the soldiers even recalled that Lacy had told the men how many lashes of the whip they would receive.[39]

William Lacy was hardly less belligerent when the *Den Keyser* arrived. He refused to let anybody from the ship land, leaving them anchored offshore for four days. The boatload of convicts could only sit it out, bobbing away on the tide. When they were finally allowed ashore they were rounded up on the parade ground, where Mackenzie and Katenkamp's men had first experienced Africa the previous year, and where Armstrong, Upton and Patterson had so recently been whipped. They stood there, surrounded by the soldiers of the island, waiting to hear their fate.

Patrick Madan, veteran of a trip to Tyburn's fatal tree, long periods in Newgate and other jails, revered gang leader and escape artist, was there that December day. Charles Thompson was there too, along with his young partners in crime, John Ruglass and Samuel Woodham. John Knowles had been part of a gang that had robbed a house in Grosvenor Square and had been impeached by one of his mates who was caught in the act.[40] John Herring and Thomas Griffin were both sheep thieves— one from York, the other from Hertford—while Thomas Davis had committed the rather expert crime of robbing a man while they were both already shackled in New Prison for previous offences.[41]

Rumour always had it that some women convicts were also left at Gorée and were there waiting for Lacy's pronouncement too. When the ship arrived at Cape Coast Castle, Richard Miles believed that women had already been disembarked from it, and stories swept the Senegambia region of white women who had been abandoned there. In America the *Providence Gazette and Country Journal* printed a story the following year which told of the captain and two sailors from a slave ship who escaped to Gorée in a boat after their human cargo had revolted and murdered the rest of the crew. The captain had afterwards got a vessel to carry him to Barbados, where he reported to have seen some convicts from England abandoned at Gorée and to have heard stories 'that three women, one [advanced] in years, perished for want'. Yet only Sarah Jordan and Ann Evans are mentioned on the two lists of convicts aboard the *Den Keyser*—Jordan with the Newgate felons, Evans with those from outside of London, and two women disembarked at Cape Coast Castle. It can only be assumed that either this was a rumour put about to make the affair seem even more sordid than it already was, or that some additional women had been embarked after the muster roll was completed on 1 November.[42]

Convicts had been sent to this part of West Africa as soldiers since at least the late 1770s, but this was the first time that felons were dispatched there as civilians, and what they were supposed to do after they arrived was far from clear. Some, like Thomas Davis, Bill Gregory, and the boys John Ruglass and Samuel Woodham, had specifically been 'pardoned on condition of Entering and Serving during Life in His Majesty's Corps of Foot stationed on the Coast of Africa'. Evidently they were supposed to serve in the manner of Mackenzie's troops. But others, like jewel thief Benjamin Harvey, alias Herbert, and John Knowles had received respites which stated only that they had to go to Africa, not what they were expected to do when they got there. If it seems obvious that they were supposed to join the British garrison, then what was meant by sending women aboard the *Den Keyser*? In the 1780s a women had no role in the armed forces other than camp follower or unpaid nurse.[43]

Even for the men willing and able to act as soldiers, there was a major problem. Earlier in 1782, before the wet season had arrived with its crippling diseases and daily burials of the dead, Gorée had been short of soldiers, having only 150 men of its standard contingent of 200. By June, they were down to 140. But Lieutenant Lacy did not want the twenty men who stood before him, any more than the governors at Cape Coast Castle and all the other Gold Coast forts wanted the *Den Keyser*'s criminals. 'It was very hard that he should have a parcel of men on the island,' Lacy complained.[44]

According to one of the men who stood there that day, his first day on Africa's alien shores, Lacy told them that 'his troops were starving already on the island'. He then decreed that they were 'all free men, and that we were to do the best we could, for he had no victuals'. Another said more simply, 'Governor Lacey ... sent them off, and would not give them any victuals'.[45]

If these sound like the excuses of men who would have dearly loved for Lacy to declare them free that day, they have more than a ring of truth to them. Gorée was notorious for running short of food; it had been since the days of Charles O'Hara, when he had sold slaves to a passing ship to feed his men.[46] Things grew much worse after Robert Browne, the man who had previously held the contract to victual Gorée's soldiers (and who had protested the sending of convicts to the region), was deposed by Joseph Wall and forced to declare bankruptcy. In December 1780, long before Wall left the island, William Lacy had written to the Treasury in London complaining that the soldiers were still short of subsistence items.[47]

The story also fits with that told by the captain of the slave ship who had been cast off his vessel. He reported not only that three women convicts had starved to death for want of food, but that all of them, men included, 'had been turned loose', Lieutenant Lacy 'having no provisions to give them'. The whole garrison had been starving when they arrived at Gorée, the captain reported.[48]

Admittedly, Captain Waddington reported that the convicts had been put to work at Gorée and that even Madan had eventually succumbed to his fate. But that does not square with the other evidence. The story that the convicts had been refused entry to the garrison became widely known, with most observers believing that most had subsequently sailed away. The West Indies was considered to be the most likely destination.[49]

Although few British slave ships purchased their cargo at Gorée, a small number did, like the *Providence* of London in 1780. Other vessels, both slave ships and those involved in other branches of commerce, called there on their way further south. Given the mortality rate of sailors in West Africa, it is entirely possible that some ships would have been in need of men to fill the gaps in their ranks by the time they reached Senegambia. For skilled men like Bill Gregory or William Harry, who had been convicted of plundering, the chances of being rescued in this manner were high.

John Ruglass and Samuel Woodham, friends since their days robbing sailors in London, decided to get away however they could. Ruglass's back already bore the marks of a whipping for theft the previous year and he was only too happy to escape the kinds of punishment he heard were inflicted at Gorée. When they saw a ship arrive they seized their chance and went aboard asking for employment and offering to work their passage to wherever the ship was headed. It did not matter where in the world it was going, so long as it was away from Gorée.[50]

Another young convict also fled on a ship. Thomas Limpus had been sentenced to seven years' transportation to Africa for the crime that was to become almost apocryphal during the long years of transportation to Australia: he had been found guilty of stealing a single cambric handkerchief worth only 10d. He was an old offender, though, having only begun his life of crime at fifteen when he spent three years doing hard labour on the hulks for the theft of another single handkerchief. He had been there when some of his fellow prisoners had joined the independent companies of Katenkamp and Mackenzie and he had been there during a mutiny in 1778 which had seen the guard fire on the ringleaders.[51]

Now, aged only twenty and transported for picking another pocket of another handkerchief, Thomas Limpus wasted no time in taking Lieutenant Lacy at his word. If he was a free man, he would leave. After going to the mainland near Gorée, Limpus continued to struggle to feed himself and was delighted when he one day saw a British ship close by. He lost no time in going aboard and offering his services, perhaps masquerading as an unfortunate sailor left behind in those parts. As Limpus put it, 'I did not chuse to go into the hands of the enemy.'[52]

Rumour had it that another man got away too. Patrick Madan, sly as a fox, multiple escapee, was thought to have taken flight yet again. News spread that he had posed as an American sailor who had been shipwrecked and had led the other convicts in making distress signals to attract the attention of passing ships. Some claimed that he had escaped to the French West Indies, or perhaps that he had managed to get aboard a ship bound for Cork in Ireland and was now hiding in his homeland.[53]

In London, too, many wondered how a man who had dodged the gallows at the last moment and had already escaped being sent to Africa once had not managed to make it home again when others had. When both Limpus and then Woodham returned the newspapers speculated as to where Madan was and when he would show himself once again. By July 1783, the *Morning Chronicle* reported, 'Patrick Madan has got [back] to town from Africa. He has, it is said, been drunk with some of his old companions at a public house in Fleet Lane, and another in Old Bailey, but how he escaped Africa, he will not tell.' It would have been just Pat Madan's style to have gone drinking right under the noses of the Old Bailey judges. Warrants were issued to search his usual haunts for the wily survivor, but if he ever did make it back to Britain, this time he miraculously escaped both the law and his own proclivity for trouble. Patrick Madan was never heard from again.[54]

Chapter Eleven

'NAKED AND DISEASED ON THE SANDY SHORE'

Aboard the *Den Keyser* those who had not been disembarked at Gorée sailed onwards, around the bulge of West Africa's coastline, ever further away from Britain and home. There were still more convicts aboard than Richard Miles and the Company of Merchants had agreed to take, and at Fort Commenda Captain Waddington ordered four men to disembark.

Added to Commenda's muster roll was John Prime, who had originally been sentenced to three years' hard labour on the Thames for theft. Like so many of Mackenzie's troops before him, he had swapped dredging for service in the African corps. John Sones and John Petty were both horse thieves who had been sentenced to death and then allowed to live on condition of going to Africa. James Aldred, who had been with Prime and Sones since they were in Wood Street Compter, also joined the Commenda garrison. They were all listed as 'convicts acting as soldiers'.[1]

They worked alongside one of the remaining men from Katenkamp's independent company. Only nineteen when he had stood in the dock at East Grinstead for stealing £5, William Harris had been reprieved from his original date with the hangman to labour on the Thames, and then had exchanged that for a lifetime in Africa.[2]

Meanwhile, the fifteen convicts still aboard the *Den Keyser* sailed on the short distance to Cape Coast Castle. Having seen the reception they had received at Gorée, where they had been made to wait four days to land, they must have wondered what on earth would greet them. Seeing the grand walls of the Castle as the ship dropped anchor, perhaps they were reassured that they would be protected from the savages, strange man-eating animals and head-boiling cannibals many still thought lived in Africa. Equally, though, the high castle walls, fortifications and armaments were their new jail.

For Richard Miles and his fellow Company officers watching from the fortress as the ship hove into view, this was their worst nightmare come to pass. They had protested furiously against having Mackenzie and Katenkamp's men on the coast, but this was much worse. These men—they were as yet unaware of the presence of the women aboard—who were not even sent to them under the auspices of the British Army, would be entirely under Company control. Just as the men of the independent companies were decreasing in number so that there were fewer troublemakers left, here were more.

Since the day of Murray's execution, there had been fewer and fewer of Mackenzie's men to discipline. By September 1782, two months before the *Den Keyser* set sail, Captain Mackenzie lamented that he had only ten men fit and present. The carpenters at the various forts were kept busy putting together rudimentary coffins for them as ever more succumbed to the malaria, yellow fever and dysentery which besieged the coast. By October, so few were left that Mackenzie, not even having a fit man to wield the cat-o'-nine-tails, had to request help from the castle to flog a soldier. In typical fashion, he never bothered to state the man's offence.[3]

Relations between Mackenzie and Miles had not improved either. In September of 1782 Philip Quaque wrote to his employers, the Society for the Propagation of the Gospel, that Mackenzie and his men had 'created irreparable Confusion, Disorder and Mismanagement'. Little did he know but things were about to sink to an all-time low.[4]

At Mori the situation had become progressively worse since the murder of Murray as the men starved, sickened and died while Captain Mackenzie lost his mind; anger and frustration keeping his already short temper at permanent boiling point. His own frequent fevers—the headaches, alternate profuse sweating and then chills, nausea and even delirium which made him think that death was close at hand—only made things worse. He was quite possibly also suffering from mercury poisoning from the medicine taken for the venereal disease he had contracted years before. Its side effects include extreme sweating, kidney problems, headaches, insomnia, memory loss, fits of anger and a general decline in brain function. Whatever the cause, he was certainly losing his mind.

Trusting none of his soldiers, he prevented them all from having weapons and standing guard and simply kept Fort Mori's door locked. He raged at the thought that his own noble attempt to help out the British Government in its time of need had cost him so dearly. Now the American war was lost and he was stuck in Africa, ailing and close to bankrupt, and with only a few sick, filthy and insolent men left of his grandiose dream.[5]

Although his earlier decision to let his men steal food from the local population had ended so badly, the issue still infuriated him. It seemed that the locals were eating well, food he thought should rightfully be feeding his men. Thomas Randall, a cattle thief from Norfolk, had already reported that Captain Mackenzie encouraged his men to pillage for anything they could and had made a necessity out of looting.

Mori was a small fishing village in the 1780s, dependent on the men going out each day across the treacherous breakers in their canoes. Every day the local people worked together down on the beach to land the catch. If Mackenzie stood on the battlements of Fort Mori he had a bird's-eye view of the small beach where this activity took place. The evocative singing which accompanied the hauling in of the nets and the turnout of all able-bodied men, women and children looking so contented was a red rag to Mackenzie's rampaging bull.

In early September he roused what remained of his bored, jaded men. Perhaps (ironically, it would have been one of the few times he and Richard Miles were in agreement) he talked of Britain's superiority, reminding the men that they were valiant soldiers of the British Army while the fishermen were just Africans, scarcely more sophisticated than beasts. Most likely, with hunger gnawing in the pits of their stomachs, the men needed no urging at all to go on the attack. One afternoon, when the canoes started to arrive on the beach, Captain Mackenzie led his troops hugger-mugger down the cliff. It was the last time the 101st and 102nd Independent Companies would go into battle, even if this was a most unorthodox fight.

Against unarmed opponents who were surprised by the attack, the soldiers quickly got the fish. If they had left it at that perhaps the matter would have come to nought. Never a man who knew when to stop, alas, Captain Mackenzie began to station soldiers on the beach every day to take what they wished from the day's catch. After this had gone on for some time, the locals had a meeting to decide what action to take. They decided on a path of passive resistance and simply stopped fishing.

Of course this only increased Mackenzie's ire, and he ordered his soldiers to destroy the Fante canoes and fishing equipment. They then went on to 'plunder their Houses & Markets of Goats, Fowles, Sheep,

Cankey &c'. As the men in the fort feasted on their spoils, the local people were left to starve.

As the English and other Europeans had discovered throughout their long centuries of slave trading, Africans simply would not accept such conduct. This time they took radical action. They established a blockade to prevent food and water from getting into Fort Mori. Inside, the fish-eaters held out for a short while out of a mixture of pride, stubbornness and sheer terror at what might meet them if they left. 'I am determined to die with the Fort,' Mackenzie rashly declared, but though he tried to keep the few men who could still stand and hold a weapon resolute, eventually hunger and thirst overwhelmed them. Governor Miles, although fuming at this turn of events, sent Captain Egyir to negotiate for peace, but to no avail.

When they could hold out no longer, Kenneth Mackenzie 'madly opened the Gates and rushed out' to find himself surrounded by a crowd of '2 or 3,000 enraged inhabitants'. It was humiliating enough to be defeated by a village full of African civilians, but now the crowd made it clear that they would have 'their own satisfaction' of him. The mob beat him up and then 'turned him out of the town, naked as nature formed him'. His attackers threatened that 'if ever he returned to Mouree they would cut him to pieces'. Raging at this indignity, Mackenzie had no choice but to throw himself on the mercy of his archenemy Richard Miles. He got to Cape Coast Castle as fast as he could, presumably finding some clothes to cover himself somewhere along the way.[6]

Richard Miles reluctantly took him in, unable to turn away a fellow Briton in his hour of need despite the havoc he had wreaked. He gave Kenneth Mackenzie the use of an apartment at the castle. Some of the men who had arrived with him were again garrisoned with the other soldiers but remained under the sole command of their captain. The incredible events were the talk of the coast for weeks.

A small note, written in the margins of a Cape Coast Castle account book by Dr Ormsby, tells of the desperate situation the men were in even after they had left Mori. 'It is really distressing to see those poor Men of Captain MacKenzies Starving, for three days they complain that they have not received any Sustenance, and during this time lived on a Bisquit [sic] and a little Canky.'[7]

There it was, the crux of the problem cast off as a few words of marginalia. The men were starving, which was a disgrace to the British Army, but, worse still, in their hunger they ate African food. While biscuit was a basic foodstuff, much like hardtack on ships, cankie was a kind of savoury pudding made from cassava, plantain or sweet potato, native to West Africa. With little to eat, they had traded what goods they had for cankie and palm wine.

It was not the fact that they were procuring extra provisions from the locals around the forts which chiefly troubled the Company of Merchants, although this in itself was a disruption to the usually closely controlled interaction between European and African. Of more concern was what they were giving in exchange. The convict-soldiers were bartering their weapons away in order to feed themselves and to obtain alcohol to numb the pain of their appalling conditions. This illicit trafficking was so successful that they had, lamented Richard Miles, 'not a Musquet among the whole of them'.[8]

Others, meanwhile, used their old skills at picking locks, breaking and entering, and stealthy pilfering to feed themselves from the castle's stores. Richard Miles became desperate. He wrote to London begging, 'for God's sake send us good Locks, for we have already experienced that those we now have here are not proof against the Villainy of these Wretches … indeed unless a power is sent out to try the most Notorious of them and to hang them, they must be kept always in Irons'. Of course, their captain was equally untrustworthy. In truth, implied Miles, he was little better than the cutpurses he commanded.

By December 1782, ten months after the troops had arrived in Africa and just as the *Den Keyser* sailed into view with more convicts aboard, the rumours of insurrection among the remaining convict-soldiers with Mackenzie were so numerous that it was hard to be certain what was truth and what hearsay. There were reports that the situation was so bad that Mackenzie's men at Mori would no longer accept him as their commander even if the local people allowed him to return. The writing was on the wall for Captain Kenneth Mackenzie. He had effectively given up all pretence that he was still in charge of the independent companies.[9]

In his absence trouble still brewed at Mori. Another mutiny was exposed by Thomas Randall, the cattle thief. Randall claimed that John Plunkett had grown disillusioned with Sergeant Robert Andrews.[10] Andrews beat Plunkett and in retaliation Plunkett imprisoned Andrews which, as Andrews was his senior officer, constituted an act of mutiny. Andrews escaped to Cape Coast Castle, where Kenneth Mackenzie ordered the soldiers to take Andrews back and sentenced John Plunkett to one of his favourite punishments: incarceration in the slave hole. There John Plunkett, former seafarer and a man who had been forced to commit far worse crimes as a member of His Majesty's army than he ever had as a criminal in London's lawless back allies, contracted malaria and died. Although he, as well as Kenneth Mackenzie, would eventually be indicted for William Murray's murder, he was dead and buried before he could ever give his version of events.[11]

Then, into this maelstrom, sailed the *Den Keyser* with its cargo of fifteen convicts as well as the goods to purchase a cargo of slaves. It must have been the least welcome slave ship to ever arrive at the castle.

Richard Miles wrote to the Colonial Office about the convicts' arrival. Despite having paid a great deal of attention to what the government intended and duly noted the instructions sent out to him with the ship, he took issue with 'the evident defect there is in the mode of transporting them'. He must have been horrified at the sight of white captives being unloaded from a slave ship in a place where the proceedings could be observed by local Fante merchants. Miles recognised that while some had originally been sentenced to death, so transporting them saved their trips to the hempen halter, he remonstrated that 'the grand consideration seems to be, *to get them out of Europe at all events*, without ever once adverting to the evil consequences that must attend this mode'. The old arguments that convicts would disrupt the trade in slaves had never gone away.[12]

Miles also addressed the problem inherent in the *Den Keyser* voyage: what were these people supposed to do in Africa? The Company had received no direction from the government about what to do with them and he had not been instructed to take them as soldiers. '[I]s it natural to infer that Government understand it is just simply landing these people in Africa, to let them shift for themselves, and get their bread in the best manner they can,' he queried, quite justifiably. 'In some other parts of the world they might by their Industry maintain themselves, but here, it is impossible, we have no employment for them but that of Soldiers ... the Natives have none; how then are they to be maintained?'[13]

Even if they would work as soldiers, Miles knew this would not be without problems. Reflecting on Rutherford's instruction to keep them separate from the main body of castle soldiers, Miles now wrote that the convicts would set a bad example to the Company's employees. Plus, he had every reason to think that instead of defending the Company and its possessions, they would run off to the enemy as the convict-soldiers of the independent companies had done. And there was another problem.

Miles could not obey the rules of both the government and the Company. Contrary to their usual state of being desperate for soldiers, the war had created a situation where they had an excess. A year before Miles had written home that he actually had too many men as there had been some Dutch deserters he had felt it prudent to add to the muster. So, as he complained in January 1783, 'putting these convicts on the Establishment as Soldiers is a breach of our orders'.[14]

Miles had another contention, though, one which is fascinating for its seeming bare-faced hypocrisy. If the convicts were employed as soldiers, 'Punishments also must be much more frequent among such Men, than is consistent with our feelings.' It was an interesting argument coming from a man who presided over a dungeon full of slaves. But perhaps Miles did not intend it to be insincere. He just saw no correlation between the way the slaves gathered beneath his castle's sturdy floors were treated, and those who strode the ramparts. This, indeed, was the biggest tragedy of all.[15]

As far as the newly arrived convicts were concerned, Miles acted the alarmed humanitarian. 'They are landed ... naked and diseased on the sandy Shore,' he wrote to London. He reported their progress thus: 'the more hardy of them probably will plunder for a living for a few days untill [sic] the climate stops their progress, and then shocking to humanity, loaded with the additional diseases incident to the Country, these poor Wretches are to be seen dying on the Rocks, or upon the Sandy Beach, under the scorching heat of the Sun, without the means of Support of the least relief afforded some'.[16]

This comment was rather disingenuous. While he reported having seen several convicts dying on the rocks, only one of the ship's convicts is recorded as having died in the first days they were ashore.[17] And far from having no work for them, the Company did have plans for the remaining twelve men, or at least it quickly formulated them.

Deciding that they may as well be used to bolster the thinly manned forts, despite all the disasters with the convicts that had arrived with Mackenzie, Miles divided them into two groups. Half would go to Fort James at Accra, the other half to Ouidah, which the English knew as Whydah. These forts had the advantage of being beyond the territory that Mackenzie had dispatched his men to, and therefore far away from the troublemaking captain himself. Richard Miles gladly paid a passing Portuguese ship to take the men off his hands. As the twelve remaining men embarked on another ship which would take them away, their number almost immediately shrank to eleven. One man, having evidently been the victim of an infected mosquito, succumbed to his fevered pains and was swiftly sewn into a piece of cloth. His companions watched as his body was dropped into the waters of the Gulf of Guinea.[18]

At Accra, where Thomas Shirley and his men had fought a desperate battle against the Dutch fortress close to the British establishment, six convicts left the ship, their travels now at an end. Among these was John Staples, convicted of stealing two heifers at Cumberland, sentenced to death, and offered a respite on condition of going to Africa for life. John Brown had been found guilty of stealing oxen and other cattle at York. He too was reprieved from his death sentence, although his term of banishment was seven years.[19] With them were Thomas Greenwood and John Cockroft, two of the men who had been sentenced to death at York for coining. They had been respited on condition that they go to 'one of our Settlements on the coast of Africa' for the rest of their lives.[20] That would not prove to be too long.[21]

The wages list reveals the truth of their situation after they arrived at Fort James. Paid in 'brandy, tobacco, pork, and cowries' they took up their posts at the fort, surviving the endless ringing of the bell which marked their duties and interrupted their sleep with its ceaseless calls to patrol.

But they did not endure it for long. The first to succumb to the diseases of the coast were the other two convicts who had gone to Accra. John Tebble died on 4 March 1873, followed by Thomas Whittle from Peterborough on 17 March. John Staples died two weeks later. April was less deadly, with the remaining three convicts surviving. Then, on 2 May, John Brown was added to the coast's death toll, followed by Thomas Greenwood on 29 May. With the death of John Cockroft on 1 July, all the convict-soldiers stationed in Accra were gone.[22] Whether their sentence had been seven or fourteen years' transportation or banishment for the term of their natural life had proven immaterial. None of them had lasted a year, never mind seven.

With six men having left the ship at Accra, only five were left alive to be disembarked at Ouidah. Edward Matthews, from the town of Salisbury—famous in the eighteenth century for music as well as for its markets, which had been held since the thirteenth century—went to the rather less cultured community of Ouidah's English fort.[23] William Deadman and William Marshall, old partners in crime who had been convicted at Southampton of sheep stealing, also found that Ouidah was to be their new home.[24]

After spending time between the vast, heavily fortified walls of Cape Coast Castle, Matthews, Deadman and the others must have been rather shocked to find that their new fortress home was a mud-and-thatch affair. Although it was a two-storey building towering over a sea of single-storey African dwellings, it was really more of a glorified storeroom for slaves and other goods than a true military post. There were plenty of other things interesting about their new situation too, as although there was no Dutch fort in the vicinity, the British 'castle' at Ouidah was positioned between the French and Portuguese forts in the town, only a stone's throw from each.[25]

Surely most bizarre of all to the new arrivals was the presence within the fort complex of a fetish temple. Ouidah, centre of the Vodun religion (commonly called Voodoo), had at least thirty fetish temples in the early 1780s, of which the most popular was that dedicated to Dangbe, the python. Dangbe was not as powerful as Hu, the sea god, but nevertheless drew the largest crowd of followers. The temple within the British fort grounds was dedicated to Nana-Buruku, a form 'of the supreme creator deity'. Quite what a young man from Salisbury (where the town was dominated by a cathedral tracing its roots back to the days before the Magna Carta, with a tower of over 400 feet testifying to the local omnipotence of a Protestant god) made of it all can only be imagined.[26]

The man in charge of the British fort at Ouidah, Lionel Abson, was none too pleased about the influx of convicts. Abson, who had been in Africa for fifteen years when the *Den Keyser*'s passengers arrived, would go on to be among the longest-serving British residents of all, living at Ouidah for thirty-six years, until his death in 1803. He knew only too well, then, that his profits were well down in 1783, affected by the American war just like those on other parts of the coast. He had less need for the convicts as soldiers than ever, and worse still had little to feed them with.[27]

Not long after they arrived Abson complained to Miles, in a comment reminiscent of Lacy's complaints at Gorée, that he did not have enough food for the convicts. 'I have hithertoo [sic] been put to it to find them Provisions for every thing even black's Provisions are both scarce & dear'. Evidently even as convicts, unwanted and little regarded, they were still white men and accordingly had to be fed the 'appropriate' food. Belts had been tightened because of the war and the resulting reduction in shipping, and Abson grumbled that his 'Allowance from the Capital for 2 Years past has been very scanty'.[28] In sending convicts away to African forts in this haphazard manner, the government was essentially outsourcing them, leaving others to find some way to profit from their existence. It was a strange state of affairs.

Despite his reservations, Abson 'entered them on the Garrison Ledger at £27 per Annum'. If he was hoping that by using them as soldiers he would be in profit, he did not get value for money. 'Most of them been sick,' he wrote to Miles, and although they had largely recovered from their first bouts of coastal diseases by March, Abson was still worried about feeding them. 'They are so many Mouths I have to provide for & if my Allowance in the Provision Way is not more considerable from you than hithertoo [sic] they will not I am sure like their Quarters,' he said.

Whether they 'liked their quarters' is extremely doubtful, but in fact they probably had some advantages over those at other parts of the coast. Ouidah had long enjoyed a more positive image in the British imagination than virtually anywhere else in West Africa. Thomas Phillips, who had visited the region as captain of a slave ship at the end of the seventeenth century, had written that it was 'the pleasantest country I have seen in Guinea, consisting of champaigns and small ascending hills beautify'd with always green shady groves of lime, wild orange and other trees, and irrigated with divers broad fresh rivers'. This was despite the fact the area was excessively hot and humid, the mosquitoes fierce and the area full of 'noisome stinks'. The following century, the *Universal Modern History* had written that Ouidah was, 'In a word … the true image of what the poets sing of the Elysian fields'. Having read all that had been written about the place, the authors did not want to 'speak of all its perfections' as it would seem as if they were exaggerating.[29]

There was certainly the odd break from routine, as Paul Erdmann Isert, who visited the fort in 1785, reported. Sitting by a window he had seen the viceroy riding past with a large procession and then stopping in the courtyard and dancing. He then saw the dignitaries kiss the ground before opening some 'crown-shaped basins' in which were seven heads and a right hand which had apparently been preserved by being smoked with straw. 'The entire performance appeared to me to be like one of our masquerades,' Isert rather implausibly wrote.[30]

The market at Ouidah was also one of the largest and best-supplied on the coast, attracting traders from all over the region. Cowry shells, imported to the coast from the Maldives as currency, formed part of the wages of those stationed at Ouidah and Accra, and could be bartered for all kinds of food. Some years later an egg cost ten cowries at the Ouidah market, an orange only three. A chicken was prohibitively expensive at around 280 cowries, but interestingly enough the attentions of a prostitute cost little more than the single egg. If that didn't appeal, there was, reported one European visitor to the coast:

Pork, beef, mutton; cotton cloth, native and English; thread, beads, gun-flints, tobacco-pipes, iron, pepper, elu [a composition to destroy mosquitoes], chuchume, bill-hooks, Badagry pipes, flints and steel, raw native cotton; tanacam, a medicinal root resembling ginger; goora and kolla nuts; eyo-nuts … skins of the alligator [crocodile], deer, bush-pig, and cat; dried rats and mice; raw and dried fish; fish cooked in palm oil; kootatuffee, a root resembling onion but very bitter; cocoa and dego-nuts, for making oil; boiled and raw Indian corn; country pots and calabashes …

And so it went on. The convicts could have purchased anything from 'porcupine quills' to all kinds of medicinal roots if they had goods to offer in exchange. Perhaps, though, all the stalls selling food ready to eat were just torturous to men who had insufficient goods to trade, even if they did not recognise the ingredients let alone the finished products.[31]

Certainly Abson remained concerned about feeding the convicts with adequate European food. In another letter to Miles in July, he complained rather improbably that he had to give others more to eat than he had for himself. 'The poor Convicts too have regularly shared at meals with me ever since their falling Sick and withal my Assistance they are in Debt for you know they arrived naked,' he wrote. By then, though, he had only three men to worry about. Edward Matthews had died on 13 May, William Marshall on 28 June. Ouidah, situated beside a lagoon which attracted mosquitoes in droves, was deadly for malaria.[32]

Back at Cape Coast Castle the remaining two convicts, the two whom the Company had most definitely not agreed to accept and who had not been sent away to either Ouidah or Accra, were causing great consternation. They reason was that they were women, the female of the species who had no real role in West Africa's slave trading forts. The majority of the castle officials thought that Africa was no place for any white woman, let alone female convicts. When Philip Quaque had brought his white wife with him when he returned to the coast, the current governor had written: 'she becomes [the] theme of dispute, the cause of idleness, and a spring of disease among your officers'.[33]

As horrified as he was by the other convicts and their bad behaviour, Governor Richard Miles was utterly aghast by the arrival of the women. The convict men could be put to work at least, but what on earth did the British government intend the women to do? He wrote home urgently, stating that the events were almost too 'shocking' to him to relate—the women had turned to prostitution 'among the blacks'.

Whether the two women, probably Sarah Jordan and Ann Evans, actually did become prostitutes at Cape Coast is impossible to know, although certainly their options were probably limited to that or theft if they were not supported by the fort. The accusation in Miles's letter, though, could equally easily have just been muckraking, playing on the one thing which might just tweak the government's conscience. After all, the idea that white women had to be protected from African men, who were considered to be particularly libidinous, had been commonly held since the earliest meetings of Europeans and Africans.

Richard Miles's horror at the women's alleged descent into whoredom certainly implied that what alarmed him was that they were prostituting themselves not to the white men of the fort but to black men in the local town. Many white men in Africa—Miles among them—had black mistresses, but for a white woman in Africa to take a black lover was unheard of. There were, after all, very few white women in West Africa to begin with, and those few were the wives or daughters of fort officials or soldiers. A woman left a widow after her soldier husband died either returned to Britain or found herself another spouse from among the garrison. But miscegenation was not considered in a particularly negative light by London's working class, the very community from which Sarah Jordan had come. Possibly she had taken a local African man as a lover and supporter in this intensely alien environment—though this would undoubtedly have been condemned as prostitution by Miles. (We can only imagine how a mixed-raced trader or a local merchant might have regarded the prospect of a white 'wife'.)[34]

One of the women did not live long enough to find out what the British authorities had intended her to do out in Africa. On 24 April 1783 one of Governor Miles's expenses was the cost of wood and nails 'to make a Coffin for a Woman'.[35] It is not clear that the dead woman was either Evans or Jordan, but given the timing it seems probable.

Two weeks before the woman's death, somebody else's destiny had begun to draw near. On 8 April 1783, Captain John Wickey of HMS *Rotterdam* arrived on the West African coast having been sent out from

Britain to investigate the state of the forts and protect trade. Successful trade meant a good relationship with the local people, which he found at all the places he called bar one. 'At all the settlements on the Coast I touch'd at,' he wrote, 'a general Peace and tolerable good understanding at the Natives prevails, excepting in the Neighbourhood of Cape Coast'. There, the problem was all too apparent to Captain Wickey. He did not mince his words. At Cape Coast Castle he had 'found a *Captain McKenzie*, who hath been guilty of such cruelties, and Depredations, bordering so near upon *Piracy* and *Murder*' that he had thoroughly alienated the locals.[36]

When Wickey arrived, true to form it was Kenneth Mackenzie who made the first protest. He went swiftly aboard the *Rotterdam* and complained that he had been badly treated by the Company's servants and the natives. Wickey invited him to make a formal protest the following day, but when he did not hear from him for another ten days he sought him out, finding him hiding out at Cape Coast Castle, so hated by the local people that he 'durst not' go beyond where the castle's cannons could protect him.[37]

But the story Wickey heard from others was quite different of course. He listened to long reports of how, at Mori, Mackenzie had stolen the people's fish and destroyed their canoes, so angering them that they had 'surrounded the Fort and cut of[f] all supplies from the [plaintiff] who thereupon rushing out amongst some hundreds of them was seized stript Naked and beat very much'. He learned that the two ships which Mackenzie had taken as prizes had been identified as neutral before he seized them. Of the Portuguese vessel, it was alleged that he had allowed his men to 'Rob the Crew of all their Cloaths, Books, charts and necessaries' even though the Company's men told him this was prohibited. He also heard from Richard Miles, among others, that Mackenzie had not paid his men nor given out the clothes provided for them by the government. 'He had cruelly punished them for small offences seldom giving less than 1000 and often 1500 Lashes and ... had put one of his soldiers to Death without any Trial by Court Martial or otherwise'. So it was that the murder of William Murray came to Wickey's attention.[38]

On 4 May John Wickey ordered Lieutenant Columbine of HMS *Rotterdam* to go to Cape Coast to collect Mackenzie who was already 'under a Guard of Marines for Piratical depredation &c on the High Seas or the Coast of Africa'.[39] At first he was reluctant to deal with the situation himself, as he explained the following week in a letter. If he took Mackenzie into his care, then he would be 'charged with him & every expense attending besides a great deal of trouble'. 'What do I get in return,' he reasoned; 'perhaps his Life' but no other reward.[40] Eventually, however, Wickey was prevailed upon to take charge of Mackenzie after Richard Miles implored him to do so.

Even so, Wickey did not think it fair to remove Captain Mackenzie from the coast without letting him sort out his affairs, nor was it sensible to take him away without seeking testimony from his former soldiers. Having arrested him at Cape Coast Castle, Wickey decided to return him to Mori. When they arrived there, though, the Fante prevented their old adversary from landing. Wickey and some of his officers went to the fort, where they found Daniel Munro, the former castle gardener, in charge and the soldiers complaining about their treatment on Mackenzie's plantation and the lack of food. There was no option but to remove Mackenzie from Africa. Richard Miles was anyway refusing to have him back at Cape Coast Castle.[41]

As John Montagu Clarke had done earlier, Kenneth Mackenzie wrote to Lord Germain protesting his innocence. Mackenzie swore that it was only Ensign Clarke's revolt that had caused him to lose control of the two independent companies, claiming that it had 'infus'd among the Troops' a 'mutinous spirit'. He further alleged that after Murray had deserted he resolved to have him caught as he did not want him to get to the other forts, 'which were chiefly Garrisoned by Convicts over whom the said Murray McKenzie was well known to have great influence'. He also made new and unsupported allegation: that Murray's sway with the other felon soldiers reached back to England, where he had 'been concerned with many of them in their Crimes of which they stood convicted'.[42] He was so threatened by Murray's insubordination and power, he claimed, that he had no opportunity to convene a proper court-martial. As the only officer at the fort, he alone had the right to pass sentence on his underling. The sentence was intended to 'strike Terror into the rest of the Conspirators'. In his own telling words, he had made 'a striking example of him'. The last sentence at least was the unmitigated truth.[43]

Wickey sought some of Mackenzie's men to go home with him to testify to events. The problem was that he could only take those who were volunteers in the service as the convicts were forbidden from ever returning to their homeland. But the old problem of identifying the men remained, for no official note had ever been made of who was free and who was serving a lifelong sentence of banishment. The few remaining who had been volunteers quickly stepped forward to go to England and bear witness, knowing it was their way out of their predicament. And so too did all the convicts, quick to declare themselves also to be free men. Felons they might have been, but they were not fools.

Eventually Wickey settled on seven men who would return with him to give evidence about Captain Mackenzie's alleged crimes. Richard Miles, eager to absolve himself of any blame should the seven be found to be convicts after all, wrote a letter to send home with them saying that as he had never received a list of the crimes of any of the soldiers it was impossible for him to be certain that the seven were all volunteers. He recommended that their records be closely looked into before they were allowed ashore in England. In their favour was that 'their Serjeant [Robert Andrews] who is himself a Convict declares these seven Men were Volunteers'. Then again, one of those who returned claimed that 'there is two come home now that you might find out, [are] two old offenders'.[44]

Richard Miles also sent a deposition with the ship which supported the allegations that Mackenzie had cheated both his men and the government. Mackenzie was accused of having forged some of the men's pay slips, including those of Patrick Madan and one James Gable, who had died while the ship was at Cork. Kenneth Mackenzie had apparently forged a mark against their names purporting to be their signature. Miles continued, 'you'll see a scratch of mark said to be Kenneth [Murray] Mackenzie's purporting to be a receipt signed 1st Sept 1782', though it was well known that he was literate and had, by that time, been killed.[45]

John Fontaine, a Company factor, also sent an affidavit in which he confirmed that Kenneth Mackenzie had held a gun to John Plunkett's head to ensure that he would fire the cannon to which Murray had been attached. He alleged that he had asked Captain Mackenzie why he had not put Murray to death 'by a regular mode such as hanging or shooting him with musketry', to which the accused had said that he feared that if he did not 'do it in some such rapid manner his men would either act disobediently or perhaps might seize him'. Fontaine testified that in fact the manner by which their captain killed Murray had led some of men, until the final moment, to believe that he acted 'in Jest' and in fact had no intention of actually murdering his reputed kinsman.[46]

Finally, with all the evidence gathered, the *Rotterdam* sailed with Captain Mackenzie aboard. Desperate as he had been to escape his African hell for some months, being returned home in disgrace was not what he had intended. Close to despair, he could hardly believe how badly things had turned out or that he had risked his life for nought. As Africa disappeared over the horizon he felt only extreme bitterness towards the place which had been the scene of his downfall.

The ship could not go straight to Britain as it was under orders to sail for the West Indies. So Mackenzie made the same transatlantic ocean voyage as the Africans he had seen embarked on slave ships at Cape Coast Castle and the other forts. Arriving at Barbados the news only grew worse for him. Governor David Parry informed Wickey that he had received a letter from the Home Secretary, Lord North, telling him that should Mackenzie arrive at that island, he should be put under arrest and his property secured. Accordingly Wickey formally arrested Mackenzie and secured the gold dust he had taken away with him. Wickey estimated that it was worth around £5000 or £6000. After taking on enough food and water for the return voyage, Wickey and the *Rotterdam* sailed straight for England to deliver their prisoner.[47]

Before the *Rotterdam* sailed from West Africa, Lieutenant John Dowling had been ordered ashore to take control in Mackenzie's absence. He found himself in charge of a ragtag band of sick, disillusioned men. Worse still, he was charged with taking control of a situation in which the forts Apam and Senya Beraku, having been totally neglected, were being plundered by 'the Natives'. Cormantin, William Murray's old post, was also beleaguered.[48]

Wickey had reassured the remaining men before he left that from then on they would be 'treated as men and as soldiers'. But Dowling was soon out of favour with the men. Half of those left behind sent a petition to the governor. 'With the greatest deference and respect we the soldiers of the Independent Company ... most humbly beg leave to represent to your honour the great hardships we at present labour under. We had great reason to expect at the time Captain Mackenzie was removed from us for the many injuries we sustain'd and the many assurances we received, we might receive redress.'[49]

They were aggrieved that their pay had effectively been cut since Dowling's arrival, as they were now paid only in tobacco and brandy, neither of which had a high exchange value in the local markets. Perhaps they, too, were adversely affected by the lowered profits of the coast due to the American war. But Dowling was also aggrieved. Suffering from malaria, he would later complain that he had to stay in West Africa for an entire year and was never paid a penny for his tenure as commander of the forts.[50]

In fact, long before that year was up, the 101st and 102nd Independent Companies were officially disbanded. In September 1783, the seventeen men who remained became the responsibility of the Company of Merchants, each indentured for five years. They were extremely distressed by the idea. As Dowling wrote to Richard Miles in October, 'As Captain Mackenzie's troops under my command are not willing to be incorporated into the Company's service, I beg, Sir, that you will take such measures as you think proper in removing them.' Miles, of course, did no such thing. And so the men who had agreed to join the British Army, no doubt thinking themselves part of a long tradition of men who had been able to whitewash their former transgressions through military service, found themselves bound to the Company of Merchants Trading to Africa. Earning scarcely enough to buy a passage back to Britain and with little chance of surviving five years, they had every right to feel ill-treated.[51]

Those who had travelled to Africa aboard the *Den Keyser* knew their fate, however, and had little room to argue their lot. Few were left alive after the first year to complain anyway, most having succumbed to the first flush of malaria they encountered. When the independent companies were disbanded all those at Accra were already dead though three men were still alive at Ouidah. In December 1783 that number became two when Joseph Jowit died and the fort's Company slaves were paid a gallon of brandy for making his coffin and digging his grave. His death left only William Deadman, one of the sheep thieves from Winchester, and William Anderson alive. The only other of the *Den Keyser*'s convicts unaccounted for, of the fifteen left at Cape Coast Castle, was the lone surviving woman. Her fate remains a mystery.[52]

The men who had been disembarked at Commenda Fort were faring rather better. James Aldred did not survive for long, passing away on 23 September 1783. On Christmas Eve of that year, Thomas Harris, the last of Mackenzie's men at Commenda, followed him to the grave, having outlived a great many of his independent company comrades.[53] But the other three men who disembarked from the *Den Keyser* at that fort survived for much longer.

John Petty, horse thief, survived until at least April 1784, when he appeared on the fort's muster roll once again. He was missing from the rolls by January 1785, however, having either died or deserted by then. At that later date only John Prime and John Sones were both still alive and at their post at Commenda. At that time they worked alongside two mulatto soldiers and seventeen Africans who fulfilled various roles. Their wages were paid in everything from brandy and tobacco to gold, pewter, soap and cloth. Hard as their lives doubtless were, compared to most of their former shipmates, the outcome of their sentences had not been too bad.[54]

Chapter Twelve

TRYING AMERICA AGAIN

When Thomas Limpus escaped from Africa after his ghastly journey in the *Den Keyser*'s hold, it was not long before he was back in London. Having sailed away from Gorée aboard a British ship, eventually its route took him back to the capital, where Limpus could not resist a visit to family and friends. It was a foolish mistake. William Collins, who had known Limpus before his *Den Keyser* voyage, saw him in King Street, Seven Dials, and knowing him to be a transported convict tried to arrest him. Limpus, who had never committed a worse crime than stealing a handkerchief, was now a desperate man, fearing that illegally returning from transportation would earn him a death sentence. In dread of what would happen if he was recaptured, he took out two knives he was carrying and tried to stab his foe. Sidestepping smartly, Collins managed to dodge the blades and called out, 'Stop thief!' to alert the neighbourhood's honest citizens. A nearby butcher and grocer came to Collins's assistance, the butcher divesting Limpus of his weapons in no time. The escapee who had made it all the way back from Africa was once again in custody and delivered to Newgate.

In September 1783 he stood in the dock of the Old Bailey, scene of his original trial, this time charged with returning from transportation. For the crown it was really just a case of proving his identity. John Townsend, servant to Akerman, Newgate's jailer, testified that Limpus was definitely one of the convicts who had been delivered to the *Den Keyser* to be transported to Africa. Henry Wright, who had been the turnkey of Tothill Bridewell for sixteen years, also swore that Limpus was the man who had been exiled to Africa for seven years for being a pickpocket. Things looked bleak.

In his defence, Limpus recounted the sorry tale of woe that had been the *Den Keyser* experiment, at least for those deposited unceremoniously at Gorée. Lieutenant Lacy, he told the courtroom, had refused any responsibility for him or any other of the felons left there. What choice did he have but to find any means of supporting himself? With no work available in the area he had signed on a passing ship, arguing that he had only returned to Britain because the voyage had brought him back and that it was his intention to sail out again on the same vessel in the coming days. His mother had gone to ask the ship's captain to come and speak for him, Limpus told judge and jury, and the man had promised that he would come when the lading was complete. They were all ready to put out to sea again, Limpus pleaded, evidently hoping that he would be released if he could guarantee not to linger in Britain. It was not to be. The judge sentenced him to death.[1]

The judge may have shown little compassion for Limpus's plight due to the fact that a whole host of other men and women had already appeared before him in that court session charged with having illegally returned from transportation, normally one of the more unusual of offences. The session had begun in the customary manner with the trials of a thief, a gang of burglars, a forger and then a highwayman, but had then progressed to hear the cases of no less than twenty-five illicit returnees. Limpus alone had escaped from Africa; the others were all part of a cargo of felons who had mutinied aboard the *Swift* transport.

A madcap attempt to resume convict transportation to America, the *Swift*'s voyage had its origins in the aspirations of a Maryland trader named George Salmon who was in cahoots with London merchant George Moore. Moore, promised £500 by the British government if he would take a shipload of convicts away, and with the added incentive of being able to sell them for their labour upon arrival, leaped at the potentially profitable scheme. He was under no illusion that the Americans would want a cargo of felons—it had, after all been such a bone of contention before the revolution—and he had written to Salmon to enquire about the best way to sneak the convicts into Baltimore. Salmon had reassured his new partner, reminding him that no law existed prohibiting the importation of felons. What was more, he believed that the governing men of the state, friends and business partners of his, could be brought around to the idea, perhaps with the inducement of a few well-placed gifts. He reassured Moore that the voyage would be profitable, telling him that he did not 'know any thing would bring more money here ... than a parcel [of] Servants or Convicts'. Nevertheless, it seemed prudent to class the convicts as free indentured servants rather than felons and to list the ship's destination as Nova Scotia.[2]

Aboard the ship were some colourful characters. Martha Ingleston, known to the ne'er-do-wells of London—and the watch—as Gallows Pat, had stolen promissory notes and money from a man's breeches. She had distracted him by provocatively unbuttoning his trousers in a pub where the landlord was clearly her associate. Her nickname was well deserved as the notes alone, worth over £70, were enough to have sent her to the gallows. Also with her were Thomas Dudfield and Levy Hart, two daring fellows who specialised in stealing trunks from carriages and were also lucky not to have hanged. More pitiful was Frederick William Ealias, second footman to a gentleman, who had pawned some of his master's silver cutlery in a desperate attempt to buy himself the 'very genteel' clothes required to keep his job and so feed his family. The lady of the house had complained that she was embarrassed to be seen with Ealias as her footman but 'loath to expose my poverty to my master' he had taken the terrible decision to pawn some items which were not his.[3]

Only a few days out, Captain Pamp rather injudiciously began allowing around twenty convicts on deck at a time 'in compassion of their sufferings'. On the third day of this scheme, those out of irons liberated the rest and seized the ship. A convict with seafaring experience took command and soon forty-eight made off in the ship's boats. They landed on the coast of Kent and Sussex and 'plundered some houses' as they ran towards freedom. Alarm spread through the countryside and thirty-nine were recaptured, some putting up furious resistance, thinking they would be hanged for the mutiny. In one rather comi-tragic scene, when five mutineers were found together hiding in a house, one shouted 'we shall be hanged if taken' and attacked the policemen with a knife while two others lowered themselves out of a bedroom window using bed sheets.[4]

Although this had ostensibly been a scheme to restart transportation to America, Africa loomed large in the sorry saga. One of the ringleaders, Charles Keeling, swore in court that it was the rumour that they were to go to Africa that had provoked them to mutiny and take the ship. Some of the seamen had apparently also fanned the flames of this fear by telling the convicts that their orders were to deposit them in Africa if nowhere in America could be found to accept them. The authorities denied the existence of any such plan, and sailors were certainly not above tormenting their unwilling passengers, but given that American ports had refused to take any more convicts it is far from certain that this rumour had no basis in fact. If Charles Keeling was aware of Thomas Limpus's story that day in September 1783 as they were both tried at the Old Bailey, he certainly had reason to think that his story had substance. In fact even some years later, many in Britain thought that the *Swift* had been bound for Africa.[5]

For the judges on that early autumn day, though, there was no merit in this plea for leniency. Keeling, along with his brother John Herbert— another who had been 'one of the first … in taking arms'—and a further twenty-four mutineers were, like Thomas Limpus, sentenced to death for returning from transportation. It was not long before respites were offered, however. Despite the judge's claim that the brothers had 'a very principal share' in the mutiny, neither of the Keelings hanged. Instead Charles Thomas, butter thief, Thomas Millington, shoplifter, and William Matthews, who had run off with a hamper of dead pigeons, were the men who, along with three others, went to the hangman to atone for their part in the *Swift* affair. The rest were offered respites to go to America for the term of their natural lives. Thomas Limpus was presented with a reprieve on the same terms.[6]

This might have been a reasonable condition of their respites from the hangman if the rest of the *Swift*'s prisoners, those left aboard after the revolt, had been sold in Maryland as planned. But George Moore's scheme had met with no such profitable outcome. By the time the *Swift* arrived at Baltimore claiming that a shortage of provisions prevented it from going on to Nova Scotia, the entire conspiracy had already been revealed to authorities. Instead of willingly receiving the felons, as Salmon had predicted, the state assembly had been stirred up 'into a Flame on the Supposition that England should Empty their Jails on them'. It was like the pre-Revolutionary era all over again. What had the war and all that vitriol been for if King George still felt that the former American colonies were fitting recipients of his evildoers? All the same, the state did not immediately pass a law prohibiting them, perhaps because Salmon gave a few hasty Christmas presents of cheese and porter to those concerned.[7]

Salmon, meanwhile, succeeded in selling twenty of the convicts for between £20 and £35 each, a lower figure than he had anticipated, due in part to the fact that another ship had just unloaded free indentured servants from Ireland into the Baltimore labour market. Those Salmon sold were all on indentures of five years, which, in a land far less deadly than Africa, give or take the odd cruel master, was a substantially better deal than that received by those who had sailed just before them aboard the *Den Keyser*.

Just when things looked reasonably promising for Salmon and Moore's fortunes, though, winter set in and the demand for labour lessened substantially. By January 1784, only thirty of the 104 who had reached Maryland had been sold. The others, still aboard ship, were sickening or contemplating making their escape across the thick ice. By 4 February, Salmon wrote to Moore that he was thinking of cutting his losses. 'I thought several times it would be almost as good to let the Villains go on shore and so have done without them ... if I cannot sell them for some price or other, I will turn them adrift.' Eventually most were sold, but Salmon and Moore suffered serious losses from the venture.[8]

Clearly the undertaking had not been planned as a one-off event as George Salmon, alarmed not just by his financial losses but by his damaged reputation and news that the Maryland legislature was belatedly going to outlaw convict importation, then wrote to Moore begging him to 'send no more'.[9] It was too late. Moore had already contracted with the government to transport a new cargo of convicts aboard another of his ships, the *Mercury*. He had even agreed to take some of the men known to be subversive, including Thomas Limpus and ten of the *Swift* rebels.

The *Mercury*'s passengers were not all previous returnees. Male convicts aboard the *Censor* and *Justitia* hulks were sent aboard at the end of March 1784 after Lord Sydney wrote a letter to the contractor stating that 'our Trusty and Wellloved [sic] George Moore' had signed an agreement to transport them away from Britain's shores. Others who joined the ship were from outside London, their jailers eagerly petitioning the government to relieve the overcrowding by finding space aboard for some of their inmates. Finally, 179 felons, of whom only twenty-two were women, sailed with the ship. Another two were not men at all but just boys. James Grace, aged eleven, and John Hudson, only nine years old, had both received seven-year sentences for housebreaking. Hudson had reported at trial that his parents were both dead and he had no means of support other than occasionally working as a chimneysweep. He had aroused suspicion when washing the soot from himself after the robbery. This was strange behaviour in a profession where 'Boys ... served Four or Five Years without being at all washed'. The poor little tyke was the youngest to sail in the ship's hold.[10]

The *Mercury*'s destination was unclear. By one report it was sailing for Georgia, by another just for some unidentified American port. The steward, meanwhile, claimed that they were sailing to Baltimore, Honduras, Virginia and only then on to Nova Scotia, where the convicts would be disembarked. Africa was mentioned too, at least in the rumours and increasingly fantastic tittle-tattle which raced between those fettered below decks, terrified as to where there final destination might be. Apart from the sailors among them and Thomas Limpus, the rest had never left Britain.[11]

For some it would hardly matter where the ship was bound. At 8 am on 8 April 1784, about twenty-five leagues from England, the convicts revolted. They had managed to conceal small spring saws beneath their clothes, and using these and some nitric acid they managed to remove their shackles. Attacking captain and crew, after a 'bloody and short Resistance' they had total control of the ship. 'I had then the pleasure of wearing what the gentlemen here call darbies,' the steward would later recall sardonically, using a slang name for fetters. The rebels threatened to cut Captain Arnott's ears off and 'the scissars [sic] were put to his head' but he was saved by one of the convicts who intervened.[12]

For six days the mutineers were in command of the ship. Many of them had been imprisoned for long periods and threw a wild party to celebrate their sudden release. They 'stove the wine' and proceeded to get very drunk. Less explicably (although all that wine could account for it) they threw the bread overboard. They appear to have had no plan beyond taking the ship. Nor were there many seafarers among them who knew how to manage the vessel. On 13 April, when the weather turned squally, they sailed back to Torbay. Two fishermen tried to warn them that the ship was anchored dangerously close to shore, and must have been rather shocked when the reply to this friendly advice was 'Bourgre your Eyes'. The next morning the two fishermen saw passengers climbing down from the ship and, thinking they needed help, again approached. This time their welcome was even less charming, as a mutineer told them he would blow their brains out if they came any closer. Nonetheless the surgeon and Captain Arnott managed to escape into the fishermen's boat and raised the alarm.

Quite why they had received only cursing and threats in return for their proffered help immediately became clear to the two fishermen. But they had to think quickly, as shoplifters, housebreakers, pickpockets, highwaymen and countless other undesirables were already making their way ashore, exhilarated by finding themselves unexpectedly breathing the air of free men in their homeland and resolutely determining not to be recaptured. There was no help available ashore, the fishermen told Arnott, but by an astonishing piece of good fortune HMS *Helena* was only a couple of miles away. The four men put their backs into rowing there with all haste, and told the story to a flabbergasted Captain Cadman.[13]

Immediately Cadman sent armed men to do what they could to assist the stricken vessel. Arriving back at the *Mercury* the naval men fired shots and promptly drove the rowdy convicts who were still aboard back down into the hold. Then, while some joined the few crew members still aboard in an attempt to stop the ship foundering on the rocks, others went off in pursuit of those who had already fled the ship.

They were too late to catch some. A few of the rebels managed to reach London, if only briefly. John Harris was taken from the coach carrying him from Exeter as it arrived back in the capital. He claimed in court that he had been forced by his fellow convicts to leave the *Mercury* just as, quite coincidentally, those aboard the *Swift* had also coerced him into joining that escape. John White was recaptured only three hours after arriving in London. He too claimed to have been an innocent party whose rebellious shipmates had threatened with a blunderbuss to force him overboard as they needed him to mend one of the boats. Nathaniel Collier managed a longer sojourn in the capital but was soon back in the Old Bailey's dock. After escaping from the *Swift* he had asked for his good behaviour in jail and aboard ship to be taken into account. This time, doubtless fearing that his credibility was at an end, he stated his guilt.[14] The judge had little sympathy with any of the men. He wore the black cap when reading each of their sentences.

Few of the *Mercury* rebels made it further than the nearest pub. Between the armed men of HMS *Helena* and the local authorities, the majority were rounded up within hours or days of stepping ashore. Others never even reached the shore and instead were deposited back aboard the

Mercury, where Arnott and his crew were once again in control. Later, this would lead to legal questions as to whether these men and women could actually be said to have 'returned' from transportation, but for those who were captured ashore there was no question. They were soon crowding the jail cells of Exeter awaiting the further course of the law.

Among them was Thomas Limpus. He was one of five men committed to 'His Majesty's High Gaol' on 19 April. Twenty-seven other convicts from the ship had been taken there three days earlier. Forty-nine other escapees, including some of the female prisoners, had also been caught and were held in the local bridewell. By May more than ninety *Mercury* rebels were held in Devon's jails and Robert Sidaway, who had been dangerously wounded when the *Helena*'s men had retaken the ship, was under guard in Exeter hospital. Little John Hudson was among those packed into Exeter jail's subterranean 'night-dungeons'.[15]

Grossly unsuited to housing such a sizeable influx of prisoners, fears soon arose of another mass escape attempt or a typhus outbreak. A suggestion that a naval ship then waiting to transport 'Hanovarian troops' home should collect the recaptured *Mercury* and transport them away from England (to where was unclear) came to nothing, and as an interim measure an old ship was converted into a hulk. The *Dunkirk*, once a sixty-gun naval vessel, was fitted out to receive the convicts and William Cowdry, a former jail warden, appointed overseer. It was moored at Plymouth.[16]

In June the convicts began to be transferred to Plymouth, two or three at a time 'so as not to alarm the county', to go aboard the new hulk. Eventually the 70th Regiment of Foot was on hand to accompany the prisoners and they could be transferred in bigger numbers. But it was August before some men, including Thomas Limpus and *Swift* ringleader Charles Keeling, were in their new home. Eventually ninety of the *Mercury*'s former passengers were aboard the *Dunkirk*, including ten women.[17]

To all the horrors of the hulks moored in the Thames, the *Dunkirk* added a novel twist. As with the *Den Keyser* convicts at Cape Coast Castle, it was the presence of women which presented new challenges. An appalled observer wrote that 'as soon as Mr Cowdry leaves the ship, the officer, serjeant & the whole Guard has recourse to the women', noting that it was all 'too shocking to describe'. One of Cowdry's lieutenants, Levings Ivie, seems to have been particularly blameworthy. On one evening he is said to have demanded that two of the women go and 'entertain' some private guests he had aboard. The *Dunkirk* apparently doubled as gaming hall and brothel, and that was only what the guards cooked up, never mind the scams and trickery the convicts contrived.[18]

By November, things turned from bad to worse. On the fifth, as bonfires raged across the country in celebration of the crushing of another, much older insurgent, Guy Fawkes, the convicts used the festivities as a cover to attempt a mass escape. The endeavour was quickly overwhelmed but it alarmed the law nonetheless. It was now almost seven months since the *Mercury* mutiny and autumn had turned to a bitter winter. Around the county fears grew that they would soon attempt another escape if matters were not resolved.

J.P. Bastard, Member of Parliament for Devon, wrote to Lord Sydney about his county's reluctant guests. 'I suppose your Lordship cannot be ignorant [of the fact] that many of the prisoners are nearly if not quite naked', he wrote, though clearly he was more concerned about security than the convicts' health, complaining that 'at present they are under no Controul [sic] whatever either civil or military'. '[T]he most licentious acts are committed on board notably by the Prisoners, but also by the Soldiers, many of whom are nearly connected, if not old Accomplices with the Convicts.'[19]

The problem of what to do with the convicts was so serious by this time that Lord Sydney could not even offer any hope that Devon would soon be rid of the *Dunkirk* and its residents. The best he could offer Cowdry was one guinea per convict to provide them with some winter clothing. It was hardly enough, but at least Limpus and the other male convicts each got two shirts, one pair of stockings, a jacket, trousers, a cap and some shoes. John Hudson signed for his with the cross of one who had never been inside a school room.[20]

Even so, as desperate as local authorities were to get rid of the convicts, at least one man was ready to protest when word came that they 'shall forthwith be removed … to the coast of Africa'. John Nicol, Lord Mayor of Plymouth, believed that whatever they had done, this was unjustifiably harsh. He wrote to the Home Office asking whether 'any Person brought before you for a Petit Larceny should suffer *so severe a Sentence as that of Transportation*' to '*the Coast of Africa*'. Such a punishment, he continued, was '*in the routine of Punishment … considered as next in degree to that of Death*'. He begged instead that they be sentenced to the vaguer punishment of transportation 'beyond the seas' and also asked the recipient to keep the matter secret as 'it would likely create trouble were the intentions of Government known, with respect to the destination of the convicts'. If rumours that they were going to Africa spread to the convicts, they would no doubt try yet again to escape. Thomas Limpus was able to describe to the others his experiences of transportation to that continent and what had happened to his old shipmates from the *Den Keyser*.[21]

In fact the prospect of Africa loomed large even for some *Mercury* mutineers who had managed to reach London, thereby avoiding the fate of being incarcerated aboard the *Dunkirk*. Held in London's jails, at their new trials they too found themselves condemned to go to Africa. Initially sentenced to death for returning from transportation, Nathaniel

Collier was reprieved on condition of going to Africa for fourteen years.[22] Charles Courcey and Nathaniel Byers, who had originally been convicted at Winchester, were also now destined for Africa.[23] John Barker, sentenced to death in September 1783 for being one of the footpads who had stolen a watch and money from Jeremiah Branson, was recaptured in August of 1784 after his escape from the *Mercury*. This time his punishment was set at seven years in Africa.[24]

Even if the convicts on the *Swift* and the *Mercury* had not mutinied, the attempt on the part of the British government to find an American colony willing to accept convicts had been an unmitigated disaster. After the *Mercury* was repaired, it set sail again in May 1784, having now added some unlucky convicts awaiting transportation from Devon to the fifty-eight of its original contingent still aboard.

Its destination was no more certain than it had been the first time. In the event, it sailed first to mainland America, where the ship and its felons were turned away. There was no way that the newly liberated Americans would agree to receive more convicts after the *Swift* controversy. There were few options left for Captain Arnott, but he was not yet reduced to landing the chained men and women in Africa as some had feared. Instead, he turned the ship south, towards a small speck of British territory in Central America. In mid-July, they landed at Honduras Bay.[25]

The origins of the Honduras Bay settlement—now part of Belize— are shrouded in myth. Some suggest a shipwrecked English crew were the earliest non-Spaniards on the coast but Peter Wallace, a Scotsman who had previously served under Sir Walter Raleigh, is generally credited with establishing the lawless community, having sailed his ship *Swallow* there in 1634. He had narrowly escaped from the pirate stronghold of Tortuga during a Spanish attack and was on the lookout for a new base for his buccaneering operations. The mangrove-dense, scarcely explored tributaries and bays of the Honduran coast were perfect lairs to return to after each orgy of plunder on the Caribbean seas. So much was he a part of the formation story that some credit him with giving the region its name, Belize conceivably being a Spanish corruption of Wallace.[26]

The myth of colonisation maintains that the indigenous Maya had long since left the scene, the landscape being dotted with the remains of their ancient cities. This was not the case, although the Mayan population had been decimated by the diseases brought by the Spaniards and, later, other Europeans. Nevertheless some remained when the British arrived and into the late 1780s the coastal settlements suffered an 'attack of the Wild Indians'.[27]

Another legend of colonisation, more believable than the idea that the Maya had left unclaimed land calling out for settlement, was that of the loutish frontiersmen, men as rough and ready as England created. A mariner who was shipwrecked there in 1719 described the Baymen as 'generally a rude, Drunken crew', some of whom had been pirates and many of them sailors, and all of whom were inordinately fond of liquor. In 1768, a visiting Lord of the Admiralty wrote that they were 'a most notorious lawless set of Miscreants [who] pursue their licentious conduct with impunity'. Rather evocatively, one early visitor misspelled the name Belize, terming it 'the river of Bullys'.[28]

Throughout its first century of existence the British government never officially recognised the territory so informally held by a few of its expatriates. The general suppression of piracy in the early eighteenth century affected the settlement, making it rather more respectable as many of the settlers living on the coast turned to logwood cutting. By the early eighteenth century the 'Baymen', as they called themselves, were supplying almost all of the logwood Europe imported. Logwood, 'used in dying Colours, Such as Blacks, Blues and Purples' and essential to the wool and cotton industries in Britain, became the settlement's raison d'être.[29]

Not fully recognised, though, the settlement was endangered whenever Britain went to war with Spain. It was destroyed several times and it was only after the Baymen returned to the region after the Seven Years' War that they had any legal right to be there. Even then, although they were allowed to occupy the region for the purposes of cutting and shipping away logwood, they were permitted no British military fortifications and no rights of land cultivation. Rather ironically, they gained the right to cut logwood just as their attentions turned to a more profitable alternative. Soon mahogany, used in the luxury furniture industry, was far more important to the settlement than logwood. The logging of that remained illegal despite the fact that they were partly supplying a whole new industry in Britain. Thomas Chippendale was at the forefront of luxury mahogany furniture-making; William Murray had often walked past his St Martin's Lane shop while on his nefarious travels around London.[30]

During the American conflict the old issues between Britain and Spain arose. Officially the charge against the settlers was that they had 'daily encroached upon the old [Spanish] establishments' and had 'prevailed upon the Indians to revolt; furnishing them with arms'. The former may have been true; the latter seems unlikely. But that was hardly the point; it was disputed territory and definitely fair game in eighteenth-century warfare. On 19 February 1779 the Spanish approached the main settlement on St George's Cay. The alarm had been raised on the mainland only two hours earlier 'by an Indian runner' and the men hurried to launch boats, eager to go and protect wives, children and property. By the time they got there it was too late. With no military fortifications at all, the assault was more of a rout than a battle, though the 'half-dozen white men and a few negroes' who were there fought to the death. The 101 whites,

40 mixed-race people and 250 or so people of African origin left alive were all captured. Some of the men who had been working on the mainland had only the bodies of their loved ones to return to.[31]

In 1784, as the *Mercury* set sail, the Honduras Bay settlement was just being re-established as the chaos of the war years receded. Those who had been captured in the 1779 attack had suffered terribly, some being put in shackles, others blindfolded and marched to Merida. After being held in Cuba, they were only freed to travel to Jamaica in July 1782, but from there the survivors began to make their way back to Honduras Bay. The tiny town on St George's Cay, with whites' houses facing the sea to get the sea breeze and their black slaves' dwellings behind, began to be reconstructed.[32]

Under the Treaty of Versailles the Spanish agreed to respect the settlement and guaranteed the rights of the Baymen to be there, but in a restricted region. Rather than the whole area from Cape Catoche on the Gulf of Mexico to Cape Honduras, which the Baymen rather preposterously considered their own, they were instead confined to the territory between Rio Hondo and the Belize River. They still had no right to cultivate the land, theirs being the privilege of usufruct rather than the right of ownership. It was hardly what the Baymen believed themselves entitled to. Neither was restitution for their losses in 1779—they claimed to be £100,473 11s 1d out of pocket, around £10 million in today's values—forthcoming from London.[33]

At this extraordinarily inauspicious moment, the *Mercury* appeared on the horizon. It sailed not so much into the crude, frontier settlement the government imagined, but rather into a raging storm. Admittedly an Irish colonel, Edward Marcus Despard, had just been appointed Superintendent of the Bay Settlement with a view to regulating the affairs of the colony. But in spring 1784, when the *Mercury* was making its way across the ocean, he was touring the territory with Juan de Aguilar, Governor of Yucatan, drawing up the borders between Spanish and British territory. Even after he eventually arrived to take up the post some two years later, his would prove an impossible and thankless task.[34]

The newly recreated settlement was as unorthodox as before. Governed on the principles of Burnaby's Code, a set of rules hammered out some years earlier, the settlement was run by public meetings which met three times a year and comprised all the free men in the area. The main tenet by which they lived was, first and foremost, that anybody heard to have been guilty of 'profane cursing and swearing' would pay 2s 6d or the equivalent in logwood. That participants at the public meetings had to be free was a vital corollary, for this was a society with slaves. But this provision made the citizenry a tiny minority. The first public meeting of the re-formed settlement had been held in June 1784, only a few weeks before the convicts' arrival. At that first June meeting only twelve men were in attendance. There was simply no way that they could safely incorporate eighty-six felons into their society. There would be more than seven malefactors for each free male citizen.[35]

Whenever the *Mercury*—or, in fact, any other convict transport—had sailed into view, it was unlikely that the Honduras settlement would have been a suitable community to accept a shipment of convicts. Most other slave societies had vehemently rejected the idea of using convict labour long before, afraid of their rebellious tendencies and preferring black slave workers who both society and the law allowed masters to own in perpetuity and to treat pretty much as they wished. As the nearby island colony of Jamaica and the eastern Caribbean islands of Barbados, St Kitts, Nevis and the others had become wealthy enough, they had all rejected convict labour in favour of purchasing African slaves. It was far too late in the day for the British government to introduce another experiment in convicts and slaves working side by side in the Caribbean region.

Admittedly Honduras Bay was unlike any other society with slaves in the Americas. The vast majority of those who passed through the dungeons of the African castles where British convicts were masquerading as redcoats did not end up in a society anything like the community at Honduras Bay. There was, after all, little cultivation of the land and so no tobacco or sugar plantations requiring their labour. No agriculture was officially allowed, and although one visitor reported that each house had a 'plantain-walk' of great 'beauty and richness' interspersed with melons and pineapples, this illicit activity hardly compared to the mass plantations of other American slave colonies. Plus there was only the most makeshift sort of society, so it could hardly afford to operate on the strict racial lines common to other American slave societies. By the 1790s mixed-race and free blacks were some of the largest slave owners in the settlement.[36]

All the same, these factors ultimately made the settlement less appropriate a place for the *Mercury*'s men and women, not more so. The work slaves performed, cutting mahogany and logwood in gangs of up to fifty men, meant minimal supervision and great freedom of movement. What was more, sale to the region was seen as a hardship posting for slaves, a place that Caribbean masters could send those who were particularly rebellious, insubordinate and intractable. 'It is notorious that Honduras is at this hour the mart for every black villain that is transported from the British Islands,' it was said.[37]

When taken together, these two factors meant that the tiny white minority lived in constant fear of a slave attack, despite professing, as other slave owners did, that their slaves were ceaselessly dedicated and devoted. Their fears were not unfounded. Slaves held in the region rebelled at least three times between 1765 and 1773, on each occasion killing several white members of the community before making their way to the Spanish. In 1773, the settlement spent five months under siege when the slaves staged a mass revolt, an uprising which was ultimately subdued only with naval support from Jamaica. When the settlement was attacked by the Spanish in 1779 during the American War of Independence, some of their own runaway slaves were among those leading the assault.[38]

The Baymen, then, were clinging tentatively to the precipice of oblivion in 1784, surrounded on all sides by the ever-present threat that the Spanish might renege on their treaty agreement, that their slaves might rebel and kill them and their families as they slept, or that the 'wild Indians' might launch an attack. Struggling to maintain control were those twelve men who attended the public meeting in June 1784 and, more specifically, five magistrates who had been voted into office the previous year when there had been only seven names on the electoral roll to choose the five from.[39]

Unsurprisingly, the arrival of the *Mercury* with eighty-six convicts aboard horrified the fledgling community. They saw not a newly arrived supply of labour, much less a way to bolster the tiny free white population, but rather that the ship represented a 'most daring attempt to ruin, and destroy the Peace of our little Settlement'. As they could not feed such a large number of men and women with no agriculture permitted and a vastly reduced territory under their control, they foresaw a future in which the felons simply rampaged around stealing what food they could, then probably taking off to sea with all available boats.

Nevertheless, apparently with the permission of Magistrate James McAulay, some of the convicts were landed at a place called Haulover. There, the urban thieves, those who had been captured during the revolt before they made it to shore, and the unlucky later additions who had been awaiting transportation in Devon's jails at the most inopportune of moments, cleared a small area of land and even put up some rudimentary huts. It was a brief respite of calm before the storm.[40]

In early August another public meeting was held to decide how to deal with the crisis. This time numbers were bolstered to fifteen men, three more than two months earlier, but still showing a vulnerability which doubtless firmed their resolve. They declared that anybody buying a convict would be fined £100. The ship itself, along with all her unwilling passengers, was given fifteen days to sail away and leave them alone. They cared not at all where they went. Robert White, the agent to the settlers who was based in London, had a suggestion for Lord Sydney though. Seeing 'no proper Refuge for them in the West Indies ... I beg leave to submit the propriety of sending them in that same line of Conveyance to Affrica [sic], as has been practiced in disposing of other Convicts,' he wrote. Whatever the expense, it would be worth it for 'Clearing the West Indies of their Company'.[41]

Daniel Hill, the *Mercury*'s chief mate, feared that he could not realistically re-embark all the convicts and sail away with them. What remained unsaid was the question of where on the face of the earth he could possibly take them to. Rather than actually going away as the attendees of the public meeting had demanded, he settled for a river only slightly to the north of the main settlement. There, out of sight of the majority of Baymen, he put about twenty of the convicts to work cutting wood, gang-labour style, just like the slaves.

Henry Jones, a settler who logged that part of the river, quickly became aware of Hill's actions. Jones got an affidavit to stop the convict work gang and Hill was taken into custody. One of the five magistrates was so enraged that he announced from the 'bench', using hardly the most magisterial language, that Hill 'was a damned old rascal, and if it was not for his years he would break his head'. Meanwhile, in Hill's absence, Jones 'decoyed' the convicts away with promises of freedom and transported them to Cay Chapel, a small islet in the Spanish territory where they were apparently left to starve. The magistrates, meeting at McAulay's house, heartily approved Jones's action, others rushing to declare that they would have acted in just the same way given half a chance.[42]

The problem was, though, that if they were just left there on Cay Chapel the convicts would be 'driven to acts of desperation by the calls of hunger and nakedness'. The Baymen reiterated their former demand. Hill and Captain Arnott were to re-embark all 'the poor, starving wretched convicts', those on Cay Chapel included, and sail away with them to somewhere, anywhere else. The settlers would be only too pleased to contribute towards the costs.[43]

By this point all trust and cooperation between Daniel Hill and Captain Arnott, the only two men left in charge of the *Mercury* after the supercargo's death not long after they reached Honduras Bay, had broken down. By October, according to Hill himself, Arnott led a group of his sailors and some of the felons in an attack on Hill at his hut, and armed with cutlasses and blunderbusses forced him back aboard ship. He claimed to have then been held prisoner on the ship for six weeks, during which time some of the convicts were finally sold to settlers. By the time Hill emerged from his captivity, some were 'running wood' for magistrate McAulay, others were toiling for Magistrate Thomas Potts or for a settler named Davis. According to a half-pay officer who arrived just at this time, the change of heart had been brought about by the suggestion that if the convicts were divided up among the residents and made to work, the danger they posed could be kept to a minimum. Somehow they had been persuaded that their efforts to make the ship sail away were futile and the convicts escaped the threat of Africa.[44]

George Moore lost £4500 as a result of this debacle. Rumours flew that he was bankrupt as a result. He attempted to place some of the blame for the fiasco on Captain Arnott and had him arrested and imprisoned upon his return to England a few years later. It was all in vain; Arnott had only 'some trifle' to give to Moore as a result of the affair. Daniel Hill claimed that he was never paid for the *Mercury*'s voyage, despite having been with the ship for two years.

But Moore was either a glutton for punishment or exceptionally foolhardy, as he believed that the only way to recoup these losses was to assemble another, third, shipment of convicts. One of the very few men who supported his actions was the half-pay officer, who had decided that if the mahogany, logwood and sarsaparilla trades could be built up, the Honduras Bay settlement could receive large numbers of convicts. It was all pie in the sky, as the next of Moore's ever-more-disastrous shipments was to show.[45]

Lord Sydney was growing increasingly desperate, however, and quickly latched on to the idea. The very same day that the case of Captain Arnott vs Daniel Hill was being heard in a Honduras Bay hut before a magistrate and eight jurors, far away in Whitehall Lord Sydney was writing a letter to Governor Clarke of Jamaica. He claimed to have heard from Vice-Admiral Gambier that the *Mercury* convicts 'were likely to have been well received in the Bay of Honduras'. He certainly hoped so, for as he wrote, 'the more I consider the matter the greater difficulty I see in disposing of these people in any other place in the possession of His Majesty's Subjects'.[46]

Chapter Thirteen

THE ONCE MIGHTY ARE FALLEN

By 1784 the chickens were coming home to roost. The war years now over, Britain turned its attentions to the wrongs done in the name of its noble army. Both Kenneth Mackenzie and Joseph Wall stood charged with murdering soldiers who had been under their command on the coast of Africa and with having committed those murders in the most unusual, inhuman ways.

Predictably, neither man took the news well. Joseph Wall, who in 1783 returned to Britain, where his troops were disbanded at Chichester, was put under arrest as 'several charges had been preferred against him by two officers of the African corps'. Wall was taken before a court-martial, but the case fell apart as the ship bringing the witnesses from Africa was believed to have been shipwrecked with the loss of all aboard. Wall, less relieved at his escape than indignant at the whole affair, promptly went to Bath. Perhaps he intended to take the waters for which the town was famous or spend a social season among the country's leading lights, but Bath also had its fair share of gambling opportunities, a vice Wall was well known to enjoy.

Whatever his leisure activities, they were short-lived. With the troops back in Britain, news of his misdeeds spread. Feeling that such gross misdemeanours could not go unpunished another attempt was made to arrest him. Two king's messengers set off to Bath and lost no time placing him in custody. The party set off back to London in a post-chaise but stopped at Reading 'to sup' and rest for the night. There, ale tankard in hand, Wall learned that the new charges against him were not just the crimes alleged by the two officers who had served under his command but a far more serious matter. Joseph Wall found himself under arrest for murder.

After the two messengers had drunk their fill and gone to rest for the night, Wall saw his chance. He climbed out of an open window at the inn and made off into the night. He was by now forty-five, an old man by eighteenth-century standards and his hair, previously said to have been as flame red as his temper, had now faded to a light brown. His determination had not deserted him though. He walked sixty miles away from his captors, only then feeling himself safe to take a coach to Scotland. There he charmed his way into society, quickly becoming enamoured with Frances Mackenzie, sixth daughter of Lord Seaforth. Unaware that the noble gentleman was on the run, Frances's family were apparently happy with the match and the two married. His new wife was a distant cousin of Kenneth Mackenzie, another alleged murderer.

Joseph Wall and his new bride took off for the continent, creatively combining the old tradition of a grand honeymoon tour with life as fugitives. In March 1784 Wall wrote to Lord Sydney, offering to turn himself in as soon as witnesses had been brought from Gorée. By October he wrote to Evan Nepean, Undersecretary of State, that he had applied to the French court for some eyewitnesses he needed for the case to be sent to England and was living 'in daily expectation of its being complied with'.

Such offers were disingenuous, and he and Frances continued life as exiles. Throughout 1785 he wrote letters home from Rome, Turin, Mannheim and Coblenz, mostly dealing with money problems. Even on the run a gentleman had to keep up his lifestyle. He still maintained a servant.[1]

Meanwhile, Kenneth Mackenzie had seen no such opportunities of escape. Arriving back in Britain aboard the *Rotterdam*, he was confined in Newgate, the very place so many of his own former soldiers had once been held. Joseph White, solicitor to the Treasury, was given the job of looking into the case to determine for what, if anything, he should be indicted. Despite vehement protests from authorities in both Lisbon and Ostend about the illicit seizure of their vessels and the mate of the Portuguese ship offering to travel to Britain to state his case, White concluded that they should try him only for the murder of William Murray. The preliminary hearings into that rested largely on the testimony of John Jones, a man who had been serving on the *Active* ordnance ship and had been near Mori at the time of Murray's death.[2]

The prosecution papers charged that Captain Kenneth Mackenzie had murdered Murray by firing him out of a nine-pound cannon. The accusations were more comprehensive than this lone offence, though, and many of Mackenzie's misdemeanours were laid out on the charge sheet. He had been interested solely in his own financial gain, the prosecution alleged, and not only in the matter of making his men work on his plantation. He had not supplied the soldiers 'with Claoths [sic] or necessaries' provided by the government for them and had instead 'appropriated that Subsistence to his own use'. The fact that the troops had been made to labour alongside his newly purchased black slaves was also noted.[3]

Mackenzie was no more broken by these events than Wall, now his distant relative by marriage. Like Wall, he thought himself hard done by and, instead of going on the defensive, came out fighting. As he lingered in jail awaiting his trial, he launched a lawsuit against John Wickey for allegedly stealing his gold dust when he had arrested him. The court notes state that Kenneth Mackenzie 'commenced an Action of Trover against the Def[endan]t late Commander of His Majesty's Ship Rotterdam for 5000 ounces of Gold Dust and 6000 pounds weight of Ivory 1000 Gallons of Brandy 1000 Gallons of Wine & 1000 Gallons of Rum of the value of £10000'.[4] What had happened to the gold dust and the ensuing profits would be a continued source of disgruntlement for Mackenzie long after other matters had been settled.

While in Newgate, Kenneth Mackenzie entertained various visitors in his cell on the masters' side of the jail. Humphrey Bustle, a clerk with the military's Sick and Hurt Board, visited often; a barber named John Patten attended to his hair.[5] In December 1783 he also had another visitor. Jean Hageuron, captain of the *Comte de Flandres*, visited him in Newgate to hear his deposition about the case.[6] He was displeased that the British authorities had decided against prosecuting Mackenzie for piracy.

Into mid-June 1784, Kenneth Mackenzie stayed in jail awaiting trial. The delay was partly self-inflicted as he kept appealing for further witnesses to be brought from Africa. He begged trader Pindar Crawford and two further soldiers to journey home for his defence, a judge having decreed that Mackenzie could not get a fair trial without their evidence.[7] Crawford did not travel to London to testify, having apparently gone 'to leeward' when the request came, but two additional soldiers, William Copeland and Thomas Maple, did return to England. Both convict respites, the two thieves were allowed to set foot in the country from which they had been eternally banished.[8]

It was unsurprising that Mackenzie wanted other men for his defence, as those who had travelled home with him certainly did not have many positive things to say about their captain. William Reeves swore that he had not been paid while in Africa, had received few clothes and had been sick for much of the time. When asked about the soldiers' general treatment, Reeves replied, 'he never gave himself much trouble about us, but let us go about as we liked.' Florence McCarthy, who had originally been with Katenkamp, claimed that he had not been paid while in Africa and neither had he received the money he had been promised from the seizure of the *St Antoine Almas*. His grievances included the fact that the clothes he had with him while in Chatham Barracks were stolen by Mackenzie aboard HMS *Mackerel* and given to those who had arrived from jail.

All the men claimed that they had been treated badly, had not been paid, and had been given insufficient food. The issue of men being put in the slave hole was also raised, with the claim that John Mullory, one of the witnesses, had been punished in this way.[9] During the long months that Mackenzie awaited trial, four of the seven men who had originally been sent home with him disappeared from the case, presumably either dying or, more likely, taking their one chance to abscond and so make sure that they would never be returned to Africa.

Eventually, on 10 December 1784, Kenneth Mackenzie had his day in court. He dressed 'in a full suit of black' and his hair, carefully attended by John Patten for those months in jail, was 'powdered … *à le Grenadier*' (in a queue or plait tied with a ribbon). He cut quite a dash. An observer who saw him that day wrote, 'he is a well made tall man, much pitted with the small pox, and about 30 years of age.'[10] He was actually thirty-six.

Mackenzie had retained two barristers, William Adam and Sir John Silvester, as his defence team. Hiring lawyers for legal defence was just becoming common practice in the 1780s and his employment of them showed that he knew how very serious a predicament he was in. In his hour of need he had turned to an old friend, for Adam was a Scotsman from Kinross and a close friend of Francis Mackenzie, Baron Seaforth. Francis Mackenzie's older brother Thomas had once fought with Kenneth Mackenzie at Ouen's Bay in Jersey, back in the accused man's glory days. John Silvester was a less obvious choice, but was probably a good fit for Mackenzie, being said by one of his contemporaries to be 'vulgar and ineloquent'. Although one of the first members of the London bar, his record at the Old Bailey was poor and he was later known as Black Jack and accused of asking sexual favours from women who asked for his help.[11]

They faced a formidable prosecution team. John Lee, a former solicitor-general and attorney-general, had built up an impressive legal practice after his noteworthy performance in support of the radical John Wilkes. Then there was John Wilson, soon to be Sir John and appointed judge. Of Wilson it was said that 'no man of the profession is held in superior estimation'. The third member of the legal team was William Fielding, son of Sir Henry Fielding, magistrate and author. While some thought him lazy and lacking ambition, others believed that Fielding had inherited his father's brilliance and certainly the name alone was enough to strike fear into the opposing counsel.[12]

In court, standing at the bar where his victim, William Murray, had stood so many times, Mackenzie faced judge and jury. William Fielding opened the indictment, stating that Captain Mackenzie, 'a man of some rank', had gone out to Africa in 1782 and become commander of Fort Mori. He had become enraged by Murray's desertion and after he was recaptured he had sentenced him to immediate death. This much was hardly in doubt. It was the manner of the death, though, to which Fielding drew the court's attention. It was 'an execution performed in a manner totally unheard of in any country': the prisoner had been 'sent … out of the world eagle fashion'. 'I cannot at all figure to my mind,' said Fielding, 'any legal excuse for such an act.'

After the court had ascertained that the original co-accused, John Plunkett, was dead, they moved on to the first witness. John Jones, formerly of HMS *Argo* and HMS *Active*, claimed to have been in Black Town when Mackenzie had starting firing on the local houses in order to have Murray returned. He had then, he said, gone up to Fort Mori and watched the execution as part of a crowd of African observers. Right away, Mackenzie's wisdom in hiring Adam and Silvester was obvious. They doggedly attacked Jones, casting doubt on all his assertions and suggesting that Jones was a dishonest, disreputable man. They had been helped by the fact that Mackenzie knew what Jones's testimony would be, having heard it before at the pre-trial hearing.

Then it was the turn of the three remaining men of the seven who had originally returned from Africa with Captain Mackenzie. William Mortimer was sworn in under his alias, John Mortimer. He testified that he knew that there had been a falling-out between Kenneth Mackenzie and his supposed nephew, but that he did not know what it concerned. At the time he had been at Cape Coast Castle, where he was so sick that he 'never thought to live for a minute'. Having recovered, he was back at Mori in time to witness the events which followed. Captain Mackenzie had threatened to flog 'to death' the soldier who had let Murray escape and had then sent all available men, including himself, to look for him. Mortimer had also been among those whom Mackenzie had ordered to fire the cannons into Black Town when the locals failed to return the runaway.[13]

Mortimer's tale was gripping, with details such as the fact that they had not had any rope to tie Murray to the cannon and had to cut down the rope used to fly the fort's flag. He recalled Murray changing from his 'snuff-colour' coat into his red jacket and his dramatic declaration: 'if I am going to be shot like a dog, let me be shot like a man.' Mortimer added another titbit: Captain Mackenzie's nightcap had been too small for Murray's head and they had struggled to cover his eyes with it. Then, at the last moment, Murray had shouted, 'O for God's sake have mercy on me! … good bye to you all, comrades, and God bless you all.' Adam and Silvester doggedly cross-examined, but Mortimer's testimony was powerful.

Job Cooper next took up the story. Cooper's own part in the proceedings had been to fetch Murray's prayer book for him immediately before his death. Afterwards he had gone down to where 'the carcase [was] after it was shot away' and had 'helped to gather it up'. 'The legs and head were left', he related, 'but the middle part of the body was tore to pieces.' Then the defence struck a blow. Questioned by John Silvester, Cooper admitted that he had heard Murray planning to kill Captain Mackenzie.[14]

Next Phillip Brookes faced John Lee. He had a different tale to tell, as he was the sentry who had let Murray go to the gate at Mori, thereby allowing him to escape. He had done so, he reported, so that Murray could go and get some brandy and he had made Murray promise to return before Captain Mackenzie got up. But he did not return, and Phillip Brookes was given 'near fifteen hundred lashes' for letting him escape. So it was that Brookes was a prisoner when Murray was returned to the fort and put to death. It was astonishing that he had survived to go to London to tell his tale.[15]

Brookes's evidence was the first time that another issue was heard by the court. Two days before the trial started, the defence attorneys had apparently spoken to all the witnesses in a pub called the White House. Quite what had occurred is uncertain, but accusations of bribery and corruption circled the court room.

The next witness was Daniel Munro, the castle gardener who had worked as an overseer on Mackenzie's plantation and had then been in charge at Mori after Mackenzie fled. His report was inconsequential, although he claimed to have once inadvertently sat on the gun from which Murray had been fired. The real importance of his testimony concerned whether he had been bribed by Captain Mackenzie to find out what the other witnesses would say.

William Copeland and Thomas Maple, who had been brought home to testify at Mackenzie's insistence, both gave evidence in defence of their former commander. Copeland had previously complained that he had not been paid or given sufficient food, and had been made to labour on the plantation rather than as a soldier. But in court he related that the other soldiers had approved of Murray having been put to death and had signed a paper to go home on the *Rotterdam* with their captain to that effect.[16]

Then Thomas Maple's evidence established that Murray was a dangerous man. 'He wanted every man to desert out of the fort,' stated Maple on the stand; Murray had particularly encouraged him to work for the Dutch at Elmina in the capacity of a clerk. At the time that Murray was fired from the cannon Maple had in fact been a prisoner in the slave hole, apparently because Kenneth Mackenzie feared that he too was about to run off.

After a couple of army men testified to how dangerous the convict-soldiers had been, Sir John Silvester closed the case for the defence. Afterwards the judge summed up the evidence, excluding that of John Jones, which had been discounted as having been successfully challenged. Then Captain Kenneth Mackenzie himself spoke. He claimed that Job Cooper and William Mortimer had visited him in Newgate and there threatened that if he did not give them £100 each they would assure that he was hanged. On the contrary, Mortimer countered, it was Mackenzie who had invited them to visit and then had offered them money to give positive testimony at the trial.[17]

It was all immaterial. The judge had heard enough. 'Murray Mackenzie was executed by order of the prisoner, in the manner that has been described,' he concluded; it was now for the jury to decide whether he was justified in having done so either by martial law or because it was necessary for his own self-defence. At least the dead man should have been allowed to defend himself, he stated, and could have been sent to Cape Coast Castle for a fair trial. Martial law did not extend to firing men from the mouth of a cannon, the judge declared, 'and though we may have heard of such a kind of punishment in Asia, I am afraid it will not be warranted by any law existing in this country.'[18]

The judge was more inclined to be sympathetic to the charge that Murray's death was required because of the threat he caused to the company's security. It was acknowledged that Kenneth Mackenzie's command over so many convicted felons was a difficult one, and rumours of mutinies had swept through the ranks from the time they had left England. The judge made the following analogy to support the self-defence claim:

> I will put a case, which might have happened something like the present: supposing this Captain, sailing to the coast of Africa, had heard of an insurrection amongst the slaves, and one of them, more desperate than the rest, had threatened to take away his life; if he had sent for the man up, and if upon deck he had taken a pistol and shot him, perhaps it would have been thought self-defence.

In death, William Murray Mackenzie, who had held himself such a gentleman and had once gazed superciliously on Virginia's slaves, was compared to one himself.[19]

It took barely two hours for the jury to reach a verdict. When they returned the outcome was clear, for the judge slipped on the black cap of doom. Kenneth Mackenzie was found guilty of wilful murder. He had, the clerk of the court stated, 'without a trial, and without a hearing, by a violent and hasty order, in a most new and unprecedented manner, hurried an unfortunate wretch into eternity, untried, unheard, and unprepared.' An Old Testament condemnation was uttered: 'Whoso willfully and maliciously sheddeth man's blood, by man shall his blood be shed!' Captain Kenneth Mackenzie was ordered to be hanged by the neck until he was dead and, in the additional punishment reserved for murderers, his body would then be 'dissected and anatomized'. The *Edinburgh Advertiser* reported that he nonetheless 'evinced a most steady composure through the while of this trying scene, and calmly submitted to the verdict'.[20]

It was not the end of the matter. The jury had recommended the defendant for mercy 'in consideration of the wicked persons [he] had under his command' and the following day Mackenzie was given leave to appeal. By January letters began appearing in the media in his favour. A man calling himself 'a constitutional crown lawyer' stated that as the jury had recommended the prisoner to His Majesty's mercy, it would not become the humanity of England to hang him.[21] In his native Scotland the *Caledonian Mercury* published some letters in support of his case making similar claims. It was argued that he should have been tried by a military not criminal court and that his conviction meant that no other officers would now agree to go to Africa, where, as the writer put it, 'nauseous vapours ... in which an European can scarcely exist' already made it difficult enough to find willing men.[22] His supporters compared him with everybody from Captain Cuzens, who had once been wrecked on the Patagonian shore with a band of mutinous midshipmen, to Oliver Cromwell.[23]

In early January, newspapers began reporting that a free pardon was expected for Captain Mackenzie any day. He had been given the 'Royal promise', stated *The Daily Universal Register* on 8 January. But it was not to be a quick procedure. Although more and more short-term respites were offered, Mackenzie languished in Newgate.

In the midst of reports on Captain Mackenzie's trial and his various respites, *The Times* published another short notice. A former slave ship was at Deptford ready to take more convicts to Africa. Those who would sail aboard it, or those on the masters' side at least, were Mackenzie's fellow prisoners at Newgate.[24]

In fact on 14 December 1784, only four days after Kenneth Mackenzie's death sentence was handed down, Lord Sydney had again written to the Company of Merchants begging them to consider taking some more felons at their West African forts. His request was small: he wanted them to take only twenty men.[25] It would hardly make a difference to the vast prison population but Sydney was growing increasingly desperate to show that he was making any progress at all in emptying the overflowing jails.

Sydney had not actually abandoned altogether his earlier idea that Honduras Bay would resolve the convict dilemma, but the media seems largely to have missed or ignored another small group of convicts leaving the country. Towards the end of the previous year George Moore, contractor of the mutinous *Swift* and *Mercury* transports, had sent his third shipment of convicts away. Twenty-nine convicts, only a little more than half the fifty Sydney had agreed to, had been embarked aboard the *Fair American* under the command of Captain Thomas Callow, bound for Honduras Bay.

At first this entirely wrongheaded scheme had seemed a cause for optimism. Lord Sydney had written to Edward Marcus Despard, superintendent of the Honduras Bay settlement, instructing him that the shipment had the 'approbation of government' and that the convicts should 'be employed in cutting Logwood, and the Others to be disposed of, as opportunities may offer'. Despard was ordered to give the ship's captain all the help he required. Also with the ship was a letter from Moore directing Callow not to let the convicts even speak to the seamen nor to let the crew 'on any pretence to pass thro' the barracade [sic]' in an effort to prevent a third insurrection. Whether on account of these precautions or not, Moore managed to send off a shipload of convicts without their raising a mass revolt while still in English waters.[26]

Moore must have breathed a sigh of relief when it passed out of sight of the British coast without incident. It sailed on to Jamaica, where it met with Edward Marcus Despard, who was then visiting the island, and loaded some more unwilling passengers. The ship's records listed them as 'indentured negroes', but what exactly this meant in Jamaica in the mid-1780s is unclear. Most likely it was a euphemism for slaves. So for the first time since earlier in the century, British transported convicts and black slaves sailed aboard the same vessel.[27]

Then, however, rather predictably, things started to go wrong. Arriving back at Honduras Bay in January 1785, Despard told the settlers about the convicts and of Sydney's 'unequivocal' orders that they be accepted. He personally wrote to magistrates and other prominent citizens asking them to employ the convicts. But the community, still reeling from its earlier troubles, refused the new shipment. The ship was ordered to leave within ten days. There were even reports that the Baymen had refused to land those picked up from Jamaica.[28]

Forced to leave Honduras Bay, Callow wrote to Moore, 'We must now proceed to Cape Gracias a Dios [on the] Musquito [sic] shore as the only place likely to land the Convicts.' In other words, they would go to possibly the only place in the Americas where a more marginal British settlement existed. 'I am exceeding Sorry to find your plan, from which you had so great hopes turns out so contrary and is loaded with a train of misfortunes,' Callow sympathised.[29]

Like Honduras Bay, the Mosquito Shore had once been a refuge for buccaneers and misfits, although the Puritans of New England had also briefly flirted with the idea of securing influence in the region. Englishmen in particular settled in the area, their relationships with the local Miskito people bolstered by a mutual hatred of all things Spanish. During the 1720s and 30s a man named William Pitt, distant relative of the Prime Minister of the same name, had decided to leave the Honduras Bay settlement and establish an unofficial colony in the region. By the time the convicts arrived it contained around 2500 British subjects scattered along the coast. The centre was Black River.[30]

The main industry was again logwood and mahogany felling, although equally important to the Mosquito Shore's economy was running contraband to and from the Spanish areas. By the 1760s settlers there were also working sugar plantations, cattle farms and indigo cultivation. At one time during the 1770s Olaudah Equaino, soon to be the most famous black man in Britain, had managed what was intended as a model plantation scheme in the settlement. Disrupted by the American war just like their neighbour to the north, the trouble was still brewing with Spain when the *Fair American* arrived. At just the same time, the governor of Jamaica had been forced to send 600 men and arms to the Mosquito Shore to ensure the settlement's safety. Like the *Mercury*'s earlier arrival at Honduras Bay, it could not have come at a worse time. Although, rather miraculously, the convicts were landed, news that this undertaking was also a disaster would filter back to Britain in the coming months.[31]

So with the idea of America as a convict haven having to be abandoned once more, Lord Sydney turned his attentions back to Africa. After a 'pressing application', the Company agreed to take twenty men despite its long resistance to convict workers. In the end, twenty would go as transported convicts, plus another two as soldiers. The presence of the additional two men raised all the old questions. What, after all, were the twenty convict-workers supposed to do in Africa? What role were they intended to fill if not that of soldier or guard? If only two were specifically marked out as convict-soldiers, the role of the other twenty was decidedly ambiguous. The idea of unoccupied miscreants running wild on the African coast had always made the Company employees' collective blood boil.

The Company had driven a hard bargain. They would pay nothing for the labour of these men, with the British government paying for their 'Maintenance and Earnings', for which it would be invoiced twice yearly. The Company men's sole responsibility, as Lord Sydney wrote to them, was 'to receive and dispose of the said Twenty Men Convicts in the safest and best manner'.[32]

With this agreed upon, Sydney eagerly looked for a ship to transport the chosen twenty men. He wanted them sent off as quickly as possible, away from the heaving jails and out of his remit. First he asked the Company of Merchants to embark the men on their annual storeship. The government would pay the Company for their passage, he assured them.[33] But Gilbert Ross from the Company quickly put paid to that idea. He claimed that other Company members would not agree to the scheme, as they 'entertain such strong Apprehensions of danger from the proposed Passengers'. In view of that, he was 'exceedingly doubtful' that the Company would approve the measure. Finally, the Company told Sydney that the storeship was too full to take the men.[34]

Sydney next tried to get various Royal Navy ships to transport the convicts to Africa. He endeavoured to persuade Captain Edward Thompson to deliver them to their place of banishment, but he and other navy men applied to all refused. Unfortunately for Sydney, it was beyond his powers to compel them to do so.[35]

Finally, early the following year, Sydney found a solution. He contracted with Anthony Calvert, merchant and slave trader, for twenty-two men to be delivered to West Africa. He wrote to the Lords Commissioners of Treasury informing them that he had agreed with Calvert that they would be sent out on his ship *Recovery*, which would be captained by Andrew Hewson. The government would pay £12 each for the twenty men whose upkeep would continue at the government's expense, and the reduced rate of £8 8s for the two who would serve the Company as soldiers. Half would be paid at the time the convicts embarked on the ship and the remainder when the ship brought home proof that the men had 'been landed and delivered into the Custody of the Company's Servants'. The total bill came to £256 16s.[36]

For Calvert this marked an interest in convict transportation that would take his ships to New South Wales in the earliest days of that settlement. In the meantime, though, he was playing all angles. For some years he had contracted to deliver goods to the Company's forts in Africa and this year was no exception.[37] In fact, the *Recovery* had already been contracted to the Company to send out their stores for that year. By agreeing to take the twenty-two convicts aboard as well, he was deliberately going against the Company's wishes. The Company was incensed.

The Company of Merchants held a meeting in late January 1785 and composed a letter to send to Thomas King, Anthony Calvert's business partner, part owner of the *Recovery* and a former slave trader who had once been tried for murdering his human cargo. They demanded that King meet them to discuss the convicts then aboard the *Recovery*, 'contrary to your express Agreement'. They claimed to be worried about the insurance for the ship and demanded that a new policy be implemented to take account of the presence of the felons aboard. The cost of the new policy they would charge to King, Calvert and Captain Hewson.[38]

They also instituted a legal challenge against Andrew Hewson. They claimed that under the terms of the agreement they had signed with King, only goods and passengers agreed by the Company were to be taken aboard the ship. King and Hewson had particularly agreed, it was alleged, not to load anything on their own account, nor anything to which the Company had not specifically consented. Regardless, Hewson had embarked the twenty-two convicts while anchored in the Thames. The convicts were 'people of the most profligate and abandoned Character', leaving them 'apprehensive that they would sustain great Damage by their said Goods and Merchandise being stole, plundered or otherwise destroyed'.[39]

If these stratagems were a last-ditch attempt to have the convicts removed from the ship the Company failed in its objective. Twenty-two men were already earmarked to go. The majority were transported to Gravesend at a cost of £2 2s each, plus the costs of the guard hired to watch them. The travel of the two who were to work as soldiers had been arranged directly through the Treasury solicitors Chamberlayne and White, the same attorneys who had been part of the prosecution team against Kenneth Mackenzie.[40]

At the time of the *Den Keyser*, *Swift* and *Mercury* shipments, any discernible pattern in who was sent aboard and who stayed behind is very hard to see. It was as if the government merely ticked off enough names to fill the spaces and that was that. This time, though, perhaps stung by the criticism of how harsh life was for convicts in Africa, authorities selected the men carefully, choosing the most dangerous offenders. No less than five of the twenty-two were highwaymen. Gone were the days when Englishmen saw highwaymen as chivalrous descendants of Robin Hood; they were generally regarded as profligate and malign offenders.[41]

Irishman Robert Cross, who claimed to have been a naval captain and master-at-arms of HMS *Gibraltar*, had bailed up Sir William Jarvis Twissden in Friern Barnet, which was then to the north of London (and long ago subsumed into the urban sprawl). Brandishing his pistol, Cross had forced Twissden to hand over a gold watch, his purse, his 'red cornelian seals set in gold' and some black silk ribbon. Cross got away but one of the post boys bravely gave chase and caught him before he made Highgate. At the Half Moon pub in Holloway he was searched and found to have Twissden's stolen goods. He produced several character witnesses at trial but was found guilty and sentenced to death, although the court recommended he be shown mercy. Cross's respite had stated that he had to go to Africa for seven years so he had been left behind when some of his fellow prisoners were loaded aboard the *Mercury*. Now he found himself put aboard the *Recovery*.[42]

Another two highway robbers bound for Africa in 1785 were old accomplices. Peter Airey and James Davis had been found guilty of attacking two men in Crouch End, not far from Friern Barnet. They had held up Alderman Henry Kitchen and his travelling companion with pistols and demanded money. Davis's language was merely said to be 'illiberal' while Airey, the more 'outrageous' of the pair, had such an inventively ignoble turn of phrase that Kitchen declared that he had 'never heard such a number of oaths in my life'. Lucky to escape the hangman after initially being found guilty of theft with violence, the terms of their respites were severe. Both were to be transported to Africa for the term of their natural lives. They too went aboard Calvert's *Recovery*.[43]

Not all of the *Recovery* convicts were highwaymen. Against Daniel Hickman's name, the charge read simply 'sodomite'. This was something of a misnomer as he had actually been charged with blackmailing a man over his alleged sodomy rather than the offence itself. In July 1783, he had been found guilty of extorting money from John Miller by using menaces. Miller testified that coming home one night he had found Hickman in his doorway and out of pure good nature had invited him in for a drink. Miller gave his visitor bread and cheese, and when Hickman left afterwards he thought it was the end of the matter.

About two weeks later Miller returned to his apartment late at night to discover Hickman waiting for him. Hickman claimed he had come for 'satisfaction' over what had happened on his previous visit. Miller professed ignorance, causing Hickman to declare he was 'a sodomite ... a thing I abhor above all things on earth'. He threatened prosecution and demanded money from Miller, who, being only a servant himself, had to borrow to pay Hickman off.

A few days later, Hickman made a further demand. He sent a note to Miller:

Sir, I am sorry to acquaint you, that the young man is not entirely satisfied with what you gave me, and if you do not make me ample satisfaction, I will certainly expose you; consider the crime you have committed is dangerous, therefore if you do not chuse [sic] to satisfy me in a handsomer manner than what you have done, I shall to-morrow take a further method.

In court Hickman did not debate the basic facts, saying that he had been on sentry duty when he had begun a conversation with Miller, asking him for some food and water because soldiers' pay was so meagre. A few weeks later he had returned because Miller had been so kind to him and on that occasion he had decided to stay the night. When he had climbed into Miller's bed—hardly an unusual occurrence in the eighteenth century, where many slept cheek-by-jowl with strangers in boarding houses—the man had acted inappropriately. 'He began to act as a Sodomite to me; the same as a man would, if he had a woman in bed with him,' Hickman said. It is unclear if he was alleging seduction or attempted rape, but it hardly mattered in an era when homosexuality was generally abhorred. The money was given to him as Miller begged Hickman not to expose him, the alleged blackmailer claimed.

With the note of demand presented in court, Hickman's story was not believed. Interestingly enough, the judge seemed indifferent to the matter of whether Miller actually had attempted to commit a homosexual act, despite the fact that those convicted of sodomy regularly suffered at the hanging tree. In 1780, Edmund Burke had harangued parliament that sodomy was 'the most detestable' of all offences; at a 1785 trial for sodomy—the next time such a case was heard at the Old Bailey after Hickman's trial—the judge struggled even to articulate the word. He preferred to say that the charge was an 'abominable and detestable crime (not to be mentioned by Christians) called buggery'. Despite such contemporary views, the judge at Hickman's trial concentrated instead on the allegations of blackmail. During the extortion attempts Hickman had apparently declared that 'he did not value his life a damn'. It was just as well, as the sentence delivered at the end of his relatively long and complex trial was death.[44]

The crime was so unusual, however, that the original judge asked for the case to be reviewed. The following January a different judge ruled that Hickman had very properly been found guilty of robbery. Theft was 'a man's being forced to part with his property' which Hickman had done by 'threatening to charge him [Miller] with the greatest of crimes'.[45] The original death sentence stood, but in April of that year he was given a respite on condition of his being transported to Africa for fourteen years. He was also embarked on the *Recovery*. The mistaken marking of his crime as sodomy rather than theft or blackmail can hardly have made his life easy among his new shipmates.[46]

If only the most hardened criminals sailed aboard the *Recovery*, there was still a great deal of chance in the matter of who sailed away to Africa and who remained in jail. Two men who went aboard left their partners in crime behind. Alexander Kennedy and Henry Horne had been condemned to death for highway robbery and their subsequent respite sentenced them to seven years' transportation to Africa, yet only Kennedy was aboard the *Recovery* when she sailed.[47] Similarly William Maynard and William Richardson, sentenced to death for mugging and then offered respites to go to Africa, were separated when the ship sailed; Maynard was aboard while Richardson was left behind. Both Richardson and Horne remained aboard the *Ceres* hulk.[48]

When Cross, Airey, Davis and Hickman went aboard the *Recovery* there was another convict waiting in Newgate with a sentence of transportation to Africa who was not loaded aboard the ship. Mary Humphries, better known as Hell-Fire Moll, had been convicted of robbing a man she claimed was soliciting her sexual services, but whom she did not go with on account of his youth. Sentenced to death, she was reprieved to be transported to Africa for fourteen years. Yet when her fellow Africa respites were delivered to the *Recovery*, Mary Humphries remained in Newgate. It seems that the experiences of Sarah Jordan and Ann Evans, coupled with the extreme reluctance of the Company in Africa to receive women convicts, saved Mary Humphries from that fate.[49]

Like the *Den Keyser*'s, the *Recovery*'s journey was swift and uneventful, the owners, captain and crew eager to get to Africa and get rid of their troublesome cargo without delay. This time there was no outraged Richard Miles to meet the cargo and fire off a disgusted letter to London; he had returned to Britain where, along with Jerome Bernard Weuves, he had set up the company Messrs Miles & Weuves, merchants trading to Africa. His replacement as Governor of Cape Coast Castle was James Morgue, who had been based at Tatumquerry during Mackenzie's time. Like his predecessors he had a bevy of coastal wives, one of whom would bear him a son who would go by the evocatively dual names of James Morgue Jnr and Kofi Koom, and would become a prominent coastal merchant.[50]

The American war was still having a negative effect on the coast when the *Recovery* arrived. The previous year an American rum ship had caused Morgue and his men significant trouble when the vessel's captain had 'used every argument to inflame the minds of the blacks and instil into them that spirit of republican freedom and independence, which they through rebellion have established for themselves, as no arguments are so powerful with the natives as a plentiful supply of rum'. When the ship had sailed close to Anomabu, the governor there had fired on it, causing the local people to dissent against the British, or to become 'insolent' as Morgue imperiously described it. He must have been extremely glad that Mori was no longer the hotbed of discord and duplicity it had been during Kenneth Mackenzie's rule.[51]

Some of Mackenzie's men were still there, though, and they now became the co-workers of the newly arrived *Recovery* men. David Street, who had been injured in the original battle at Elmina, had recovered from his wounds and, showing remarkable resilience, had survived the bouts of malaria which had carried off so many of his shipmates. William Cheatham was still alive and working for the Company. John Sones and John Prime from the *Den Keyser* were also still employed at Commenda. However, the twenty-two convicts just arriving can hardly have missed the grim future foretold by so few survivors.[52]

Another one of the original convict-soldiers was also still in the region. Having testified at the Old Bailey to his ex-captain's conduct, Thomas

Maple, apron-and-teaspoon thief, had been returned to Africa to complete his sentence of army service for the rest of his natural life.[53]

The newly arrived were divided up between some of the smaller forts which had not previously been the home of any convicts. Blackmailer Daniel Hickman was sent to Dixcove at Cape Three Points to the west of Cape Coast. It was a small outpost and in 1785 held few white men. The entire garrison comprised of only two officers ruling over four privates and a gunner. Hickman found that his main circle of acquaintances was now nine African men and boys plus eighteen women, all of whom worked within Dixcove's walls.

He must have been pleased to have had an ally at the fort. Twenty-eight-year-old Richard Buxton had been sentenced to hang for stealing £7 10s from a man in Maidstone, Kent, but was then reprieved on condition that he spend the rest of his days in Africa. Originally the sentence was intended as Fort James in the Gambia River but anywhere in Africa was obviously considered close enough and he had sailed on the *Recovery* bound for Cape Coast. He too then found himself stationed at Dixcove, where he and Hickman were listed on the fort records below the other Europeans but above the Africans, their crimes having apparently committed them to a racial netherworld between the two.[54]

Hickman and Buxton, like the other *Recovery* men, were paid £2 5s per month which occasionally dropped to £2 4s 8d as punishment for some infraction. This was paid not in currency but in 'goods which [their] superiors did not want' and then had to be traded for food and anything else they should need. It meant that the thieves, swindlers and highwaymen quickly had to learn the art of bartering and what foodstuffs to eat, or they would starve. As with any fort soldier, 'blows and curses were a regular part of his education ... and unless he possessed both a tough frame and stout heart, one to stand against the climate and the other to keep him from despair, his days were likely to be both short and miserable.'[55]

It certainly proved a very short life for most of the *Recovery*'s migrants. The first couple of months passed in a blur as the men tried to inure themselves to their new situations, but then the rains set in, cloudbursts and deluges which totally changed the landscape and were nothing like Britain's damp drizzle. With the rain came the mosquitoes and the dying began.

First to succumb was highwayman Peter Airey on 15 July. Nathaniel Wallis, thief, followed him to the grave nine days later. Ephraim Abrahams, who was known to the Old Bailey as Ephraim Ephraims and had been found guilty of a mugging, died on 9 August. His respite from death had granted him less than seven extra months of existence. Two days later Alexander Kennedy followed him to the grave. On the final day of August a hole was dug for the body of James Roberts, another of the highwaymen aboard the *Recovery*. After an interval in September, in October the dying began again. Robert Cross, who had terrorised Sir William Jarvis Twissden, died on 21 October.[56]

By the end of the year only a few of the *Recovery*'s felons were left on the Company's books. John Harvey, alias Seagrave, had stolen clothing, silver buckles and a gold and diamond pin from Sir George Onesiphorus Paul, who was staying at Boodle's club. Unfortunately for Harvey the pin was distinctive and word quickly spread that it had been stolen. He was apprehended trying to pawn it. At trial Sir George's valet was asked whether the stolen goods had amounted to more than the forty shillings which brought an automatic death penalty. 'Yes, my Lord,' he replied, 'for they were almost new.' Harvey, given a capital sentence, was reprieved to go to Africa, but the buckle and pin proved fatal anyway. He died on 16 December 1785.[57]

Daniel Hickman was still alive at Dixcove, another couple of men named Davis and Barker were stationed at Anomabu, and Thomas Turner was working at Cape Coast Castle. Turner had stolen a large number of household items from an apartment above a mews and had nearly escaped punishment on the grounds that the premises did not constitute a dwelling house. But after the judges had considered the legal fine print, he was convicted and sentenced to go to Africa for fourteen years.[58]

Turner was joined at the castle in late 1785 by John Miles, a single convict sent out on the Company's annual storeship *Commerce*. With him had gone a letter simply stating that 'at the particular Desire of Government' the Company was to 'receive and employ [Miles] as you see best for the Publick Service'. There appears to be no record of protest at the government's demand, but they took the instructions lightly. By April of the following year, having spent only a few scant months' serving the Company, Miles left their employ and went to work for a private merchant recorded only as 'mr. M'. On 8 June 1786 Thomas Turner succumbed to some unknown disease. At Cape Coast, none of the latterly transported convicts remained.[59]

The government was certainly not giving up on the idea of transporting convicts to Africa, however. At the same time the *Recovery* was being dispatched, the British government was devising a plan to found a convict colony in a different part of Africa. Countless convicts were having their sentences changed in preparation. The government had settled on an area in the Gambia River.

Chapter Fourteen

LEMANE ISLAND

By 1785 another part of Africa was the chosen destination for a large-scale convict scheme, one which it was hoped would prove a long-term solution to the prisons crisis. Given the opposition among a number of concerned parties to sending convicts to the continent it was a bold move. Only two years earlier even a high court judge, Edward Willes, had declared that he would rather hang prisoners than send them to Africa.[1] But with few other options the British government proceeded with their plan.

The idea to form a convict colony on Lemane Island in the Gambia River was largely the brainchild of one John Barnes, former merchant and resident of the Senegambia region. Sometime at the end of 1784 he had detailed the island's many benefits for this purpose and the plan had landed on the desk of the increasingly desperate Lord Sydney.

Barnes had never set foot on the island which now became the focus of government hopes, and though he had passed it twice, it had been some twenty-eight years since he had been there. Lemane, he now reported, obviously casting about in his memory, had 'appeared to him a very fine

Island, 10 or 12 Miles in Length', which did not seem to flood in the rainy season and was already partly cultivated with rice and corn. He thought that the island could support three or four thousand people and that two or three hundred armed Europeans could not 'liberate' themselves from it, 'on Account of the different Rivers running into the Gambia, and because the Blacks would not suffer them to be in their Country'. Away from all 'Means of Debauchery' the convicts could soon be reformed, he wrote optimistically.[2]

Barnes's plan reflected a suggestion already put forward by Edward Morse, who had been the Chief Justice of Senegambia from 1772. In June 1784 Morse had written a list of pros and cons about making the Gambia River region into a colony, though his scheme did not focus specifically on Lemane Island. Morse believed that many convicts could be employed in the region 'to great Advantage'. Another idealist who believed that idleness rather than evil was behind most of the crime in Britain, he had expressed his opinion that:

> I am not singular in opinion that Convicts may be made useful People. I conceive that the great, and perhaps only, Inducement to Theft are Idleness, and the Facility with which stolen Goods are disposed of in London. In Gambia they would not have much Opportunity or temptation to steal, or if they had, it would be impossible for them to dispose of the Things stolen without being detected. The Cause being removed the Effect will cease, and it is reasonable to conclude that a major part of them would get into an habit of Industry, the sweets of which they would soon feel the Effect of, and having a Property to defend would become useful Members of Society.[3]

In the coming years Morse would refine these plans. Reflecting all those old ideas about gold and untold wealth which went back to the legends of

King Solomon's mines and the days of the disastrous Senegambia colony, Morse believed that if Britain shipped its convicts to the Gambia they could quickly bring profit to the motherland. 'It is very well known that the great, if not the major part of the Gold purchased by the natives of Africa is collected by them at, and near the Rivers and Waterfalls, the violence of which washes down great quantities of Earth which carry the Gold with it,' he reported. He told the story of a London merchant who had requested a slave-ship captain to bring a firkin of sand (about forty-one litres) from the River Gambia home with him, from which he claimed to have extracted so much gold that it had sold for £30. Morse's imaginings led to the prospect of countless unwanted British miscreants gathering gold by hand on the African coast, their every movement watched over by guards who would be collecting the gold for some higher imperial purpose.[4]

Sydney can hardly have imagined such a golden utopia but he was remarkably quick to adopt the outline of Barnes's scheme, the lack of viable alternatives causing optimism to prevail over a cooler head. It was rather ironic, though, as just at this time John Roberts, former Acting Governor of Cape Coast Castle, finally became a defector in the Company's long-running opposition to accepting convicts there. The plan he submitted to the government involved the taking of 200 convicts annually at the castle, where they would be put to work in chained labour gangs, guarded over by African 'bomboys', producing cotton. He calculated that within five years they would pay back the government's investment. Roberts admitted that many people would be surprised at this sudden reversal in the Company's position on convicts at the castle, but if Britain's felons were going to be shipped to Africa, much better that they be put to use in cotton cultivation than being sent as soldiers. Mackenzie's men had showed all too well the foolishness of that.[5]

Ignoring this plan, Sydney instead began putting the Lemane scheme into action. Robert Heatley, a merchant who had been to the region two years earlier as captain of the slaver *Ferret*, offered to go as captain of a ship to guard the settlement as long as he received an annual salary of £700. It would be enough, he explained, to mean that he would not have to be engaged in the slave trade to supplement his income. The island itself could be rented from local chiefs for about £100 to £150 per annum, he estimated, while the costs of setting up the penal outpost 'would not exceed 1000 pounds'.[6]

Anthony Calvert, London merchant and slave trader, tendered to ship 150 convicts to Lemane. Having shipped the twenty *Recovery* convicts to Cape Coast Castle, he now proposed to charge the government £8 per convict to take the unwanted felons and their belongings to the island—or as near as his ship could get—plus a demurrage charge to be paid for a month after the ship's arrival.[7]

Most staggeringly of all, Richard Bradley had already been dispatched to 'buy' or rent—the details were sketchy, as in so many of Britain's overseas dealings with 'natives'—the island of Lemane for the purpose of settling convicts there.[8]

With far more than the proposed 150 initial convicts to choose from, officials also set about deciding which of the men, women and children from the bursting jails were to suffer this particular form of punishment. Top of the list was John Martin, the African-American seaman who had been put aboard the *Den Keyser* but then removed as he was suffering from typhus. Now recovered, with both a sentence of transportation directly to Africa and dark skin, he was the first man to be considered a suitable candidate.

William Richardson and Henry Horne were also among those officials selected. Their partners in crime, Alexander Kennedy and William

Maynard, had already gone to Africa aboard the *Recovery*, and there had paid the ultimate price for their offences. Mary Humphries, a.k.a Hell-fire Moll, the woman sentenced to transportation to Africa who had been left behind when the *Recovery* felons had been embarked, was now also on the first list of those who were sentenced specifically to Lemane.

John Ruglass and Samuel Woodham, the two young boys who had escaped from Gorée after being delivered from the *Den Keyser*, were also now marked down to go to Lemane. Both had been recaptured in London and sent back to Newgate, where they had again appeared in court, this time charged with having returned from transportation. Held at His Majesty's pleasure until the government could decide what to do with them, it was over a year before Woodham heard his fate and only slightly less for Ruglass. Then came the news that they would be 'pardoned on condition of serving for life in his Majesties [sic] Corps of Foot on the Coast of Africa'. They were ideal candidates for Lemane.[9]

Among the initial ninety-seven names chosen one was missing. Thomas Limpus, whiling away the years aboard the *Dunkirk* hulk at Plymouth, was not one of the convicts originally destined for Lemane. Possibly because conditions in the jails were a more pressing problem than those on the hulks, candidates were more likely to be drawn from the nation's prisons. At Newgate, Adair would choose twenty-two who 'appear[ed] to be the most proper to be treated with severity' to be banished to Lemane. To send some of those chosen to Africa required an Order of Court as their respite had sentenced them to America and to change that required official sanction, but Sydney ploughed ahead, unconcerned by this stricture.[10]

If Sydney was trying to keep the scheme quiet his attempts failed. By early February 1785 it was reported in the media, with the *Bristol Journal* writing that 'Government have contracted with the African Company to transport 150 felons to the coast of Africa.' 'What will be the fate of these unhappy wretches?,' it asked, before answering the rhetorical question with its own dreadful image. 'As soon as the natives hear of their arrival,' it supposed, 'they will steal their tools, fishing tackle, &c. and afterwards murder them one after another.' It was another interesting take on who exactly would be a threat to whom if a penal colony were founded in Africa. British felons were apparently far too evil and malign for civilised England, but would be no match for murderous 'natives'.[11]

A week later the citizens of London heard the news from the *Chronicle and Daily Advertiser*. An anonymous 'correspondent' had told the paper that between two and three hundred felons were going on the *Grampus* to 'an island about 500 miles up the river Gambia, and there left to provide for themselves as they can'. The writer railed against these rumours on many grounds: the risk that they would become 'an asylum and nursery for pirates and thieves', the trouble they would cause to the 'almost defenceless factories of the African Company', the fact that the local French, Dutch and Portuguese would not allow such a settlement, and of course that they would have 'no protection against the treachery and savage dispositions of the natives'. The only thing which could protect the convicts against the wild Africans, the journalist suggested, was if a government was formed on the island to protect them, but then the problem would be that the colony ran the danger of becoming 'opulent'. Two days later the *General Evening Post* expanded on the theme, warning that the locals around Lemane 'sacrifice to their idol deities such white men as fall into their hands, and whose bodies they devour'.[12]

As a new hulk, the *Ceres*, was established for those who were destined for Lemane, Edmund Burke addressed the rumours of a planned African penal colony in parliament. Attacking the government's record in transportation, he alleged that 100,000 convicts were awaiting removal—a ludicrously high estimate—and stated that he hoped they were not destined for Gambia, which he called 'the capital seat of plague, pestilence and famine. The gates of Hell were there open night and day to receive the victims of the law,' he told the House.[13]

By early April Lord Beauchamp was also raising the matter in parliament, calling for an inquiry into any such scheme. It was mocking the idea of the mercy of respites, Burke again claimed, to send felons away to a place where their death would be far worse than anything they might suffer at the hands of Britain's hangmen. Pitt protested at the two men's allegations, but it was decided that a committee would be held into the matter with Beauchamp as chairman.

The committee began its inquiry at the end of the month, beginning with a series of testimonies as to the state of the severely overcrowded jails. Then Evan Nepean, Undersecretary to Sydney, reported on details of the Lemane plan. Asked whether the island had been settled upon, Nepean reported that it was 'preferred to every other Plan tho' is not finally resolved upon'. The idea was that 200 of the most notorious felons—so dangerous they were every day expected to launch a jailbreak—would go on a ship supplied by Anthony Calvert. They would be supplied with 'framing for their Inhabitants[,] Tools to construct them and for cultivating the Land— Merchandize to provide stock and Grain for sowing' and 'with a Proportion of Provisions till they could raise Stock for themselves'. There would be women as well as men, and Nepean even held out the preposterous image of convicts who had been trained in the medical profession working as doctors and tending to the needs of the sick. To questions about the local people, Nepean replied that the 'Natives contiguous are inoffensive'.

John Barnes, the scheme's advocate, gave a glowing report on the area, as could be expected. 'The Natives are the best disposed people in the World,' he enthused, also arguing that the climate was far less deadly than at the coast. On these two points, however, believed to be crucial during the era of transportation to Africa, the committee heard many far less positive reports. Boone, an army surgeon who had lived at Senegal, testified that 'fevers and fluxes' carried off two-thirds of the men stationed under him each year and that no European made to do agricultural labour would survive longer than a month unless he had a good surgeon to attend him. Far from the native people being friendly, Boone offered the opinion that they would soon rob the convict settlers of all their tools, leaving them unable to grow their own food.

John Call, who had lived in Africa in the 1750s and who offered as his credentials that he had seen the mouth of the Gambia River, added to this image of mass death and murderous Africans. Having arrived at the settlement already debilitated, Call foresaw, the convicts would soon either die from the diseases or at the hands of the natives, or would revolt and could take a ship trading in the river. Sending a naval ship to guard the island would mean 'sacrificing 50 or 60 good Subjects annually to taking care of 2 or 300 Convicts'.

The negative reception to the plan was continued by Sir George Young, who told the committee that he considered the Gambia River region to be the least healthy part of the West African coast for Europeans. Any white men who did labour in such a climate 'would be killed if they were to continue in the Sun an Hour', he argued, reaffirming the belief that if a naval ship had to be sent out to guard the settlement, it would mean 'Death to all the Crew'. Young's other objections were equally firm and reflected those of Company men from the beginnings of the scheme so long ago when Kenneth Mackenzie had led two independent companies to Africa. A colony of convicts would cause 'riot & Confusion', he suggested, and would lead to Europeans being devalued in Africans' eyes, as they 'would take every White man then for an English Thief'.

The Mackenzie debacle was also partially relived for the committee by a man named Stuart who had been with the initial party led by Captain Shirley. He revived some of the less successful parts of that expedition for those of the committee who had not heard of the disaster: the deaths on the way from typhus, the lack of discipline, the eagerness with which the convicts had run away to the Dutch, the escape of those aboard the *Comte de Flandres* (who may or may not have become pirates). As Stuart correctly intimated, it hardly boded well.

The next man to testify had rather more of an interest in any prospective penal colony than he publicly allowed. Edward 'Ned' Thompson was the third surviving son of a prosperous 'sugar-baker' from Hull, an aspiring poet, an avowed republican in a country of monarchists, a hater of all things Scottish, and a naval captain. He was now also in all expectations of being chosen as governor of the new African penal colony.[14]

On 23 July 1783, Thompson had been appointed to overall naval command of the coast of Africa, a post Lord Keppel had apologised over as he offered it, 'saying he was sorry, he had nothing better, but this should be followed by some thing superior'. Nonetheless, Thompson had immediately set about making the best of his assignment, offering to make an exploration of south-west Africa, the unclaimed region sandwiched between the Portuguese to the north and the Dutch to the south, where he claimed there were natural harbours, fertile land and a healthy climate. If Britain should acquire such territory it would prove invaluable 'for our Indiamen to call at to refit & to come up with SE trade in war to avoid the enemy—without returning the beaten road from the Cape & necessity of putting into the Rio de Janeiro'. This magical unspoken-for location was, thought Thompson, 'between Cape Da Sierra & Cape Das Voltas'.[15]

Lord Keppel was interested in the plan but, unwilling to risk any conflict so soon after the end of the American war, advised Thompson to wait until the following year to begin his survey of the region. So Thompson sailed around the coast further north, meeting many of those who had played a role in the convict affair so far, and some of the remainder of the convict-soldiers still alive on the coast. At Mori he performed an inventory of all the weaponry, furniture and other items left behind when Mackenzie and his men had departed the fort. He found there a 'gold headed cane' which had belonged to Captain Mackenzie. More ominously, Thompson became involved in trying to soothe feathers still ruffled as a result of Mackenzie's actions, meeting Africans who complained that they had never been paid the promised amount for fighting in the various conflicts Mackenzie had engaged in.[16]

A man of education, Thompson also set about studying Africans. To this end, at Anomabu he purchased a 'ballad-singing monkey', whom he named Jenny Oakum, and hired a servant to care for it. His interest in Jenny was not purely as a pet, as the ideas of French naturalist the Comte de Buffon, then among the most progressive in the world, suggested that man had descended from chimpanzees. Hoping to teach Jenny to talk, Thompson wrote in his diary: 'Buffon proves the anatomy progressive from Monkey to Negro to man, and that there is no difference but what is in the brain, being smaller in both, than in the European.' Jenny died of a 'bloody flux' he too had been suffering from before she mastered any of his poems.[17]

In these travels Thompson saw no area of the mainland which he thought suitable for a penal colony. In fact he thought the whole idea untenable. 'A Negro's first passion is Jealousy,' he wrote one day while anchored off Appolonia, 'and though he [may] suffer you to build a Fort— yet the Attempt of extending that Power to a Town, or *Colonization* would rouse every latent Resentment in the Negroe & thwart every Plan of such Intentions.' Worse still, even for those who survived the inevitable ravages of disease, there would really be no hope of convicts producing enough children to form a real settlement, Thompson feared. British women could never survive let alone reproduce in Africa, he believed, writing that 'the Heat of the Climate is so intense, that it is immediately fatal to English Women, it stops the Menses & they expire in Madness'.[18]

Returning home in August 1784 he immediately reported these concerns to Pitt, only to be told to report to Sydney. Instead of Africa, he promoted the idea of Britain taking Demerara and Essequibo on the Caribbean coast of South America, which he thought would compensate Britain for the loss of her other American colonies. His poetic tendencies came to the fore, writing of 'that Country which Sir Walter Raleigh named Golden'. He also for the first time linked the settlement of Britain's convicts with another pressing problem: where to put the loyalists who had left the now-independent territory of North America out of devotion to George III. Both groups, Thompson suggested confidently, could be settled in Demerara and Essequibo, a place which would be 'joyfully embraced' by the loyalists and offer an 'advantageous asylum' for those crowded in Britain's jails.[19]

The only West African location Thompson advocated for a convict colony was São Tomé, a small island in the crook of the Gulf of Guinea which had been claimed by the Portuguese for centuries. Now an 'elegant wilderness', the island had, as Thompson reported to an Undersecretary of State, once been cultivated and had produced considerable sugar. The Portuguese had largely abandoned their plantations there in favour of the larger scale agriculture of Brazil, but Thompson thought that the island's soil could once again be cultivated, this time using British convict labour. He saw an island paradise of transported convicts working as 'Mechanics & Husbandmen' being useful to their home nation, which was all a far cry from the likely outcome if they were shipped to mainland Africa, where they were 'doomed to be Soldiers & their lives are but of very short duration'.[20]

Edward Thompson was one of the men who had been party to Lord Sydney's Lemane scheme before it had become general knowledge. On 3 January 1785 he had 'a long conference with Lord Sidney about the state of the public jayles [sic] & the disposal of the convicts', during which he had heard about the planned penal settlement on Lemane Island. He was unequivocal in his opinion. 'I answered his Lord,' he wrote later that day in his diary, that 'there was an inhuman appearance in the style of the business, & it would never be received by the people of England—it was in one word an African grave, & they went there devoted to Death.' It was a retort so shockingly bold that Pitt himself showed up to hear Thompson's objections. Pitt and Sydney stressed again the importance of emptying the jails and Thompson, seeking to appease, offered to investigate the Sierra Leone region as a possible alternative.[21]

In the following months Thompson remained in London, however, frequently meeting with various government officials to discuss the convict problem. In February he again saw Lord Sydney and discussed the Gambia region; in March, still opposed to the Lemane plan, he returned to his much earlier idea of a penal settlement in south-west Africa. He went so far as to provide Sydney with 'a sketch of a plan, on the settling Cape Voltas for the Loyalists of America & the Convicts' to that end. 'This exile to Gambia,' he still believed, 'is more than death.' In April he came up with another suggestion: sentencing more hanged men and women to have their bodies dissected after death would deter crime, he argued, conjecturing that it was the mutilation of their bodies, with its attendant fears for an afterlife, which would frighten the 'criminal classes'.[22]

It was at this juncture that Thompson appeared before the committee investigating the Lemane proposal. His earlier vehement objections to the plan and his alternative suggestions remained unvoiced as he gave his evidence, now far more temperately worded than in his private meetings

with Pitt and Sydney. Nevertheless his evidence was unambiguous—
Lemane would simply not do. A settlement there would 'incense the Native
to be more Barbarous', he stated, and be of no use whatsoever to Britain.
He painted an image of the male convicts taking local brides while female
convicts would ail and die in short order. Again invoking the disaster of
Mackenzie's independent troops, Thompson told the committee that a
Lemane colony could only end in doom and ruination.

After Thompson's testimony, various other schemes and suggestions
were then put before the committee as it finished its collection of evidence.
.Mr Call returned with another suggestion—the settlement of south-
west Africa—which mirrored Thompson's 'Cape Voltas' idea. Henry
Smeathman, a botanist and fly-catching enthusiast, suggested the Banana
Islands in the Sierra Leone estuary, 'reckoned the most healthy part of the
Country', as a more suitable alternative to Lemane.

Then two men made an even more outlandish suggestion. James Mario
Matra and Sir Joseph Banks suggested that New South Wales, a land seen
some fifteen years earlier by Captain James Cook, could be settled by the
convicts, plus some willing ladies from Tahiti to keep them company. Part
Elysian dream of Tahitian beauties, which had captivated European men
for some decades, part myth of empty southern lands which balanced out
the crowded northern hemisphere, this was perhaps the most eccentric
idea of all, notwithstanding its noble advocate. More sensibly, Charles
Thomas Coggan gave answers on the feasibility of shipping the convicts
to India.[23]

On 9 May, the committee placed its report before the House of
Commons, providing no definitive recommendation to go with the mass
of evidence. A newspaper reported that the whole scheme had been shown
to be 'a means for establishing a nest of pirates which afterwards might
be a piratical state'. In late July, however, it issued a second report, this

one with a far more interpretive account of the evidence and suggestions for the future. It reiterated what had been one of the main objections to transportation to Africa all along. Quite simply, if convicts were just sent away to die, then it raised serious questions about the meaning of the Royal pardon. Moreover, and harking back to the frequent complaints of slave traders, discipline for any convict settlement would be essential. It was not sufficient to merely drop off the expelled in the chosen location and leave them to fend for themselves; such a deed would only end in carnage. Something far more concrete was required; after all, 'the outcasts of an old society would never serve as the sole foundation of a new one'.[24]

The committee must have seen and admired Edward Thompson's plans for a convict colony at Das Voltas, submitted the previous March, as it now turned its attentions to a similar scheme. It even adopted some of his sentences verbatim in its new report. Near the 'great river of Das Voltas' it imagined 'a rich copper vein', hospitable natives, abundant cattle, sheep and horses, a climate where 'not a cloud appeared in the sky', fine harbours where Royal Navy ships could anchor safely and fertile soil. Envisaging a colony where Britain's unwanted miscreants could rise to some greater good when put to use by the American loyalists who would also be in this new utopia, the settlement would soon benefit Britain as a place from where to run whaling expeditions to the South Seas and ships could break up their long voyages home from India and even further east. There would be a superintendent, a forty-gun ship, two additional guardships and no less than three companies of marines, all costing an estimated £18,669. Somehow, the Lemane plan of abandoning the unwanted dross of Britain to fend for themselves somewhere up the Gambia River had become an all-out scheme of colonisation somewhere in south-west Africa at some isolated spot the British believed had so far been mysteriously overlooked by their European rivals.[25]

It was just as well that the Lemane plan had been abandoned, as Richard Bradley's efforts to buy the island for the crown had descended into farce. Stopping to purchase some goods to take upriver as 'dashes'—that is, gifts or bribes—he had been blackmailed by a local trader into buying far more merchandise than he had intended. Then he had been made to pay a large number of 'barrs', or small iron bars worth five shillings each, to local figures. Bradley paid barrs not only to such dignitaries as the 'King of Barra' and the 'master of Gilifree' but to two 'Key Keepers', the 'Tobabmanser of Jancacunda' and to the latter's retinue of fifty servants. The Tobabmanser was unable to conduct any negotiations without his 'singing Man' (who also required payment in barrs of course), and when the 'King of Lemain' arrived he also brought a large retinue of servants, including the requisite key keeper, singing man and principal marabout. The whole negotiations cost much more than Bradley had anticipated, and during the palaver, wilting in the West African rainforest, he sickened and died. Later, his brother Henry would proudly announce to Sydney that the island had been purchased, only to discover that he had laboured in vain as the government had abandoned the plan.[26]

The move to establish a colony in southern rather than western Africa may have been pushed along by a letter received by the government from Mrs Diana Dalrymple, the wife of Colonel Dalrymple of the 73rd Regiment, written sometime in the summer of 1785. Forced to leave his station in India because of bad health, her husband had sailed aboard the Indiaman *Pigot*, hoping to return to the cooler climate of England, his loving wife and good health. Instead, by the time the ship was rounding the coast of southern Africa, so many of the seamen were sick and the ship was so leaky that all aboard feared for their safety if they faced the notorious storms and huge seas of the Cape of Good Hope in that condition. After a public meeting aboard, all agreed to stop at the Cape to allow the crew to recover their strength. Four days later it became apparent that even this was an optimistic scenario. They had no choice but to put into any bay they could find and soon found themselves in an area of a few remote Dutch settlers, far to the east of the main Cape colony.[27]

There, amid the dead bodies as their shipmates continued to succumb to scurvy, Colonel Dalrymple became enchanted with this part of Africa. 'It is the finest soil I ever saw, with a divine Climate,' he enthused, imagining the cultivation of 'Wheat, Corns, Cabbages, Potatoes &c &c' in addition to the fish which was easily caught in the bay, fine oranges and even 'a tolerable Wine'. They were, he believed, about forty or fifty leagues eastward of Plettenberg Bay, in a place he called Gromarivire [Krom River] Bay.

He began to dream of a settlement there, using many of the same arguments for its strategic importance for ships heading out to India as had attracted Edward Thompson to the region of Das Voltas. The indigenous people were, if not friendly, then at least 'ignorant of the use of Fire Arms' and hostile to the Dutch, whom Dalrymple knew would oppose any such settlement in the region. A colony could compensate Britain for the loss of her American colonies and it could be a 'paradise' to her transported convicts, who could surely find valuable employment in such an Eden. Quite convinced, Dalrymple had written to his wife, telling her to write to the government of his plans. He himself would go with 200 men to found the colony and, presumably, to act as its governor. Diana Dalrymple dutifully sent on his detailed plans for this glorious colony.[28]

It hardly mattered at that moment, though, as anything other than further evidence that a settlement in southern Africa might answer their needs. Edward Thompson was going out to survey the Das Voltas region and find a suitable spot, and hopefully that would mean the beginning of the end of the crisis. He left at the end of September, the King's younger brother Prince William Henry visiting Spithead just before the expedition set off to wish them luck.

Thompson could not sail directly for the south-western coast of Africa, however, first having to return to West Africa to continue the work of rectifying the harm done by Kenneth Mackenzie during his time on the coast. He believed that if he could satisfy the Fante people then those all along the coast might be appeased, and though they claimed to have been promised £1000 in goods by Mackenzie, Thompson eventually settled with them to the tune of £400. But the people at Cape Coast and Commenda demanded the same as the Fante plus eight ounces of trade 'dead Money' for the men they had lost during the battles over Elmina and the Dutch fort at Commenda. Thompson offered £100 and a puncheon (over 300 litres) of alcohol but this was rejected and the locals began a blockade of Cape Coast Castle. Edward Thompson, eager to leave the Gold Coast and begin his survey of south-west Africa, was forced into a hasty compromise. It should have been a timely reminder that mixing convicts and the slave trade was an extremely bad idea.[29]

Thompson and his crew also met the remainder of Mackenzie's men who were still living and working on the coast, having lost so many of their former brothers in arms. At Prampram fort, in such bad repair that they recommended it be demolished, they found William Cheatham, grown to adulthood in West Africa's harsh climate. At Cape Coast Castle they met six of the independent companies' convict-soldiers, including Thomas Randall and David Street, plus Thomas Turner, who had arrived aboard the *Recovery*. Visiting Commenda, they discovered that *Den Keyser* men Prime and Sones were still alive, while at Anomabu they met with Thomas Barker and James Davis, shipmates from the *Recovery*. Dixcove, they reported, also had one unnamed convict who had been promoted to sergeant. It was a scant number from the close to 250 souls who had been sent there to atone for their crimes.[30]

In December 1785, as Thompson was meeting with the survivors of the independent companies disaster, their former commander was finally leaving jail. He had been imprisoned in Newgate for two years by this time, the first year awaiting trial and the second as a series of reprieves had been granted. There was more to his long wait than that however. All throughout 1785, during the Lemane inquiry and the government's prevarication over where to send its banished criminals, the media had kept the country informed of the twists and turns in the saga of Captain Kenneth Mackenzie.

In May, having been allowed the 'indulgence' of walking around the jail—a right not normally granted those capitally convicted—he had contracted a 'bilious fever' and was dangerously ill. By June it was said that he had suffered 'a paryletic stroke' and was 'miserably emaciated'. It was *The Times* which finally informed the population what was causing the hold-up in releasing the prisoner. Mackenzie had refused to pay the fees of the jail which any prisoner had to disburse. He had, the paper alleged, 'written a letter to the Secretary of State in a stile [sic] of disrespect becoming a man in his situation'.[31] Captain Kenneth Mackenzie was never a man who quit when he was ahead.

In fact Mackenzie was in jail long enough that a short book, *An Address to the Officers of the British Army*, was written which argued his case on several points. It ridiculed his having been tried by a civilian court, remarking that 'the expedients of the Commander of a Garrison of convicts on the coast of Africa, can be little understood by [a jury of] London tradesmen'. The author visited Mackenzie in jail and may well have been an old acquaintance, for he reported anew the captain's defence of his actions, how terrible his men had been, and the threats made to his life.[32] Whether it made a difference or not is unclear, but certainly the government could eventually delay his pardon no longer. In December 1785, Kenneth Mackenzie was finally given a free pardon. As his father had died in May while he was still in jail, he walked out of Newgate bearing the title Redcastle.[33]

Whatever the justice of his pardon, there was certainly plenty of irony involved from a wider perspective. Mackenzie was, after all, shown clemency for committing a crime far more heinous than those of the men who had served under him in Africa. Among his ranks had been handkerchief and ribbon thieves, sheep and cattle rustlers, and petty forgers. Some of the robbers had used violence in their crimes but very few indeed had been convicted of actual crimes against the person. They, nonetheless, had been sent to Africa to atone for their sins, where many had quickly died from malaria, yellow fever and dysentery, while Kenneth Mackenzie walked from Newgate a free man.[34]

The man who signed Mackenzie's final pardon was Thomas Townshend, who signed with his title, meaning that Captain Kenneth Mackenzie's pardon rather prophetically bore the single word 'Sydney'.[35] But as 1785 drew to a close, the idea that the land christened New South Wales by James Cook would be the future of convict transportation was as far away as ever.

As the cold Christmas season progressed, it seemed clear what the future held. Captain Edward Thompson would seek a location in south-west Africa where he would found a colony which would be a new home to both American loyalists and transported convicts. Thompson, who believed Americans were his brothers and had accordingly refused to fight in the American Revolutionary War (though he had quickly entered the fray when the dastardly, non-fraternal French had joined in) had enthusiastically made the convict crisis his business and was evidently expecting to be governor.[36]

The government had already begun asking for tenders to ship the convicts out to the new colony. The company of Turnbull, Macaulay and Gregory calculated it would cost fifteen guineas per head to ship 500 convicts to '30° south on the coast of Africa'. Anthony Calvert tendered to take 850 men and 150 women there for £20 per head. Ever the successful slave trader, he mentioned specifically that the felons would have 'sufficient airings, gratings, security etc' during their journey. Duncan Campbell, keeper of the hulks, matched Calvert's figure.[37]

Whatever his visions of this loyalist–convict utopia might have been, Thompson was clearly not intending to call any new settlement after the Secretary of State. When the man he knew as Tommy Townshend had taken his title in 1783, Ned Thompson had been driven to poetry to express his derision. He had written that day in his diary:

> To hither Tommy, tell one what's thy claim
> Did ever Sense or Honour hear thy name
> Or art thou mention'd in the paye of Fame?
> Blush if thou hast a blush upon thy skin
> For this preposterous, patriot putrid Sin;
> I add the name of Sidney to thy scroll
> Without one Virtue of his noble soul!
> So the great Patriots of the World are sham'd
> When Curs, are Cato, Brutus, Sidney nam'd.[38]

Chapter Fifteen

THE END OF THE AFRICAN DISASTER

The plan for the south-west African colony remained unchanged for exactly sixteen days into the new year of 1786. Then, aboard HMS *Grampus* anchored offshore from Cape Coast Castle, Captain Edward Thompson became feverish and very sick. The ship was loaded with monkeys, parrots and other African animals which the crew were taking back to Britain as exotic pets. When the ship's surgeon appeared on deck and suggested that the stench from the animals had increased the captain's sickness, his loyal crew threw every living creature overboard and hastened to scrub every cranny and crevice of the vessel. But their efforts were in vain. Edward Thompson breathed his last at quarter past four in the afternoon of 17 January. The following day the body of their captain was dropped into the Gulf of Guinea by his devoted crew, the service accompanied by a volley of small arms and cannon fire. His will left only £100 to Mary Thompson, 'my ungrateful wife', but he did not forget a bequest to the woman who had instead been in his thoughts through his long periods at sea, his 'beloved Emma'.[1]

Five years earlier a friend and colleague had summed up the man who aspired to be governor of the new penal colony thus:

> He is perfectly honest in his friendships; not rich by any means: unfortunate in his Marriage; an excellent companion; very enterprising with good Judgement; he is grateful in every sense of the word: but he is violent in Politics, but that would be less objectionable were he less a friend to Republican Principles—Whig-ism, in a degree, excuses the mistake, but unluckily he carrys [sic] the Idea, a little too far. You will find him much your friend, & he is a bold advocate, as well as able in Argument.[2]

Now his talents and attributes, and his perceived failings, were lost to any prospective penal settlement. George Tripp took over command of the *Grampus* and the Africa station while captaincy of the second ship, HMS *Nautilus*, passed to nineteen-year-old Thomas Boulden Thompson, Ned's nephew and heir. With this post Boulden Thompson also inherited the mission to survey the south-western coast of the continent with a view to finding a suitable site for his uncle's dream colony.[3]

The younger Thompson was rumoured to be Edward's illegitimate son, his unhappy marriage being common knowledge. He was actually a nephew by marriage, the son of Mary Thompson's sister Sarah, who had married one Richard Boulden. Not nearly such a judicious marriage as her sister's, at least in economic terms, the poverty-stricken Bouldens had many children prior to Richard's early death, so the childless Thompsons were only too happy to take on the precocious Thomas as a sort of unofficial stepson. Ned Thompson certainly took an avid interest in the boy's education, instructing that Ovid, Virgil and Horace be read daily when Thomas was only nine years old, recommending that he study how Rome flourished as a republic, and sending Latin texts for him to translate. More importantly, he groomed him for a life at sea, following in his footsteps. Gossip had it that the Bouldens had exchanged their son for a fat pig to feed their other hungry children. More likely, Ned needed an heir, and Thomas Boulden, who added the name Thompson to his own, was simply the most likely candidate.[4]

At the age of twelve his shore-based education was abandoned and, rigged out as a sailor boy, he had gone to sea aboard the *Hyena* with his uncle and guardian. Four years later he was promoted to the rank of lieutenant. Now, still some weeks shy of his twentieth birthday, he was to command an expedition his uncle had fervently advocated, and all without the advice, seamanship and counsel of the older man. 'My only friend & parent' he had called Ned at the time of his death.[5]

Nevertheless the teenager—who would one day be a vice-admiral, made a KCB (Knight Grand Cross of the Order of Bath), elevated to the baronetcy and lose a leg in battle—rose to the challenge. On 1 February, less than two weeks after his bereavement, Boulden Thompson had the *Nautilus* loaded with supplies from the *Grampus* and set sail on the voyage of exploration. Among his crew were two men who would also go on to have notable careers: botanist Anton Pantaleon Hove, a Pole whose achievements included taking the first mangosteen to Britain, and Lieutenant Home Riggs Popham, who would go on to have a distinguished naval career and become a member of parliament. Also sailing with him was a surgeon's mate named William Balmain, who would later give his name to part of the settlement in New South Wales.

It was a very slow passage, fifty-two mind-numbingly long days from São Tomé, during which time they did not set eyes on a single other vessel. The nights were worse, 'raw and cold'. On one of these days, with nothing but blue sky and various birds to amuse, Thomas Boulden Thompson celebrated his twentieth birthday. Finally, on

21 March, they anchored in St Helena Bay, only some hundred miles north of Cape Town. Four days later Boulden Thompson sent Popham ashore to investigate and find the Berg River. It proved to be salt water, a Dutch fisherman 'found on the beach with 3 or 4 Hottentot servants' telling them that there was no fresh water for some fifty or sixty miles up river. 'Much chagrined', the ship was forced to hire 'water bullocks' to go and fetch water. To console themselves, back aboard ship they broached a cask of rum.[6]

Catching fish and waiting for the water party to return, Boulden Thompson wrote in his journal, 'I look upon St Hellen's Bay to be the northernmost of the Dutch settlements of the Cape of Good Hope.' In fact there is little question that in 1786 the Dutch would certainly have laid claim to any territory south of the Orange River, well to the north of where Boulden Thompson wrote those words, and possibly even beyond that. But his words show the confusion apparent in the entire exploratory voyage. Although they had undertaken to survey the whole coast from 33°0'0" to 16°0'0" south, there is little question that it was the 'Das Voltas' region which was thought particularly suitable for the convict colony. The question was, where exactly was that?[7]

Edward Thompson's information on Das Voltas had come from disparate sources which included some old, flawed Portuguese charts, the journals of two English ships which had landed significantly to the north of the area in question, and some reports from the Dutch East India Company. The latter included the intelligence of Hendrik Hop, a man who had led an expedition overland from the Cape which had crossed the Orange River, but who had passed some distance inland from the coast. Another source of information was Colonel Hendrik von Prehn, who had never been to the region and based his evidence on earlier, even less reliable information.[8]

A better source was Robert Jacob Gordon, a Dutch-born soldier of Scots descent stationed for some years at Cape Town. He had at least visited the relevant region, having journeyed overland from the Cape to the Orange River in October 1779, though rather inland from the coast. He had noted the lack of water in the region, but that small trees and mimosa grew, and he saw and drew some fine images of birds, flowers, giraffes, other animals and the local people, as well as scenes of the river itself. The wildlife kept the party going as well as being the subject of his art: rhinoceros 'was as tasty as veal', he wrote. More bizarrely, he wrote that most of the local men were 'half castrated', having only a single testicle. He thought the region suitable for settlement despite the scarcity of water, and it seems to have been based largely on this information that Edward Thompson had conceived his scheme.[9]

Nevertheless, even the name of the place they were looking for was confusing. In 1487, Bartholomeu Diaz had named the bay at 26°36' south Angra Das Voltas (the site of the present town of Lüderitz, Namibia), and erected a cross or *padrao* to mark that he claimed the region for the Portuguese crown. But this was not the place which the *Nautilus* and her crew were actually seeking. The bay at 28°40' south, at the mouth of the Orange River (the present day border between South Africa and Namibia, site of the towns of Alexander Bay/Oranjemund), was sometimes known as Cape Voltas. It was this which Edward Thompson had rather confusedly advocated for settlement, following Gordon, even if his information had been both sketchy and unclear.[10]

After having secured some oxen, sheep, goats, cabbages and onions from a farmer, with water casks filled and Popham's survey completed, the *Nautilus* went in search of this location. They had been told it was a place 'well watered' with 'many Rivers of great length and breadth, and some navigable' of which only the greatest was 'that called Das Voltas which communicates with a great Lake that supplies Rio Espirito Santo'. Heading northwards, Boulden Thompson and his men instead found 'entire barren loose sand, rocky beaches and cliffs'. It was nothing like the verdant oasis he and his men were expecting.[11]

At 28°40' south, Boulden Thompson saw what he recorded as 'two remarkable square rocky clumps about half a mile from the beach' and 'concluded that this must be ... Cape Voltas'. He sent Popham ashore to investigate, but the lieutenant returned with the news that he had failed to find any opening to the grand river. In April the Orange River would have been very low and difficult to find. Boulden Thompson wrote in his diary, 'We had been so often disappointed in our researches for de Voltas, that I now began to despair of there being such a place, tho' from draughts I have seen of it, it appeared a large open bay with a broad river.' He was beginning to believe, contra to his uncle, that no such place existed. He set sail to proceed further north along the coast.[12]

They did find the bay of Angra Das Voltas (Lüderitz), which was also known by the name Angra Pequeña, and which both Popham and Boulden Thompson drew charts of using this second name. At first the seas were too rough even to enter the bay but eventually, at noon on 14 April, they sailed in, marking the entrance Pedestal Point as they sailed past. Finally, the second day after their arrival, Popham saw life. Some local people along with their dogs led him to what appeared to be a freshwater spring. 'Elated at this discovery', their hopes that they could salvage the mission revived, they filled a cask. It proved to be only a small reservoir of rainwater. Back aboard ship, they instead opened a new cask of wine.[13]

Having met some native people Boulden Thompson concluded that they were 'Iaggas', 'cunning and savage' and in possession of 'the smallest feet I ever saw'. But despite these signs of life, the news was overwhelmingly negative. Hove found only a variety of geranium growing and the land, far from the easily cultivated pasture imagined, was 'barren, unfruitful soil, apparently doomed to everlasting sterility'. Nor was the harbour the safe shelter they had hoped for. Instead, the most interesting things seen were the *padrao* erected by Diaz centuries earlier on which they could still make out the Portuguese arms, along with a pine spar they thought to have been assembled by Monsieur Bart of the French ship *Venus* in 1733.[14]

His hope growing as barren as the landscape, Thomas Boulden Thompson ordered the sails set to go even further northwards. On the evening of 27 April they anchored in Walvis Bay, effectively their last chance of finding a place to found a colony. Immediately things looked up when Boulden Thompson and Popham encountered four local people who 'as a token of friendship rubbed each of us in the cheeks and breast with rancid stinking grease, that they had in a cow's horn' and issued some statements which the visitors took to be an invitation to their town. The following day they went ashore again to find this place, which they discovered to be a hard march over the 'barren hills of loose sand'—the famous colossal sand dunes of the area—after which they found only a village of twenty huts resembling 'the halves of bee hives, with the backs to the wind'.[15]

Typically of many men of his era, Boulden Thompson wrote in his diary about the people they found there in the most disparaging manner: 'Both sexes are very ugly, having thick lips, flat noses, low foreheads, bad teeth, small eyes and high cheek bones.' Their 'woolly' hair they 'begrime with stinking grease' which, along with their perceived affinity for 'any filth they can find', caused them to 'stink most intolerably'. Finding little to celebrate in a people who plainly eked out an existence in a desolate, inhospitable land, Boulden Thompson instead found them to be 'slothfull [sic], dull, & filthy to a great degree'.[16]

Any such life—wandering as tribesmen, eating lice off each other for nourishment, as Boulden Thompson imagined—was hardly what Uncle

Ned had envisaged for his convict colony. Worse still, there was no potable water to be found. Not long after, he gave up. There was no 'regret at leaving so dreary a coast, along which we had sailed nearly 1200 miles in a direct line, without seeing a tree, or procuring a drop of fresh water, altho' every effort and diligent attention was exerted by all and everyone'. Disillusioned, he sailed home to report to the government that the plan to found a convict colony anywhere in the region was utterly hopeless. They arrived home in June 1786, delighted to once again breathe their 'native air'.[17]

When the *Nautilus* reported that the south-western region of Africa was utterly unsuitable for convict development, the final nail was being hammered into the coffin of another disastrous convict scheme. Revealing just how peripheral and isolated the Mosquito Shore really was, it had taken eighteen months for the true scale of the *Fair American* calamity to filter back to London. The whole expedition had been another disaster for George Moore. By 1786 he had begun writing to the State Department pleading for the government to 'indemnify me from the losses', a claim that Nepean and Sydney treated with disdain. 'The measure was undertaken entirely at your own risque [sic],' Nepean countered, noting that 'your Agent had, without the permission of Government, proceeded with convicts to Cape Gracias a Dios, on the Mosquito Shore, with an intention of landing them and employing them at that settlement'. Lord Sydney had found it 'incumbent to disapprove of that proceeding' and declared that Moore and Callow 'must not expect the support or protection of this Country, whatever consequences may happen'. Sydney and Nepean thus effectively washed their hands of the whole affair.[18]

What this meant for the twenty-nine convicts involved was clear. To all intents and purposes they had been abandoned at the Mosquito Shore just as earlier twenty felons had been left at Gorée to fend for themselves. In fact their situation was probably even more precarious, if that was possible. Nine days after Nepean wrote to Moore denying all responsibility for what happened to the *Fair American* and its passengers at the Mosquito Shore, representatives of George III signed the Convention of London, which agreed with the Spanish monarch to evacuate all Britons from the settlement. If anybody chose to stay behind, they would do so at their own peril, vulnerable to attack by the Spaniards at any time. Understandably, most chose to leave, and in 1787 2650 settlers left the Mosquito Shore colony, most for Honduras Bay, where they added exponentially to the problems there. Presumably some convicts went there with them, perhaps meeting with the earlier cohort who had been landed there from the *Mercury*. Their fate ultimately remains uncertain.[19]

What was certain by the time of Moore's protests and as the *Nautilus* arrived back in Britain was that neither Africa nor America seemed to be the answer to Britain's convict dilemma. It was just as well, then, that the government was holding another scheme in reserve.

The seemingly outlandish sketch of an idea given before the Lemane Committee that New South Wales, the land visited fifteen years earlier by Cook and his expedition, would be a suitable place for settlement actually had a far more solid basis in reality than that testimony had suggested. Like Edward Thompson, Sir Joseph Banks and James Mario Matra had far more detailed plans for a new colony than they had divulged to Lord Beauchamp and his team of investigators. Lord George Young, who had also developed a plan to colonise New South Wales, had not even mentioned this before the inquiry and restricted his evidence to condemning Lemane.

Sir Joseph had been the botanist on Captain James Cook's first voyage, when the existence of a great south land had been proven to the people of Britain once and for all. He had first suggested back in 1779 that the country he called New South Wales be settled. As part of an investigation at the time that the Hulks Act was instituted, he had recommended that up to 300 convicts could be sent out to the land he had seen while on the *Endeavour*'s momentous voyage. Banks had suggested that as long as they were provided with seeds, livestock, arms and ammunition, they could be left to their own devices and could govern themselves through their own civil government. The climate, he thought, was similar to that of Toulouse, France. The scheme had attracted attention at the time but had not been approved.[20]

Matra had then submitted a proposal in August 1783 for settling New South Wales, back when George Moore had hopes of reopening convict transportation to America and before Kenneth Mackenzie's trial had made public to the British people the disaster he had led. In many ways the plan had advocated New South Wales on the same grounds that Thompson used the following year to promote a settlement at Das Voltas. The proposed settlement would 'atone for the loss of our American colonies'; it had fertile soil which could quickly produce 'sugar-cane, tea, coffee, silk, cotton, indigo, tobacco'; it was 'peopled only by a few black inhabitants'; and in addition to these benefits it could produce flax. Just as Thompson believed that Das Voltas would be a crucial strategic point which would bolster Britain's trade routes to the east and could be a base for whaling, so Matra had recommended that New South Wales could prove vital, geographically speaking, to the mother country. In short, it could be a home for both the American loyalists and those awaiting transportation in the nation's jails.

Matra had been born in New York of Corsican heritage and educated in England before joining the Royal Navy. In 1768, he had signed on board the *Endeavour* as an able seaman and set off on its voyage—passing through Rio de Janeiro, enduring the torrid seas of Cape Horn, enjoying the famous charms of Tahiti, skirmishing with cannibals in New Zealand and 'discovering' Australia. Of the inhabitants of the land named New South Wales he had written at the time that they were 'entirely naked and black, but they differed from the negroes in Africa in having long straight hair instead of wool on their heads'. Further north on the Australian coast he had again compared the indigenous people to Africans, writing in his journal that 'many of them had flat noses, thick lips, bandy legs, like the negroes of Guinea. They were ignorant, poor, and destitute, not only of the conveniences, but of many of the necessaries of life.' The land he now promoted as extremely fertile he had at the time regarded as 'rocky and sandy', though with some parts where grass grew 'luxuriantly'.[21]

Matra was not at all popular with Captain James Cook, who suspected him of cutting off part of the ears of another man during a prank, being all too fond of 'drunken frolicks' and generally 'good for nothing'. But despite this, Matra was a favourite of Sir Joseph Banks and Daniel Solander, the expedition's botanists. Back in London he became part of their circle and, though he left to become consul at Tenerife and then Constantinople, he and Banks kept in touch. It was largely through them that the first plan to settle New South Wales came into existence. It was only one of Matra's schemes. Returned to London from Constantinople because of illness he had set himself up as an informal adviser to the government about possible colonisation schemes. He promoted imperial ambitions from Demerara to Gibraltar, Florida to the Canary Islands, and his ancestral homeland, Corsica. But he had quickly become convinced that the settlement of the great south land was the most pressing matter and wrote 'many letters ... pestering on the subject of New South Wales'.[22]

Matra had heard rumours as early as July 1783 that Sir George Young was promoting 'a settlement in the South-Seas', but Young had concerned himself only with the impracticality and inhumanity of the Lemane proposal when he had given his testimony to the committee investigating the plan to settle that island. It was not until 13 January 1785 that Young had forwarded a plan for the colonisation of New South Wales to the government. His plan relied heavily on the attractiveness of possible flax cultivation in any such settlement, but the other positives—the fine climate, the fertile soil which would produce 'all kinds of spice ... fine Oriental cotton, indigo, coffee, tobacco, with every species of the sugar-cane', a strategic base for shipping—were also there. It would be a fine home for both the American loyalists and the convicts, Young suggested. At that time this plan had been summarily rejected in favour of an African solution.[23]

By the time the *Nautilus* returned with the news that the Das Voltas region was utterly unsuitable for the proposed purpose, however, New South Wales was the only viable alternative remaining. By 18 August, Lord Sydney wrote to the Treasury informing them that Botany Bay had been decided upon. There were few real choices left. Some of the proposals which had streamed in to the government were so outlandish they made a penal settlement at the end of the world seem positively bland by comparison. Honest citizens had suggested employing felons in the North Sea herring industry, anchoring a hulk off the coast of Africa, and a host of other bizarre ideas. William Eden's idea of swapping criminals for Britons held as slaves in North Africa was again resurrected. One anonymous plan had even suggested that as Christianity decreed that sinners should suffer eternal darkness, convicts should be worked in mines up to a hundred fathoms below ground where they would be as cut off from the living as though 'they had already crossed the River Styx'.[24]

With Sydney's letter announcing that Botany Bay had been chosen was a 'list of Tools, Utensils, &c, necessary for the Convicts', and a list of clothing each man would need. The famous 'Heads of a Plan' revealed all. The settlement would have a ship of war manned by 'discreet officers', two companies of marines for protection against both the convicts and the local people, a chaplain, a surgeon and at least one surgeon's mate. The plan was one for ridding themselves of the convicts, although it hopefully noted that flax might be produced there and even that New Zealand might prove invaluable for getting wood for ships' masts.[25]

By September the newspapers were reporting the scheme to the British people. Applications for tenders had appeared in various papers on 1 September, but it was the *London Chronicle* which first really mentioned the plan on 7 September. A week later the *Daily Universal Register* told its readers of the project and, although placing it in the Indian Ocean instead of the Pacific, wrote approvingly of a land of 'exquisite beauty' where a beast named the 'Kangazoo' roamed free. The next day the *Morning Chronicle* went further by reporting that there would be no way for convicts to get home from a place so far away, and any who tried to escape overland would encounter the local cannibals who were 'extremely fond of human flesh'. On 23 September came the first objection, printed in the *Morning Herald*. Unlike the various African schemes, which had been thought of as just a roundabout sentence of death, Botany Bay by contrast was condemned as a paradise, and thus unsuited to a penal settlement. The main criticisms in the coming weeks, though, regarded the possible fate of the indigenous people should the plan go ahead, and some concern about the expense.[26]

So plans began for shipping many of the felons then in the jails and hulks off to Botany Bay; 'a settlement for the purpose of exonerating this country of its obnoxious members', as William Eden called it. In September, William Richards entered into a contract with the government to transport the convicts thither. Five ships were chosen for the prisoners and another three for stores. It was still a considerable time before the fleet would be ready, however. The ships needed adapting to carry non-free passengers and the outfitting and victualling of the vessels to be suitable for such a vast undertaking was no easy feat. In the end, the ships originally chosen would prove insufficient and others would be added to the fleet destined for the great south land.

It was 1787 before those to be sent away finally went aboard the various ships of the fleet. Those who for so long had endured the prospect of Africa now knew that they would be banished to a different continent, much further away and almost totally unknown. Did any dare to hope that it might also prove less deadly? African-American John Martin, who had been aboard the *Den Keyser* but then deemed too sick to travel, had been removed from Newgate to the *Ceres* hulk in 1785, where he had been labouring for over a year when he finally heard about another ship which was to transport him away. In January 1787 he was sent on board the *Alexander*, destined to be a founder of the new penal settlement rather than to be returned to his ancestral homeland.[27]

John Ruglass and Samuel Woodham, who had been fellow gang members in London's slums and delivered to Gorée while still only teenagers, had managed to stay together. They too had been sent from jail to the hulk *Ceres* in 1785, but escaped that purgatory when, on 24 February 1787, they were embarked on the *Scarborough*, bound for New South Wales.[28]

At Plymouth, Thomas Limpus and the other recaptured *Mercury* mutineers had been aboard the *Dunkirk* hulk for almost three years when they were embarked on the First Fleet ships. Limpus was marked as 'quiet' on the hulk records; many others had been refractory. Boredom had likely provoked tempers to flare, but this was no death ship, like some of those anchored in the Thames. Although there were said to be many convicts suffering from venereal diseases, dropsy and consumption, the *Dunkirk* had been relatively healthy. Still, when they were taken aboard either the *Friendship* or *Charlotte* for the long voyage to their new home, few can have been sorry to leave. Limpus was aboard the *Charlotte*; John Hudson, chimneysweep, who had celebrated his tenth, eleventh and twelfth birthdays aboard the *Dunkirk*, was loaded onto the same ship.[29]

The two men whose partners in crime had gone to Africa aboard the *Recovery* but who had inexplicably escaped that fate themselves also now boarded ships of the First Fleet. Mugger Henry Horne, whose ally Alexander Kennedy had died in August 1785 only weeks after arriving in Africa, was aboard the *Alexander*. Also with him on that ship was William Richardson, whose old criminal associate William Maynard had sailed with Kennedy aboard the *Recovery*. Unless word had somehow filtered back to London, they likely never knew how lucky they were to have escaped having gone with their former friends to Africa. Mary 'Hell-fire Moll' Humphries, intended for Africa but also left behind when the *Recovery* sailed, now found that she too would go to New South Wales. She was aboard the *Lady Penrhyn*.

It was, of course, the end of the African era of convict transportation, but that was far from apparent to those at the time. When Martin, Limpus, Ruglass, Woodham and the others went aboard the ships of what has become known as the 'First Fleet', there was no sense that there would ever be a 'Second Fleet', let alone all the other ships which would follow in their wake. And, if the Botany Bay experiment had failed, as it stood more than a fair chance of doing, it is entirely possible that the British government would have looked to other parts of the world. In the years after the 'Botany Bay decision', places as diverse as Tristan da Cunha (in the south Atlantic Ocean), New Zealand, Chile, Peru and New Caledonia were all nominated as possible homes for Britan's unwanted criminals.

In 1786 Admiral John Blankett advocated Madagascar if anything went wrong with the New South Wales colony, believing that the Africans there were 'Bold, Sociable & Friendly'. This idea would survive into the 1790s, when a man named Alexander Davison wrote that the island was 'capable, at any time, to receive all the future Convicts'.[30]

The New South Wales plan could not immediately escape from its African past in another way too. For some years the convict problem had been attached to the plight of the American loyalists, with many schemes planned to house both groups of people. Some, such as Edward Thompson, had imagined that the convicts could work for the displaced loyalists in a newly founded colony. But in 1786, with loyalists spread out through Canada, Britain, Nova Scotia, the Bahamas and other parts of the Caribbean, it was one particular segment of that group which was causing particular consternation. They were black loyalists, and it was these men and women, starving on the streets of London, who played a strange part in the whole story of the African penal settlement.

The 'black poor', as they quickly became known, were mostly runaway slaves who had freed themselves by escaping from their masters to the British during the American Revolutionary War. Others were freemen who had fought on the British side. John Martin, bound for Botany Bay, was one of their number. Like him, many had found themselves destitute when they reached Britain, and their plight had attracted the attention of a group of philanthropists. It was proposed that a new settlement be founded for them, and after Nova Scotia was mooted and discussed, Henry Smeathman recommended Sierra Leone. Smeathman had already recommended a similar area for the convicts. When he had given evidence before the inquiry discussing the merits of Lemane as a penal settlement, he had suggested instead that the small Banana Islands near Sierra Leone would be far more suitable.

So it was that the New South Wales colonisation scheme always had a twin, and one which stayed in Africa. The idea that Africa was simply unsuited to white (convict) settlers did not apply to the black loyalists, whose skin colour was (erroneously) considered to give them some genetic protection against the continent's diseases. Nor did the Company of Merchant's long-standing complaint that mendacious white men would ruin the slave trade matter in the least, as not only were the majority of the proposed settlers neither criminals nor white, the philanthropists behind the scheme were the archenemies of the slave traders. Additionally, many of the black poor, as they were known, wanted to go to Sierra Leone, having believed Smeathman's positive reports. So as it turned out, the Sierra Leonean 'First Fleet' was loading at just the same time as that bound for the great southern land.

The ties between the two schemes went back to the time when Lemane was the intended destination of the convicts. Incredibly, despite the fact that one plan was ostensibly to assist a group of men and women whose loyalty to Britain had left them destitute, while the other was a scheme of punishment, the white/convict/Lemane plan and the black/free/Sierra Leone plan had been 'remarkably similar'. The government had proposed that both places would be governed, or rather not really governed, in the same way. Plus, it was thought that the same ships could deliver supplies to both groups of settlers. Then, when doubts had initially been raised about the suitability of Sierra Leone, it had been suggested that 'the Negroes' could go to the Gambia instead as they would be 'more contented and happy under a regular Government'. That is, it was rather extraordinarily argued that they would enjoy a penal settlement more than living under their own authority.

Even after Botany Bay was chosen for the convicts as an alternative to an African destination, ideas that the convict colony and the Sierra Leone scheme were intertwined would not die. This was hardly surprising as such notions were promoted in the media and elsewhere. Of the handful of black convicts bound for New South Wales, it was reported that five men and one woman were appealing to go instead to Sierra Leone. As late as 1786 the *Register* reported that the convicts were going to Africa to serve the 'black masters' at Sierra Leone. It would, the paper suggested, be 'a greater punishment than death'.[31]

Botany Bay it was, however, for all the criminals aboard the First Fleet ships. The *Register*'s report was merely the work of a scandalmonger. The days of African schemes for Britain's convicts were over.

Finally, on 12 May 1787, Arthur Phillip ordered the flagship *Sirius* to weigh anchor and the fleet set sail. The scheme had grown to far greater proportions than any of its African predecessors, and more than 700 convicts were aboard the ships, along with marines, seamen, various officers and some of the free men's families. The voyage was one of the longest any Englishman, let alone woman, had ever embarked upon and the place they were going was unimaginably remote.

As Robert Hughes has written, 'if they had been told they were off to the moon, the sense of loss, deracination and fear could hardly have been worse—at least one could see the moon from England, which could not be said for Botany Bay'.[32] Undoubtedly the fear and sense of foreboding was immense. Yet for those like Limpus, Ruglass and Woodham, and perhaps too for John Martin and Hell-fire Moll Humphries, there could possibly have been the faintest glimmer of hope. After all, they had known what awaited them in Africa, and that was the overwhelming likelihood that they would very quickly be nothing more than a memory. Botany Bay was unknown to be sure, but the rumours which swirled told not only of death, cannibals and whippings but of something else too. The idea, first circulated in the media, that Botany Bay was unsuitable because it was a paradise never completely disappeared. In fact, it never would. Down by the docks and in the urban slums, ditties were sung about this new land. As one reported:

> They go to an Island to take special charge
> Much warmer than Britain, and ten times as large:
> No customs-house duty, no freightage to pay,
> And tax-free they'll live when at Botany Bay.[33]

AFTERWORD

The year 1788 would prove momentous. The first day of the new year saw the inaugural publication of what would become one of the world's pre-eminent newspapers, *The Times* of London.[1] By the end of the year George III was enduring one of his bouts of 'madness'—now known to be porphyria—which saw him confined to a straitjacket and restraining chair. In the intervening months Georgia, Connecticut, Massachusetts, Maryland, South Carolina, New Hampshire, Virginia and New York all ratified the American constitution, thereby becoming states of the new union. In April, the Comte de Buffon, whose words about man being descended from chimpanzees had inspired Edward Thompson while he was in Africa, died in Europe.

In January the First Fleet, with more than a thousand men, women and children aboard, arrived at Botany Bay. After only a few days Arthur Phillip, dismayed at finding nothing like the verdant pastures Cook had reported, sailed a few miles northwards and through the heads of Port Jackson. He had unwittingly found the 'finest harbour in the world'. In awe of the vast twists and turns, coves and headlands, sandy bays and glorious promontories, he decided that a place he named Sydney Cove would be the site of the new colony. When the other ships followed to the chosen site and the flag was raised, the most remarkable colonisation project in British history was underway.

There were the usual firsts of settlement. The first interactions with the indigenous people ranged from what the new arrivals considered to be innocuous dances of welcome to far less benign meetings after distrust, profound misunderstandings and cynicism took hold. The first sermon ashore was preached on 3 February, when Psalm 116 was heard by the displaced flock: 'what shall I render unto the Lord, for all his benefits towards me?' Three days later things were thought organised enough for the first women convicts to go ashore. Most were dressed in their most attractive outfits and the sailors requested extra rum to 'make merry' with them. By later that day almost everyone ashore was joining in the debauchery, giving rise to the common perception that Sydney's first public gathering was an orgy. Next day, all the convicts, many with sore heads, stood to hear the governor's commission read for the first time. There was a volley of cannon and cries of 'God Save the King!' Unsurprisingly, there was soon also the first hanging as seventeen-year-old Thomas Barrett swung from a newly constructed gibbet.[2]

Things were very difficult in the early months and years as Phillip and his officers discovered that they were missing many kinds of food, tools and others supplies which would have made things easier. Few of the convicts had the skills needed in building, farming and animal husbandry, and they struggled ceaselessly with British ideas about crops, trees and plants in this vastly different climate, and floundered as relations between the invaders and the locals worsened.

In the new colony, some of those who had been embroiled in African convict schemes got off to shaky starts. Black prisoner John Martin, once destined for the *Den Keyser*, soon found that the law was as adamantine in the new country as in the old. Martin was arrested one night when a flickering light betrayed the fact that he had a fire burning in his hut, something deemed an offence. He was sentenced to twenty-five lashes. Samuel Woodham, escapee from Gorée, could not escape the law's grasp in the new settlement. He soon found himself back in court at Sydney Cove, charged with breaking into the house of Richard Cartwright. He was, however, acquitted.

Elizabeth Barber, the prostitute who had stolen a watch and sold it to publican William Woodley and who had sailed aboard the *Den Keyser* for this misdemeanour, was constantly in trouble during the long voyage out. Always feisty, she did not take her treatment lightly and wrote a letter to Major Robert Ross protesting that her punishment was 'fixious'. Her reputation for unruliness would be hard to shake off in the new colony. Things were hardly helped when, married to Thomas Brown soon after arrival, her first two children by him both died within days of their birth.

Worst of all was Woodham's former gang-mate John Ruglass. He was employed cutting timber to build shelters, but soon found himself in serious trouble. The new setting had not dampened his keenness for knives, a propensity he had shown years before as a young teenager on the streets of London. His victim this time was Ann Fowles, transported for stealing clothing, and with whom Ruglass had set up home in New South Wales. In January 1789, a year after their arrival, he stabbed Ann in a rage. Hauled before the newly created court, he was found guilty and sentenced to a potentially deadly 700 lashes.

Despite all this, things were nowhere near as bad as they had been for the convicts who had been sent to Africa. This much was clear from the overall success of the colony and from the fact that whatever trouble they were in, all the convicts who had so narrowly escaped dying in Africa did survive in the new settlement.

Sydney's successes contrast starkly not only with the disease and deaths of those who had gone to Africa as convicts, but also with the unfortunates who had gone to the twin colony at the mouth of the Sierra Leone River. The 'black poor' and the other settlers who had gone to establish an African utopia found instead a hellish graveyard. Just like the convicts who had been banished to the African coast, the Sierra Leone settlers quickly succumbed to the diseases of the region. Their skin colour did not, as had been believed, give them innate resistance to malaria or yellow fever. Such immunity had to be acquired through years on the coast, so the settlers died just as quickly as the convicts once had.

What was more, unlike at Port Jackson, where the local people had only spears to use against the new arrivals, in Africa the centuries of the slave trade had ensured that the indigenous people had plenty of firearms with which to hold the invaders at bay. They burned the settlers' formative town to the ground in 1789. Similarly, while distance may have been Australia's 'tyranny', it was also its early saviour, as New South Wales remained safe from European warfare when the French destroyed the Sierra Leone colony in 1794. If anyone in Australia ever wanted to see what might have been if the Lemane or Das Voltas plans had not been abandoned, they always had their disastrous colonial twin to look towards.

The new southern colony could not immediately escape its catastrophic African past, however, despite the great distance separating it from that continent. In 1790, that dreadful history came calling when the Second Fleet sailed into Sydney Harbour, bringing with it scenes unlike anything seen on the First Fleet vessels. Under the governance of Arthur Phillip the inaugural voyage had had a miraculously low death rate and had generally been remarkably healthy. The only ship which had arrived in the meantime, the female convict transport the *Lady Juliana*, had likewise delivered its passengers in astonishingly good health, regardless of the sniping about it being a 'floating brothel'.

But the three ships of the Second Fleet were utterly different. After watching them arrive, Judge-Advocate David Collins wrote, 'both living and dead exhibit more horrid spectacles than has ever been witnessed in this country'.[3] Reverend Richard Johnson, on visiting his new parishioners, thought that 'The misery I saw among them is unexpressible' [sic], noting that many were all but naked, were so ill they could hardly move and were 'covered over almost with their own Nastiness'. One convict had, Johnson believed, 10,000 lice in his bed and on his body; some had scurvy or dysentery, others 'violent fevers'.[4]

If it seemed as though the horrors of transportation to Africa had come to visit, they indeed had. The three muck-ridden, infested, death-plagued vessels had been contracted for by none other than the London slave-trading company of Calvert, Camden and King. They had become embroiled in convict transportation during the days when Africa had been the chosen destination, Anthony Calvert first becoming involved when he had rather preposterously offered to buy Kenneth Mackenzie's fledgling plantation when the latter was removed from Africa to stand trial for murder. Following that, Calvert had tendered for the contract to ship convicts both to Lemane Island and Das Voltas, plans which had never come to pass. Both he and Thomas King had been involved in the *Recovery*'s convict voyage, with King being accused by the African Company of acting wrongly on that occasion. Now they had dispatched ships to New South Wales and the result, as Arthur Phillip wrote, was 'a scene of misery'.[5]

The captain of the worst of the three ships, the *Neptune*, had also played a tangential role in the African convict fiasco. Donald Trail was a former slave trader who knew the coast from Cape Coast Castle along to Ouidah well, and had almost certainly met some of those transported there for their crimes. He was a former partner of Andrew Hewson, captain of the *Recovery* when it had delivered twenty-two felons to the coast, and was married to a relative of Hewson's. When he returned to London from Sydney Cove he would stand trial along with his chief mate William Ellrington for having murdered some of the convicts and the ship's cook. They would ultimately be acquitted, but after Calvert, Camden and King's Third Fleet ships proved to be little better, the government never again contracted slave traders to transport convicts to Australia.[6]

As the Second Fleet ships arrived in Sydney, William Hill, a soldier with the New South Wales Corps, wrote a letter claiming that 'the slave trade is merciful compared to what I have seen in this fleet'. To modern eyes it is an inappropriate comparison perhaps, but Hill believed that he was contributing to a debate which had raged when he and the rest of the Second Fleet had set sail. As the morality and legality of the transatlantic slave trade was increasingly called into question, its defenders sought to justify it by comparing it with convict transportation. Lieutenant John Matthews, writing of his voyage to Sierra Leone, claimed that, 'a pretty close parallel may be observed between the African condemned for some offence against the laws of his country, to be sold to a white man, and the English felon transported to a wild uncultivated country; for such is Botany Bay represented.'[7] Slave trader Robert Norris likewise argued that Africans had sold their countrymen for centuries and 'had never entertained any more doubt of their right to do so, than we do of sending delinquents to Botany Bay'.[8]

These were the opening gambits of the anti-abolitionist campaign, decrying the crusade of William Wilberforce, Thomas Clarkson and their allies which would soon galvanise large swathes of the British population in righteous indignation. But these comparisons between British convicts and slaves also provided a rather strange coda to the years of convict transportation to Africa, an era when however grim their personal circumstances, however cavalier the British government had been with its felons' lives, they had nonetheless seen nothing absurd about using their malefactors to guard African captives. What was, surely, an extremely inappropriate though telling punishment—to dress in a redcoat, be armed with a musket and stand guard over human merchandise—was forgotten in the rush to attack and defend the trade in which they had been involved. The inherent imprudence in the suggestion that sending convicts to 'Botany Bay' was the equivalent of a slave trade could have been shown with only a cursory glance at what had gone before. The abolitionists chose not to point this out, however, perhaps feeling that it would muddy the waters of their noble argument. The information that convicts had been transported, shackled, aboard slave ships to their place of banishment would hardly have helped their cause, even given they had then become the guards of captive slaves.

When the British parliament launched its inquiry into the slave trade in the years immediately after the settlement of Australia, many of the men who had been part of the 'convicts in Africa' debacle were called to testify. Richard Miles, Jerome Bernard Weuves, independent trader John Fontaine, the *Brookes*'s captain Clement Noble, Thomas Boulden Thompson, Sir George Young, John Barnes and Thomas King all bore witness. From May 1789 onwards the men paraded past the committee giving evidence which drew on their own knowledge of the transatlantic slave trade. Young and Boulden Thompson told of slave-ship seamen seeking refuge from cruel captains, but most of the other men were avid supporters of the trade. John Fontaine, whom Kenneth Mackenzie had once sought for the defence at his murder trial, told the committee that

African captives were entirely content with their lot on slave ships. 'I never saw a people happier than when they were on board,' he claimed, rather ludicrously. None mentioned the convicts who had been sent to Africa, some aboard slave ships, to guard African captives.

Yet in Africa, a handful of convicts were still alive. Thomas Maple, brought back to Britain to testify at Kenneth Mackenzie's trial, had been returned to Africa and was employed at Cape Coast Castle. He died sometime in the late 1780s or early 1790s. Thomas Randall, who had also given evidence at Mackenzie's trial, was discharged from Company service on 31 August 1786, less than a year after he returned to Africa. Presumably he worked as an independent trader from then on. David Street, who had been wounded in the original failed attempt to take St Jago, was also still alive in these years and working alongside Maple at Cape Coast Castle.[9]

A few of the convicts endured into the 1790s. William Bolton, known as Billy the Flat, survived for almost a decade before breathing his last in early April 1791, still shy of his thirtieth birthday.[10] John Prime, one of the three men disembarked from the *Den Keyser* at Fort Commenda, survived there for years, only being sent away to Accra in 1791. Whether it was the change of scene or just coincidence is unclear, but it was the end for Prime. He survived only a matter of months at his new workplace.[11]

A few others were also alive in the new decade, although they slip from view as they slowly became incorporated into the main body of fort employees, no longer noted separately as convicts. Thomas Phillips, the former highwayman, was still working in Africa as the 1790s dawned. Almost ten years after arriving on the coast he remained on the Company's books, marked down in 1791 as having been transferred to Anomabu. William Cheatham, too, still alive in Africa a decade after he had stood in the dock alongside Patrick Madan. He only disappears from the historical record in October 1791, when he was sent to Accra to serve at Fort James.[12]

The last man to slip from view was John Morris. Having been saved when his half-brother Enoch Fleming had been hanged for being part of the mob during the Gordon Riots, Morris survived while the majority of his mess-mates sickened and died. He endured through it all: the death of his original captain, George Katenkamp; the madness of Kenneth Mackenzie; the runaways and the starvation, the floggings and the slave hole, the mutinies and the piracy, and the later years when he found that he had no say in becoming an employee of the African Company. In 1791, a year when all the convicts were relocated to new forts, Morris moved from Prampram to Anomabu on 1 April. Like Cheatham and Phillips, he was still a young man, and having now built up some immunity to malaria through constant bouts of the deadly disease, there was every chance that he could survive for a relatively long period. Nevertheless, he pined for home. In 1794, after thirteen years in Africa, and after it was clear that New South Wales would be the place of transportation henceforth, he petitioned to go home.

He had been only seventeen at the time of the Gordon Riots, he wrote to London, and had been swept along with the crowd at Woodstock Road near Oxford Road. He admitted that he had been part of the mob that attacked a house and, captured that night, had been taken along with his elder half-brother to Horse Guard Parade in Whitehall. After his brother was hanged he had been pardoned, he claimed, in exchange for serving for only three years in the army. In the intervening years, the decade after he had expected to be released, he had often begged his superiors in Africa to be discharged. He longed to 'return to his Native Country'. His plea did make it back to London and to the Secretary of State, but there it was firmly rejected. John Morris was destined to remain in Africa for the term of his natural life. He would be shown no mercy.[13]

Kenneth Mackenzie himself had not lived long enough to see the new colony at New South Wales flourish. He was dead before Martinmas (11 November)1789. After his discharge from Newgate he had returned to Edinburgh, where he had remained long enough to pose for a portrait by the artist John Kay as one of four 'young bucks' of the city. It is the only known image of him. He was reported to be unhappy with the outcome and, seeing the print in a bookshop window, raged against the artist, believing himself portrayed in unfit company. The other sitters pictured with him—Dr Eiston, an army surgeon and 'macaroni', or dandy, Hieronymo Stabilini, an Italian musician and Francis MacNab, the laird of MacNab—he considered to be 'fiddlers and madmen', and he offered Kay half a guinea to change the work.[14]

It was money he could scarcely afford to throw away, his always precarious finances now being in dire straits. The sequestration of the Redcastle estate had begun at the time of his father's death in 1785 and, though Mackenzie desperately hoped to pay off the debts and regain the property, he had few means available to him. With no skills but as an army officer, and unable to rejoin the British Army, he took a step other Mackenzies had taken before him. He joined the Russian military. Rumour had it that he had to flee the country anyway, having been caught up in a duel.

Mackenzie had not been gone long when another report about him reached Scotland. The story related how the irate and increasingly desperate Mackenzie had somehow heard that a man named John Smith was in Constantinople and he had followed him there, determined to get what he claimed he was owed. Smith, former captain of the slaver *Little Pearl*, was accused by Mackenzie of having stolen gold dust and other belongings at

Fort Mori when he had been charged with murder and removed from his post. Now, so the people of Scotland heard, Mackenzie had challenged Smith to a duel and, no longer the hotshot he fancied himself, had been killed in the contest. Captain Kenneth Mackenzie, convicted murderer, was said to have taken his last breath in Constantinople, apparently still raging about how his life had gone so wrong in Africa.[15]

At the time of his death his finances told the story of a life lived badly, of mistakes made and foibles unchecked. He owed his former wife £621 6s 1d, meaning he had not paid her alimony for more than six years. He also owed money to two of his daughters, Boyd and Hannah, and £15 15s for the upkeep of his 'natural son', born to one of his many mistresses. Most revealingly of all, the £800 borrowed from George Ross back in 1781 to raise his company had not been repaid, or at least not in full. Together with money owed to Lieutenant Colonel Colin Mackenzie, formerly of the 92nd Regiment, and John Peter du Roveray, London merchant, the total amount in deficit on his military loans was more than £4000.[16]

There was nothing for the trustees to do but sell Redcastle, Kenneth Mackenzie's beloved ancestral home. James Grant of Shewglie purchased the castle, made of 'red' stone and set on the banks of Beauly Firth, for £25,450. For those left behind, it was the end of an era. Kenneth's son and heir, Roderick, went to live in Jamaica and upon his death in 1798 the Redcastle dynasty ended. At Fortrose Cathedral a carved stone mural, dating back to 1800, shows a member of the Mackenzie clan and is entitled 'Death holding on to his castle of Redcastle'.[17]

Kenneth Mackenzie's death did not quite signify the end of the African convict debacle, however. The denouement did not occur until Joseph Wall finally returned to Britain and stood trial for murder. Quite why he went back to London after his years on the run is unclear, but rumour had it that he was trying to regain some money belonging to his wife which was being held because of the charges against him. He apparently lived incognito for some years on Tottenham Court Road under the alias of Thompson, along with his wife and son, now aged nine, before anybody realised his true identity and had him rearrested.[18]

His trial before a special commission at Hick's Hall began on 20 January 1802. He asked for permission to sit near his counsel instead of at the bar but this was denied. He was to be treated like all other common criminals. He must have been horrified by the coarseness of the men in whose hands his fate lay. Among the prospective jurors were a lighterman, a shoemaker, a baker, a tailor, a bricklayer and an ironmonger. Of the forty-eight men gathered there to comprise the jury, only two gave their status as 'gentleman'.[19]

Two of the witnesses to events in Gorée all those years earlier showed the opposing sides of criminal life in Britain. Henry Fawcett, one of the men who had been flogged by the black slaves that fateful day under orders from Joseph Wall, but who had survived the whipping, was not there to testify. Demobilised back in Britain, he had become involved with a notorious housebreaker named Thomas Burdett, who mocked the court at one of their trials in 1786 by stating, after their acquittal for lack of evidence, that 'one house we robbed was my Lord Grantham's, of all the gold medals, he had the Speaker's gown, and the grand seal'. Fawcett and Burdett escaped that time, but both soon hanged for burglary. Meanwhile another witness from Gorée, Edward Lewis, was now an officer at Bow Street, the equivalent of a policeman.[20]

William Lacy's fate was also characteristic of the African disaster. The man who had once dismissed the *Den Keyser* felons, telling them he had no food, had died in 1784, but for three years before that he had been insane, which his widow attributed to *coup de soleil*, or sunstroke. Those rumours about white men going mad under the tropical sun just would not go away.[21]

Despite the fact that he was alleged to have killed more than one man, Wall was charged only with the murder of Benjamin Armstrong. 'Seduced by the instigation of the Devil', Joseph Wall had ordered his victim to be severely whipped, the court heard. But the whole sorry saga came out in the courtroom: the black slaves who had done the actual flogging; the allegations of mutiny by the poorly paid and starving soldiers; contentions that Wall cheated his men out of their pay; the misery and the violence of Gorée. Like Kenneth Mackenzie before him he was accused of having inflicted a cruel and unusual punishment—the atypical rope used for the flogging and the fact that it was not administered by the men's brother soldiers—and charged that he should have held a court-martial instead of unilaterally declaring the men guilty. Wall, 'much agitated', took to the stand in his own defence, but it was in vain. The judge did not instruct the jury about their verdict, but it took them only half an hour to return and declare Wall guilty. He was sentenced to death.[22]

After his conviction the Old Bailey was 'a scene of tumult and confusion'. Wall, returned to Newgate and incarcerated in the condemned cell, was visited by his wife, the former Frances Mackenzie, whom the papers fawningly reported to be 'a near relative of a nobleman'. He had been advised by the judge to make 'his peace with heaven' and prepare himself 'for that place in which no crime was too great to be forgiven'. He took the judge's advice, spending his last days in 'prayer most fervent'.[23]

But the following day a respite was given and it seemed as if Joseph Wall, like Kenneth Mackenzie so many years earlier, might escape punishment. When that reprieve expired, another followed. But Britain in 1802 was a different place from 1785. Less than two weeks later, no further reasons could be found to keep Joseph Wall from the scaffold. The evening before his execution the artist J.T. Smith, under commission from the Duke of Roxburgh, visited Wall in the condemned cell to draw his final portrait. Smith flinched when he set eyes on his subject: 'tall, shrivelled [sic], and pale … his soul shot so piercingly through the port-holes of his head that the first glance of him nearly petrified me.' The condemned man was, thought Smith, 'death's counterfeit'. An image of Wall in his final days shows the former governor stooped, reading a Bible and 'contemplating his unhappy fate'.[24]

Joseph Wall finally appeared before the 'immense' crowd at 8 am on Thursday, 28 January 1802, the Ordinary (chaplain) of Newgate at his side. He was dressed in a grey coat with black collar and 'black pantaloons'. His appearance was 'rather mean', said one witness, evidently accustomed to condemned men going off to their deaths in their wedding attire with nosegays, buttonholes and other little flourishes of individuality and defiance.[25]

As so many of those in this story witnessed, hanging days were always events of mass public revelry, but even by the standards of the day Joseph Wall's visit to the hangman was extraordinary. Sixty thousand people turned out to behold the spectacle and their transparent hostility rocked the condemned man's fortitude. As the halter was being placed around his neck the crowd broke out into uproarious cheers. An observer wrote: 'as if in contemptuous triumph [the crowd] gave three distinct huzzas; pulling off their hats at the same time, accompanying their shouts and exclamations by groans and hisses; as if in detestation of the prisoner's conduct.'

Nor was it a quick end for Joseph Wall. Hanging was never a particularly efficient way to kill a person, and Wall's execution was a fine example of what happened when things went wrong. As the platform dropped beneath his feet and he fell, the knot of the noose slipped to the back of head. He swung there for fifteen very painful minutes, his body convulsing and twitching involuntarily, until the hangman took pity on him and pulled on his legs to hasten his demise. The crowd, so belligerent when he first appeared, were 'awed ... into a dead silence when they saw the object of their hatred in the act and agony of death'. But the hush did not last long. Before his corpse could even be cut down from the scaffold, some Irishwomen began 'drinking his damnation in a mixture of gin and brimstone'. Decent society was outraged. 'The barbarous exultation of the populace ... resembles the horrid BRAVOES of the French Guillotine,' wrote one witness.[26]

By the time of Wall's death the penal colony at New South Wales was flourishing. After the earliest years, when the settlers feared themselves forgotten by Britain and faced starvation, the place had undergone a quite remarkable turnaround. A report of the colony printed in October 1802 told Britons that their least likely offspring was 'in a very progressive and prosperous condition'. The harvest the previous year had been so abundant that they had been able to export grain. More remarkably still, the 'convicts, transported under the worst circumstances of vice and depravity, [had] become sober, industrious, and respectable farmers'. The report's authors even began to envisage a day when the reformed criminals would proselytise to the indigenous, teaching them not just about Christianity but showing them 'European arts' and 'policy'.[27]

And therein, encapsulated in those last words, was the downside to these triumphs. The fact that the new colony had flourished had cost the indigenous people very dearly. While the arrivals had found the continent remarkably healthy, in great contrast to Africa, the fact was that their diseases had wreaked devastation on the native population. The colony's successes, especially when viewed in comparison to their 'twin' colony at Sierra Leone, had been won at the expense of the Eora and the other Aboriginal people of the region. The smallpox which felled so many soon after January 1788 may or may not have come from the First Fleeters, but that hardly mattered in the scheme of things. The general picture was of a people who had no resistance to the invaders' microbes, no weaponry to match European guns, and little to countermand the onslaught of 'westernisation'.[28]

There was something perhaps more destructive still implicit in those words of 1802. All the early comparisons of the people's blackness and the straightness of their hair compared to Africans took on a terrible weight as notions of race increased in importance. While Britons were being persuaded that Africans were 'men and brothers', as the abolitionist slogan exhorted, Australia's native people were depicted as the lowest form of life. They were seen as 'the very nadir of human degeneration, just before the species left off its human form and turned bestial'. Racism against people of African origin continues to be a scourge around the world, of course, but, ironically, while the many peoples of Africa and their descendents were devastated by their role in European profitability, the Aboriginal people faced the horrendous void of being irrelevant to those same forces. The corpses continued to pile up. For the Eora, 1788 had marked the end of life as they had always known it to be. Nothing would be the same ever again.[29]

But for those who were members of the fledgling colony, however hard things were, they were never as bad as the fate they had so narrowly escaped. After their early troubles in New South Wales, the three men who had actually been transported to Africa and escaped, thrived in their new home.

More than ten years after arriving in the colony—a decade of hard labour—Samuel Woodham was given a conditional pardon in October 1799. With his freedom came a grant of thirty acres of land at Mulgrave Place on the Hawkesbury River. Trying to coax a living from New South Wales's soil was certainly no easy life, but compared to the sufferings of the other convicts left at Gorée, it was a dreamland. Woodham settled down to a quiet life and lived out his days on the beautiful Hawkesbury.[30]

In March 1790, recovered from his latest flogging, John Ruglass was sent to Norfolk Island, the small Pacific Island colonised directly after New South Wales was settled. There Ruglass began to clear some land to farm and soon had sufficient success to co-own a pig. Having been convicted of a crime in the colony, he was not granted a conditional pardon until 1804, five years after his old gang mate Woodham. He finally had some control over his life for the first time virtually since boyhood. He decided to act upon his new-found sovereignty, and a few years later left Norfolk Island for Van Diemen's Land (Tasmania). And there he stayed for many years, living a life far away from his tumultuous, law-breaking past. Unlike his former shipmates who had not managed to get away from Africa, most of whom had barely survived for a couple of months, John Ruglass lived to the grand age of eighty.[31]

Thomas Limpus, veteran of two previous transportation voyages, also lived into the nineteenth century, far longer than his former *Den Keyser* shipmates who had stayed in Africa. After arriving in New South Wales, Limpus, like Ruglass, went to Norfolk Island. There he began clearing land and was evidently productive and thought trustworthy as he earned a conditional pardon relatively quickly, being judged to have served due time by 1796. He appears to have lived out the rest of his days on Norfolk Island.[32]

Those who had so very nearly gone to Africa also fared comparatively well in the new colony. Mary Humphries left her 'Hell-fire' ways behind her and married John King, a convict who did well enough to be given a conditional pardon; he became overseer of the brick and tile makers. Never again troubling lawmakers, Mary lived in Sydney and remained married to King, though childless. She died at the age of about sixty in 1810 and was buried in Sydney.

Henry Horne, sentenced at the Old Bailey along with Alexander Kennedy for a mugging, also survived far longer in New South Wales than his old ally had done at his place of exile. Whereas Kennedy had died within weeks of stepping ashore in Africa, Horne went on to have a son in Australia and, after becoming free, was appointed the coxswain of the government boat. In the 1790s he disappeared from the records, but is not thought to have died at that time. As a man who had learned seafaring skills in his colonial job, he would have had no difficulty in finding work aboard a passing ship. Chances are, Horne went on to have a successful free life, an opportunity which had been denied Kennedy.[33]

Perhaps the most remarkable turnaround of all was achieved by the other man whose former partner in crime had been transported to Africa. Why William Richardson was left behind in jail when William Maynard was sent aboard the *Recovery* is not clear, but it is evident which man was the more fortunate of the pair. While Maynard soon died in Africa, Richardson married in New South Wales and acquired a decent job working for Captain James Meredith. Then, after having at least two children of their own, William and Isabella Richardson set up a fledgling school, teaching basic literacy skills and the gospel to the colony's young.

From 1793 onwards they received a small salary from the Society for the Propagation of the Gospel and the Reverend Richard Johnson wrote that 'so far as their ability & opportunity wd [sic] permit, they have been attentive to their duty'. Richardson also farmed seventy-five acres and was successful enough to lease a plot in the town besides; in addition, he acted as a sergeant in the New South Wales Corps for more than sixteen years. In 1810, the Richardsons managed what few First Fleeters ever could. They returned to England. After that William was a witness at the parliamentary committee investigating transportation, the former convict now so respectable as to be called to give evidence about his experiences. He gave no hint of the earlier scheme he had escaped by only a hair's breadth—a disaster by then largely airbrushed from history.[34]

The last word, however, should go to John Martin and his descendants. In Sydney Martin married Ann Joy, a convict who arrived in 1790 aboard the deadly Second Fleet, having been convicted of pawning a stolen violin. By 1795 his farm was doing so well that he was able to support himself, although Ann still received rations from the public store. Martin was said to be 'a sober industrious man, yet very poor', still working his land when others in the area had given up.

By 1802, the year that Joseph Wall was hanged in London, Martin held fifty acres of land which he planted with wheat and maize, and he owned two hogs. Four years later, with Ann now living off their produce too, he had twelve hogs and also owned two sheep. He had also become a constable of the local watch. It seemed as if John Martin, despite being 'very poor', was really one of the colony's success stories. Then, in 1806, tragedy struck when Ann died.

Martin soon remarried, this time to Mary Randall, the daughter of John Randall, another of the black convicts who had been First Fleeters. Having had no children by his first wife, five were now born to John and Mary: John, Sophia, Francis, Henry and Hannah. And so a pleasant family life continued for John Martin in the following decades as his children grew up and his wealth steadily increased. By the time he was in his seventies he owned sheep and two horses, and even employed a convict labourer to work on his farm. He died at the incredible age of eighty-eight, all five of his children outliving him, and was buried at Parramatta.

Today the Martin–Randall descendants number in the thousands and are spread across Australia and the wider world. Some of them identify themselves as Aboriginal (and indeed some of their progeny may have intermarried with indigenous people), some think of themselves as 'white', and others are aware of their African-American heritage too. They are the story of Australia. But the very fact of their existence is also testament to how very lucky John Martin was to have been removed, at the very last minute, from the *Den Keyser*, and how very much more fortunate the convicts who arrived in Australia were than their predecessors who had been banished to Martin's ancestral homeland.[35]

From the perspective of the early twenty-first century it seems incredible that Great Britain once had the effrontery to ship its convicts away at all, whether here to the United States or anywhere else. But that having lost its American colonies, it briefly sought a home for them in Africa among the slave traders and the captive Africans is less explicable still.

Standing on the shores of Sydney Harbour, surrounded by the wealth and beauty of a large, gleaming city, or here, wandering down Pennsylvania Avenue in the world's wealthiest and most powerful nation, it is amazing that the two nations which received most of Britain's unwanted pickpockets, forgers, shoplifters and ne'er-do-wells have become two of the most successful nations on earth.

Amazing too that the place which Britain initially hoped to be a 'New America' was Africa, still burdened with poverty and disease. And that, of course, is largely why the story of the convicts banished to Africa has been forgotten. No historians from Ghana or Senegal have sought them out as their ancestors; they play no part in any wealthy nation or state's founding story.

Two hundred and twenty-two years after the last British convicts arrived in Africa and almost 200 years since the American abolition of the slave trade, Africa still awaits a rosy future.

The tragic truth is that while America and Australia have become two of the world's wealthiest nations, Africa is still considered by many in the west to be as deadly, 'uncivilised' and uninhabitable as it ever was.

The legacies of this story are present in the faces of the people of African origin who walk past me today in Washington, and in the genes of others who are descended from convict forebears. They are apparent in the celebrations of Australia Day every 26 January, commemorating the arrival of the First Fleet into Sydney Harbour in 1788, and the protests of native peoples that the date instead marks the start of their demise. And it is apparent too in the fact that long after the mysteries of Africa's deadly diseases have been unravelled and understood, the old stereotypes of the place remain.

ACKNOWLEDGEMENTS

During the long years it has taken to research and write this book I have benefited from the help of many people. I'd like to firstly thank my agent, Mary Cunnane, my publisher, Jane Palfreyman, and also Ann Lennox at Allen & Unwin, for their encouragement, wise advice and commitment to this project.

Colleagues at Monash University, Melbourne and the University of Sydney have provided support, a wealth of expert knowledge and have been wonderful friends during the completion of this work. In particular Bain Attwood, Barbara Caine, Maria Nugent, Mark Peel, Marion Quartly, Barbara Russell and Sue Taffe at Monash, and Robert Aldrich, Alison Bashford, Frances Clarke, Clare Corbould, James Curran, Peter Denney, Kate Fullagar, Cindy McCreery, Mike McDonnell, Penny Russell, Richard Waterhouse and Shane White at Sydney, have been especially supportive. A special note of thanks must go to Iain McCalman for his infallible advice on all manner of things, to Kirsten McKenzie for always being willing to chat over questions of convict history and how to write history books, and to Cassandra Pybus who read the first few chapters of this work and offered her usual helpful critiques.

Other historians have also helped in diverse ways. Marcus Rediker kindly sent a reference he came across to convicts in Africa, Simon Devereux very generously shared his work on Patrick Madan, Ty Reese advised on where to find more information about Richard Miles, and Randolph Vigne sent me his unpublished work on the plans to settle the Das Voltas region of Africa. Hamish Maxwell-Stewart has been my default authority on all convict matters and has been a huge support in many ways. Additionally, Marika Sherwood and Peter Linebaugh answered emails about the mysterious fates of John Glover and Benjamin Bowsey, Anna Berkes answered questions about convict labourers at Monticello, Nigel Penn discussed the extent of Dutch claims at the Cape in the 1780s (while driving me around Cape Town's beautiful surrounds), Lucy Rutherford sent on the wording on the Katenkamp tomb at Bath Abbey, and Peter Turner travelled to the West Glamorgan Archives to track down information on convict butcher William Harry. I could not have finished this book without Susan Guy Holyoak who photocopied various documents for me in London after I had moved to Australia and was too far away to nip back for things I had missed, and who generously gave me a place to stay whenever I returned to London. And while I'm sure he doesn't remember this, I am also grateful to Paul Lovejoy who long ago, on a night out in Toronto, heard about my initial findings with regard to convicts in Africa and encouraged me to research further. All mistakes, of course, remain my own.

The many librarians and archivists who have helped me locate documents and books during the course of this research have each helped to make this book what it is. Graeme Mackenzie, genealogist for the clan Mackenzie, and Graham Clarke of Redcastle in Scotland, were tremendously welcoming and helpful in assisting me to track down the two Kenneth Mackenzies and also took me to see Captain Mackenzie's 'red castle'. I am indebted to them for their interest in this story. Moreover, I owe a great debt to the people (who remain nameless at their own request) in the still semi-closed De Beers diamond town of Oranjemund, Namibia who extended an extraordinarily generous hand of welcome and provided a means for me to go and see where the Das Voltas settlement would have been. That visit helped me to understand the nuances of the story I was researching and also, due to their boundless hospitality, was great fun.

Funding, at various stages of the project, has been provided by Monash and Sydney universities, the Mellon Foundation, the Huntington Library, the National Maritime Museum in London, and especially the Australian Research Council. I am very grateful for their faith in me and this project.

Finally, as ever, I would like to thank my family—especially my parents who selflessly tore themselves away from the delights of winter in the north of England to visit me in beautiful Ghana during one research trip there—and friends too numerous to name, who helped in ways only they know. Without them none of this would have been at all possible.

LIST OF ABBREVIATIONS

*All records held by the National Archives, London,
except entries in* **bold**

ADM	Admiralty Papers		**Archives**
AO	Archives Office	**LSP**	**London Session Papers**
ASSI	Records of the Justices of	**ML**	**Mitchell Library, Sydney**
	Assize	**NMM**	**National Maritime Museum,**
BT	Board of Trade Papers		**London**
CLRO	**Corporation of London**	**OBSP**	**Old Bailey Sessions Papers**
	Records Office	PC	Papers of the Privy Council
CO	Colonial Office Papers	PCOM	Prisons Commission Papers
HCA	High Court of the Admiralty		PRO Domestic Records of
HO	Home Office Papers		the Public Records Office
HRNSW	**Historical Records of**	T	Treasury Papers
	New South Wales	TS	Treasury Solicitors' Papers
KB	Records of the Court of the	WO	War Office Papers
	King's Bench	ZHC	Publications of the House of
LMA	**London Metropolitan**		Commons

NOTES

Introduction

1   WO 34/172 f. 156.
2   Joseph Wall, *Genuine and Impartial Memoirs of the Life of Governor Wall, Who Was Tried and Convicted at the Old Bailey* (London: J. Davenport, 1802) pp. 8–9.
3   M.B. Schedvin and C.B. Schedvin, 'The Nomadic Tribes of Urban Britain: A Prelude to Botany Bay', *Historical Studies: Australia and New Zealand* 18:71 (October 1978) pp. 254–76.
4   L.D. Schwarz, 'Income Distribution and Social Structure in London in the Late Eighteenth Century', *Economic History Review* 32:2 (May 1979) pp. 250–9.
5   Peter Ackroyd, *London: The Biography* (London: Vintage, 2001) pp. 131–43.
6   Clive Emsley, *Crime and Society in England, 1750–1900* (Harlow: Pearson Education, 2005) p. 120; *Daily Gazetteer* 23 September 1736; V.A.C. Gatrell, *The Hanging Tree: Execution and the English People, 1770–1868* (Oxford: Oxford University Press, 1994) p. 81; Greg Dening, *Mr Bligh's Bad Language: Passion, Power and Theatre on the Bounty* (Cambridge: Cambridge University Press, 1992) p. 248.
7   Emsley, *Crime and Society in England*, pp. 33–4; Peter King, *Crime, Justice and Discretion in England, 1740–1820* (Oxford: Oxford University Press, 2000) pp. 161–6; Douglas Hay, 'War, Dearth and Theft in the Eighteenth Century: The Record of the English Courts', *Past and Present* 95 (May 1982) pp. 117–60.
8   J.M. Beattie, *Crime and the Courts in England, 1660–1800* (Princeton: Princeton University Press, 1986), pp. 227–8n; King, *Crime, Justice and Discretion*, p. 155.
9   Emsley, *Crime and Society in England*, pp. 58–62; Beattie, *Crime and the Courts*, pp. 208, 218–23, 233–4.
10 Hay, 'War, Dearth and Theft'. On arguments about a criminal class see, for example, Kirsty Reid, 'Moving On: Resolving the Convict Origins Debate', *Australian Studies* 12:1 (1997) pp. 139–55. For a discussion of wheat prices and crime, see King, *Crime, Justice and Discretion*, pp. 145–52.

11 Norma Myers, 'The Black Presence through Criminal Records, 1780–1830', *Immigrants and Minorities* 7 (1988) pp. 292–307; Gretchen Holbrook Gerzina, *Black London: Life Before Emancipation* (New Brunswick: Rutgers University Press, 1995) p. 14.

12 *Morning Herald and Daily Advertiser* 27 January 1785; Gerzina, *Black London*, pp. 15–16; Amelia Rauser, 'The Butcher-Kissing Duchess of Devonshire: Between Caricature and Allegory in 1784', *Eighteenth-Century Studies* 36:1 (2002) pp. 23–46; *Morning Herald and Daily Advertiser* 2 February 1785.

13 Adam Hochschild, *Bury the Chains: The British Struggle to Abolish Slavery* (New York: Pan Books, 2005) pp. 3, 7.

14 George E. Boulukos, 'Olaudah Equiano and the Eighteenth-Century Debate on Africa', *Eighteenth-Century Studies* 40:2 (2007) pp. 241–55; Anthony J. Barker, *The African Link: British Attitudes to the Negro in the Era of the Atlantic Slave Trade, 1550–1807* (London: Frank Cass, 1978) pp. 128–34; Robin Law, 'Human Sacrifice in Pre-Colonial West Africa', *African Affairs* 83:334 (January 1985) pp. 53–87.

15 Barker, *The African Link*, p. 120.

16 *Exeter Flying Post* 13 December 1780; Gerzina, *Black London*, p. 15. The *Oxford English Dictionary* states that 'satyr' is a rare term for an orang-utan, an animal frequently confused with chimpanzees in the eighteenth century.

17 Peter Fryer, *Staying Power: The History of Black People in Britain* (London: Pluto Press, 1984) pp. 228–9; OBSP T17790915–69.

18 I. Chukwukere, 'Akan Theory of Conception: Are the Fante Really Aberrant?', *Africa: The Journal of the International African Institute* 42:2 (1978) pp. 135–48.

19 Ibid; Margaret Priestley, *West African Trade and Coast Society* (London: Oxford University Press, 1969) pp. 10–24; James Sanders, 'The Expansion of the Fante and the Emergence of the Asante in the Eighteenth Century', *Journal of African History* 20:3 (1979) pp. 349–64.

20 Chukwukere, 'Akan Theory'; www.uiowa.edu/~africart/toc/people/Fante.html.

21 *Eora: Aboriginal Sydney*, www.sl.nsw.gov.au/discover_collections/history_nation/indigenous/eora/index.html; M. Donaldson, 'The End of Time? Aboriginal Temporality and the British Invasion of Australia' available online at http://ro.uow.edu.au/artspapers/150.

22 Emma Christopher, '"The slave trade is merciful compared to [this]": Slave Traders, Convict Transportation and the Abolitionists' in Emma Christopher, Cassandra Pybus and Marcus Rediker, *Many Middle Passages: Forced Migration and the Making of the Modern World* (Berkley: University of California Press, 2007); Cassandra Pybus, *Black Founders: The Unknown Story of Australia's First Black Settlers* (Sydney: University of New South Wales Press, 2006); Ian Duffield, 'From Slave Colonies to Penal Colonies: The West Indian Convict Transportees to Australia', *Slavery and Abolition* 7 (1988) pp. 25–45.

23 Recently even the fact of any convicts going to Africa has been called into question. Gregory Durston says, 'Few, if any, went from London to that continent [Africa].' Gregory Durston, 'Magwitch's Forbears: Returning from Transportation in Eighteenth-Century London', *Australian Journal of Legal History* 9 (2005) pp. 137–58.

CHAPTER ONE: BOUND FOR AMERICA

1 Philip Rawlings, 'Fielding, Sir John (1721–1780)', *Oxford Dictionary of National Biography* (Oxford: Oxford University Press, 2004).

2   Helen Berry, 'Polite Consumption: Shopping in Eighteenth-Century England', *Transactions of the Royal Historical Society* 12 (2002) pp. 375–94; Deirdre Palk, 'Private Crime in Public and Private Places: Pickpockets and Shoplifters in London, 1780–1823' in Tim Hitchcock and Heather Shore (eds), *The Streets of London: From the Great Fire to the Great Stink* (London: Rivers Oram, 2003) pp. 135–50.

3   OBSP T17730908–7, LMA OB/SP/1773/09/018.

4   Iain McCalman, 'Newgate in Revolution: Radical Enthusiasm and Romantic Counter-culture', *Eighteenth-Century Life* 22:1 (1998) pp. 95–110; LMA OB/SP/1772/013.

5   OBSP T17720715–62; OBSP T17711023–80; *The Life and Complete Trial of Kenith Mackenzie, Esq* (London: Robert Turner, 1785) p. 39.

6   Douglas Hay, *Albion's Fatal Tree: Crime and Society in Eighteenth-Century England* (London: A. Lane, 1975), p. 17. But see also John H. Langbein, 'Albion's Fatal Flaws', *Past and Present* 98 (Feb 1983) pp. 96–120, who argues that these were not individual statutes but rather amendments.

7   OBSP T17730908–7, LMA OB/SP/1773/09/018.

8   Douglas Hay, 'The Laws of God and the Laws of Man: Lord George Gordon and the Death Penalty' in John Rule and Robert Malcolmson (eds), *Protest and Survival: Essays for E.P. Thompson* (London: Merlin Press, 1993) pp. 60–111; Beattie, *Crime and the Courts*, pp. 146, 585; Gatrell, *The Hanging Tree*, pp. 20, 7–8; Tony Rayner, *Female Factory, Female Convicts* (Dover, Tasmania: Esperance Press, 2004) p. 19; Emsley, *Crime and Society in England*, pp. 260–2, 264; King, *Crime, Justice and Discretion*, pp. 273–8.

9   Stephen Conway, 'From Fellow Nationals to Foreigners: British Perceptions of the Americas, circa 1739–1783', *William and Mary Quarterly* 59:1 (2002) pp. 65–100.

10   SP 44/91 ff. 286–8; Hay, 'The Laws of God and the Laws of Man' in Rule and Malcolmson (eds), *Protest and Survival*, pp. 60–111; Emsley, *Crime and Society in England*, pp. 260–2, 264; King, *Crime, Justice and Discretion*, pp. 273–8; Gatrell, *The Hanging Tree*, pp. 7–8, 20; Simon Devereaux, 'Transportation, Penal Practices and the English State, 1770–1830' in Carolyn Strange (ed.), *Qualities of Mercy: Justice, Punishment and Discretion* (Vancouver: University of British Columbia Press, 1996) p. 57.

11   OBSP T17731020–62; OBSP T17730908–32; OBSP T17730908–43; OBSP T17730908–27; OBSP T17731208–12; OBSP T17731020–63; OBSP T17731208–19.

12   Christopher Jeaffreson, *A Young Squire of the Seventeenth Century*, John Cordy Jeaffreson (ed.) (London: Hurst and Blackett, 1878) vol. 1, p. 159.

13   ML MSS Campbell Letterbooks; Gwenda Morgan and Peter Rushton, *Eighteenth-Century Criminal Transportation: The Formation of the Criminal Atlantic* (Hampshire: Palgrave Macmillan, 2004) pp. 33–4; Dan Byrnes, 'Emptying the Hulks: Duncan Campbell and the First Three Fleets to Australia', *The Push From the Bush* 24 (1987) pp. 2–23; Eltis, David, Stephen D. Behrendt, David Richardson and Herbert S. Klein, *The Trans-Atlantic Slave Trade: a CD-Rom* (Cambridge University Press, 2000); now updated online at www.slavevoyages.org; Abbot Emerson Smith, *Colonists in Bondage: White Servitude and Convict Labor in America, 1607–1776* (Chapel Hill: University of North Carolina Press, 1947) p. 122. Byrnes claims that Campbell shipped 900 convicts per annum, but Morgan and Rushton suggest this is the total for the whole country rather than just London and the south-east.

14   Bruce Kercher, 'Perish or Prosper: The Law and Convict Transportation in the British Empire', *Law and History Review* 21:3 (2003) pp. 527–84.

15 OBSP t17681019–40; OBSP t17580222–31; OBSP t17250513–45; OBSP t17290226–90; OBSP t17460226–7; OBSP s17460226–1; Peter Wilson Coldham, *Emigrants in Chains: A Social History of Forced Migration to the Americas 1607–1776* (Stroud: Sutlou, 1992).

16 Morgan, 'English and American Attitudes Towards Convict Transportation 1718–1775, *History*, 72 (1987) p. 417.

17 Quoted in Roger A. Ekirch, 'Bound for America: A Profile of British Convicts Transported to the Colonies, 1718–1775', *William and Mary Quarterly* 3rd Series XLII: 2 (April 1985) p. 199 and Farley Grubb, 'The Market Evaluation of Criminality: Evidence From the Auction of British Convict Labor in America, 1767–1775', *American Economic Review* 91 (2001) p. 298.

18 *Maryland Gazette* 10 August 1767.

19 J.C. Ballagh, *White Servitude in the Colony of Virginia* (New York: Burt Franklin, 1965) pp. 23, 35; Hilary McD. Beckles, *White Servitude and Black Slavery in Barbados, 1627–1715* (Knoxville: University of Tennessee Press, 1989) p. 57; Peter Wilson Coldham, *British Emigrants in Bondage, 1614–1788* (CD-Rom) (Genealogical Publishing Company, 2005); Jeaffreson, *A Young Squire*; David Eltis, *The Rise of African Slavery in the Americas* (Cambridge: Cambridge University Press, 2000) p. 52.

20 Hilary McD. Beckles, 'The Colours of Property: Brown, White and Black Chattels and their Responses on the Caribbean Frontier' in Paul E. Lovejoy and Nicholas Rogers (eds), *Unfree Labour in the Development of the Atlantic World* (Essex: Frank Cass, 1994) pp. 38–9.

21 Warren B. Smith, *White Servitude in Colonial South Carolina* (Columbia: University of South Carolina Press, 1961) p. 39.

22 Morgan and Rushton, *Eighteenth-Century Criminal Transportation*, p. 36; Eltis, *The Rise of African Slavery*, p. 69; David W. Galenson, 'White Servitude and the Growth of Black Slavery in Colonial America', *Journal of Economic History* 41 (1981) pp. 39–47; Eugene I. McCormac, *White Servitude in Maryland, 1634–1820* (Baltimore: Johns Hopkins Press, 1904); Beckles, *White Servitude and Black Slavery in Barbados*, pp. 56, 90; Smith, *White Servitude in Colonial South Carolina*; Emerson Smith, *Colonists in Bondage*; Lorena S. Walsh, 'The Chesapeake Slave Trade: Regional Patterns, African Origins, and Some Implications', *William and Mary Quarterly* 58:1 (2001) pp. 139–70.

23 Fredrick Hall Schmidt, 'British Convict Servant Labor in Colonial Virginia', unpublished PhD dissertation, College of William and Mary (1976) pp. 5–6.

24 Ibid.

25 *Maryland Gazette* 30 July 1767; Schmidt, 'British Convict Servant Labor' pp. 5–6.

26 Morgan and Rushton, *Eighteenth-Century Criminal Transportation*, pp. 59–60; [Purdie and Dixon] *Virginia Gazette* 24 March 1774.

27 *Virginia Gazette* [Purdie and Dixon] 10 March 1774.

28 Quoted in Rushton and Morgan, *Eighteenth-Century Criminal Transportation*, p. 131.

29 Rind's *Virginia Gazette* [Rind] 10 March 1774. On Hodge see Schmidt, 'British Convict Servant Labor' pp. 86–8.

30 *Virginia Gazette* [Rind] 10 March 1774.

31 Grubb, 'The Market Evaluation of Criminality', pp. 295–304; Kenneth Morgan, 'Convict Transportation to Colonial America', *Reviews in American History* 17 (1989) pp. 29–34; R. Kent Lancaster, 'Almost Chattel: The Lives of Indentured Servants at

Hampton-Northampton, Baltimore County', *Maryland Historical Magazine* 94 (1999) pp. 341–62.

32   OBSP T17710911–78, OBSP T17730908–24; OBSP T17730707–19.

33   OBSP T17731208–74; OBSP T17730908–93; OBSP T17731020–27; OBSP T17730113–30; OBSP T17731020–20; OBSP T17731020–20; *Virginia Gazette* [Rind] 12 May 1774.

34   William Green, *The Sufferings of William Green, Being a Sorrowful Account of his Seven Years Transportation* (London: J. Lond, 1774) pp. 4, 6.

35   James Revel, *Poor Unhappy Felon's Sorrowful Account* (London c.1800) pp. 4–6. Revel's account is probably a composite of other convict stories. For a more measured account of convict lives in North America, see Lancaster, 'Almost Chattel'.

36   He was also known by the names Woolford and Davis. Alan Atkinson, 'The Free-Born Englishman Transported: Convict Rights as a Measure of Eighteenth Century Empire', *Past and Present* (1994) p. 91; Coldham, *Emigrants in Chains*; OBSP T17190903–7; OBSP T17210301–61.

37   Morgan and Rushton, 'Running away and returning home: The Fate of English in the American Colonies' *Crime, Histoire et Sociétiés*: 7:2 (2003), pp. 61–80; Coldham, *Emigrants in Chains* p. 84; Atkinson, 'The Free-Born Englishman'; Frederick Hall Schmidt, 'Sold and Driven: Assignment of Convicts in Eighteenth-Century Virginia', *Push from the Bush* 23 (October 1986) pp. 2–27.

38   John J. McCusker, *Money and Exchange in Europe and America, 1600–1775: A Handbook* (Chapel Hill, NC: University of North Carolina Press, c1978); Liza Picard, *Dr. Johnson's London* (London: St Martin's Press, 2002) p. 297.

39   *The Life and the Complete Trial of Kenith Mackenzie.*

40   T.H. Breen, *Tobacco Culture: The Mentality of the Great Tidewater Planters on the Eve of Revolution* (Princeton: Princeton University Press, 1985) pp. 46–55.

41   J.H. Soltow, 'Scottish Merchants in Virginia 1750–75', *Economic History Review* 21:1 (1959) pp. 83–98; Breen, *Tobacco Culture*, pp. 22–3, 60–70.

42   A.G.L. Shaw, *Convicts and the Colonies: A study of penal transportation from Great Britain & Ireland to Australia and other parts of the British Empire* (Dublin: Irish Historical Press, 1998), p. 32.

43   Coldham, *British Emigrants in Bondage*; Morgan, 'Convict Runaways in Maryland, 1745–1775', *English Historical Review* (1989) p. 262.

44   Peter A. Dorsey, 'To "Corroborate Our Own Claims": Public Positioning and the Slavery Metaphor in Revolutionary America', *American Quarterly* 55:3 (2003) pp. 353–86.

45   Shane White and Graham White, 'Slave Clothing and African-American Culture in the Eighteenth and Nineteenth Centuries', *Past and Present* 148 (1995) pp. 149–86; Lois Green Carr, 'Emigration and the Standard of Living: The Eighteenth-Century Chesapeake' in John J. McCusker and Kenneth Morgan (eds), *The Early Modern Atlantic Economy* (Cambridge: Cambridge University Press, 2000) pp. 319–63; Lois Green Carr and Lorena S. Walsh, 'Changing Lifestyles and Consumer Behavior in the Colonial Chesapeake' in Cary Carson, Ronald Hoffman and Peter J. Albert (eds), *Of Consuming Interests: The Style of Life in the Eighteenth Century* (Charlottesville: University Press of Virginia, 1994) pp. 66–9.

46   Ernest M. Eller (ed.), *Chesapeake Bay in the American Revolution* (Centreville: Tidewater Publishers, 1981) p. 399; Michael A. McDonnell and Woody Holton,

'Patriot vs. Patriot: Social Conflict in Virginia and the Origins of the American Revolution', *Journal of American Studies* 34:2 (2000) pp. 231–56.

47 *Virginia Gazette* [Pinkey] 1 June 1775.

48 *Virginia Gazette* [Purdie] 2 June 1775; *Virginia Gazette* [Pinkey] 28 September 1775.

CHAPTER TWO: MR JEFFERSON AND PATRICK MADAN

1   OBSP т17740706–18; OBSP т17740907–62; OBSP т17740706–19; LMA OB/SP/1774/07/021; LMA OB/SP/1774/07/021; LMA OB/SP/1774/07/027a; LMA OB/SP/1774/07/028;LMA OB/SP/1774/07/029a. LMA MJ/SP/1774/04/109 also apparently relates to Madan's crimes in early 1774, but according to the library catalogue is 'unfit to consult'.

2   Ackroyd, *London*, pp. 293–4; *Public Advertiser* 20 August 1774; Stephen Halliday, *Newgate: London's Prototype of Hell* (Stroud: Sutton Publishing, 2006) pp. 63–6.

3   Quoted in Gatrell, *The Hanging Tree*, pp. 45–6 (emphasis in original). Kenneth Morgan, 'Petitions against Convict Transportation, 1725–1735', *English Historical Review* (1989) pp. 110–13.

4   Gatrell, *The Hanging Tree*, pp. 29–40, 56–7; Michel Foucault, *Discipline and Punish: The Birth of the Prison* (New York: Random House, 1995) pp. 50–3; George Rudé, *Hanovarian London, 1714–1808* (London: Secker and Walburg, 1971) p. 94; Alan Brooke and David Brandon, *Tyburn: London's Fatal Tree* (Stroud: Sutton, 2004) p. 188.

5   *Public Ledger* 20 August 1774.

6   OBSP т17740907–62; Coldham, *Emigrants in Chains*; *Morning Chronicle* 20 August 1774, 11 January 1775; *London Chronicle* 23 August 1774, 10 January 1775; *Morning Chronicle and London Advertiser* 12 September 1774.

7   *London Evening Post* 7 February 1775; *London Chronicle* 9 February 1775; *Morning Post and Public Advertiser* 9 February 1775; *Lloyd's Evening Post* 10 February 1775; *Bingley's London Journal* 11 February 1775; *General Evening Post* 14 February 1775.

8   *Morning Chronicle and London Advertiser* 25 February 1775; *Middlesex Journal and Evening Advertiser* 29 April 1775; *St James's Chronicle or British Evening Post* 29 April 1775.

9   Dror Wahrman, 'The English Problem of Identity in the American Revolution', *American Historical Review* 106:4 (October 2001) pp. 1236–62; Eliga H. Gould, 'The American Revolution in Britain's Imperial Identity' in Fred M. Leventhal and Roland Quinault, *Anglo-American Attitudes: From Revolution to Partnership* (Aldershot: Ashgate, 2000) pp. 23–31; Conway, 'From Fellow Nationals to Foreigners'; Mary Beth Norton, *The British-Americans: The Loyalist Exiles in England, 1774–1789* (London: Constable, 1974) pp. 37, 42–61. The lists of pensions for returned loyalists do not begin until 1776 (AO 12 and AO 13) by which time Murray would surely have been struck off even if he had earlier been successful in claiming.

10 There is no evidence that Murray was ever employed by Thomas Jefferson. See Lucia C. Stanton, 'Indentured Servants at Monticello', unpublished report prepared for the Jefferson Library. I am grateful to Anna Berkes at the Jefferson Library for assisting with this query.

11 Hallie Rubenhold, *The Covent Garden Ladies: Pimp General Jack & The Extraordinary Story of Harris's List* (Stroud: Tempus, 2005); Tony Henderson, *Disorderly Women in*

Eighteenth-Century London: Prostitution and Control in the Metropolis, 1730–1830 (London: Longman, 1999) pp. 32–3.

12 Picard, *Dr Johnson's London*, pp. 253–7.

13 Gillian Russell, 'The Peeress and the Prostitutes: The Founding of the London Pantheon 1772', *Nineteenth-Century Contexts* 27:1 (March 2005) pp. 11–30.

14 Oxford Road is now Oxford Street. The Pantheon was on the site of the present day Marks and Spencer store of that name. The building in which the masquerades were held burned down in 1792. OBSP T17760417–3; LMA OB/SP/1776; LMA OB/SP/1776; uncatalogued additional papers.

15 John Howard, *The State of the Prisons in England and Wales with Preliminary Observations and an Account of some Foreign Prisons and Hospitals* (Warrington: William Eyres, 1780) pp. 163–4; Randall McGowan, 'The Well-Ordered Prison: England 1780–1865' in Norval Morris and David J. Rothman (eds), *The Oxford History of the Prison: The Practice of Punishment in Western Society* (Oxford: Oxford University Press, 1998) pp. 73–5.

16 Howard, *The State of the Prisons*, pp. 1, 5–10, 17–19.

17 H.M. Scott, 'Thynne, Thomas, third Viscount Weymouth and first marquess of Bath (1734–1796)', *Oxford Dictionary of National Biography* (Oxford: Oxford University Press, 2004).

18 James Oldham, 'Murray, William, first earl of Mansfield (1705–1793)', *Oxford Dictionary of National Biography* (Oxford: Oxford University Press, 2004).

19 *Morning Chronicle and London Advertiser* 11 December 1778. Perhaps we have to suspect Beauchamp or Cornwall as they were the only men, other than North himself, to hold the office throughout the period of Murray's escapes from the law.

CHAPTER THREE: LONDON IN FLAMES

1 Wilfred Oldham, *Britain's Convicts to the Colonies* (Sydney: Library of Australian History, 1990) pp. 34–6.

2 SP 44/94 ff. 1, 2–5.

3 Campbell Letterbooks, Mitchell Library, A3225 f.503; PCOM 2/168.

4 OBSP T17850406–81.

5 OBSP S17770910–1; ASSI 31/12; SP44/96.

6 A3225 ff. 357, 364, 503, 513–4, 521; A3226 ff. 72, 156–7, 184; A3231 part 2, ff. 4, 13–4; W. Branch Johnson, *The English Prison Hulks* (London: Christopher Johnson, 1957) pp. 1–17; Suzanne Rikard (ed.), *George Barrington's Voyage to Botany Bay* (London: Leicester University Press, 2001) p. 11.

7 *London Chronicle* 19 August 1777.

8 *Morning Post and Daily Advertiser* 22 August 1777.

9 OBSP T17780115–66; Devereaux, Simon, 'Patrick Madan: One Man's Odyssey through England's Penal Crisis, 1774–1784', unpublished Paper. *Morning Chronicle* 15 September 1777; *The General Evening Post* 19 August 1777; *Morning Chronicle and London Advertiser* 8 September 1777; *London Evening Post* 11 September 1777; *Gazetteer and New Daily Advertiser* 9 February 1780.

10 *St James Chronicle or British Evening Post* 28 February 1778.

11 Later that year Thomas Colcomb's warehouse would be 'stripped of everything in it', including a lock of hair from his infant son who had died a few days before, OBSP

T17761204–13; *The Life and Complete Trial of Kenith Mackenzie*, pp. 39–40; *Morning Chronicle* 11 December 1778.

12 OBSP T17781021–4; OBSP T17790519–22; *The Life and Complete Trial of Kenith Mackenzie*, p. 40; OBSP T17790404–52; *Morning Chronicle* 7 January 1779.

13 *Morning Chronicle* 11 December 1778, 7 January 1779; Rickard, *George Barrington's Voyage*, pp. 3–5.

14 *General Advertiser and Morning Intelligencer* 1 July 1779; *Public Advertiser* 1 July 1779.

15 OBSP T17790707–32; Beattie, 'Scales of justice: Defense Council and the English Criminal Trial in the Eighteenth and Nineteenth Centuries', *Law and History Review* 9:2 (Autumn 1991); Beattie, *Crime and the Courts*, pp. 167–70; *Morning Chronicle* 8 July 1779. Morris too would be found guilty for his part in these events, OBSP T17790707–35.

16 Tim Hitchcock, 'Begging on the Streets of Eighteenth-Century London', *Journal of British Studies* 44:3 (July 2005) pp. 478–98; LMA MJ/SP/1779/001; OBSP T17790707–33; OBSP T17790707–34.

17 Howard, *The State of the Prisons*.

18 OBSP T17800510–13.

19 Colin Haydon, 'Gordon, Lord George (1751–1793)', *Oxford Dictionary of National Biography* (Oxford: Oxford University Press, 2004).

20 Peter Linebaugh, *The London Hanged: Crime and Civil Society in the Eighteenth Century* (London: Penguin, 1991) pp. 331–4; Thomas Babington Macaulay, *The History of England in the Eighteenth Century* (London: the Folio Society 1980, first published 1848) 175*n*; Nicolas Rogers, 'Crowd and People in the Gordon Riots' in Eckhart Hellmuth (ed.), *The Transformation of Political Culture: England and Germany in the Late Eighteenth Century* (Oxford: Oxford University Press, 1990) pp. 39–41; Eliga H. Gould, *Persistence of Empire: British Political Thinking in the Age of the American Revolution* (Chapel Hill: University of North Carolina Press, 2000) p. 175.

21 LMA LSP/1780/5; John Ashton, *The Old Bailey and Newgate* (New York: James Pott and Company, 1902) pp. 204–19; Knapp and Baldwin, *New Newgate Calendar, Comprising Interesting Memoirs of the Most Notorious Characters vol. 4* (London: J. Robins and Co, 1825) pp. 144–8; George Rudé, 'The Gordon Riots: A Study of the Rioters and their Victims', *Transactions of the Royal Historical Society* 5th series, 6 (1956) pp. 93–114; Halliday, *Newgate*, p. 119; Linebaugh, *London Hanged*, pp. 333–42; OBSP T17790915–74; OBSP T17790915–65; OBSP T17790707–8; Linebaugh mentions Murray and Doyle as being escapees, but is mistaken in thinking the former was an Irishman.

22 OBSP T17790707–8; Linebaugh, *London Hanged*, p. 341; Ashton, *The Old Bailey and Newgate*, pp. 204–19.

23 LMA LSP 1780/5.

24 LMA LSP/1780/5; OBSP T17800628–26; Linebaugh, *London Hanged*, p. 364; *Lloyd's Evening Post* January 3–5 1781; *General Evening Post* 10 June 1780.

25 OBSP T17800628–94; OBSP T17800628–33; OBSP T17800628–110; OBSP T17800628–71; OBSP T17800628–26; CO 267/10, Petition from John Morris, Cape Coast Castle 29 July 1794.

26 Gatrell, *The Hanging Tree*, pp. 20, 31–2; PCOM 2/169.

27 OBSP T17801206–45; OBSP T17801206–46; *Gazetteer and New Daily Advertiser* 1 November 1780; *General Evening Post* 7 November 1780.

28 OBSP T17810110–18. The book could, alternatively, have been an attack on Samuel Foote by the Reverend William Jackson which lampooned the cork-footed Foote as homosexual. Called *Sodom and Onan*, it had included *The Devil Upon Two Sticks* as a subtitle as well as a picture of a foot, to make sure that all readers knew the allusions were to Foote, who had previously produced the Le Sage play very successfully at the Haymarket Theatre.

29 Peter Linebaugh writes that Bowsey and Glover hanged for their crimes, but they were clearly still alive beyond the date he believes that they hanged and were offered respites. WO 1/874 f. 347; SP 44/95 f. 1, pp. 114–15; LMA LSP 1781/4; LMA LSP 1781/4.

CHAPTER FOUR: THE 'BEST SACRIFICES FOR DEATH'

1 G.C. Bolton, 'William Eden and the Convicts, 1771–1787', *Australian Journal of History and Politics* 26:1 (1980) pp. 30–44; A.J. Draper, 'William Eden and Leniency in Punishment', *History of Political Thought* 22:1 (Spring 2001) pp. 106–30.

2 Michael Ignatieff, *A Just Measure of Pain: The Penitentiary in the Industrial Revolution, 1750–1850* (London: MacMillan, 1978).

3 Ignatieff, *A Just Measure of Pain* pp. 45–7, 61–3, 81, 93–6; Draper, 'William Eden'.

4 William Eden, *Principles of Penal Law* (London: B. White and T. Cadell, 1771) p. 34.

5 J.M. Gray, *A History of the Gambia* (Cambridge: Cambridge University Press, 1940) pp. 158–9; Daniel Defoe [Charles Johnson], *A General History of the Robberies and Murders of the Most Notorious Pyrates* (New York: Garland Publishing, 1972) pp. 152–4; James F. Searing, *West African Slavery and Atlantic Commerce: The Senegal River Valley, 1700–1860* (Cambridge: Cambridge University Press, 1993) p. 103–4. Much to Prime Minister William Pitt's chagrin, Gorée was not included in the colony as it had been handed back to France by the Treaty of Paris. Gray, *A History of the Gambia*, pp. 230–3; Walter Frewen Lord, 'Gorée: A Lost Possession of England', *Transactions of the Royal Historical Society* 11 (1897) pp. 139–52; Pierre H. Boulle, 'Eighteenth-Century French Policies Toward Senegal: The Ministry of Choiseul', *Canadian Journal of African Studies/Revue Canadienne des Études Africaines* (1970) pp. 305–20.

6 Thora G. Stone, 'The Journey of Cornelius Hodges in Senegambia, 1689–90', *English Historical Review* (1924) pp. 89–95; E. Ann McDougall, 'The Quest for "Tarra": Toponymy and Geography in Exploring History', *History in Africa* 18 (1991) pp. 271–98; Gray, *A History of the Gambia* pp. 27–8; R. Hallett, *The Penetration of Africa: European Enterprise and Exploration Principally in Northern and Western Africa up to 1815*, (London: Routledge & Kegan Paul, 1965) pp. 67, 129, 143.

7 Christopher Brown, *Moral Capital: Foundations of British Abolitionism* (Chapel Hill: University of North Carolina Press, 2006) pp. 269–75, quotes pp. 272, 275; Adam Smith, *An Inquiry into the Nature and Causes of the Wealth of Nations*, Library of Economics and Liberty, www.econlib.org/library/Smith/smWN20.html.

8 'Act Vesting Senegal in the Crown, 1765', 'Propositions for forming a civil government and military establishment, 1 November 1765', 'Instructions to Colonel Charles O'Hara, 6 February 1766' all reprinted in Fredrick Madden and David Fieldhouse

(eds), *Select Documents on the Constitutional History of the British Empire and Commonwealth, vol. 3, Imperial Reconstruction, 1763–1840* (New York: Greenwood Press, 1987) pp. 496–501.

9   Ibid; Brown, *Moral Capital*, pp. 274–7.

10   Hallett, *The Penetration of Africa*, pp. 144–5.

11   William D. Griffin, 'General Charles O'Hara', *Irish Sword* 10:40 (1972) pp. 179–87.

12   Searing, *West African Slavery*, p. 97.

13   Mark Harrison, *Climates and Constitutions: Health, Race, Environment and British Imperial India* (Oxford: Oxford University Press, 1999), especially pp. 58–75, quote p. 59; Mark Harrison, '"The Tender Frame of Man": Disease, Climate, and Racial Difference in India and the West Indies, 1760–1860', *Bulletin of the History of Medicine* 70:1 (1996) pp. 68–93; Karen Ordahl Kupperman, 'Fear of Hot Climates in the Anglo-American Colonial Experience', *William and Mary Quarterly* 41:2 (April 1984) pp. 213–40.

14   PD. Curtin, '"The White Man's Grave": Image and Reality, 1780–1850', *Journal of British Studies*, 1:1 (1961) pp. 94–110; Harrison, '"The Tender Frame of Man"'; Roger Norman Buckley, *Slaves in Red Coats: The British West India Regiments, 1795–1815* (New Haven: Yale University Press, 1979) pp. 7–8.

15   CO 267/1; Eltis et al, *Trans-Atlantic Slave Trade* Database.

16   Curtin, *Economic Change in Precolonial Africa: Senegambia in the Era of the Slave Trade* (Madison: University of Wisconsin Press, 1975) pp. 110–1, 174; Boubacar Barry, *Senegambia and the Atlantic Slave Trade* (Cambridge: Cambridge University Press, 1988) p. 68.

17   Searing, *West African Slavery*, pp. 152–3; Curtin, *Economic Change*, pp. 126–7; Gray, *A History of the Gambia*, pp. 239–42, Barry, *Senegambia*, pp. 87, 102–3.

18   CO 267/1; Buckley, *Slaves in Red Coats*, pp. 33–8.

19   Peter Way, 'Class and the Common Soldier in the Seven Years War', *Labor History* 44:4 (2003) pp. 455–81; Stephen R. Conway, 'The Recruitment of Criminals into the British Army, 1775–81', *Bulletin of the Institute of Historical Research* 137 (May 1985) pp. 46–58; Roger Norman Buckley, *The British Army in the West Indies: Society and the Military in the Revolutionary War* (Gainesville: University of Florida Press, 1998) p. 58; Richard Holmes, *Redcoat: The British Soldier in the Age of Horse and Musket* (London: HarperCollins, 2002) p. 138.

20   Arthur N. Gilbert, 'The Recruitment of the East India Company Army, 1760–1800', *Journal of British Studies*, 15:1 (1975) pp. 89–111; Andrew O'Shaughnessy, 'Redcoats and Slaves in the British Caribbean' in Stanley L. Engerman and Robert Paquette, *The Lesser Antilles in the Age of European Expansion* (Gainesville: University of Florida Press, 1996) p. 111.

21   Buckley, *The British Army*, p. 95.

22   British Library ADD MSS 34413 ff. 11–12; O'Shaughnessy, 'Redcoats and Slaves', p. 110.

23   OBSP T17680706–28; WO 1/874; George Rudé, *Wilkes and Liberty* (London: Lawrence and Wishart, 1983).

24   OBSP T17681207–20; WO 1/874.

25   OBSP T17690222–52; OBSP T17680907–14; OBSP T17690112–15; WO 1/847; Stephen Nicholas and Richard H. Steckel, 'Heights and Living Standards of English Workers

during the Early Years of Industrialization, 1770–1815', *Journal of Economic History* 51 (1991) pp. 937–57.

26   WO 1/874 ff. 69–71.

27   OBSP T17680907–7; OBSP T17690405–44; OBSP T17680907–14; WO 1/847; Coldham, *British Emigrants in Bondage.*

28   WO 1/992, 15 June 1776.

29   John Joseph Crooks, 'A Statement of Events at Senegal and Gorée, 1758–1874', *United Service Magazine,* 173 (1916) p. 420; Arthur N. Gilbert, 'The Recruitment of the East India Company Army, 1760–1800', *Journal of British Studies* 15:1 (1975) pp. 89–111.

30   CO 267/16.

31   SP 37/13.

32   *House of Commons Journal* vol. 37; Oldham, *Britain's Convicts to the Colonies,* p. 70; Crooks, 'A Statement of Events at Senegal and Gorée', pp. 418–9.

33   *House of Commons Journal* vol. 37; Oldham, *Britain's Convicts to the Colonies,* p. 70.

34   By the time the African plan was implemented, Eden's penal ideas had moved on. See Draper, 'William Eden' and Bolton, 'William Eden'.

35   Arnold Lawrence, *Trade Castles and Forts of West Africa* (London: Johnathan Cape, 1963); William St Clair, *The Grand Slave Emporium: Cape Coast Castle and the British Slave Trade* (London: Profile, 2006).

36   Eveline C. Martin, *The British West African Settlements, 1720–1821* (London: Longmans, Green and Co, 1927) pp. 5–6, 9–10, quote p. 11.

37   Ibid., p. 18.

38   St Clair, *The Grand Slave Emporium.*

39   Lawrence, *Trade Castles and Forts,* p. 59

40   Ty M. Reese, 'Toiling in the Empire: Labor in Three Anglo-Atlantic Ports, London, Philadelphia and Cape Coast Castle, 1750–1783', unpublished Ph.D dissertation, University of Toledo (1999) pp. 79, 134; St Clair, *The Grand Slave Emporium,* pp. 130–1.

41   Lawrence, *Trade Castles and Forts,* p. 59.

42   CO 267/20 ff. 37–8.

43   Ibid.

CHAPTER FIVE: AFRICA

1   WO 34/172 f. 156.

2   WO 12/8314; Angus Fairrie, *Queen's Own Highlanders (Seaforths and Camerons): An Illustrated History* (published for the Queen's Own Highlanders Trust, 1998) pp. 1–2; Douglas Watt, '"The Laberinth of Thir Difficulties": The Influence of Debt on the Highland Elite, c.1550–1700', *The Scottish Historical Review* 85:1 (April 2006) pp. 28–51; Andrew Mackillop, *More Fruitful than the Soil: Army, Empire and the Scottish Highlands, 1715–1815* (East Linton: Tuckwell Press, 2000).

3   Jim Stockton, *Seaforth Highlanders: A Fighting Soldier Remembers* (Somerset: Crécy Books, 1987) pp. 2–3.

4   *Morning Chronicle* 30 September 1778; H. Paton, *A Series of Original Portraits and Caricature Etchings by the Late John Kay* (Edinburgh: Adam and Charles Black, 1877) pp. 294–5.

5   Ferdinand Brock Tupper, *The History of Guernsey and its Bailiwick, with Occasional Notices of Jersey* (London: Simpkin, Marshall and Co., 1876) pp. 411–2; *Edinburgh Advertiser* 14–17 December 1784.

6   National Archives of Scotland, CS 8/5/16: Decreet of Divorce Mrs Jean Thomson ag[ain]st Kenneth Mackenzie 1780; Leah Leneman, '"Disregarding the Matrimonial Vows": Divorce in 18th and Early 19th Century Scotland', *Journal of Social History* 30:2 (Winter 1996) pp. 465–82.

7   National Archives of Scotland, CS 96/4733; National Archives of Scotland, CS 271/31041; Leneman, '"Disregarding the Matrimonial Vows"'.

8   David Alston, 'Ross, George, of Cromarty (1708/9–1786)', *Oxford Dictionary of National Biography* (Oxford: Oxford University Press, 2004); National Library of Scotland, CS 96/4733 f. 20.

9   SP 46/151 ff. 173–4; I am grateful to Dr Lucy Rutherford, archivist at Bath Abbey, who sent me details of the full inscription from the tomb. David Hill Radcliffe, 'Hole, Richard (bap. 1746, d. 1803)', *Oxford Dictionary of National Biography* (Oxford: Oxford University Press, 2004).

10 George Eyre-Evans, 'Exeter Academy, 1760–1771', *Devon and Cornwall Notes and Queries* 4 (Jan 1906–October 1907) pp. 108–111; Anonymous, *A List of All the Officers of the Army: Viz. the General and Field Officers* (London: War Office, 1780) p. 71.

11 A. Michael Brander, *The Royal Scots: the Royal Regiment* (London: Leo Cooper Ltd, 1976) pp. 21–2; Lawrence Weaver, *The Royal Scots* (London: Country Life, 1915) p. 116.

12 Charles Fraser-Mackintosh, *Letters of Two Centuries: Chiefly Connected with Inverness and the Highlands* (Inverness: A. & W. Mackenzie, 1890) p. 20; Duncan Warrand, *Some Mackenzie Pedigrees* (Inverness: Robert Caruthers & Sons, 1965) p. 78.

13 WO 34/172, ff. 38, 970.

14 WO 34/172, ff. 156–7.

15 WO 34/172 ff. 295, 104.

16 WO 34/172 ff. 102, 106.

17 Treasury Paper, TNA 70/1545; Stephen Conway, 'The Recruitment of Criminals', pp. 46–58; T 1/564.

18 CO 267/7.

19 Ibid.

20 WO 34/225 f. 487 [no date].

21 T 1/564 ; ASSI 33/6; OBSP T17790113–40; OBSP T17781209–16.

22 OBSP T17770702–4; SP 44/95; T 70/1545.

23 OBSP T17781021–4.

24 OBSP T17810110–5; OBSP T17810110–2.

25 OBSP T17810110–7.

26 OBSP T17810222–41; OBSP T17810222–2; PCOM 2/169.

27 *London Chronicle* 10 February 1781.

28 *Morning Chronicle and London Advertiser* 22 May 1781; WO 34/225 f. 363; *Gazetteer and New Daily Advertiser* 22 May 1781.

29 CO 267/20.

30 PC 1/3103, Mackenzie's testimony, 23 October 1783.

31 Duncan Campbell Letterbooks A 3231 [part 2] f. 4; OBSP 017811205–1.

32 OBSP 017800628–1; OBSP T17800628–71.

33 Rudé, 'The Gordon Riots', p. 105; Marika Sherwood, 'Blacks in the Gordon Riots', *History Today* 47:12 (December 1997) pp. 24–8; *Gazetteer and New Daily Advertiser* 3 October 1780. I am grateful to Marika Sherwood for the suggestion that Glover went on the *Sylph*, but I have been unable to find him in the ship's logbook at ADM 34/735. There are no records for Poultry Compter prior to 1782 so the exact history of the two men is hard to trace.

34 *Whitehall Evening Post* 29 November 1781; *Morning Chronicle and London Advertiser* 30 November 1781.

35 CO 268/3.

36 Keith P. Herzog, 'Naval Operations in West Africa and the Disruption of the Slave Trade during the American Revolution', *The American Neptune* 55:1 (1995) pp. 42–8.

37 *Craftsman or Say's Weekly Journal* 21 July 1781.

38 *Craftsman or Say's Weekly Journal* 21 July 1781; *London Chronicle* 28 July 1781; *Morning Chronicle* 31 August 1781; *Public Advertiser* 25 October 1781.

39 OBSP 017820109–2; Gentleman of the Inner Temple, *Authentic Memoirs of the Life, Numerous Adventures and Remarkable Escapes of Patrick Madan* (London, 1782) 37–8; WO 35/225 ff. 321, 344, 327, 330, 333, 421, 430, 448.

40 Thomas Shirley had once had charge of twelve-year-old Philip Gidley King, who would later sail to New South Wales with Arthur Phillip as one of the founders of modern Australia and eventually be Governor of New South Wales. Arthur Phillip, *The Voyage of Governor Phillip to Botany Bay . . .* (London, 1789).

41 HO 42/6 ff. 373–382 ; OBSP т17780115–48; T 70/1549 part 1; OBSP т17780115–48; OBSP 017781021–1. Patrick Madan would later claim to have escaped while at Cork and this story has been generally believed by historians. The weight of evidence would suggest otherwise, however.

42 T.F. Henderson, 'Cranstoun, William Henry (bap. 1714, d. 1752)', *Oxford Dictionary of National Biography* (Oxford: Oxford University Press, 2004); www.electricscotland. com/history/nation/cranston.htm.

43 CO 267/20 ff. 180–7; John Joseph Crooks, *Records Relating to the Gold Coast Settlements from 1750 to 1874* (Dublin: Brown & Nolan, 1923), pp. 52, 61; Robert B. Shoemaker, 'The Taking of the Duel: Masculinity, Honour and Ritual Violence in London, 1669–1800', *The Historical Journal* 43:3 (2002) pp. 525–45, *The Times* quote p. 535.

44 ADM 36/9915.

45 Crooks, *Gold Coast Settlements*, p. 53; CO 267/19; CO 268/3 Germain to Wall, 30 May 1782.

46 Crooks, *Gold Coast Settlements*, p. 53.

47 T 70/1545.

CHAPTER SIX: THE BATTLE FOR THE COAST

1 St Clair, *The Grand Slave Emporium*, p. 10.

2 Eltis et al, *Trans-Atlantic Slave Trade* Database, voyage *Brooks*: 80663, *Molly*: 82768, *Nancy*: 82847, *Gascoyne*: 17907, *Gregson*: 81669.

3 Eltis et al, *Trans-Atlantic Slave Trade* Database, 80663; Marcus Rediker, *The Slave Ship: A Human History* (New York: Viking, 2007) pp. 308–10.

4   Samuel Robinson, *A Sailor Boy's Experience Aboard a Slave Ship in the Beginning of the Present Century* (Wigtown: GC Books, 1996) pp. 76–7.

5   St Clair, *The Grand Slave Emporium*; Crooks, *Gold Coast Settlements*, p. 49.

6   T 70/69 f. 143.

7   Ludewig Ferdinand Rømer, *A Reliable Account of the Coast of Guinea*, Selena Axelrod Winsnes (trans. and ed.) (Oxford: Oxford University Press, 2000) pp. 51–2.

8   Lawrence, *Trade Castles and Forts*, pp. 164–79; St Clair, *The Grand Slave Emporium*, pp. 64–5, 72.

9   CO 268/3, Germain to Mackenzie, 30 May 1781; ADM 2/1340, Sandwich, Penton and Gascoyne to Thomas Shirley, 2 July 1781; Crooks, *Gold Coast Settlements*, pp. 49–50; Piers Mackesy, 'Germain, George Sackville, first Viscount Sackville (1716–1785)', *Oxford Dictionary of National Biography* (Oxford: Oxford University Press, 2004).

10   Crooks, *Gold Coast Settlements*, p. 51; Kwesi J. Anquandah, *Castles and Forts of Ghana* (Paris: Atalante, 1999) pp. 52–61; Lawrence, *Trade Castles and Forts*, p. 97.

11   Crooks, *Gold Coast Settlements*, pp. 54–5; Lawrence, *Trade Castles and Forts*, pp. 80–2.

12   L/L/282, Lieutenant's log of HMS *Leander*, National Maritime Museum, London; ADM 36/9570.

13   ADM 36/10021; T 70/30; T 70/1341; George Metcalf, 'Gold, Assortments and the Trade Ounce: Fante Merchants and the Problem of Supply and Demand in the 1770s', *Journal of African History* 28:1 (1987) pp. 27–41.

14   ADM 36/10021.

15   ADM 36/9560; NMM L/L 282.

16   Crooks, *Gold Coast Settlements*, p. 54.

17   NMM ADM L/L/282.

18   NMM ADM L/L/282; Crooks, *Gold Coast Settlements*, pp. 54–5 (emphasis in original); Ty M. Reese, 'Liberty, Insolence and Rum: Cape Coast and the American Revolution', *Itinerario* 28:3 (2004) pp. 18–37.

19   ADM 36/9570; ADM 36/10021; BT 98/43; BT 98/44; NMM ADM L/L/282; Reese, 'Liberty, Insolence and Rum'.

20   SP 44/96 ff. 109–112; T 1/564; T 70/1545; ADM 36/10021; OSBP T17750913–9; OBSP T17780916–69; OBSP T17790519–22; OBSP S17780916–1; OBSP S17790519–1; WO 34/172.

21   CO 267/20 f. 180; www.electricscotland.com/history/nation/cranston.htm.

22   CO 267/20 ff. 180–187; Crooks, *Gold Coast Settlements*, p. 55.

23   Crooks, *Gold Coast Settlements*, p. 55.

24   T 70/1545, Weuves to Mackenzie, 3 March 1782 and Mackenzie's reply, same date.

25   Harvey M. Feinberg, 'Africans and Europeans in West Africa: Elminas and Dutchmen on the Gold Coast During the Eighteenth Century', *Transactions of the American Philosophical Society*, 79:7 (1989) pp. 30–1.

26   Lawrence, *Trade Castles and Forts*, p. 42.

27   OBSP T17841210–1.

28   NMM ADM L/L/282; Crooks, *Gold Coast Settlements*, pp. 56–7.

29   Lawrence, *Trade Castles and Forts*, pp. 245–9, 333–6, 341–5.

30   *Gentleman's Magazine* (July 1782) p. 355.

31   T 70/1545; T 70/1546.

32   T 70/153 ff. 8–10.

33   T 70/1546.

34 Ibid.

35 van Dantzig, *Forts and Castles of Ghana* (Accra: Sedco, 1980) p. 63; Crooks, *Gold Coast Settlements*, p. 58.

36 NMM ADM L/L/282.

37 CO 267/7; Crooks, *Gold Coast Settlements*, pp. 58–60.

CHAPTER SEVEN: DESERTING TO THE ENEMY

1   On Charlton see Prob. 11/1109, at www.captaincooksociety.com.

2   St Clair, *The Grand Slave Emporium*, pp. 11–12; Metcalf, 'Gold, Assortments and the Trade Ounce'.

3   T 70/1545, Weuves to Mackenzie, 9 April 1782.

4   Reese, 'Liberty, Insolence and Rum'.

5   TS 11/1016.

6   PC 1/3103.

7   T 70/33; T 70/1546; CO 267/20 f. 189; FO 95/8/2 ff. 34–7; HCA 30/672; HCA 32/296 part 2 ff. 1–16; HO 42/5 ; PC 1/3103, Examination of Kenneth Mackenzie. The number of men on the ship is given as both twenty-eight and forty in different documents.

8   T 70/1546.

9   T1/564; ASSI 31/12 ; ADM 36/10021; T 70/1642.

10 SP44/96 ff. 140–4; OBSP T17771203–44.

11 CO 267/20 f. 191.

12 T 70/1545, Weuves to Mackenzie, 24 April 1782; T 70/1546 Weuves to Mackenzie, 18 April 1782; Tobias Smollett, David Hume et al, *The History of England from the Revolution to the American War and the Peace of Versailles, Designed as a Continuation of Mr Hume's History* vol. 6 (Philadelphia: Robert Campbell, 1798) p. 238.

13 ADM 51/19; ADM 36/9948; Crooks, *Gold Coast Settlements*, p. 66; HO 42/5.

14 P1C 3/10/1, letter dated 22 January 1783, Political and miscellaneous correspondence of the 3rd Duke of Portland, 1738–1809, Portland Collection, University of Nottingham; CO 267/20 f. 191.

15 T 70/153 ff. 8–10.

16 'J.S.G., the last Commandant of Commenda', *The Detector Detected: Or, the State of Affairs on the Gold Coast, and the Conduct of the Present Managers Consider'd* (London: printed for the author, 1753) pp. 40–1.

17 T 70/1545, Weuves to Hawkshaw, 3 April 1782 and Hawkshaw's reply, same date.

18 T 1/564; ASSI 31/12, Norfolk Summer Assizes; OBSP T17780429–12; OBSP T17780429–75; S17780429–1.

19 T 70/1545, Weuves to Hawkshaw, 3 April 1782; T 70/1546.

20 OBSP T17841210–1.

21 Ibid.

22 See Jan Dalley, *The Black Hole: Money, Myth and Empire* (London: Penguin/Fig Tree, 2006).

23 T 70/153 ff. 8–10; T 70/1545, Miles to Mackenzie, 14 July 1782; T 70/1552 ; T 70 1545, Beard to Mackenzie, 4 May 1782.

24 CO 267/7.

25 T 70/1546; OBSP T17801206–46.

26 T 70/1545; T 70/1546.
27 T 70/33.
28 OBSP т17841210–1.
29 T 70/1546.
30 T 70/153 ff. 8–10; T 70/1546.
31 T 70/1545, letters from Miles to Hawkshaw; CO 267/20 Clarke to Germain, 12 June 1782.
32 T 70/1545, Mackenzie to Cape Coast Castle, 11 April 1782 and Smith to Mackenzie, 12 April 1782; Silke Strickrodt, 'A Neglected Source for the History of Little Popo: The Thomas Miles Papers, c. 1789–1796', History in Africa 28 (2001) pp. 293–330.
33 T 70/1545, Richard Smith to Kenneth Mackenzie, 9 April 1782.

CHAPTER EIGHT: A PLANTATION WITH SLAVES

1 T 70/33.
2 Extracts from an Account of the State of the British Forts, on the Gold Coast of Africa Taken by Captain Cotton of His Majesty's Ship Pallas in May and June 1777, to Which are Added Observations by John Roberts, Gov of Cape Coast Castle (London: J. Bew, 1778) pp. 16–17.
3 J.S.G. The Detector Detected, pp. 41–2 (emphasis in original).
4 Anne McClintock, Imperial Leather: Race, Gender and Sexuality in Colonial Context (New York: Routledge, 1995) pp. 54–6; Dror Wahrman, The Making of the Modern Self: Identity and Culture in Eighteenth-Century England (New Haven: Yale University Press, 2004) p. 153.
5 T 70/153, list of complaints against Kenneth Mackenzie, 23 June 1782.
6 Patrick Cruttwell, '"These are Not Whigs": Eighteenth-Century Attitudes to the Scottish Highlanders', Essays in Criticism 15 (1965) pp. 394–413; Roxann Wheeler, Complexity of Race: Categories of Difference in Eighteenth Century British Culture (Philadelphia: University of Pennsylvania Press, 2000) pp. 192–203; David Stenhouse, How the Scots Took Over London (Edinburgh: Mainstream Publishing, 2005) pp. 199–206.
7 Eveline C. Martin, 'The English Establishments on the Gold Coast in the Second Half of the Eighteenth Century', Transactions of the Royal Historical Society 5 (1922) pp. 167–208, quote pp. 187–8.
8 Metcalf, 'Gold, Assortments and the Trade Ounce'; George Metcalf, 'A Microcosm of Why Africans Sold Slaves: Akan Consumption Patterns in the 1770s', Journal of African History 28:3 (1987) pp. 377–94.
9 Joseph E. Inikori, Africans and the Industrial Revolution in England (Cambridge: Cambridge University Press, 2002) pp. 183–93, quote p. 390.
10 Robin Law, 'Further Light on Bulfinch Lambe and the "Emperor of Pawpaw": King Agaja of Dahomey's Letter to King George I of England, 1726', History in Africa 17 (1990) pp. 211–26.
11 Ray A. Kea, 'Plantations and Labour in the South-East Gold Coast From the Late Eighteenth to the Mid Nineteenth Century' in Robin Law (ed.), From Slave Trade to 'Legitimate' Commerce: The Commercial Transition in Nineteenth-Century West Africa (Cambridge: Cambridge University Press, 1995) pp. 119–30, quote p. 126; Deirdre Coleman, Romantic Colonization and British Anti-Slavery (Cambridge: Cambridge University Press, 2005) pp. 28–30.

12 Beaver, *African Memoranda: Relative to an Attempt to Establish a British Settlement on the Island of Bulama* (London: 1792) p. 375. See also Coleman, *Romantic Colonization* on this question.
13 CO 267/7 (emphasis in original).
14 Ty M. Reese, 'The Drudgery of the Slave Trade: Labor at Cape Coast Castle, 1750–1790' in Peter A. Coclanis (ed.), *The Atlantic Economy during the 17th and 18th Centuries: Organization, Operation, Practice and Personnel* (Columbia: University of South Carolina Press, 2005) p. 283.
15 Wahrman, *The Making of the Modern Self*, pp. 87–96; Harrison, '"The Tender Frame of Man"'; Philip D. Curtin, *The Image of Africa: British Ideas and Action, 1780–1850* (London: Macmillan and Co., 1965).
16 WO 34/172; T 70/1549 part 1.
17 T 70/1546.
18 WO 34/172; T 70/1549 part 1.
19 TS 11/1016.
20 See Linda Colley, *Captives: Britain, Empire and the World, 1600–1850* (London: Jonathan Cape, c2002) pp. 56–64.
21 Robin Law, *The Slave Coast of West Africa 1550–1750: The Impact of the Atlantic Slave Trade on an African Society* (Oxford: Clarendon Press, 1991); Robin Law, '"Here is No Resisting the Country": The Realities of Power in Afro-European Relations on the West African "Slave Coast"', *Itinerario* 18 (1994) pp. 50–64; Martin, *The British West African Settlements*, p. 51.
22 T 70/153 ff. 8–10.
23 Crooks, *Gold Coast Settlements*, pp. 47–8.
24 CO 267/20 ff. 180–7.
25 T 70/1549 part 1.
26 Swanzy, 'Incident at Mouri', *African Affairs*, 58:231 (April 1959) pp. 147–52.
27 T 70/1552; T 70/153; T 70/33.
28 Margaret Priestley, 'Philip Quaque of Cape Coast' in Philip D. Curtin, *Africa Remembered: Narratives by West Africans in the Era of the Slave Trade* (Madison: University of Wisconsin Press, 1967) pp. 99–112; Christopher Fyfe, 'Quaque, Philip (1741–1816)', *Oxford Dictionary of National Biography* (Oxford: Oxford University Press, 2004); West Africa Correspondence, Society for the Propagation of the Gospel Archive, Rhodes House, Oxford, C/AFW/1, Letter from W. McFee, 1788; Ty M. Reese, '"Sheep in the Jaws of So Many Ravenous Wolves": The Slave Trade and Anglican Missionary Activity at Cape Coast Castle, 1752–1816', *Journal of Religion in Africa* 34:4 (2004) pp. 348–72; T 70/1549 part 1.

CHAPTER NINE: A MUTINY AND A MOST PECULIAR MURDER

1 WO 34/169 f. 8; CO 267/20 ff. 180–87.
2 T 70/1545, Clarke to Cape Coast Castle, 9 June 1782.
3 CO 267/20 ff. 180–7; T 70/1545, Clarke to Cape Coast Castle, 7 May 1782, Fielde to Clarke, 9 May 1782, Clarke to Cape Coast Castle same date and Cape Coast Castle to Clarke, same date.
4 T 70/153.

5   Ibid.
6   CO 267/20 ff. 180–7.
7   T 70/153 f. 5; T 70/1545, Mackenzie to Miles, 12 May 1785.
8   WO 34/ 172; T 70/153 ff. 5–7.
9   T 70/153 ff. 5–7.
10 Swanzy, 'Incident at Mouri'.
11 T 70/1545, Clarke to Cape Coast Castle, 13 May 1782.
12 ADM 36/9948. The muster notes that Clarke was discharged at Antigua in September of that year, presumably to another naval ship which would take him back to Britain.
13 T 70/1545, Quaque to Miles, 17 May 1782; Crooks, *Gold Coast Settlements*, pp. 63–4.
14 St Clair, *The Grand Slave Emporium*, p. 12.
15 Ibid, p. 67; E. St John Brooks, 'An 18th Century Slave-Owner's Estate', *Notes and Queries* (May 19, 1928) pp. 345–9.
16 T 70/153 f. 2; Reese, 'Liberty, Insolence and Rum'.
17 PC 1/3103, Examination of Kenneth Mackenzie.
18 T 70/153 f. 8–10; Eltis et al, *Trans-Atlantic Slave Trade* Database, 80663; T 70/1545, Fielde to Mackenzie, 23 July 1782.
19 T 70/1545, Mackenzie to Miles, 17 July 1782.
20 T 70/1545, Mackenzie to Cape Coast Castle, 7 July 1782, Mackenzie to Cape Coast Castle, 12 July 1782 and Miles to Mackenzie, 14 July 1782.
21 WO 34/172.
22 CO 267/20 ff. 315–20; T 70/1545, Fielde to Mackenzie, 17 June 1782.
23 See Marcus Rediker, *Villains of All Nations: Atlantic Pirates in the Golden Age* (Boston: Beacon Press, 2004) especially chapter 4.
24 T 70/153 ff. 5–7; T 70/1549 part 1; T 70/1552; CO 267/ 20 ff. 315–20; HCA 30/627; OBSP 17841210–1.
25 T 70/1545, Fielde to Mackenzie, 18 May 1782.
26 Ibid; T 70/1545, Mackenzie to Miles, 7 June 1782.
27 T 70/1545, Mackenzie to Miles, 7 June 1782.
28 Ibid; OBSP т17841210–1.
29 CO 267/7.
30 Ibid.
31 OBSP т17810110–18; OBSP т17841210–1; CO 267/7.
32 OBSP т17841210–1.
33 Ibid.
34 Ibid.
35 CO 267/20 ff. 315–20.
36 Andrew Cormack, 'The Uniform of Officers of the Independent Companies in the Later 18th Century', *Journal of the Society for Army Historical Research* 84 (2006) pp. 215–22.
37 OBSP т17760221–30; OBSP т17780916–53; OSBP т17781209–16.
38 T 70/1545; OBSP т17841210–1.
39 OBSP т17841210–1.
40 OBSP т17841210–1.
41 T 70/1545, Mackenzie to Fielde, 24 July 1782.

CHAPTER TEN: TROUBLE AT GORÉE ISLAND

1 OBSP T17811017–41; OBSP s17811017–1; *Morning Herald and Daily Advertiser* 19 October 1781.

2 OBSP s17721209–1; OBSP T17721209–8; Coldham, *British Emigrants in Bondage;* on this crime see Beattie, *Crime and the Courts*, pp. 172–3.

3 OBSP 017811205–1; OBSP 017820109–1; OBSP s17820410–1.

4 Gentleman of the Inner Temple, *Authentic Memoirs* (London, 1782) pp. 38–9. Robert Hill would later be pardoned, PCOM 2/169, 4 April 1782.

5 Gentleman of the Inner Temple, *Authentic Memoirs*, p. 39; *Public Advertiser* 25 October 1781; *London Courant, Westminster Chronicle and Daily Advertiser* 26 October 1781; *Morning Chronicle and London Advertiser* 30 October 1781; *London Chronicle* 27 November 1781.

6 *London Courant, Westminster Chronicle and Daily Advertiser* 25 October 1781; Gentleman of the Inner Temple, *Authentic Memoirs*, p. 40.

7 LMA MJ/SP/1782/02.

8 Gentleman of the Inner Temple, *Authentic Memoirs*, pp. 40–2; OBSP o17811205–1; OBSP o17820109–1; OBSP s17820410–1.

9 Gentleman of the Inner Temple, *Authentic Memoirs*, p. 46; OBSP T17820515–2; OBSP s17820515–1.

10 SP 44/95 ff. 413–15; Duncan Campbell Letterbooks, Mitchell Library, Sydney, A3227 f. 134, Campbell to Isaac Wood, 18 February 1780; A3228 f. 24, Campbell to Isaac Wood, 18 April 1782; HO 13/1 p. 2.

11 A 3228, Campbell to Justice Buller, 28 June 1782; T 70/69 f. 153.

12 Eltis et al, *Trans-Atlantic Slave Trade* Database, voyage ID 80980.

13 OBSP T17820911–38; OBSP T17820911–101; OBSP T17820911–111; OBSP T17820911–115; OBSP T17821016–34; OBSP 017830910–3.

14 OBSP T17820911–38, HO 77/1 f. 28; HO 13/1 f. 211.

15 OBSP T17810425–49; OBSP T17810530–52; HO 77/1 f. 15; *London Chronicle* 2 November 1782.

16 OBSP T17810711–56; OBSP T17820911–101.

17 *Morning Chronicle* 2 November 1782.

18 OBSP T17820703–5; Mollie Gillen, *The Founders of Australia: A Biographical Dictionary of the First Fleet* (Sydney: Library of Australian History, 1989) p. 239. The other man returned to jail was William Whittaker, OBSP T17810912–12; OBSP T17810912–42.

19 PCOM 2/170; SP 44/95 ff. 420–1.

20 *Morning Chronicle* 2 November 1782.

21 SP 44/95; ASSI 2/24; West Glamorgan Archives Service, D/D Gn/E204/1–70, accounts and depositions regarding the *Caterina* wreck 29 December 1781. Why Harry was tried in Hertford after this crime is unclear. Nevertheless his trial stated that this was the wreck he had plundered and he is named in the West Glamorgan documents. None of the other convicted plunderers went to Africa.

22 ASSI 2/24; SP 44/95 ff. 377–8

23 OBSP T17830910–41.

24 ZHC 1/82 85, Evidence of John Knox.

25 HO 42/1 f. 384.

26 T 70/69 ff. 154–6.
27 *Parker's General Advertiser and Morning Intelligencer* 14 January 1783; *London Chronicle* 28 June 1783.
28 OBSP T17810711–6; SP 44/95 ff. 337–40.
29 Wall, *Genuine and Impartial Memoirs*, pp. 10–11; David Dean, 'Joseph Wall of Gorée Island', *African Affairs* 57:229 (October 1958) pp. 295–301. Like Dean, I have been unable to confirm the veracity of this story, or to find a convict named Paterson, sentenced in the relevant time period, who had ever worked as a hatter. Patrick (or Paget) Wall did die at Gorée on 10 July 1780, however. See Crooks, 'A Statement of Events at Senegal and Gorée', p. 533.
30 *The Life, Trial and Particulars of the Execution of Governor Wall, Who Was Executed … for the Murder of Benjamin Armstrong* (London: J. Davenport, no date) p. 2; Wall, *Genuine and Impartial Memoirs*, pp. 8, 11.
31 CO 267/20 f. 361; Lord, 'Gorée'; TS 11/984.
32 PC 1/3536B; TS 11/984; *The Life, Trial … of Governor Wall*, p. 5.
33 TS 11/984; CO 267/20 ff. 230–1.
34 TS 11/984; Colley, *Captives*, p. 330.
35 TS 11/984; *The Trial of Lieutenant-Colonel Joseph Wall for the Murder of Benjamin Armstrong on 10ᵗʰ July 1782 at Gorée* (London: Messrs Blanchard and Ramsay, 1802) p. 25.
36 Colley, *Captives*, pp. 329–30; J.R. Dinwiddy, 'The Early Nineteenth-Century Campaign against Flogging in the Army', *English Historical Review*, 97 (1982) pp. 308–31; Peter Burroughs, 'Crime and Punishment in the British Army, 1815–1870', *English Historical Review*, 100 (1985) pp. 545–71.
37 CO 267/20 f. 373. This allegation that Joseph Wall was trading in slaves was later backed up by Captain Hills of the *Zephyr*, the ship which had sailed with Kenneth Mackenzie's fleet as far as Gorée. He claimed that Wall 'drove a considerable trade in that species of commerce' and had even kidnapped some Africans to give him as slaves when he had complained that his ship was short of crew. Thomas Clarkson, *Substance of the Evidence* (London: James Phillips, 1789) pp. 281–9.
38 TS 11/984.
39 *The Life, Trial … of Governor Wall*, pp. 19–20; CO 267/20 f. 373.
40 OBSP T17820220–12; OBSP T17820220–13; SP 44/95 ff. 337–40; HO 77/1 f. 33.
41 SP 44/95 ff. 413, 566–7, 277–8; OBSP T17810912–18; SP 44/95 ff. 334–5.
42 CO 267/7, Richard Miles to Colonial Office, 1 February 1783; *Providence Gazette and Country Journal* 27 December 1783, also printed in the *Norwich Packet* (Connecticut) 1 January 1784. I am grateful to Marcus Rediker for this information. HO 42/1 f. 384. It seems likely that other women could have been added after the muster as two men suddenly appear on records in Africa directly after the *Den Keyser*'s arrival who are not on either the Newgate or the Waddington list, which suggests they were not comprehensive.
43 HO 77/1 ff. 33, 45.
44 WO 17/228, Monthly Return of African Corps 25 May to 24 June 1782; Crooks, 'A Statement of Events in Senegal and Gorée', p. 533; OBSP T17830910–41.
45 OBSP T17830910–41; OBSP T17830910–41; OBSP s17841208–1.
46 Curtin, *Economic Change*, pp. 110–1, 174; Barry, *Senegambia and the Atlantic Slave Trade*, p. 68.

47 T 1/449 ff. 226–8; T 1/562 f. 145; T 1/567 f. 52; T 1/567 f. 57; T 1/567 f. 117.
48 *Providence Gazette and Country Journal* 27 December 1783.
49 *London Chronicle* 28 June 1783, 26 February 1784.
50 Eltis et al, *Trans-Atlantic Slave Trade* Database, voyage ID 77865; OBSP T17810425–49.
51 OBSP T17830910–41; ML MSS A3226 Duncan Campbell Letterbooks, Campbell to Lord Suffolk, 1 October 1778.
52 OBSP T17830910–41; *Morning Chronicle* 14 September 1783.
53 *London Chronicle* 26 February 1784; *General Evening Post* 11 September 1783.
54 *Whitehall Evening Post* 24 January 1784; *London Chronicle* 17 July 1783, 13 September 1783; *Morning Chronicle* 8 July 1783.

CHAPTER ELEVEN: 'NAKED AND DISEASED ON THE SANDY SHORE'

1   SP 44/95 ff. 339, 400–1, 409, 413; HO 42/1 f. 384 ; T 70/1552, Muster Roll of Commenda Fort.
2   ASSI 31/12.
3   T 70/153, Miles' complaints against Mackenzie, 26 July 1782; T70/1545, Miles to Kenneth Mackenzie, 14 July 1782.
4   West Africa Correspondence, Society for the Propagation of the Gospel, Rhodes House, Oxford, C/AFW/1, Phillip Quaque to SPG, 1 September 1782.
5   OBSP T17841210–1.
6   T 70/33; TS 11/892; PC 1/3103, Wickey to Stephens, 22 July 1783; T 70/1545, Mackenzie to Miles, 11 September 1782 and Miles to Mackenzie, 12 September 1782; Reese, 'Liberty, Insolence and Rum'.
7   T 70/1545, George Ormsby, Cape Coast Castle sick list, 6 October 1782.
8   HO 42/5; T 70/1546; CO 267/20 f. 189.
9   T 70/1546.
10 ASSI 33/6; SP 44/96 ff. 140–4; T 1/564.
11 T 70/1545; OBSP T17841210–1.
12 CO 267/7, Miles to Colonial Office, 1 February 1783.
13 Ibid.
14 T 70/1341, Cape Coast Castle Garrison Ledger 1782; T 70/153 f. 14.
15 CO 267/7, Miles to Colonial Office, 1 February 1783.
16 Ibid.
17 Of the thirteen men landed, eleven are accounted for and another one died on the Portuguese ship sent to take them away.
18 T 70/1552.
19 SP 44/95 ff. 566–7.
20 SP 44/95 ff. 364–5.
21 SP 44/95 f. 413; T 70/1552; T 70/1554; HO 42/1 f. 384. As Greenwood and Cockroft's old accomplice John Wood had sailed with them on the *Den Keyser* but was no longer with them, he is likely to have been either the man who died on the rocks at Cape Coast Castle—as witnessed by Richard Miles—or the man who died the first day aboard the Portuguese ship.
22 T 70/1552, Muster Fort James, Accra.

23 T 70/1552, Muster Roll, William's Fort Whydah; ASSI 24/26. Strangely, Edward Matthews is not listed aboard the *Den Keyser* in HO 42/1 f. 384.

24 T 70/1552, Muster Roll, William's Fort Whydah; SP 44/95 ff. 368–9.

25 Robin Law, *Ouidah: The Social History of a West African Slaving 'Port', 1727–1892* (Athens: Ohio University Press, 2004) p. 36, and map, p. 72.

26 Ibid., pp. 88–93.

27 Robin Law and Kristin Mann, 'West Africa in the Atlantic Community: The Case of the Slave Coast' in Gad J. Heuman and James Walvin, *Slavery Reader* (New York: Routledge, 2003), p. 746; Law, *Ouidah*, p. 75.

28 T 70/1545.

29 Barker, *The African Link*, p. 102.

30 Paul Erdmann Isert and Selena Axelrod Winsnes (eds), *Letters on West Africa and the Slave Trade: Paul Erdmann Isert's Journey to Guinea and the Caribbean Islands in Colombia, 1788* (Oxford: Oxford University Press, 1992) pp. 107–8.

31 Quoted in Law, *Ouidah*, p. 83.

32 T70/1545; T 70/1552; Law, *Ouidah*, p. 80.

33 Quoted in Reese, 'Sheep in the Jaws', p. 358.

34 This was, of course, an allegation made against many of the female convicts during the years of transportation to Australia. See Deborah Oxley, *Convict Maids: The Forced Migration of Women to Australia* (Cambridge: Cambridge University Press, 1996) pp. 4–7.

35 T 70/1552.

36 PC 1/3103.

37 TS 11/892; T 70/1549 part 1.

38 Ibid.

39 T 70/1548.

40 T 70/1549 part 1.

41 T 70/153 ff. 16–17; T 70/1549 part 1; PC 1/3103.

42 CO 267/7.

43 CO 267/20 f. 197.

44 T 70/1549 part 1; OBSP T17841210–1.

45 T 70/1549 part 1.

46 CO 267/20 ff. 315–20.

47 PC 1/3103.

48 ADM 51/ 777 f. 19.

49 Swanzy, 'Incident at Mouri', p. 152.

50 Ibid., p. 152; T 1/610/251–2; PC 1/3103.

51 Crooks gives the date as 4 September, Oldham as 24 September. Crooks, *Gold Coast Settlements*, p. 69; Oldham, *Britain's Convicts to the Colonies*, p. 79; T 70/1549 part 2; Swanzy, 'Incident at Mouri', p. 152.

52 T 70/1162; T 70/1552.

53 T 70/1552, Commenda Muster Roll.

54 T 70/1462; T 70/1564 part 1; T 70/1550; T 70/1552.

CHAPTER TWELVE: TRYING AMERICA AGAIN

1 OBSP T17830910–41.

2   A. Roger Ekirch, 'Great Britain's Secret Convict Trade to America, 1783–1784', *American Historical Review* 89:2 (1984) pp. 1285–91.
3   PCOM 2/169; PCOM 2/170; OBSP т17830723–73; OBSP т17830226–6; OBSP т17830226–3; OBSP т17830430–16.
4   Mollie Gillen, 'His Majesty's Mercy: The Circumstances of the First Fleet', *The Push* 29 (1991) pp. 49–109; Knapp and Baldwin, *New Newgate Calendar*, pp. 124–6. Knapp and Baldwin erroneously name Limpus as a *Swift* mutineer.
5   OBSP т17830910–20; OBSP т17850511–10.
6   OBSP т17830910–9; S17830910–1; s17830910–1; Knapp and Baldwin, *New Newgate Calendar*, p. 125; OBSP т17830226–50; OBSP т17830723–36; OBSP т17830430–78; о17831210–1
7   Ekirch, 'Great Britain's Secret Convict Trade'.
8   Bob Reece, *The Origins of Irish Convict Transportation to New South Wales* (Basingstoke: Palgrave, 2001) pp. 68–9; Ekirch, 'Great Britain's Secret Convict Trade'.
9   Ekirch, 'Great Britain's Secret Convict Trade'.
10 HO 77/1, 23 July 1783, Middlesex; HO 13/2 ff. 16–17; Gillen, *The Founders of Australia*, pp. 435–6; Gillen, 'His Majesty's Mercy'; HO 13/2 ff. 10, 16–17; OBSP т17831210–19; Robert Holden, *The Orphans of History: The Forgotten Children of the First Fleet* (Melbourne: Text Publishing, 2000) p. 31.
11 OBSP т17840707–6; *Morning Herald and Daily Advertiser* 29 July 1784.
12 HO 42/4 ff. 166–7; OBSP т17840707–6; Gillen, 'His Majesty's Mercy'.
13 HO 42/4 ff. 166–7; OBSP т17840707–6; Gillen, *The Founders of Australia*, p. 435; ADM 51/675 f. 340.
14 OBSP т17840526–58; OBSP т17840707–100; OBSP т17830910–23; OBSP т17840526–59.
15 Devon Records Office, QS32/62; Devon Records Office, QS32/63, both available online at http://genuki.cs.ncl.ac.uk/DEV/CourtRecords/Prisoners.html; Gillen, 'His Majesty's Mercy'; Holden, *Orphans of History*, p. 79.
16 ADM 1/1451, letter dated 29 May 1784; HO 13/2 f. 129, 169–70, 203–5.
17 HO 13/2 ff. 169–70.
18 Gillen, 'His Majesty's Mercy', p. 95.
19 ADM 1/1451, Letter from J.P. Bastard, dated 5 November 1784.
20 HO 13/2 ff. 292–3.
21 HO 42/5 ff. 461–2 (emphasis in original); Holden, *Orphans of History*, p. 82.
22 OBSP s17830910–1; OBSP т17840526–59; OBSP о17850112–1.
23 CLRO, Sessions Papers, Home Circuit, Pardons, 1783; Mollie Gillen, 'Lemain Island', *The Push* 30 (1992) pp. 3–9. Note, however, that Gillen does not name either of these men as *Mercury* mutineers in her previous works *The Founders of Australia* or 'His Majesty's Mercy'.
24 OBSP т17830910–36; OBSP т17840915–54; OBSP о17831210–1; Gillen, 'His Majesty's Mercy'.
25 HO 13/2 ff. 57–8; Oldham, *Britain's Convicts to the Colonies*, p. 88.
26 Steven Forbes, *The Baymen of Belize, and How They Wrested British Honduras From the Spaniards* (London: Originally published by the Society for the Propagation of Christian Knowledge, 1914) p. 9; Herbert F. Curry, 'British Honduras: From Public Meeting to Crown Colony', *The Americas* 13:1 (July 1956) pp. 31–42; Bolland, 'Social

Structure and Social Relations in the Settlement in the Bay of Honduras (Belize)'
Journal of Caribbean History, 6 (1973) p. 4.

27 Bolland, 'Social Structure'.

28 Bolland, 'Social Structure', pp. 4, 8–9.

29 Bolland, *Colonialism and Resistance in Belize: Essays in Historical Sociology* (Kingston: University of West Indies Press, 2004), p. 20.

30 Bolland, 'Social Structure' p. 7; Linebaugh and Rediker, *The Many-Headed Hydra: Sailors, Slaves, Commoners, and the Hidden History of the Revolutionary Atlantic* (Boston: Beacon Press, 2000) p. 269.

31 *A Full Answer to the King of Spain's Last Manifesto Respecting the Bay of Honduras and the Mosquito Shore* (London: T. Cadell, 1779) p. 7; Forbes, *The Baymen of Belize*, pp. 13–14, 24–8. Both the anonymous source in *A Full Answer to the King of Spain's Last Manifesto* and Richard White in *The Case of the Agent to the Settlers on the Coast of Yucatan and the Late Settlers on the Mosquito-Shore* (London: T. Cadell, 1793) give the date of the attack as September 1779. It is unclear which version of events is correct.

32 White, *The Case of the Agent*, p. 3; Forbes, *The Baymen of Belize*, p. 20.

33 Curry, 'British Honduras'; Bolland, 'Social Structure'; Lieutenant Cook, *Remarks on a Passage from the River Balise in the Bay of Honduras to Merida* (London: C. Parker, 1769) p. 6; White, *The Case of the Agent*, p. 6. A large part of the rest of White's book records attempts to get restitution.

34 Mike Jay, *The Unfortunate Colonel Despard* (London: Bantam, 2004) pp. 149–50; Bolland 'Social Structure'; Robert A. Naylor, *Penny Ante Imperialism: The Mosquito Shore and the Bay of Honduras, 1600–1914* (Rutherford: Fairleigh Dickinson University Press, 1989) pp. 64–6.

35 Jay, *The Unfortunate Colonel Despard*, p. 150; Oldham, *Britain's Convicts to the Colonies*, p. 88.

36 Quoted in Melissa A. Johnson, 'The Making of Race and Place in 19th Century British Honduras', *Environmental History* (October 2003).

37 HO 42/6 f. 36.

38 CO 123/10 ff. 104–6; Bolland 'Social Structure'; A *Full Answer to the King of Spain's Last Manifesto*, pp. 18–20. See Forbes, *The Baymen of Belize* for his opinion of his slaves' dedication and contentment with their lot in life.

39 Bolland, 'Social Structure'.

40 CO 123/3 ff. 84–5; CO 123/11.

41 CO 123/3 ff. 84–5; Oldham, *Britain's Convicts to the Colonies*, p. 91; CO 123/3 f. 86; John Alder Burdon, *Archives of British Honduras* (London: Sifton, Praed & Co., 1931) vol. 1, p. 146.

42 CO 123/10 ff. 99–101; CO 123/11; Oldham, *Britain's Convicts to the Colonies*, p. 92; Burdon, *Archives of British Honduras*, pp. 147–8.

43 Burdon, *Archives of British Honduras*, pp. 147–8; Oldham, *Britain's Convicts to the Colonies*, p. 92.

44 CO 123/11; CO 123/3 ff. 137–42.

45 CO 123/11 ff. 161–6; Oldham, *Britain's Convicts to the Colonies*, p. 93.

46 Burdon, *Archives of British Honduras*, p. 149.

CHAPTER THIRTEEN: THE ONCE MIGHTY ARE FALLEN

1   *Murder Shall Not Go Unpunished: The Trial of Governor Wall for a Murder, Committed nearly Twenty Years ago, at Gorée, in Africa* (London, 1802), p. 19; National Army Museum, Joseph Wall Papers, MS 9310–216, letters dated 5 October 1784, 5 March 1785, 24 May 1785, 9 July 1785, 13 July 1785; Spain, Jonathan, 'Wall, Joseph (1737–1802)', *Oxford Dictionary of National Biography* (Oxford: Oxford University Press, 2004). Frances Mackenzie's letter of 7 May 1798 at the National Army Museum names Lord Seaforth as her brother.
2   CO 267/7; T 70/1548; PC 1/3103.
3   TS 11/1016.
4   TS 11/892.
5   OBSP т17841210–1.
6   HCA 32/962 part 2 ff. 1–36.
7   CO 267/8.
8   LMA, LSP, 8 December 1784, LSP/1784/9; OBSP T17810110–18.
9   T 70/1545; T 70/1549 part 1.
10 *The Life and Complete Trial of Kenith Mackenzie*, p. 2.
11 David Wilkinson, 'Adam, William (1751–1839)', *Oxford Dictionary of National Biography* (Oxford: Oxford University Press, 2004); Allyson N. May, 'Silvester, Sir John, first baronet (1745–1822)', *Oxford Dictionary of National Biography* (Oxford: Oxford University Press, 2004).
12 G.M. Ditchfield, 'Lee, John (1733–1793)', *Oxford Dictionary of National Biography* (Oxford: Oxford University Press, 2004); Allyson N. May, 'Advocates and Truth Seeking in the Old Bailey Courtroom', *Journal of Legal History* 26:1 (2005) pp. 83–90.
13 OBSP т17841210–1.
14 T 10/1549 part 1; OBSP т17841210–1.
15 OBSP т17841210–1.
16 Ibid.
17 OBSP т17841210–1.
18 Ibid.
19 Ibid.
20 Ibid.; *Edinburgh Advertiser* 11–14 December 1784.
21 *Edinburgh Advertiser* 11–14 December 1784; CO 267/20 f. 360; *The Times* 19 January 1785.
22 *Caledonian Mercury* 10 January 1785; *The Times* 11 January 1785.
23 *Caledonian Mercury* 29 January 1785; *The Times* 24 January 1785.
24 *The Times* 18 February 1785; PCOM 2/172.
25 HO 43/1 ff. 353–4.
26 HO 13/3 f. 214; FO 72/6, 15 September 1785, Nepean to Despard; Burdon, *Archives of British Honduras*, p. 147.
27 FO 72/7, Moore to Nepean, 21 April 1786; CO 123/10 ff. 101–3. For some examples of earlier ships possibly carrying slaves and convicts see Morgan and Rushton, *Eighteenth-Century Criminal Transportation*, pp. 24, 30.
28 CO 123/10 ff. 104–6, 107–8; FO 72/7, Moore to Nepean, 21 April 1786.
29 FO 72/2, Moore to Nepean, 21 April 1786.

30 Nicolas Rogers, 'Caribbean Borderland: Empire, Ethnicity, and the Exotic on the Mosquito Coast', *Eighteenth-Century Life* 26:3 (Fall 2002) pp. 117–38; Frank Griffiths Dawson, 'William Pitt's Settlement at Black River on the Mosquito Shore: A Challenge to Spain in Central America, 1732–87', *The Hispanic American Historical Review* 63:4 (November 1983) pp. 677–706.

31 Dawson, 'William Pitt's Settlement'; Paul E. Lovejoy, 'Alternatives to Revolution and Insurrection: Gustavus Vassa, alias "Olaudah Equiano", and the Abortive Plantation Scheme of Dr. Charles Irving on the Mosquito Shore', in Rina Cáceres Gómez and Paul E. Lovejoy (eds), *Revolución, Independencia y emancipación: La lucha contra la esclavitud* [Revolution, Independence and Emancipation: The struggle against Slavery] (San José: UNESCO, 2005).

32 CO 267/20 f. 307.

33 HO 43/1 f. 355.

34 CO 267/20 ff. 309, 311.

35 Ibid.

36 T 1/614; HO 42/6 f. 36.

37 T 70/1550.

38 T 70/145; Eltis et al, *Trans-Atlantic Slave Trade* Database, ID 83296; HCA 1/24 ff. 57–9.

39 T 70/1553.

40 HO 42/6 f. 36.

41 Robert B. Shoemaker, 'The Street Robber and the Gentleman Highwayman: Changing Perceptions of Robbery in London, 1690–1800', *Cultural and Social History* 3 (2006) pp. 381–405.

42 OBSP t17831210–6; OBSP o17840225–5; PCOM 2/169; PCOM 2/172.

43 OBSP t17820911–5; OBSP o17821204–3; PCOM 2/171.

44 OBSP t17830723–5; Jodie Greene, 'Public Secrets: Sodomy and the Pillory in the Eighteenth Century and Beyond', *The Eighteenth-Century: Theory and Interpretation* 44 (2003) pp. 203–32.

45 OBSP o17840114–2.

46 OBSP S17840421–1; HO 77/1 f. 180; PCOM 2/171; HO 13/2 f. 14; *Morning Herald and Daily Advertiser* 24 July 1783.

47 OBSP t17831210–5; OBSP o17840225–5; Gillen, *The Founders of Australia*, p. 179.

48 OBSP t17831210–8; OBSP o17840225–5; PCOM 2/171; Gillen, *The Founders of Australia*, pp. 307–8.

49 OBSP t17831210–9; OBSP o17840225–5; PCOM 2/171; Gillen, *The Founders of Australia*, p. 184.

50 Strickrodt, 'A Neglected Source for the History of Little Popo', p. 295; T 70/1545, letter from Richard Smith, 9 April 1782; W.S. Kwesi Johnston, 'Notes on the Old Houses of Cape Coast', unpublished manuscript (c.1960) available at www.archimedes. free-online.co.uk/ghouses.htm. This source erroneously gives the date of Morgue's governorship as 1734 instead of 1784.

51 Quoted in Reese, 'Liberty, Insolence and Rum', p. 30.

52 T 70/1462; T 70/1552.

53 OBSP t17810110–18; T 70/1462.

54 ASSI 31/13; CLRO Sessions Records, Home Circuit, Pardons, 1783; T 70/1552.

55 Elizabeth Donnan, 'English Establishments on the Gold Coast', *Transactions of the Royal Historical Society* 5 (1922) pp. 166–7.

56 T 70/1642; OBSP t17840915–5; OBSP o17850112–1; OBSP t17831210–2; OBSP o17840225–5; PCOM 2/172; HO 13/1 f. 325.

57 OBSP t17831210–15; OBSP o17840225–5.

58 OBSP t17840225–29; OBSP o17840707–1; OBSP o17850112–1; T 17/1552.

59 T 70/69 f. 166; T 70/1462; HO 13/2 ff. 326–7.

CHAPTER FOURTEEN: LEMANE ISLAND

1 Gillen, 'His Majesty's Mercy', p. 78.

2 T 1/614, Barnes to Treasury, 9 February 1785.

3 CO 267/8, Edward Morse to Lord Sydney, 28 June 1784.

4 HO 42/11 ff. 142–3.

5 HO 42/5.

6 T 1/614; Eltis et al, *The Trans-Atlantic Slave Trade* Database, voyage ID 81444; Oldham, *Britain's Convicts to the Colonies*, p. 97.

7 T1/614; Oldham, *Britain's Convicts to the Colonies*, p. 97.

8 HO 42/6 ff. 9–10, 33; Gillen, 'Lemain Island', pp. 6–7.

9 *Whitehall Evening Post* 24 January 1784; OBSP o17850223–2; OBSP s17841208–1; HO 47/3 ff. 114; HO 13/3 ff. 14–15.

10 HO 47/3 ff. 118; Oldham, *Britain's Convict to the Colonies*, pp. 98–9.

11 Quoted in Gillen, 'Lemain Island', p. 6.

12 *Chronicle and Daily Advertiser* 12 February 1785. The *Morning Herald and Daily Advertiser* had a shorter report on the matter the same day. *General Evening Post* 14 April 1785.

13 Oldham, *Britain's Convicts to the Colonies*, p. 99.

14 NMM THM/301, unpublished and unfinished manuscript of Lady Ellinor Thompson's biography of the 'Poet Thompson'.

15 British Library ADD MSS 46120, Journal from 1 April 1783 to 25 March 1785 of Captain Edward Thompson, entries for 23 July 1783, 29 July 1783.

16 Ibid.; ADM 1/2594.

17 Ibid., 25 September 1784.

18 ADM 1/2594, Thompson's Remarks and Observations on the State, Commerce and Condition of the African Settlements … May 1784.

19 NMM, TMH/G, letters dated 1 August 1784, 3 August 1784, 8 August 1784.

20 Ibid., letter dated 1 August 1784, Thompson to Rose.

21 British Library ADD MSS 46120, entry dated 3 January 1785.

22 Ibid., various entries on his meetings, 9 March 1785 on the plan; NMM THM/G, Thompson to Sidney [sic], 6 April 1785.

23 HO 7/1.

24 HO 42/7 ff. 11–17; *Morning Post and Daily Advertiser* 30 June 1785, Oldham, *Britain's Convicts to the Colonies*, p. 104.

25 HO 42/7 ff. 11–17; Oldham, *Britain's Convicts to the Colonies*, pp. 105–6.

26 Gillen, 'Lemain Island', pp. 8–9; CO 267/9, letter dated 9 November 1785.

27 PRO 30/8/128 ff. 67–8, letter from Diana Dalrymple, no date but annotated 17 September 1785; India Office Library, L/MAR/B/503D-F, log of the *Pigot*.

28 Ibid.

29 Gillen, 'His Majesty's Mercy', p. 101; ADM 1/2594, Thompson to War Office, 28 July 1784 and letter from Commenda, 25 December 1785; Reese, 'Liberty, Insolence and Rum'.

30 ADM 1/2594. This number includes the volunteers among Mackenzie and Katenkamp's troops, but as they were not distinguishable from their convict fellow soldiers out in Africa, this is the total number of all who had been sent out as part of the various experiments.

31 *The Times* 30 May 1785, 9 June 1785.

32 *An Address to the Officers of the British Army, Containing a Sketch of the Case of Capt. Kenneth Mackenzie* … (London: George Kearsley, 1785).

33 *The Times* 9 December 1785.

34 HO 47/3 f. 152; Crooks, *Gold Coast Settlements*, p. 71; Oldham, *Britain's Convicts to the Colonies*, pp. 76–7.

35 HO 47/3 f. 152.

36 NMM THM/301, p. 243.

37 T 1/632, letters dated 10 May 1786, 1 June 1786, 10 June 1786, 13 June 1786.

38 British Library ADD MSS 46120, Journal from 1 April 1783 to 25 March 1785 of Captain Edward Thompson, entry for 23 April 1783.

CHAPTER FIFTEEN: THE END OF THE AFRICAN DISASTER

1 ADM 51/382; NMM THM/301, pp. 2 (quoting from the *Historical Magazine*), 18–24, 247.

2 PRO 30/20/26/3 ff. 16–18.

3 ADM 51/382.

4 NMM THM/301 24–8; NMM THM/119, Edward Thompson to Thomas Boulden Thompson, letters dated 6 September 1775, 10 September 1775. Thomas Boulden Thompson's parentage is said by his reviewer in the *Oxford Dictionary of National Biography* to be uncertain, but the author whose unfinished manuscript about Edward Thompson is kept at the National Maritime Museum, THM/301, seems to have shown that Mary Thompson's sister was his mother, Richard Boulden his father. See K. Laughton, 'Thompson, Sir Thomas Boulden, first baronet (1766–1828)' rev. Roger Morriss, *Oxford Dictionary of National Biography* (Oxford: Oxford University Press, 2004).

5 Laughton, 'Thompson, Sir Thomas Boulden'; ADM 1/2594, letter from Thomas Boulden Thompson 30 January 1786.

6 NMM, TRN/18, Thompson, Narrative of a Voyage Performed in His Majesty's Sloop *Nautilus*, p. 2; ADM 51/627, Log of the *Nautilus*.

7 Thompson, Narrative of a Voyage, p. 2. I am grateful to Nigel Penn for discussing the possible extent of Dutch territorial claims in 1786 (private correspondence).

8 Jill Kinahan, 'The Impenetrable Shield: HMS *Nautilus* and the Namib Coast in the Late Eighteenth Century', *Cimbebesia* 12 (1990) pp. 23–61.

9 Peter E. Raper and Maurice Boucher (eds), *Robert Jacob Gordon: Cape Travels, 1777–1786* (Houghton, South Africa: The Brenthurst Press, 1988) vol. 1,

pp. 19–21, vol. 2, pp. 308–27; Jill Kinahan, *Cattle for Beads: The Archaeology of Historical Contact and Trade on the Namib Coast* (Uppsala: Uppsala University, Studies in African Archaeology, 2000) p. 15. See also the reproduction of Gordon's diaries at http://web.uct.ac.za/depts/age/people/Gordon.

10 Kinahan, 'The Impenetrable Shield'; Unpublished booklet 'Historical Review of Lüderitz', available at the tourist information bureau in that town.

11 NMM, TRN/18, 3–4; HO 42/7 f. 19.

12 NMM, TRN/18, 4–5.

13 Ibid.; ADM 51/627.

14 NMM, TRN/18, 3–4; HO 42/7 ff. 7–10.

15 NMM, TRN/18, 10–11.

16 Ibid., 11–14.

17 Ibid., 13–14, 17–18, 20.

18 CO 123/10 ff. 107–8; FO 72/8 Nepean to Moore, 5 June 1786.

19 Frank Griffiths Dawson, 'The Evacuation of the Mosquito Shore and the English Who Stayed Behind, 1786–1800', *The Americas* 55:1 (July 1998) pp. 63–89; Dawson, 'William Pitt's Settlement'.

20 Alan Atkinson, *The Europeans in Australia: A History* (Melbourne: Oxford University Press, 1997) vol. 1, p. 50; Oldham, *Britain's Convicts to the Colonies*, p. 119.

21 Alan Frost, *The Precarious Life of James Mario Matra, Voyager with Cook, American Loyalist, Servant of Empire* (Melbourne: The Miegunyah Press, 1995) pp. 1–5, 58–9, 63.

22 Frost, *James Mario Matra*, pp. 5, 99; Ged Martin (ed.), *The Founding of Australia: Arguments about Australia's Origins* (Sydney: Hale and Iremonger, 1978) p. 16.

23 Frost, *James Mario Matra*, pp. 100, 110; Martin (ed.), *The Founding of Australia*, pp. 18–21.

24 Alan Atkinson, 'Whigs and Tories and Botany Bay' in Ged Martin (ed.), *The Founding of Australia: Arguments about Australia's Origins* (Sydney: Hale and Iremonger, 1978), p. 188, (orig. in *Journal of the Royal Australian Historical Society* 61:5 (1976) pp. 289–310); Mollie Gillen, 'The Botany Bay Decision, 1786: Convicts, Not Empire', *English Historical Review* 97 (1982) pp. 740–66; Oldham, *Britain's Convicts to the Colonies*, pp. 109–16; Shaw, *Convicts and the Colonies*, pp. 47–51.

25 *HRNSW* vol. 1:2, pp. 17–20.

26 Gillen, 'The Botany Bay Decision'; Alan Atkinson, 'Whigs and Tories and Botany Bay', pp. 201–4; Ged Martin, 'A London Newspaper on the Founding of Botany Bay, August 1786–May 1787' in Ged Martin (ed.), *The Founding of Australia*, p. 171; Alan Atkinson, 'The Ethics of Conquest, 1786', *Journal of Aboriginal History* 6:2 (1982) pp. 82–91.

27 Gillen, *The Founders of Australia*, p. 239.

28 Gillen, *The Founders of Australia*, pp. 317, 392.

29 Holden, *Orphans of History*, p. 84; Gillen, *The Founders of Australia*, p. 221.

30 Atkinson, *The Europeans in Australia*, pp. 59–61; Oldham, *Britain's Convicts to the Colonies*, pp. 114–6; CO 201/8 f. 149; NMM London, HOW/3, letters dated 6 August 1786 and 6 November 1786.

31 HO 42/11 f. 81; Alan Atkinson, 'The First Plans for Governing New South Wales, 1786–1787', *Australian Historical Studies* 24:94 (April 1990) pp. 22–40; Stephen J. Braidwood, *Black Poor and White Philanthropists: London's Blacks and the Foundation*

of the Sierra Leone Settlement, 1786–1791 (Liverpool: Liverpool University Press, 1994) pp. 129–36; Cassandra Pybus, Epic Journeys of Freedom: Runaway Slaves of the American Revolution and their Global Quest for Liberty (Boston: Beacon, 2006) pp. 112–13; General Evening Post 16 December 1786; Martin, 'A London Newspaper' in Martin (ed.) The Founding of Australia, p. 176.

32 Robert Hughes, The Fatal Shore: A History of the Transportation of Convicts to Australia, 1787–1850 (London: Collins Harvill, 1987), p. 77.

33 Quoted in Hughes, The Fatal Shore, pp. 76–7.

AFTERWORD

1 The Times of London officially began at the start of 1788, although it was preceded from 1785 by the Daily Universal Register. I have given all references back to 1785 as The Times as they can be found in that paper's online digital archive.

2 Hugh Anderson, Farewell to Judges and Juries: The Broadside Ballad and Convict Transportation to Australia, 1788–1868 (Hotham Hill: Red Rooster, 2000) pp. 92–3; Hughes, The Fatal Shore, pp. 87–91.

3 David Collins, An Account of the English Colony in New South Wales (Sydney: A.H. and A.W. Reed, 1975, first published 1798) vol. 1, p. 99.

4 CO 201/6 ff. 353–7.

5 See Christopher, 'The Slave Trade is Merciful'; CO 201/5 ff. 160–1; T 70/1549 part 2.

6 Christopher, 'The Slave Trade is Merciful'.

7 John Matthews, A Voyage to the River Sierra-Leone, on the Coast of Africa (London, 1788) p. 157.

8 Robert Norris, Memoirs of the Reign of Bossa Ahadee (London: W. Lowdnes, 1789) p. 160.

9 T 70/1462; T 70/1552.

10 T 1/564; T 70/1462.

11 T 70/1462.

12 T 70/1462.

13 ADM 1/2594; T 70/1642; T 70/1555; CO 267/10, Petition of John Morris, Cape Coast Castle 29 July 1794; St Clair, The Grand Slave Emporium, p. 131.

14 National Archives of Scotland CS 96/4733; Paton, A Series of Original Portraits, pp. 295–6.

15 Paton, A Series of Original Portraits, p. 297; Graham Clarke, 'Unpublished manuscript on the history of Redcastle' (very kindly shown to me by the author in the village of Redcastle, Scotland), p. 12; Alexander Mackenzie, History of the Clan Mackenzie (Inverness: A. & W. Mackenzie, 1879) pp. 402–3; Fraser-Mackintosh, Letters of Two Centuries, pp. 20–1. I am grateful to Graeme Mackenzie, genealogist for the clan Mackenzie, for the information that other Mackenzies had also fought with the Russian military. As regards the duel in Constantinople, John Smith was in Africa at about the time that Mackenzie was taken away, but I have found no evidence that Mackenzie entrusted his gold or any other items to him. See Eltis et al, Trans-Atlantic Slave Trade Database, voyage ID 17924.

16 CS 96/4733, ff. 4, 6, 19–20, 31, 41.

17 CS 96/4733, f. 59; Clarke, 'The History of Redcastle', p. 12; Warrand, Some Mackenzie Pedigrees, pp. 78–9.

18 Wall, *Genuine and Impartial Memoirs*, pp. 16–17; *The Times* 1 February 1802. The newspapers on this last date give his son's age as 'not more than eleven', but at the time of his hanging he was said to be nine.

19 *The Times* 21 January 1802; KB 8/85.

20 TS 11/984; OSBP т17860222–118; OSBP o17860222–3; *The Times* 21 January 1802.

21 *Murder Shall Not Go Unpunished*, p. 20. Lacy had apparently given some testimony on the affair before his death. See *The Times* 5 February 1802.

22 KB 8/85.

23 *The Life, Trial . . . of Governor Wall*, p. 6; *Murder Shall Not Go Unpunished*, pp. 23–4; *The Times* 29 January 1802.

24 *The Times* 22 January 1802; *The Times* 29 January 1802; Smith quote from Gatrell, *The Hanging Tree*, p. 263.

25 *The Times* 22 January 1802; *The Times* 29 January 1802.

26 *The Life, Trial . . . of Governor Wall*, pp. 7–8; Gatrell, *The Hanging Tree*, pp. 48, 75, 101; *The Times* 29 January 1802; *The Times* 1 February 1802.

27 HRNSW 1802 p. 848.

28 Alan Frost, *Botany Bay Mirages: Illusions of Australia's Convict Beginnings* (Melbourne: Melbourne University Press, 1994).

29 McClintock, *Imperial Leather*, p. 38.

30 Gillen, *The Founders of Australia*, p. 392.

31 Ibid., p. 317.

32 Ibid., p. 221.

33 Ibid., p. 179.

34 Ibid., p. 307.

35 Ibid., p. 239.

BIBLIOGRAPHY

Archives

British Library [BL]
Corporation of London Records Office [CLRO]
Devon Records Office
India Office Library [IOL]
London Metropolitan Archives [LMA]
    LSP, London Sessions Papers
    OB/SP, Old Bailey Sessional Papers
Mitchell Library, State Library of New South Wales, Sydney [ML]
National Archives (UK)
    ADM, Admiralty Papers
    AO, Audit Office
    BT, Board of Trade Papers
    CO, Colonial Office
    FO, Foreign Office
    HCA, High Court of the Admiralty
    HO, Home Office
    KB, King's Bench
    PCOM, Prison Commission
    PC, Privy Council
    SP, State Papers
    T, Treasury Papers
    TS, Treasury Solicitor's Papers
    WO, War Office
    British Parliamentary Papers (originals)

BIBLIOGRAPHY

National Archives of Scotland [NAS]
National Army Museum [NAM]
National Library of Scotland [NLS]
National Maritime Museum, London [NMM]
Old Bailey Sessional Papers (www.oldbaileyonline.org) [OBSP]
University of Nottingham
    Portland Collection
Rhodes House, Oxford
    Society for the Propagation of the Gospel Papers [SPG]
West Glamorgan Archives Service

Primary sources: Newspapers and periodicals

Bingley's London Journal
Caledonian Mercury
Chronicle and Daily Advertiser
Craftsman or Say's Weekly Journal
Daily Gazetteer
Edinburgh Advertiser
Exeter Flying Post
Gazetteer and New Daily Advertiser
General Advertiser and Morning Intelligencer
General Evening Post
Gentleman's Magazine
House of Commons Journal
Lloyd's Evening Post
London Chronicle
London Courant, Westminster Chronicle and Daily Advertiser
London Evening Post
Maryland Gazette
Middlesex Journal and Evening Advertiser
Morning Chronicle
Morning Chronicle and London Advertiser
Morning Herald and Daily Advertiser
Morning Post and Daily Advertiser
Morning Post and Public Advertiser
Norwich Packet (Connecticut)
Parker's General Advertiser and Morning Intelligencer
Providence Gazette and Country Journal
Public Advertiser
Public Ledger
St James Chronicle or British Evening Post
The Times
Virginia Gazette [Pinkey]
Virginia Gazette [Purdie]
Virginia Gazette [Purdie and Dixon]

Virginia Gazette [Rind]
Whitehall Evening Post

Primary sources: Books and pamphlets

A Full Answer to the King of Spain's Last Manifesto Respecting the Bay of Honduras and the Mosquito Shore (London: T. Cadell, 1779)

A List of all the Officers of the Army: Viz the General and Field Officers (London: War Office, 1780)

An Address to the Officers of the British Army, Containing a Sketch of the Case of Capt Kenneth Mackenzie (London: George Kearsley, 1785)

Extracts from an Account of the State of the British Forts, on the Gold Coast of Africa Taken by Captain Cotton of His Majesty's Ship Pallas *in May and June 1777, to Which are Added Observations by John Roberts, Gov of Cape Coast Castle* (London: J. Bew, 1778)

Murder Shall Not Go Unpunished: The Trial of Governor Wall for a Murder, Committed nearly Twenty Years ago, at Gorée, in Africa (London, 1802)

The Life and Complete Trial of Kenith Mackenzie, Esq., (London: Robert Turner, 1785)

The Life of Patrick Madan; Exhibiting a Series of the Most Extraordinary Transactions, Notorious Villanies, and Wonderful Escapes (London, 1781)

The Life, Trial and Particulars of the Execution of Governor Wall, Who was Executed ... for the Murder of Benjamin Armstrong (London: J. Davenport, nd)

The Trial of Lieutenant-Colonel Joseph Wall for the Murder of Benjamin Armstrong on 10th July 1782 at Gorée (London: Messrs Blanchard and Ramsay, 1802)

Beaver, Philip, *Africa Memoranda: Relative to an Attempt to Establish a British Settlement on the Island of Bulama* (London: 1792)

Burdon, John Alder, *Archives of British Honduras*, vol. 1 (London: Sifton Praed & Co, 1931)

Clarkson, Thomas, *Substance of the Evidence of Sundry Persons on the Slave Trade Collected in the Course of a Tour Made in the Autumn of Year 1788* (London: James Phillips, 1789)

Collins, David, *An Account of the English Colony in New South Wales*, orig. 1798 (Sydney: A.H. and A.W. Reed, 1975)

Cook, Lt, *Remarks on a Passage from the River Balise in the Bay of Honduras to Merida* (London: C. Parker, 1769)

Crooks, John Joseph, *Records Relating to the Gold Coast Settlements from 1750 to 1874* (Dublin: Brown & Nolan, 1923)

——, 'A Statement of Events at Senegal and Gorée, 1758–1874' *United Service Magazine*, 173 (1916) 306–319, 411–20, 530–40

Defoe, Daniel [Charles Johnson], *A General History of the Robberies and Murders of the Most Notorious Pyrates* (New York: Garland Publishing, 1972)

Eden, William, *Principles of Penal Law* (London: B. White and T. Cadell, 1771)

Fraser-Mackintosh, Charles, *Letters of Two Centuries: Chiefly Connected with Inverness and the Highlands, from 1616 to 1815* (Inverness: A. & W. Mackenzie, 1890)

Gentleman of the Inner Temple, *Authentic Memoirs of the Life, Numerous Adventures and Remarkable Escapes of Patrick Madan* (London, 1782)

BIBLIOGRAPHY

Green, William, *The Sufferings of William Green, Being a Sorrowful Account of his Seven Years Transportation* (London: J. Lond, 1774)

Historical Records of New South Wales (Sydney: Government Printer, 1892–1901) [NRNSW]

Howard, John, *The State of the Prisons in England and Wales with Preliminary Observations and an Account of some Foreign Prisons and Hospitals* (Warrington: William Eyres, 1780)

Isert, Paul Erdmann and Selena Axelrod Winsnes (eds), *Letters on West Africa and the Slave Trade: Paul Erdmann Isert's Journey to Guinea and the Caribbean Islands in Colombia, 1788* (Oxford: Oxford University Press, 1992)

Jeaffreson, Christopher, *A Young Squire of the Seventeenth Century*, John Cordy Jeaffreson (ed.) (London: Hurst and Blackett, 1878)

'JSG, the last Commandant of Commenda', *The Detector Detected: Or, the State of Affairs on the Gold Coast, and the Conduct of the Present Managers Consider'd* (London: Printed for the Author, 1753)

Knapp, Andrew and William Baldwin, *New Newgate Calendar, Comprising Interesting Memoirs of the Most Notorious Characters* (London: J. Robins and Co, 1825)

Macaulay, Thomas Babington, *The History of England in the Eighteenth Century*, orig. 1848 (London: The Folio Society, 1980)

Mackenzie, Alexander, *History of the Clan Mackenzie* (Inverness: A. & W. Mackenzie, 1879)

Madden, Fredrick and David Fieldhouse (eds) *Select Documents on the Constitutional History of the British Empire and Commonwealth*, vol. 3, *Imperial Reconstruction 1763–1840* (New York: Greenwood Press, 1987)

Matthews, John, *A Voyage to the River Sierra-Leone, on the Coast of Africa* (London, 1788)

Norris, Robert, *Memoirs of the Reign of Bossa Ahadee* (London: W Lowdnes, 1789)

Paton, H., *A Series of Original Portraits and Caricature Etchings by the Late John Kay* (Edinburgh: Adam and Charles Black, 1877)

Phillip, Arthur, *The Voyage of Governor Phillip to Botany Bay* (London: 1789)

Raper, Peter E. and Maurice Boucher (eds), *Robert Jacob Gordon: Cape Travels 1777–1786* (Houghton, South Africa: The Brenthurst Press, 1988)

Revel, James, *The Poor Unhappy Transported Felon's Sorrowful Account of his Fourteen Years Transportation at Virginia in America* (London, c 1800)

Robinson, Samuel, *A Sailor Boy's Experience Aboard a Slave Ship in the Beginning of the Present Century* (Wigtown: GC Books, 1996)

Rømer, Ludewig Ferdinand, *A Reliable Account of the Coast of Guinea*, trans. and ed. Selena Axelrod Winsnes (Oxford: Oxford University Press, 2000)

Smith, Adam, *An Inquiry into the Nature and Causes of the Wealth of Nations*, www.econlib.org/library/Smith/smWN20.html

Smollett, Tobias, David Hume et al, *The History of England from the Revolution to the American War and the Peace of Versailles, Designed as a Continuation of Mr Hume's History*, vol. 6 (Philadelphia: Robert Campbell, 1798)

Tupper, Ferdinand Brock, *The History of Guernsey and its Bailiwick, with Occasional Notices of Jersey* (London: Simpkin, Marshall and Co, 1876)

Wall, Joseph, *Genuine and Impartial Memoirs of the Life of Governor Wall, who was tried and convicted at the Old Bailey* (London: J. Davenport, 1802)

White, Richard, *The Case of the Agent to the Settlers on the Coast of Yucatan and the late Settlers on the Mosquito-Shore* (London: T. Cadell, 1793)

Secondary sources

'Historical review of Lüderitz', booklet available at the Lüderitz tourist information bureau

Acroyd, Peter, *London: The Biography* (London: Vintage, 2001)

Alston, David, 'Ross, George, of Cromarty (1708/9–1786)', *Oxford Dictionary of National Biography* (Oxford University Press, 2004)

Anderson, Hugh, *Farewell to Judges and Juries: The Broadside Ballad and Convict Transportation to Australia, 1788–1868* (Hotham Hill: Red Rooster, 2000)

Anquandah, Kwesi J., *Castles and Forts of Ghana* (Paris: Atalante, 1999)

Ashton, John, *The Old Bailey and Newgate* (New York: James Pott and Company, 1902)

Atkinson, Alan, 'Whigs and Tories and Botany Bay', in Ged Martin, *The Founding of Australia: Arguments about Australia's Origins* (Sydney: Hale and Iremonger, 1978) (orig. in *Journal of the Royal Australian Historical Society*, 61:5 (1976) 289–310)

——, 'The Ethics of Conquest, 1786', *Journal of Aboriginal History*, 6:2 (1982) 82–91

——, 'The First Plans for Governing New South Wales, 1786–1787', *Australian Historical Studies*, 24:94 (April 1990) 22–40

——, 'The Free-Born Englishman Transported: Convict Rights as a Measure of Eighteenth Century Empire', *Past and Present* (1994) 88–115

——, *The Europeans in Australia: A History* (Melbourne: Oxford University Press, 1997) vol. 1

Ballagh, J.C., *White Servitude in the Colony of Virginia* (New York: Burt Franklin, 1965)

Barker, Anthony J., *The African Link: British Attitudes to the Negro in the Era of the Atlantic Slave Trade, 1550–1807* (London: Frank Cass, 1978)

Barry, Boubacar, *Senegambia and the Atlantic Slave Trade* (Cambridge: Cambridge University Press, 1988)

Beattie, J.M., *Crime and the Courts in England, 1660–1800* (Princeton: Princeton University Press, 1986)

——, 'Scales of justice: Defense Council and the English Criminal Trial in the Eighteenth and Nineteenth Centurie's, *Law and History Review* 9:2 (Autumn 1991) 221–67

Beckles, Hilary McD., *White Servitude and Black Slavery in Barbados, 1627–1715* (Knoxville: University of Tennessee Press, 1989)

——, 'The Colours of Property: Brown, White and Black Chattels and their Responses on the Caribbean Frontier' in Paul E. Lovejoy and Nicholas Rogers (eds), *Unfree Labour in the Development of the Atlantic World* (Essex: Frank Cass, 1994)

Berry, Helen, 'Polite Consumption: Shopping in Eighteenth-Century England', *Transactions of the Royal Historical Society*, 12 (2002), 375–94

Bolland, O. Nigel, 'Social Structure and Social Relations of the Settlement in the Bay of Honduras (Belize)', *Journal of Caribbean History*, 6 (1973) 1–42

——, *Colonialism and Resistance in Belize: Essays in Historical Sociology* (Kingston: University of the West Indies Press, 2004)

Bolton, G.C., 'William Eden and the Convicts, 1771–1787', *Australian Journal of History and Politics*, 26:1 (1980) 30–44

Boulle, Pierre H., 'Eighteenth-Century French Policies Toward Senegal: The Ministry of Choiseul', *Canadian Journal of African Studies / Revue Canadienne des Études Africaines* (1970) 305–20

BIBLIOGRAPHY

Boulukos, George E., 'Olaudah Equiano and the Eighteenth-Century Debate on Africa', *Eighteenth-Century Studies* 40:2 (2007) 241–55

Braidwood, Stephen J., *Black Poor and White Philanthropists: London's Blacks and the Foundation of the Sierra Leone Settlement, 1786–1791* (Liverpool: Liverpool University Press, 1994)

Branch Johnson, W., *The English Prison Hulks* (London: Christopher Johnson, 1957)

Brander, A. Michael, *The Royal Scots: The Royal Regiment* (London: Leo Cooper Ltd, 1976)

Breen, T.H., *Tobacco Culture: The Mentality of the Great Tidewater Planters on the Eve of Revolution* (Princeton: Princeton University Press, 1985)

Brooke, Alan and David Brandon, *Tyburn: London's Fatal Tree* (Stroud: Sutton, 2004)

Brooks, E. St John, 'An 18th Century Slave-Owner's Estate', *Notes and Queries* (May 19, 1928) 345–49

Brown, Christopher, *Moral Capital: Foundations of British Abolitionism* (Chapel Hill: University of North Carolina Press, 2006)

Buckley, Roger Norman, *Slaves in Red Coats: The British West India Regiments, 1795–1815* (New Haven: Yale University Press, 1979)

——, *The British Army in the West Indies: Society and the Military in the Revolutionary War* (Gainesville: University of Florida Press, 1998)

Burroughs, Peter, 'Crime and punishment in the British Army, 1815–1870', *English Historical Review*, 100 (1985) 545–71

Byrnes, Dan, 'Emptying the Hulks: Duncan Campbell and the First Three Fleets to Australia', *The Push From the Bush*, 24 (1987) 2–23

——, 'The Blackheath Connection', *The Push*, 28 (1990) 51–98

Carr, Lois Green, 'Emigration and the Standard of Living: The Eighteenth-Century Chesapeake', in John J. McCusker and Kenneth Morgan (eds), *The Early Modern Atlantic Economy* (Cambridge: Cambridge University Press, 2000) 319–63

Carr, Lois Green and Lorena S. Walsh, 'Changing Lifestyles and Consumer Behavior in the Colonial Chesapeake', in Cary Carson, Ronald Hoffman and Peter J. Albert (eds), *Of Consuming Interests: The Style of Life in the Eighteenth Century* (Charlottesville: University Press of Virginia, 1994) 66–9

Christopher, Emma, 'Steal a Handkerchief, See the World: The Trans-Oceanic Voyaging of Thomas Limpus' in Ann Curthoys and Marilyn Lake, *Connected Worlds: History in Transnational Perspective* (Canberra: ANU Press, 2006) 77–88

——, '"The slave trade is merciful compared to [this]": Slave Traders, Convict Transportation and the Abolitionists', in Emma Christopher, Cassandra Pybus and Marcus Rediker, *Many Middle Passages: Forced Migration and the Making of the Modern World* (Berkley: University of California Press, 2007)

——, 'From The "Ballad-Singing Monkey" to the "Cunning Savages": The Voyage to Found a British Colony on the Orange River, 1785–6', *South African Historical Journal* 61–4

Chukwukere, I., 'Akan Theory of Conception: Are the Fante Really Aberrant?', *Africa: The Journal of the International African Institute*, 42:2 (1978), 135–48

——, 'Fante Information', *Art & Life in Africa Online*, www.uiowa/nafricart/toc/people/Fante.html

Clarke, Graham, unpublished manuscript on the history of Redcastle (personal property of the author)

Coldham, Peter Wilson, *Emigrants in Chains: A Social History of Forced Emigration to the Americas 1607–1776* (Stroud: Sutton, 1992)

Coleman, Deirdre, *Romantic Colonization and British Anti-Slavery* (Cambridge: Cambridge University Press, 2005)

Colley, Linda, *Captives: Britain, Empire and the World, 1600–1850* (London: Jonathan Cape, c2002)

Conway, Stephen, 'The Recruitment of Criminals into the British Army 1775–1781', *Bulletin of the Institute of Historical Research*, 137 (May 1985) 46–58

——, 'From Fellow Nationals to Foreigners: British Perceptions of the Americas, circa 1739–1783', *William and Mary Quarterly*, 59:1 (2002) 65–100

Cormack, Andrew, 'The Uniform of Officers of the Independent Companies in the Later 18th Century', *Journal of the Society for Army Historical Research*, 84 (2006) 215–22

Cruttwell, Patrick, '"These are Not Whigs": Eighteenth-Century Attitudes to the Scottish Highlanders', *Essays in Criticism*, 15 (1965) 394–413

Curry, Herbert F., 'British Honduras: From Public Meeting to Crown Colony', *The Americas*, 13:1 (July 1956), 31–42

Curtin, Philip D., '"The White Man's Grave": Image and Reality 1780–1850', *Journal of British Studies*, 1:1 (1961), 94–110

——, *The Image of Africa: British Ideas and Action, 1780–1850* (London: MacMillan and Co., 1965)

——, *Economic Change in Precolonial Africa: Senegambia in the Era of the Slave Trade* (Madison: University of Wisconsin Press, 1975)

Dalley, Jan, *The Black Hole: Money, Myth and Empire* (London: Penguin/Fig Tree, 2006)

Dantzig, Albert van, *Forts and Castles of Ghana* (Accra: Sedco, 1980)

Dawson, Frank Griffiths, 'William Pitt's Settlement at Black River on the Mosquito Shore: A Challenge to Spain in Central America, 1732–1787', *The Hispanic American Historical Review*, 63:4 (November 1983) 677–706

——, 'The Evacuation of the Mosquito Shore and the English who Stayed Behind 1786–1800', *The Americas*, 55:1 (July 1998) 63–89

Dean, David, 'Joseph Wall of Gorée Island', *African Affairs* 57:229 (October 1958) 295–301

Dening, Greg, *Mr Bligh's Bad Language: Passion, Power and Theatre on the Bounty* (Cambridge: Cambridge University Press, 1992)

Devereaux, Simon, 'Transportation, Penal Practices and the English State, 1770–1830' in Carolyn Strange (ed.), *Qualities of Mercy: Justice, Punishment and Discretion* (Vancouver: University of British Columbia Press, 1996)

——, 'Patrick Madan: One Man's Odyssey through England's Penal Crisis, 1774–1784', unpublished paper

Dinwiddy, J.R., 'The Early Nineteenth-Century Campaign against Flogging in the Army', *English Historical Review*, 97:383 (1982) 308–31

Ditchfield, G.M., 'Lee, John (1733–1793)', *Oxford Dictionary of National Biography* (Oxford University Press, 2004)

Donaldson, M., 'The End of Time? Aboriginal Temporality and the British Invasion of Australia', www.ro.uow.edu.au/artspapers/150

Donnan, Elizabeth, 'English Establishments on the Gold Coast', *Transactions of the Royal Historical Society*, 5 (1922) 166–67

BIBLIOGRAPHY

Dorsey, Peter A., 'To "Corroborate Our Own Claims": Public Positioning and the Slavery Metaphor in Revolutionary America', *American Quarterly*, 55 (2003) 353–86

Draper, A.J., 'William Eden and Leniency in Punishment', *History of Political Thought*, 22:1 (Spring 2001) 106–30

Duffield, Ian, 'From Slave Colonies to Penal Colonies: The West Indian Convict Transportees to Australia', *Slavery and Abolition*, 7 (1988) 25–45

Durston, Gregory, 'Magwitch's Forbears: Returning from Transportation in Eighteenth-Century London', *Australian Journal of Legal History*, 9 (2005) 137–58

Ekirch, A. Roger, 'Great Britain's Secret Convict Trade to America, 1783–1784', *American Historical Review*, 89:2 (1984) 1285–91

——, 'Bound for America: A Profile of British Convicts Transported to the Colonies, 1718–1775', *William and Mary Quarterly* 3rd Series XLII: 2 (April 1985) 184–200

Eller, Ernest M. (ed.), *Chesapeake Bay in the American Revolution* (Centreville: Tidewater Publishers, 1981)

Eltis, David, *The Rise of African Slavery in the Americas* (Cambridge: Cambridge University Press, 2000)

Emerson Smith, Abbot, *Colonists in Bondage: White Servitude and Convict Labor in America, 1607–1776* (Chapel Hill: University of North Carolina Press, 1947)

Emsley, Clive, *Crime and Society in England, 1750–1900* (Harlow: Pearson Education, 2005)

Eyre-Evans, George, 'Exeter Academy 1760–1771', *Devon and Cornwall Notes and Queries*, 4 (Jan 1906–October 1907), 108–111

Fairrie, Angus, *Queen's Own Highlanders (Seaforths and Camerons): An Illustrated History* (Queen's Own Highlanders Trust, 1998)

Feinberg, Harvey M., 'Africans and Europeans in West Africa: Elminas and Dutchmen on the Gold Coast During the Eighteenth Century', *Transactions of the American Philosophical Society*, 79:7 (1989) i–186

Forbes, Steven, *The Baymen of Belize, and How They Wrested British Honduras From the Spaniards* (London: Originally published by the Society for the Propagation of Christian Knowledge, 1914)

Foucault, Michel, *Discipline and Punish: The Birth of the Prison* (New York: Random House, 1995)

Frost, Alan, *Botany Bay Mirages: Illusions of Australia's Convict Beginnings* (Melbourne: Melbourne University Press, 1994)

——, *The Precarious Life of James Mario Matra, Voyager with Cook, American Loyalist, Servant of Empire* (Melbourne: The Miegunyah Press, 1995)

Fryer, Peter, *Staying Power: The History of Black People in Britain* (London: Pluto Press, 1984)

Fyfe, Christopher, 'Quaque, Philip (1741–1816)', *Oxford Dictionary of National Biography* (Oxford: Oxford University Press, 2004)

Galenson, David W., 'White Servitude and the Growth of Black Slavery in Colonial America', *Journal of Economic History*, 41 (1981) 39–47

Gatrell, V.A.C., *The Hanging Tree: Execution and the English People, 1770–1868* (Oxford: Oxford University Press, 1994)

Gerzina, Gretchen Hobrook, *Black London: Life Before Emancipation* (New Brunswick: Rutgers University Press, 1995)

Gilbert, Arthur N., 'The Recruitment of the East India Company Army, 1760–1800', *Journal of British Studies*, 15:1 (1975) 89–111

Gillen, Mollie, 'The Botany Bay Decision, 1786: Convicts, Not Empire', *English Historical Review*, 97 (1982) 740–66

——, *The Founders of Australia: A Biographical Dictionary of the First Fleet* (Sydney: Library of Australian History, 1989)

——, 'His Majesty's Mercy: The Circumstances of the First Fleet', *The Push*, 29 (1991) 49–109

——, 'Lemain Island', *The Push*, 30 (1992), 3–9

Gould, Eliga H., 'The American Revolution in Britain's Imperial Identity', in Fred M Leventhal and Roland Quinault (eds), *Anglo-American Attitudes: From Revolution to Partnership* (Aldershot: Ashgate, 2000) 23–31

——, *The Persistence of Empire: British Political Thinking in the Age of the American Revolution* (Chapel Hill: University of North Carolina Press, 2000)

Gray, J.M., *A History of the Gambia* (Cambridge: Cambridge University Press, 1940)

Greene, Jodie, 'Public Secrets: Sodomy and the Pillory in the Eighteenth Century and Beyond', *The Eighteenth-Century: Theory and Interpretation*, 44 (2003) 203–32

Griffin, William D., 'General Charles O'Hara', *Irish Sword*, 10:40 (1972), 179–87

Grubb, Farley, 'The Market Evaluation of Criminality: Evidence from the Auction of British Convict Labor in America, 1767–1775', *American Economic Review*, 91 (2001) 295–304

Hallett, Robin, *The Penetration of Africa: European Enterprise and Exploration Principally in Northern and Western Africa up to 1815* (London: Routledge & Kegan Paul, 1965)

Halliday, Stephen, *Newgate: London's Prototype of Hell* (Stroud: Sutton Publishing, 2006)

Harrison, Mark, '"The Tender Frame of Man": Disease, Climate, and Racial Difference in India and the West Indies, 1760–1860', *Bulletin of the History of Medicine*, 70:1 (1996) 68–93

——, *Climates and Constitutions: Health, Race, Environment and British Imperial India* (Oxford: Oxford University Press, 1999)

Hay, Douglas, 'War, Dearth and Theft in the Eighteenth Century: The Record of the English Courts', *Past and Present*, 95 (May 1982) 117–60

——, *Albion's Fatal Tree: Crime and Society in Eighteenth-Century England* (London: A. Lane, 1975)

——, 'The Laws of God and the Laws of Man: Lord George Gordon and the Death Penalty' in John Rule and Robert Malcolmson (eds), *Protest and Survival: Essays for E.P. Thompson* (London: Merlin Press, 1993) 60–111

Haydon, Colin, 'Gordon, Lord George (1751–1793)', *Oxford Dictionary of National Biography* (Oxford University Press, 2004)

Henderson, T.F., 'Cranstoun, William Henry (bap. *1714*, d. 1752)', *Oxford Dictionary of National Biography* (Oxford: Oxford University Press, 2004)

Henderson, Tony, *Disorderly Women in Eighteenth-Century London: Prostitution and Control in the Metropolis, 1730–1830* (London: Longman, 1999)

Herzog, Keith P., 'Naval Operations in West Africa and the Disruption of the Slave Trade during the American Revolution', *The American Neptune* 55:1 (1995), 42–8

Hitchcock, Tim, 'Begging on the Streets of Eighteenth-Century London', *Journal of British Studies* 44:3 (July 2005) 478–98

Hochschild, Adam, *Bury the Chains: The British Struggle to Abolish Slavery* (New York: Pan Books, 2005)

Holden, Robert, *The Orphans of History: The Forgotten Children of the First Fleet* (Melbourne: Text Publishing, 2000)

Holmes, Richard, *Redcoat: The British Soldier in the Age of Horse and Musket* (London: HarperCollins, 2002)

Hughes, Robert, *The Fatal Shore: A History of the Transportation of Convicts to Australia, 1787–1868* (London: Collins Harvill, 1987)

Ignatieff, Michael, *A Just Measure of Pain: The Penitentiary in the Industrial Revolution, 1750–1850* (London: Macmillan, 1978)

Inikori, Joseph E., *Africans and the Industrial Revolution in England* (Cambridge: Cambridge University Press, 2002)

Jay, Mike, *The Unfortunate Colonel Despard* (London: Bantam, 2004)

Johnson, Melissa A., 'The Making of Race and Place in 19th Century British Honduras', *Environmental History* (Oct 2003)

Johnston, W.S. Kwesi, 'Notes on the Old Houses of Cape Coast', unpublished manuscript (c 1960), <www.archimedes.free-online.co.uk/ghouses.htm>

Kea, Ray A., 'Plantations and Labour in the South-East Gold Coast from the Late Eighteenth to the Mid Nineteenth Century', in Robin Law (ed.) *From Slave Trade to 'Legitimate' Commerce: The Commercial Transition in Nineteenth-Century West Africa* (Cambridge: Cambridge University Press, 1995) 119–30

Kercher, Bruce, 'Perish or Prosper: The Law and Convict Transportation in the British Empire', *Law and History Review*, 21:3 (2003) 527–84

Kinahan, Jill, 'The Impenetrable Shield: HMS *Nautilus* and the Namib Coast in the Late Eighteenth Century', *Cimbebasia*, 12 (1990) 23–61

——, *Cattle for Beads: The Archaeology of Historical Contact and Trade on the Namib Coast* (Uppsala: Uppsala University, Studies in African Archaeology, 2000)

King, Peter, *Crime, Justice and Discretion in England, 1740–1820* (Oxford: Oxford University Press, 2000)

Kupperman, Karen Ordahl, 'Fear of Hot Climates in the Anglo-American Colonial Experience', *William and Mary Quarterly*, 41:2 (April 1984), 213–40

Lancaster, R. Kent, 'Almost Chattel: The Lives of Indentured Servants at Hampton-Northampton, Baltimore County', *Maryland Historical Magazine*, 94 (1999) 341–62

Langbein, John H., 'Albion's Fatal Flaws', *Past and Present*, 98 (February 1983) 96–120

Laughton, K., 'Thompson, Sir Thomas Boulden, first baronet (1766–1828)', rev. Roger Morriss, *Oxford Dictionary of National Biography* (Oxford University Press, 2004)

Law, Robin, 'Human Sacrifice in Pre-Colonial West Africa', *African Affairs*, 83:334 (January 1985) 53–87

——, 'Further Light on Bulfinch Lambe and the "Emperor of Pawpaw": King Agaja of Dahomey's Letter to King George I of England, 1726', *History in Africa*, 17 (1990) 211–26

——, *The Slave Coast of West Africa 1550–1750: The Impact of the Atlantic Slave Trade on an African Society* (Oxford: Clarendon Press, 1991)

——, '"Here is No Resisting the Country": The Realities of Power in Afro-European Relations on the West African "Slave Coast"', *Itinerario*, 18 (1994) 50–64

——, *Ouidah: The Social History of a West African Slaving 'Port', 1727–1892* (Athens: Ohio University Press, 2004)

Law, Robin and Kristin Mann, 'West Africa in the Atlantic Community: The Case of the Slave Coast' in Gad J. Heuman and James Walvin (eds), *Slavery Reader* (New York: Routledge, 2003), 739–763

Lawrence, Arnold, *Trade Castles and Forts of West Africa* (London: Jonathan Cape, 1963)

Leneman, Leah, '"Disregarding the Matrimonial Vows": Divorce in 18th and Early 19th Century Scotland', *Journal of Social History*, 30:2 (Winter 1996) 465–82

Linebaugh, Peter, *The London Hanged: Crime and Civil Society in the Eighteenth Century* (London: Penguin, 1991)

Linebaugh, Peter, and Marcus Rediker, *The Many-Headed Hydra: Sailors, Slaves, Commoners, and the Hidden History of the Revolutionary Atlantic* (Boston: Beacon Press, 2000)

Lord, Walter Frewen, 'Gorée: A Lost Possession of England', *Transactions of the Royal Historical Society*, 11 (1897) 139–52

Lovejoy, Paul E., 'Alternatives to Revolution and Insurrection: Gustavus Vassa, alias "Olaudah Equiano", and the Abortive Plantation Scheme of Dr Charles Irving on the Mosquito Shore', in Rina Cáceres Gómez and Paul E. Lovejoy (eds), *Revolución, Independencia y emancipación: La lucha contra la esclavitud* [Revolution, Independence and Emancipation: the fight against slavery] (San José: 2005)

McCalman, Iain, 'Newgate in Revolution: Radical Enthusiasm and Romantic Counterculture', *Eighteenth-Century Life*, 22:1 (1998) 95–110

McClintock, Anne, *Imperial Leather: Race, Gender and Sexuality in Colonial Context* (New York: Routledge, 1995)

McCormac, Eugene I., *White Servitude in Maryland, 1634–1820* (Baltmore: Johns Hopkins Press, 1904)

McCusker, John J., *Money and Exchange in Europe and America, 1600–1775: A Handbook*, (Chapel Hill, NC: University of North Carolina Press, c1978)

McDonnell, Michael A. and Woody Holton, 'Patriot vs. Patriot: Social Conflict in Virginia and the Origins of the American Revolution', *Journal of American Studies*, 34:2 (2000) 231–56

McDougall, E. Ann, 'The Quest for "Tarra": Toponymy and Geography in Exploring History', *History in Africa*, 18 (1991) 271–98

McGowan, Randall, 'The Well-Ordered Prison: England 1780–1865' in Norval Morris and David J. Rothman (eds), *The Oxford History of the Prison: The Practice of Punishment in Western Society* (Oxford: Oxford University Press, 1998), 73–5

Mackesy, Piers, 'Germain, George Sackville, first Viscount Sackville (1716–1785)', *Oxford Dictionary of National Biography* (Oxford University Press, 2004)

Mackillop, Andrew, *More Fruitful than the Soil: Army, Empire and the Scottish Highlands, 1715–1815* (East Linton: Tuckwell Press, 2000)

Martin, Eveline C., 'The English Establishments on the Gold Coast in the Second Half of the Eighteenth Century', *Transactions of the Royal Historical Society* 5 (1922), 167–208

——, *The British West African Settlements, 1720–1821* (London: Longmans, Green and Co, 1927)

Martin, Ged (ed.), *The Founding of Australia: Arguments about Australia's Origins* (Sydney: Hale and Iremonger, 1978)

BIBLIOGRAPHY

Martin, Ged, 'A London Newspaper on the Founding of Botany Bay, August 1786–May 1787', in Ged Martin (ed.), *The Founding of Australia: Arguments about Australia's Origins* (Sydney: Hale and Iremonger, 1978)

May, Allyson N., 'Silvester, Sir John, first baronet (1745–1822)', *Oxford Dictionary of National Biography* (Oxford University Press, 2004)

——, 'Advocates and Truth Seeking in the Old Bailey Courtroom', *Journal of Legal History* 26:1 (2005) 83–90

Metcalf, George, 'A Microcosm of why Africans Sold Slaves: Akan Consumption Patters in the 1770s', *Journal of African History*, 28:3 (1987), 377–94

——, 'Gold, Assortments and the Trade Ounce: Fante Merchants and the Problem of Supply and Demand in the 1770s', *Journal of African History*, 28:1 (1987) 27–41

Morgan, Gwenda and Peter Rushton, *Eighteenth-Century Criminal Transportation: The Formation of the Criminal Atlantic* (Hampshire: Palgrave MacMillan, 2004)

——, 'Running away and returning home: the Fate of English Convicts in the American Colonies' *Crime, Histoire et Sociétés*, 7:2 (2003), 61–80

Morgan, Kenneth, 'English and American Attitudes Towards Convict Transportation 1718–1775', *History*, 72 (1987) 416–31

——, 'Convict Transportation to Colonial America', *Reviews in American History*, 17 (1989) 29–34

——, 'Petitions against Convict Transportation, 1725–1735', *English Historical Review* (1989) 110–13

——, 'Convict Runaways in Maryland, 1745–1775' *Journal of American Studies* 23 (1989) 253–268

Myers, Norma, 'The Black Presence through Criminal Records, 1780–1830', *Immigrants and Minorities*, 7 (1988) 292–307

Naylor, Robert A., *Penny Ante Imperialism: The Mosquito Shore and the Bay of Honduras, 1600–1914* (Rutherford: Fairleigh Dickinson University Press, 1989)

Nicholas, Stephen and Richard H. Steckel, 'Heights and Living Standards of English Workers during the Early Years of Industrialization, 1770–1815', *Journal of Economic History*, 51 (1991) 937–57

Norton, Mary Beth, *The British-Americans: The Loyalist Exiles in England, 1774–1789* (London: Constable, 1974)

Oldham, James, 'Murray, William, first Earl of Mansfield (1705–1793)', *Oxford Dictionary of National Biography* (Oxford University Press, 2004)

Oldham, Wilfrid, *Britain's Convicts to the Colonies* (Sydney: Library of Australian History, 1990)

O'Shaughnessy, Andrew, 'Redcoats and Slaves in the British Caribbean' in Stanley L Engerman and Robert Paquette (eds), *The Lesser Antilles in the Age of European Expansion* (Gainesville: University of Florida Press, 1996)

Oxley, Deborah, *Convict Maids: The Forced Migration of Women to Australia* (Cambridge: Cambridge University Press, 1996)

Palk, Deirdre, 'Private Crime in Public and Private Places: Pickpockets and Shoplifters in London, 1780–1823', in Tim Hitchcock and Heather Shore (eds), *The Streets of London: From the Great Fire to the Great Stink* (London: Rivers Oram, 2003), 135–50

Picard, Liza, *Dr Johnson's London* (London: St. Martin's Press, 2002)

Priestley, Margaret, 'Philip Quaque of Cape Coast', in Philip D Curtin (ed.), *Africa*

Remembered: Narratives by West Africans in the Era of the Slave Trade (Madison: University of Wisconsin Press, 1967) 99–112

——, *West African Trade and Coast Society* (London: Oxford University Press, 1969

Pybus, Cassandra, *Black Founders: The Unknown Story of Australia's First Black Settlers* (Sydney: University of New South Wales Press, 2006)

——, *Epic Journeys of Freedom: Runaway Slaves of the American Revolution and their Global Quest for Liberty* (Boston: Beacon, 2006)

Radcliffe, David Hill, 'Hole, Richard (bap. 1746, d. 1803)', *Oxford Dictionary of National Biography*, (Oxford University Press, 2004)

Rauser, Amelia, 'The Butcher-Kissing Duchess of Devonshire: Between Caricature and Allegory in 1784', *Eighteenth-Century Studies*, 36:1 (2002) 23–46

Rawlings, Philip, 'Fielding, Sir John (1721–1780)', *Oxford Dictionary of National Biography*, (Oxford University Press, 2004)

Rayner, Tony, *Female Factory, Female Convicts* (Dover, Tasmania: Esperance Press, 2004)

Rediker, Marcus, *Villains of All Nations: Atlantic Pirates in the Golden Age* (Boston: Beacon Press, 2004)

——, *The Slave Ship: A Human History* (New York: Viking, 2007)

Reece, Bob, *The Origins of Irish Convict Transportation to New South Wales* (Basingstoke: Palgrave, 2001)

Reese, Ty M., 'Toiling in the Empire: Labor in Three Anglo-Atlantic Ports, London, Philadelphia and Cape Coast Castle, 1750–1783', unpublished PhD dissertation, University of Toledo (1999)

——, 'Liberty, Insolence and Rum: Cape Coast and the American Revolution', *Itinerario*, 28:3 (2004) 18–37

——, 'Sheep in the Jaws of So Many Ravenous Wolves: The Slave Trade and Anglican Missionary Activity at Cape Coast Castle 1752–1816', *Journal of Religion in Africa*, 34:3 (2004) 348–372

——, 'The Drudgery of the Slave Trade: Labor at Cape Coast Castle 1750–1790' in Peter A. Coclanis (ed.), *The Atlantic Economy during the 17th and 18th Centuries: Organization, Operation, Practice and Personnel* (Columbia: University of South Carolina Press, 2005)

Reid, Kirsty, 'Moving On: Resolving the Convict Origins Debate', *Australian Studies*, 12:1 (1997), 139–55

Rikard, Suzanne (ed.), *George Barrington's Voyage to Botany Bay* (London: Leicester University Press, 2001)

Rogers, Nicolas, 'Crowd and People in the Gordon Riots' in Eckhart Hellmuth (ed.) *The Transformation of Political Culture: England and Germany in the Late Eighteenth Century* (Oxford: Oxford University Press, 1990) 39–41

——, 'Caribbean Borderland: Empire, Ethnicity, and the Exotic on the Mosquito Coast', *Eighteenth-Century Life*, 26:3 (Fall 2002) 117–38

Rubenhold, Hallie, *The Covent Garden Ladies: Pimp General Jack & The Extraordinary Story of Harris's List* (Stroud: Tempus, 2005)

Rudé, George, 'The Gordon Riots: A Study of the Rioters and their Victims', *Transactions of the Royal Historical Society*, 5th series, 6 (1956) 93–114

——, *Hanovarian London, 1714–1808* (London: Secker and Walburg, 1971)

——, *Wilkes and Liberty* (London: Lawrence and Wishart, 1983)

BIBLIOGRAPHY

Russell, Gillian, 'The Peeress and the Prostitutes: The Founding of the London Pantheon 1772', *Nineteenth-Century Contexts*, 27:1 (March 2005) 11–30

St Clair, William, *The Grand Slave Emporium: Cape Coast Castle and the British Slave Trade* (London: Profile, 2006)

Sanders, James, 'The Expansion of the Fante and the Emergence of the Asante in the Eighteenth Century', *Journal of African History*, 20:3 (1979) 349–64

Schedvin, M.B. and C.B. Schedvin, 'The Nomadic Tribes of Urban Britain: A Prelude to Botany Bay', *Historical Studies: Australia and New Zealand*, 18:71 (Oct 1978), 254–76

Schmidt, Fredrick Hall, 'British Convict Servant Labor in Colonial Virginia', unpublished PhD dissertation, College of William and Mary (1976)

——, 'Sold and Driven: Assignment of Convicts in Eighteenth-Century Virginia', *Push from the Bush*, 23 (October 1986) 2–27

Schwarz, L.D., 'Income Distribution and Social Structure in London in the Late Eighteenth Century', *Economic History Review*, 32:2 (May 1979) 250–59

Scott, H.M., 'Thynne, Thomas, third Viscount Weymouth and first Marquess of Bath (1734–1796)', *Oxford Dictionary of National Biography* (Oxford: Oxford University Press, 2004)

Searing, James F., *West African Slavery and Atlantic Commerce: The Senegal River Valley, 1700–1860* (Cambridge: Cambridge University Press, 1993)

Shaw, A.G.L., *Convicts and the Colonies: a study of penal transportation from Great Britain & Ireland to Australia and other parts of the British Empire* (Dublin: Irish Historical Press, 1998)

Sherwood, Marika, 'Blacks in the Gordon Riots', *History Today*, 47:12 (December 1997) 24–28

Shoemaker, Robert B., 'The Street Robber and the Gentleman Highwayman: Changing Perceptions of Robbery in London 1690–1800', *Cultural and Social History*, 3 (2006) 381–405

——, 'The Taking of the Duel: Masculinity, Honour and Ritual Violence in London, 1669–1800', *The Historical Journal* 43:3 (2002) 525–45

Smith, Warren B., *White Servitude in Colonial South Carolina* (Columbia: University of South Carolina Press, 1961)

Soltow, J.H., 'Scottish Merchants in Virginia, 1750–1775', *Economic History Review*, 21:1 (1959) 83–98

Spain, Jonathan, 'Wall, Joseph (1737–1802)', *Oxford Dictionary of National Biography* (Oxford: Oxford University Press, 2004)

Stanton, Lucia C., 'Indentured Servants at Monticello', unpublished report for the Jefferson Library

Stenhouse, David, *How the Scots Took Over London* (Edinburgh: Mainstream Publishing, 2005)

Stockton, Jim, *Seaforth Highlanders: A Fighting Soldier Remembers* (Somerset: Crécy Books, 1987)

Stone, Thora G., 'The Journey of Cornelius Hodges in Senegambia, 1689–1690', *English Historical Review* (1924) 89–95

Strickrodt, Silke, 'A Neglected Source for the History of Little Popo: the Thomas Miles Papers, c 1789–1796', *History in Africa*, 28 (2001) 293–330

Swanzy, Henry, 'An Incident at Mouri', *African Affairs*, 58:231 (April 1959) 147–52.

Vigne, Randolph, 'The Botany Bay that Failed: Commodore Thompson and the Namibian Coast Scheme', unpublished paper, originally given as a paper at the Australian Historical Conference in 1988

Wahrman, Dror, 'The English Problem of Identity in the American Revolution', *American Historical Review*, 106:4 (October 2001) 1236–62

——, *The Making of the Modern Self: Identity and Culture in Eighteenth-Century England* (New Haven: Yale University Press, 2004)

Walsh, Lorena S., 'The Chesapeake Slave Trade: Regional Patterns, African Origins, and Some Implications', *William and Mary Quarterly*, 58:1 (2001) 139–70

Warrand, Duncan, *Some Mackenzie Pedigrees* (Inverness: Robert Carruthers & Sons, 1965)

Watt, Douglas, '"The Laberinth of Thir Difficulties": The Influence of Debt on the Highland Elite, c 1550–1700', *The Scottish Historical Review*, 85:1 (April 2006) 28–51

Way, Peter, 'Class and the Common Soldier in the Seven Years War', *Labor History*, 44:4 (2003) 455–81

Weaver, Lawrence, *The Royal Scots* (London: Country Life, 1915)

Wheeler, Roxann, *The Complexity of Race: Categories of Difference in Eighteenth Century British Culture* (Philadelphia: University of Pennsylvania Press, 2000)

White, Shane and Graham White, 'Slave Clothing and African-American Culture in the Eighteenth and Nineteenth Centuries', *Past and Present*, 148 (1995) 149–86

Wilkinson, David, 'Adam, William (1751–1839)', *Oxford Dictionary of National Biography* (Oxford University Press, 2004)

Websites and databases

Coldham, Peter Wilson, *British Emigrants in Bondage, 1614–1788 (CD-Rom)* (Genealogical Publishing Company, 2005)

Eltis, David, Stephen D. Behrendt, David Richardson and Herbert S. Klein, *The Trans-Atlantic Slave Trade: a CD-Rom* (Cambridge: Cambridge University Press, 2000); now updated online at www.slavevoyages.org

State Library of New South Wales, *Eora: Aboriginal Sydney* www.sl.nsw.gov.au/discover_collections/history_nation/indigenous/eora/index.html

www.electricscotland.com/history/nation/cranston.htm

www.captaincooksociety.com

http://web.uct.ac.za/depts/age/people/Gordon

INDEX

Page numbers followed by 'n' refer to endnotes.

INDEX

INDEX

forces men to sign false statements, 219
forces soldiers to work the land, 177–8
forges pay slips, 248
furious over disappearance of ship, 154
given free pardon, 319
goes ashore at Cape Coast, 131
hatches plan to capture Elmina, 197
headquarters at Mori, 19
in Newgate jail, 277, 278, 286, 318
indignant at charges, 277–8
informed of African mission, 121
instructed to capture Elmina, 133, 134
joins Russian military, 350
keen to repay debt, 172
laments lack of men, 230
leads attack on fishermen, 232–3, 245
life before Africa, 106–12
loses his mind, 231
men refuse to serve under, 235
men revolt against, 141–2
moderates behaviour briefly, 185
on conditions in Africa, 132
orders complainers to be whipped, 122
pays to repair mistakes, 183
plans exit from Cape Coast, 194–6
pre-departure apprehension, 105–6
problems with command of, 139–41,
    145–6, 165–6, 181–2
protests innocence, 246–7
punishes deserters, 159–60, 164, 199
purchases slaves, 173
puts Murray in charge of garrison, 199
questionable motives of, 165
raids Company stores, 196
recalls men sent to Vredenburg, 157
recollection of in Lemane scheme,
    308–9
recruits men for company, 112, 114
refuses to pay jail for release, 318
relations between Miles and, 231

relieved by Shirley's exit, 149
reviled by others, 6
schism between Shirley and, 142
seizes ships illegally, 151–3, 197–8, 245
sends convicts out to trade, 153
sent back to England, 248–9
sent to Africa, 67
sentenced to death, 284–5
severity of punishments by, 202, 246
starves his own soldiers, 182, 279
suffers illness, 194, 318
suffers loss of best recruits, 114–15
takes control of Fort Mori, 142–3
Thompson repairs harm done by,
    317–18
treats Africans with contempt, 180–1
trial of, 279–85, 347
turned out of Mori naked, 233, 245
ungentlemanly vocabulary of, 171
unhappy with portrait, 350
watches soldiers board ship, 118
Mackenzie, Kenneth, Earl of Seaforth, 62,
    106, 276, 280
Mackenzie, Roderick, 109, 351
Mackenzie, Thomas, 280
Mackerel (ship), 1, 4, 118–19, 122–3, 126,
    137
MacNab, Francis, 350
Madagascar, 336
Madan, Patrick
    asks Black Moll to accompany him, 212
    attempts breakout, 68–9, 117–18, 210
    attempts to scuttle ship, 122
    brought in for questioning, 75
    crimes of, 47–9, 53, 78
    escapes from Gorée, 227–8
    escapes from jail, 53
    escapes gallows, 52–3
    in Newgate jail, 53, 54–5, 60, 73, 78
    Mackenzie forges pay slip of, 248

INDEX

INDEX